The Hero Cults of Sparta

Also available from Bloomsbury

Orpheus in Macedonia: Myth, Cult and Ideology by Tomasz Mojsik
Demagogues, Power, and Friendship in Classical Athens: Leaders as Friends in Aristophanes, Euripides, and Xenophon by Robert Holschuh Simmons
Authority and History: Ancient Models, Modern Questions edited by Juliana Bastos Marques and Federico Santangelo

The Hero Cults of Sparta

Local Religion in a Greek City

Nicolette A. Pavlides

BLOOMSBURY ACADEMIC
LONDON • NEW YORK • OXFORD • NEW DELHI • SYDNEY

BLOOMSBURY ACADEMIC
Bloomsbury Publishing Plc
50 Bedford Square, London, WC1B 3DP, UK
1385 Broadway, New York, NY 10018, USA
29 Earlsfort Terrace, Dublin 2, Ireland

BLOOMSBURY, BLOOMSBURY ACADEMIC and the Diana logo are trademarks of
Bloomsbury Publishing Plc

First published in Great Britain 2023
Paperback edition published 2025

Copyright © Nicolette A. Pavlides, 2023

Nicolette A. Pavlides has asserted her right under the Copyright, Designs and
Patents Act, 1988, to be identified as Author of this work.

For legal purposes the Acknowledgements on p. xi constitute an extension of
this copyright page.

Cover image: Relief with heroes and worshippers, 540 BC, Chrysapha, near Sparta,
Greece. Peter Horree/Alamy Stock Photo

All rights reserved. No part of this publication may be reproduced or transmitted
in any form or by any means, electronic or mechanical, including photocopying,
recording, or any information storage or retrieval system, without prior permission
in writing from the publishers.

Bloomsbury Publishing Plc does not have any control over, or responsibility for,
any third-party websites referred to or in this book. All internet addresses given
in this book were correct at the time of going to press. The author and publisher regret any
inconvenience caused if addresses have changed or sites have ceased to exist,
but can accept no responsibility for any such changes.

A catalogue record for this book is available from the British Library.

Library of Congress Cataloging-in-Publication Data
Names: Pavlides, Nicolette A., author.
Title: The hero cults of Sparta : local religion in a Greek city / Nicolette A. Pavlides.
Description: London ; New York : Bloomsbury Academic, [2023] |
Includes bibliographical references and index.
Identifiers: LCCN 2023017718 (print) | LCCN 2023017719 (ebook) |
ISBN 9781788313001 (hardback) | ISBN 9781350198081 (paperback) |
ISBN 9781350198050 (pdf) | ISBN 9781350198067 (ebook)
Subjects: LCSH: Hero worship–Greece–Sparta (Extinct city) | Sparta (Extinct city)–Religion. |
Sparta (Extinct city)–Antiquities. | Excavations (Archaeology)–Greece–Sparta (Extinct city)
Classification: LCC BL795.H46 P38 2023 (print) | LCC BL795.H46 (ebook) |
DDC 292.2/13—dc23/eng20230722
LC record available at https://lccn.loc.gov/2023017718
LC ebook record available at https://lccn.loc.gov/2023017719

ISBN: HB: 978-1-7883-1300-1
PB: 978-1-3501-9808-1
ePDF: 978-1-3501-9805-0
eBook: 978-1-3501-9806-7

Typeset by Refine Catch Limited, Bungay, Suffolk

To find out more about our authors and books visit
www.bloomsbury.com and sign up for our newsletters.

For Andreas and Alexander

Contents

List of Illustrations — viii
Acknowledgments — xi
Abbreviations — xii

Introduction — 1
1 Early Heroes and Hero Cult — 11
2 Heroic Sites in Sparta: The Archaeological Evidence — 29
3 The Hero Shrines: Votives, Architectural Evidence, Topography — 61
4 Heroes and Immortality — 103
5 Honouring the Dead — 135
6 Burials and Hero Cult: Three Case Studies — 157

Conclusion — 171

Notes — 177
Bibliography — 237
Index — 279

Illustrations

Figures

0.1	Map of Sparta	xiv
2.1	Berlin, Antikenmuseen 731; stone relief of enthroned couple and a diminutive couple bringing offerings; from Chrysapha, Laconia	31
2.2	Sparta Museum 6517; stone relief of enthroned couple and snake in front; from the Bougadis plot, Sparta	32
2.3	Sparta Museum 505; stone relief with enthroned man, dog and horse; from near Chrysapha, Laconia	33
2.4	Sparta Museum 1005; stone relief of enthroned couple with snake coiling under the throne; inscription in retrograde [X]IΛON (*IG* V.1. 244); from southeast of the acropolis	34
2.5	Sparta Museum 3230; terracotta relief of seated man; from the deposit of Agamemnon and Alexandra/Kassandra at Amyklai	36
2.6	Sparta Museum 237-8; terracotta relief with standing triad; from the deposit of Agamemnon and Alexandra/Kassandra at Amyklai	37
2.7	Sparta Museum 6152-1; terracotta relief with a rider; from the deposit of Agamemnon and Alexandra/Kassandra at Amyklai	38
2.8	Sparta Museum 6225-1; terracotta relief with a warrior; from the deposit of Agamemnon and Alexandra/Kassandra at Amyklai	39
2.9	Sparta Museum 6223-1; terracotta relief with banqueter; from the deposit of Agamemnon and Alexandra/Kassandra at Amyklai	40
2.10	Sparta Museum; terracotta metopes with hoplites, riders and a female head; from the drainage ditch near the Eurotas Bridge	43
2.11	The Stavropoulos plot, Sparta	47
2.12	Plan of Stauffert Street excavation, Sparta	49
2.13	Stauffert Street burial, Sparta	50
4.1	The Menelaion	104
4.2	Menelaion plan	105
4.3	Sparta Museum 14742; bronze aryballos from the Menelaion	106
4.4	Sparta Museum 14742; detail of inscription of bronze aryballos from the Menelaion	108

4.5	Sparta Museum 1; pyramidal stele (side A) from Magoula, Sparta	115
4.6	Sparta Museum 1; pyramidal stele (side B) from Magoula, Sparta	116
4.7	Plan of the Amyklaion	122
4.8	Sparta Museum 575; stone relief with Dioskouroi and two amphorae	130

Table

| 3.1 | Summary of votives and finds | 71 |

Acknowledgements

I would like to express my thanks and gratitude to a number of people for their support in the writing of this book.

Deepest thanks to Paul Christesen for creating the map and reading and giving feedback on parts of the book. William Cavanagh, Richard Catling, Florentia Fragkopoulou, and Christos Flouris for taking the time to discuss with me various parts of my work, as well as Stavros Vlizos for conversing with me about the Amyklaion and providing the plan of the site.

Judy Barrringer, my PhD supervisor for her guidance, patience, and for her continuous support and encouragement through the years.

For their help in providing and obtaining photos and permissions to publish them, I would like to thank Gina Salapata and Chara Giannakaki.

I would like to thank the staff of the British School at Athens for an excellent space to work and creating a home away from home. I would like to acknowledge the Fondation Hardt for offering a wonderful place to immerse myself into research and where parts of the book were written.

My sisters, Rebecca, Ariana, Sharon and Naomi for their love and friendship so needed and received, my mother for the endless amount of chocolate sent through the years and wonderful dinners and travels shared together. My godfather Adonis and his wife Yianna for always being there for me. Furthermore, I would like to thank my friends Margarita, Christina, Erato, Britt, Adam, Jenny, Betul, and Vicky.

I would not be able to get my work done without the continuous support, encouragement, and love of my husband Shane and my two boys Andreas and Alexander.

Lastly, but most importantly, I would like to thank my father and grandmother who through their endless love have kept me strong.

Abbreviations

Journal abbreviations are those of *L'Année philologique*. For internal references within the book I use the form: Chapter 1, section 2=§1.2.

AAA	Αρχαιολογικά Ανάλεκτα εξ Αθηνών.
Arch	Αρχαιολογικόν Δελτίον
ABV	Beazley, J. D. 1978. *Attic Black-Figure Vase-Painters*. New York.
Add²	Carpenter, T. H., et al. 1989². *Beazley Addenda. Additional references to ABV, ARV² and Paralipomena*. Oxford.
ArchDelt	Αρχαιολογικόν Δελτίον
ARV²	Beazley, J. D. 1963². *Attic Red-Figure Vase-Painters*. Oxford.
CVA	*Corpus Vasorum Antiquorum*.
Davies, *PMGF*	Davies, M. (ed.). 1991. *Poetarum Melicorum Graecorum Fragmenta*. Oxford.
Dawkins, *Orthia*	Dawkins, R. M. (ed.). 1929. *The Sanctuary of Artemis Orthia at Sparta* (The Society of the Promotion of Hellenic Studies London, suppl. 5). London.
DK	Diels, H. 1985. *Die Fragmente der Vorsokratiker*, revised by W. Kranz. Zürich.
EGF	Davies, M. (ed.). 1988. *Epicorum Graecorum Fragmenta*. Göttingen.
FGrH	Jacoby, F. (ed.). 1923–. *Die Fragmente der Griechischen Historiker*. Berlin; Leiden.
Gerber	Gerber, D. E. (ed.). 1999. *Greek Iambic Poetry from the Seventh to the Fifth Centuries* BC. Cambridge MA.
IG	*Inscriptiones Graecae*.
IGA	Roehl, H. 1882. *Inscriptiones Graecae Antiquissimae*. Berlin.
LGS	Prott, de J. and L. Ziehen (eds). 1896. *Leges Graecorum Sacrae*. Leipzig.
LIMC	*Lexicon Iconographicum Mythologiae Classicae* I–VIII.
LSAG²	Jeffery, L. H. 1990. *The Local Scripts of Archaic Greece*. Oxford.

M/W	Merkelbach, R. and M. L. West. 1967. *Fragmenta Hesiodea*. London.
Neue Pauly	*Der neue Pauly: Enzyklopädie der Antik*. Vols 1–16. Stuttgart.
New Pauly	*Brill's New Pauly. Encyclopaedia of the Ancient World*. Vols 1–15. Leiden.
PCG	Kassel, R. and C. Austin (eds). 1991. *Poetae Comici Graeci*, Vol. II. Berlin.
Page, *PMG*	Page, D. L. (ed.). 1962. *Poetae Melici Graeci*. Oxford.
Para	Beazley, J. D. 1971. *Paralipomena, Additions to the Attic Black-Figure Vase-Painters and to Attic Red-Figure Vase-Painters*. Oxford.
POxy	Grenfell, B. P., et al. 1898–. *The Oxyrhynchus Papyri*. London.
Praktika	Πρακτικὰ τῆς ἐν Ἀθήναις Ἀρχαιολογικῆς Ἑταιρείας.
P-W	*Pauly's Realencyclopädie der Classischen Altertumwissenschaft*, edited by A. Pauly et al. Stuttgart.
Rose	Rose, D. (ed.). 1966. *Aristotle. Fragmenta*. Stuttgart.
SEG	*Supplementum Epigraphicum Graecum*.
Snell	Snell, B. (ed.). 1964. *Pindai Carmina cum Fragmentis*. Lipsiae.
ThesCRA	*Thesaurus Cultus et Rituum Antiquorum*.
West	West, M. L. 1972, 1991. *Iambi et Elegi Graeci*, Vols I–II. Oxford.

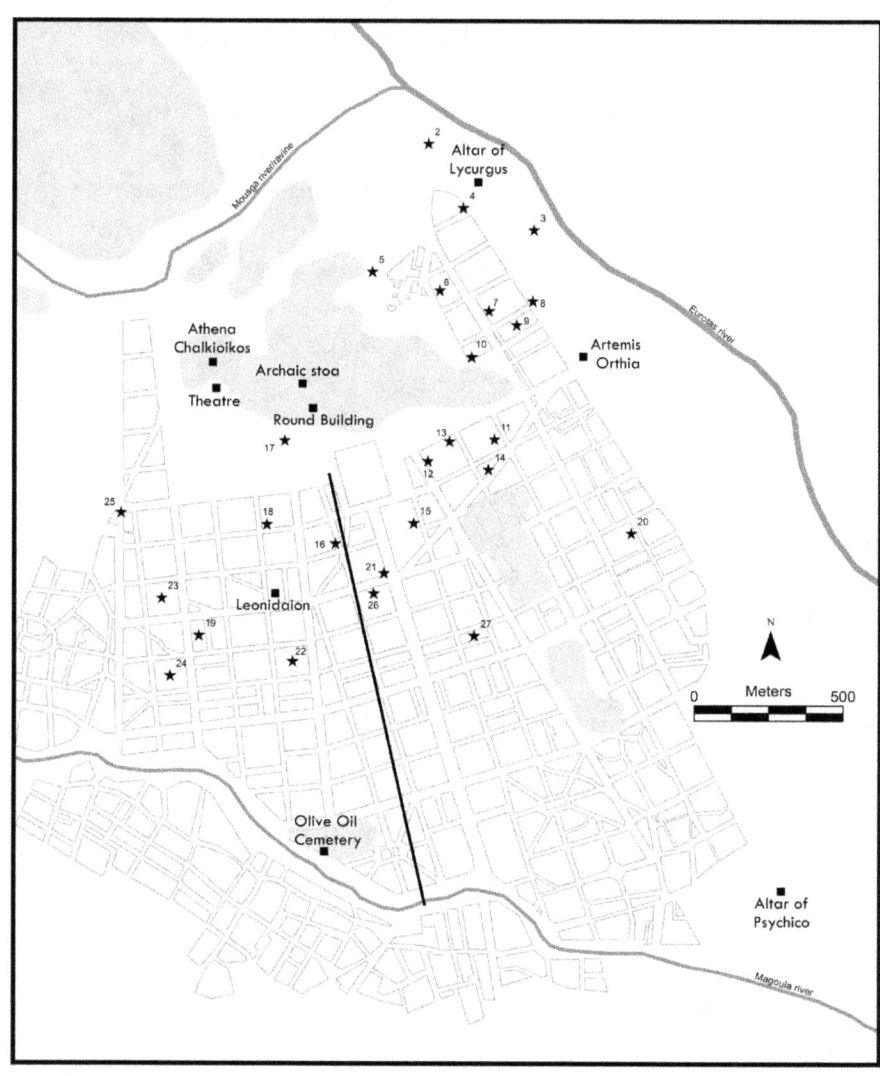

Figure 0.1 Map of Sparta. Map courtesy of Paul Christesen.

Sites:

1. The cult of Agamemnon and Alexandra/Kassandra
2. Drainage Ditch by the Eurotas Bridge
3. The Heroon by the Eurotas River
4. O 13
5. Ergatikes Katoikies
6. The Stavropoulos plot
7. The Niarchos plot
8. The cult site on Stauffert Street
9. The Lykourgos and Karela plot
10. The Bougadis plot, Gitiada street
11. The Panagopoulou plot
12. The Karmoiris plot
13. The Georganta and Petrakou plot
14. The Filippopoulou plot
15. The Tseliou plot
16. The Stathopoulos and Argeiti plot
17. The Bilida plot
18. The Kalatzis plot
19. The Markou plot
20. The Chatzis plot and Arfani plot
21. Thermopylae Street
22. The Sourli plot
23. The Psatha-Iliopoulou plot
24. The Zachariadi plot
25. The Nikolarou plot
26. The Valioti plot
27. The Stratakou plot

Introduction

Tombs, cenotaphs, temples, monuments, oral histories and poems commemorated those individuals of myth and history in Greek antiquity who were heroized after their death. The religious landscape saw hero shrines adorn civic spaces, roads, and the rural land. Heroes were tied to local and Panhellenic mythologies and histories, which were stimulated by and morphed into the collective memory of the people.

This book concerns hero cult in Archaic and Classical Sparta – a city that exhibited many hero shrines, illustrated by both textual and archaeological sources. Remains from the outskirts of the city, at Therapne, indicate that the cult to Helen and Menelaus had commenced by the late eighth century/early seventh century by a Bronze Age settlement site; it is often cited among the earliest known cults to epic heroes.[1] The early seventh century onwards saw the instigation of a number of hero cults: the cult of Agamemnon and Alexandra/Kassandra at Amyklai, the Heroon by the Eurotas, 'the cult site at Stauffert Street', and many others that will feature in this book. During the course of the Archaic period, hero cults in Sparta display a burst of dedications and building activity, as shown by votives and architectural remains. The popularity of heroes intensified in the second half of the sixth century when a specific iconographical motif for dedications in stone developed, while by the end of the sixth century a similar subject appeared on terracotta reliefs.[2] During the sixth century, reliefs dedicated to the twin heroes of Sparta, the Dioskouroi, emerged.[3] A good indication that hero cult was broadly instituted in Sparta is the appropriation of the bones of Orestes from Tegea and their burial in the Spartan agora in the mid-sixth century (Hdt. 1.67–8; Paus. 3.11.10). Other mentions of heroic cults in the Archaic period include the cult of a local hero Astrabacus outside the house of King Ariston (Hdt. 6.69.3). Hero cult of mythical heroes was widely established and there is also some evidence that Spartans, in exceptional circumstances, embraced cults to the recently dead, such as the ephor Chilon, whose stone relief dedication has been found.[4]

Determining the reason behind the early-seventh-century commencement and popularity of heroic cults in Sparta is not straightforward; it is unlikely that one explanation will encompass all. Given its unique societal organization system, its hegemonic prospects in the Archaic Peloponnese, and its Dorian background, Sparta has, for most of its scholarly history, been seen as different.[5] Thus, interpretations of Sparta's hero cults stress Sparta's Dorian 'other' and its bellicosity towards its neighbours. Because Sparta worshipped heroes who were Achaian, such as Menelaus, Agamemnon and Orestes, scholars correlate the worship of Achaian heroes in Sparta with the polis' hegemonic prospects in the Peloponnese during the Archaic period and take the view that the adoption of Achaian heroes and claiming them as Sparta's own would legitimize Sparta's dominance in the Peloponnese. In general, the commencement of some hero cults in Sparta has been viewed as the outcome of a conscious ethnic ideology applied to heroes, and it is assumed that Sparta worshipped a number of heroes to cater to its political propaganda. More specifically, because the Menelaion was set up in an area lacking settlement it is thought of as a collective project to demark the area controlled by Sparta. The establishment and promotion of the sanctuary of Agamemnon and Alexandra-Kassandra is contextualized in relation to Sparta's rivalry with Argos over the hegemony of the Peloponnese.[6] Likewise, the establishment of cults to Orestes and son Teisamenos in the mid-sixth century (Hdt.1. 67.5–68.6; Paus. 2.18.8; 7.1.7) are seen as politically motivated acts, catering to a so-called 'Achaian Policy' in Sparta.[7] While a political interpretation for the creation of cults has its merits, it can disregard the social and religious significance a cult had for the population attending a shrine or a sanctuary. A cult would have had layers of religious and social importance, and a monolithic view cannot express its significance.

The stress on Sparta's peculiarities not only affects the scholarly perception of the cults of mythical heroes, but also cults of the recently dead. Because Sparta focused on citizen militarization, scholars have seen the heroization of those who died fighting in battle as especially appealing.[8] The heroization of the Spartan kings has also been controversial, with little agreement among scholars.[9] Inasmuch as scholars disagree over the heroization of the recently dead, no examination of the heroization of the recently dead Spartans has considered local Spartan burial customs and its attitude towards its dead.

In addition to the aforementioned heroic cults, many other heroic shrines existed. A plethora of votive deposits containing terracotta reliefs, a popular and common dedication to heroes, shows that hero shrines were scattered all over the city, indicating the popularity of hero cult in the Archaic and Classical periods in

Sparta. Apart from the deposits belonging to the cult of Agamemnon and Alexandra/Kassandra, these deposits, and the architectural remains that sometimes accompany them, have not been studied or considered as a whole. When scholars remark on the city's many hero shrines, they often focus on Pausanias' Sparta.[10] Therefore, even though it is recognized that hero cults were especially popular in Sparta in the Archaic and Classical periods,[11] there is little appreciation about what kind of shrines housed the cults, what typology of votives the heroes received, and most importantly, how these shrines 'fitted' within the religious landscape of the polis and how the Spartans perceived the heroes themselves. In general, their function and position in the religious sphere of Sparta have been left relatively untouched. Most scholarly attention on Spartan religion focuses on the larger sanctuaries and cults, such as the sanctuary of (Artemis) Orthia,[12] the Menelaion, the cults of Apollo at Sparta[13] and the temple of Athena Chalkioikos.[14]

The study of hero cults offers a view of local religious traditions. The leading position on hero cult in Greek religion is that it is essentially a local phenomenon and heroes are usually tied to a place, often by legend; an obvious example from Sparta is Helen and Menelaus, Sparta's famous royal couple. Other examples may be cults to *oikistai*, who likewise have strong local connections to a specific place. Cults that formed around burials also only belong to the local community since the occupants are bound to a specific location and are physically there and not elsewhere.[15] The local nature of heroes thus tightly attaches them to the distinctiveness of the place and the community by whom they are worshipped.[16] Consequently, it can cater to sentiments of a local identity that celebrates its heroes.[17] Essentially, a hero can be an embodiment of their respective poleis; who would not think of Athens when hearing the name Theseus, or Mycenae when reading about Agamemnon?

Thus, rather than focus on external stimuli and especially political motivations, this book aims to contextualize hero cult in Sparta within the Spartan community of the Archaic and Classical periods. Some material of Hellenistic date (Chapter 6) will also be included, for a more complete view of the archaeological remains, especially in relation to cults surrounding burials. The book will explore the local idiosyncrasies of a Panhellenic phenomenon, which can help us understand the place and function of heroes in Sparta and more generally in Greek religion. The study places these cults in the context of hero cult in the wider Greek world but emphasises the need for a local reading in order to attain a view of their position in Spartan society and Spartan religious customs. It also highlights the more intimate relationship between worshipper and hero through the study of the votives and shrines of heroes in Archaic and Classical Sparta.

Setting the stage: the Archaic period

The formation of the Spartan civic and political community was a slow process, occurring over a number of centuries. By the tenth century, small amounts of pottery may indicate cult activity at sanctuaries of Sparta: the sanctuary of Athena Poliachos (Chalkioikos)[18] on the Acropolis, and that of (Artemis) Orthia in Limnai.[19] Burials and pottery deposits from Sparta demonstrate that settlement and cult activity had commenced in the areas that would gradually form the heart of the polis:[20] Limnai, near the Eurotas River, appears to have been settled first while Pitane, which included the Spartan Acropolis, probably followed soon after.[21] The other central *komai*, Kynosoura and Mesoa, were located in the southern part of the polis.[22] The last of the Spartan *komai*, Amyklai, located about 5 kilometres to the south, included the sanctuary of Apollo and Hyakinthos, where a large corpus of material suggests continuity from the Late Bronze Age to the Early Iron Age.[23] Early in its state formation, Sparta incorporated this sanctuary, together with the *kome* of Amyklai, into Sparta; a conquest attributed to the Aigeidai (Pindar *Isthmian* 7.12–15; *Pythian* 1.65) or King Teleklos during the eighth century.[24] The gradual formation of the Spartan political community saw cultic expansion in the periphery of Sparta with the cult at the Menelaion at Therapne, the Eleusinion near modern Kalyvia tis Sochas by Taygetos and the sanctuary of Zeus Messapeus at Tsakona, north-east of Sparta, all commencing in the late eighth century. Although, as Thucydides (1.10.2) informs us, in the fifth century Sparta was still not fully synoecious, the five villages of Sparta (Pitane, Limnai, Kynosoura, Mesoa and Amyklai) formed a political and civic community.[25]

Traditionally, the late eighth/early seventh century is regarded as the period in which Sparta must have undergone internal and external unrest.[26] It was a time of rapid change in Sparta, so much so that Cartledge refers to 775 to 650 as the 'Laconian Renascence'.[27] During that time, it fought the Messenian Wars, although the chronology and extent of the warfare is controversial.[28] Warfare, conquest, expansion and population relocation in Messenia and Laconia helped to consolidate and expand the area under Spartan control (e.g. Asine, which was supposed to have been populated by exiles from Asine in the Argolid).[29] Apart from the Messenian Wars, Sparta must have faced internal problems with discontented sections of the population, as evidenced by the rebellion of the Partheniai,[30] who sought equal rights with Spartans; this led to the foundation of Taras, traditionally dated to 706 BC.[31] Internal discontent also manifests in Tyrtaeus' *Eunomia*, testifying to an internal crisis and calling for redistribution of land during the Messenian Wars (Arist. *Pol.* 5. 1360b; cf. Paus. 4.18.2–3).[32] If land resources were a problem, Sparta curiously did not seem to explore the Laconian plain at the time. The *Laconia Survey*, conducted by a British–Dutch expedition under Cavanagh, Crouwel, R. Catling and Shipley, shows that new settlements were being founded in Laconia in some numbers in the sixth century and beyond.[33] After the Messenian Wars, Sparta sought expansion to the north with a failed attempt to conquer Tegea, which resulted in a series of alliances (Plutarch *Moralia* 277c; 292b; Aristotle fr.592 Rose). By the mid-sixth century, Sparta saw much of the Peloponnese under its domain (Hdt. 1.68.6).[34]

Political and cultural changes that produced the class of the *homoioi* (similars) – a term that appears by the early fourth century[35] – gradually emerge from the Archaic period as well.[36] The historicity of Lykourgos, credited with introducing the Spartan institutions, including those pertaining to the military (Hdt. 1.65.5; Xen. *Lac.* 11.1–4), is itself a much discussed subject.[37] The Great Rhetra (if accepted as genuine) can be read as a document that creates new state cults and new civic subdivisions giving further evidence for a society in transition.[38] Whatever the impetus, Sparta slowly became a polis with a unique system of organization by the end of the sixth/early fifth century, in which the Spartans preoccupied themselves with military training[39] and the helots, a form of serf slaves, tended the Spartan estates.[40]

Beyond the consolidation of Spartan territory, beginning in the late eighth/early seventh centuries, Sparta also began a religious 'consolidation' of its space. The late eighth/early seventh century establishment of the cults of the Menelaion, Zeus at Tsakona and the Eleusinion by the Taygetos, which formed a ring around the immediate territory of Sparta, shows how Spartans used religion to define themselves as a community. Likewise, the construction of the very large first peribolos wall at the Amyklaion at the hill's foot is dated to the end of the eighth/early seventh century,[41] the remodelling of the sanctuary of Artemis took place in the same period,[42] and the first phase of construction of the Menelaion dates from c. 650 to 625 BC. Being proximate to Sparta, it is suggested that the above sanctuaries created a 'sacred cordon' and may have demarked the boundaries between Spartan and perioikic territories.[43] These sanctuaries most likely served as 'visible markers of the city's ownership of its *chora* (the northern Eurotas valley) or of Lakedaimon (the Eurotas valley as a whole), under the protection of the gods'.[44] Importantly, since most of these cult sites are inter-visible,[45] they created and enhanced a visual religious landscape for visitors to the sanctuary.

The ensuing seventh and sixth centuries saw great enrichment of material culture: elaborate ivories and bronzes were dedicated at the sanctuary of Artemis

Orthia, the Amyklaion and the Menelaion.[46] More building activity materialized in the sixth century: the Menelaion's second phase of construction occurred in the mid-sixth century at the same time as building works at the temples of Apollo at Amyklai by Vathykles of Magnesia and Athena Chalkioikos in Sparta by Gitiadas. The second temple of Artemis Orthia was built *c.* 570 BC.

The Archaic period has been called 'the age of the sanctuaries', in that it saw the commencement of more cults than any other period.[47] It is also from the eighth to sixth centuries that we see an increase and profusion of dedications in sanctuaries around the Greek world.[48] The emergence of temples not only shows a drive towards monumentalization of sanctuaries but also exhibits community investment.[49] An increase of votives in sanctuaries around the Greek world from the late eighth century onwards supports this suggestion,[50] with the focus shifting from offerings as grave goods to dedications in sanctuaries.[51] It has been argued that the increase of votives in sanctuaries reflects ideas of collectivity in a community and a pattern towards the development of the polis.[52] The setting, construction of temples and elaboration of state cults in Sparta thus signifies collective projects where a community coming together would celebrate its local pantheon.

Sparta in the eighth to sixth centuries underwent a process of defining itself through warfare, expansion and internal restructuring. This was a time of tension, warfare, internal crisis and final consolidation of territory – and self-definition as a community. The Great Rhetra if genuine could be taken as evidence for a society in transition and with a need to establish identities in the citizen body as a whole and in its various official and non-official sub-divisions.[53] So, the territorial consolidation of the Spartan polis and the internal transformation of the political and social circumstances was the context in which heroic cults arose and became relevant.

As Cohen puts it, 'Symbols of the "past", mythically infused with timelessness ... attain particular effectiveness during periods of intensive social change ...'[54] Therefore, at times of historical rupture and new beginnings, sites of memory are more likely to emerge.[55] Nora has shown that symbolic systems operated behind the construction of cultural memory: landscapes, objects, buildings, practices and institutions among many.[56] Cultural memory focuses on 'fixed points of the past' but cannot preserve the past, so condenses it into symbolic figures.[57] Members of a community who share an identity will 'consolidate a sense of sameness through the articulation of communal history'.[58] As circumstances change, the need to highlight or submerge certain events from the community's history arises. Hero cult and heroes who embodied the local community came about when Sparta needed them to define itself. Thus, heroes as 'symbols of the past' became a resource for definition and unification for localities.

It is within this setting that hero cult in Sparta surfaced in the early Archaic period. The expansion of Sparta's religious topography, with the setting and embellishment of cults expressing a civic ideology and communal investment, would have extended beyond the divine sanctuaries into the foundation of hero cults celebrating the local past. Thus, some hero cults developed concurrently with Sparta's growth as a community in conceptual and physical senses. Still, we cannot expect a uniform explanation for all hero cults in Sparta. As we will see in Chapters 2 and 6, some cults were associated with Geometric graves whose occupants could have been considered ancestors to particular families. The dynamic and unsettled affairs of late eighth-/early-seventh-century Sparta would have also offered opportunities and desires for families or groups for self-definition and promotion. The late eighth / early seventh century, when hero cult first appears in Sparta, was characterized by unstable years both in terms of warfare and internal strains. The past was all around the Greeks and, when the right conditions arose, heroes came to the rescue.

Book structure

Chapter 1 deals with the use of the term 'hero' and the evidence for hero cult in early Greek thought and practice. To examine the cult of heroes in Sparta, it is necessary to establish a firm basis for the use and understanding of the terms in the Greek world. I will use the interpretation established in this chapter as a point of reference for Sparta. The use of 'hero' in the Homeric epics to describe the central protagonists is different to the term's use in later times, I therefore begin by examining its use in early literature, especially Homer and Hesiod. I then search for evidence of hero cult in early Greek literature, even when the term 'hero' is absent. I focus on the works of Homer, Hesiod and the *Epic Cycle* for mortals who gain immortality. After that, I turn to the evidence for early hero cult in the archaeological record. The large body of evidence from the tenth-century Lefkandi burial to the Archaic cults over Geometric graves provides a view of the complexity of the subject matter. It is concluded that possible references to the cult of heroes seen in the early literary sources as well as the veneration of the dead at Bronze Age tombs or over Geometric burials are probably early forms of honouring beings from the distant past even though the recipients of cults were not initially called 'heroes'. The phenomenon of worshipping the recently dead, especially in the Geometric period, highlights the mortality of heroes and their human nature. The chapter highlights the heterogeneity of the types of heroes and the changes that occur over time.

Chapters 2 and 3 deal with those sites associated with hero cult in Sparta as evidenced by finds of stone and terracotta reliefs. I first present the criteria and explain the reasons why the terracotta reliefs are a secure indicator to interpret a site as that of a heroic cult. For the definition of *cult*, I follow Zaitman and Pantel, who define it as 'a complex of religious activities concentrated on one or more deities or heroes and including prayer, ritual sacrifice and dedication'.[59] For the archaeological identification of a cult place, I follow Renfrew,[60] with my own alterations. I define a *cult place* as that of a natural spot, built structure or sacred zone that creates a boundary zone between the mortal and the 'supernatural' world, includes the presence of a deity/hero and involves the participation of an individual or a group. Identifying a cult place is not always straightforward. Naturally, large temples with inscribed dedications and statues would clearly denote the designation of a cult place. However, at other times, especially for smaller shrines, the identification of a cult place is based on the concentration of items, such as terracotta figurines, miniature vases and, in Sparta, lead figurines and terracotta reliefs.[61] This material is an identification marker for votive ritual.[62]

I analyse the finds in Chapter 3, where I discuss the votive patterns, the architecture and the topography of the sites. I conclude that many of Sparta's hero shrines were small, received mostly dedications of inexpensive items, and were often located in residential areas. Based on the finds and using comparative material from hero shrines located elsewhere in the Greek world, in particular Athens and Corinth, I propose that many of the cults investigated belonged to a more intimate part of Greek religion where people offered modest, private dedications at their local shrine. (The iconography of the stone and terracotta reliefs is dealt with in a book by Gina Salapata, who offers one of the only studies on hero cult in Sparta, that of the shrine of Agamemnon and Alexandra/Kassandra at the fifth kome of Sparta, Amyklai.[63]) Chapters 2 and 3 are accompanied by a map and a chart of the sites and finds.

This book does not treat hero cults outside of Sparta, i.e. in Laconia. This is largely due to our developing knowledge of Laconian topography in terms of both settlements and cult sites. Apart from the cult of Teimagenes shared with a female deity, possibly Artemis, at Aigies near Gytheio,[64] or the shrine at Angelona,[65] there is little archaeological knowledge of hero shrines in Laconia. A significant number of small, rural shrines attested in the *Laconia Survey*[66] and the many cult sites present in the catalogue of Laconian sites[67] may provide evidence of hero cult, but no excavation has been carried out. A recent excavation at Kladas-Voutianoi, Vordonia, north of Sparta offers new evidence of hero shrines in Laconia and may show the practice as more widespread than previously thought.[68] Therefore, I concentrate on the five *komai* of Sparta (Limnai, Pitane, Kynosoura, Mesoa and Amyklai) and will refer to sites or artefacts in Laconia only occasionally. Cults at Bronze Age tombs are generally not attested in Laconia, in great contrast to neighbouring Messenia, where such cults were prominent. Only a few Spartan examples may reveal later activity but they are infrequent when compared to other regions.[69] Because of this, I will not discuss any of the evidence of depositions at Bronze Age tombs in Laconia.

Chapter 4 presents the evidence in relation to those heroes who achieve immortality in the textual sources: the Menelaion, where Helen and Menelaus were worshipped; the Amyklaion, where Hyakinthos received cult together with Apollo; and the Dioskouroi, the legendary twins who share immortality. I present here the archaeological and textual evidence and discuss the problematic nature of these cults and the debate over the heroic or divine nature of the cult at the Menelaion, the contradicting evidence of Hyakinthos' immortality and the mortal/immortal nature of the Dioskouroi.

Chapter 5 looks into the Spartan tradition of the heroization of historical individuals, such as the Spartan kings, Leonidas and the Thermopylai war-dead, and Chilon, and discusses the social and political circumstances that may have prompted their heroization. To appreciate the motive behind the heroization of certain individuals, I look at Spartan social organization and burial customs. Therefore, this chapter begins with an overview of Sparta's social institutions and evidence of promotion of individuals in the Archaic and Classical periods, followed by a synopsis of the evidence for the treatment of the dead. I conclude that Sparta's religious tradition allowed for the heroization of the exceptional dead, especially of communal importance, and that this was within Sparta's cultural norms.

Chapter 6 resumes the discussion, touched upon in Chapter 5, on the connection between burials and hero cults. I present three case studies where archaeological remains from Sparta offer evidence of hero cults surrounding a burial: the Geometric burial from Stauffert street and two cults sites from first century BC Sparta (Ergatikes Katoikies and the Stavropoulos plot). The three cases offer varying examples in which we see that, because the nature of a hero is typically that of a dead mortal who receives rites after death, it allows for grave ritual to easily cross over into heroic cult. I explore here the themes of grave ritual and ancestor cults, cultural memory and the embrace of older burials, and elite display of power through the heroization of the recently dead.

I note here the use of the literary material as evidence on hero cult practices in Sparta and for local Spartan customs in general. The application of literary sources in the context of Archaic and Classical Sparta is not without controversy because many authors are not Spartan, such as Herodotus and Thucydides, and others are later, such as Pausanias. When possible, I try to keep to Spartan sources, such as Tyrtaeus and Alkman, or to others who visited Sparta, such as Xenophon or Stesichoros. However, given the limited Spartan literary sources, reliance on other authors is unavoidable. Nevertheless, I attempt to take into consideration their chronology: for example, Plutarch's writings can sometimes be questionable for Archaic and Classical Sparta, unless other earlier evidence can support his claims. Likewise, Pausanias visiting Roman Sparta can be consulted for evidence that is contemporary to him but his writings should be read carefully when applied to earlier periods.[70] Therefore, as with other authors, Pausanias' claims must be placed alongside other evidence.

1

Early Heroes and Hero Cult

In a critique of religious practices, Herakleitos commented that people do not recognize what gods and heroes are like (οὔ τι γιγνώσκων θεοὺ οὐδ'ἥρωας οἵτινες εἰσι, B 5 DK).[1] His observation, directed towards people's ignorance of the true nature of divinities and heroes, would be relevant today as the terms 'hero' and 'hero cult' are difficult to define, as are the origins of such cults. Some heroes existed only in myth while others only in cult and some both. There are heroes whose cults were Panhellenic, others who were worshipped only by their respective *poleis*, and others who were important to particular groups within a *polis*, such as the gene in Attica[2] or groups in a region, such as those cults at Bronze Age tombs in Messenia.[3] The chapter begins by giving the reader an overview of the views and definitions of 'hero' and 'hero cult' in scholarly thinking. The discussion examines the word 'hero' or any evidence of hero cult in Homer, Hesiod and the *Epic Cycle*. It then gives an overview of the archaeological evidence from the Lefkandi burial, cults at Bronze Age tombs, cults over Geometric burials and cults of epic heroes. The section concludes with a definition of the term 'hero' as used in this study, which will complement our interpretation of hero cult in Sparta and help contextualize the Spartan evidence.

1.1 Heroes and hero cult in the literary sources

1.1.1 Definitions of 'hero'

One of the first scholars to have investigated the topic of hero cult, Coulanges, interpreted heroes as survivals of old Indo-European institutions and thought of heroes as souls of ancestors.[4] Similarly, Rohde viewed heroes as an aspect of ancient beliefs seen in the term *daimones* as forgotten beings closely related to chthonic deities and dead mortal men.[5] He called them 'spirits of the dead', cults of souls or ancestors.[6] The older views clearly reflected the extraordinary qualities of heroes, which set them apart from ordinary humans, and highlighted their status as dead mortals who influence the lives of the living. Farnell's famous 1921 work *Hero Cults and Ideas of Immortality* confronted the views of previous scholars with scepticism.[7] He provided subsequent generations with greater clarity by creating categories of heroes: a) heroes and heroines of divine origin or hieratic type, with ritual legends or associated with vegetation ritual; b) sacral heroes and heroines; c) heroes of epic and saga; d) cults of mythic ancestors, eponymous heroes and mythic *oikistai* (city-founders); e) functional and culture-heroes; and f) cults of real and historical persons. Farnell's most important contribution rests with illuminating the concept's heterogeneity. Building on Farnell's diversity, Brelich's study went a step further to suggest that it is unfruitful to categorize heroes and instead focused on identifying the common elements that heroes have but in variable patterns.[8] Broadly, scholarship sees two kinds of heroes: one a character of epic and one 'a deceased person who exerts from his grave a power for good and evil and demands appropriate honour'.[9] Indeed, having died is a prerequisite to be a post-Homeric hero as opposed to the gods who are divine and immortal.[10] The latter definition can be found in a broad spectrum of individuals, such as, characters from mythology, for example the Dioskouroi or Theseus, and the historically or recently dead, such as Brasidas.

The hero, as a person once alive and now dead, prompted Nilsson to conceive that the original heroes were humans who had died and thus hero cult originated from the cult of the dead[11] – an idea that has sustained to recent times, with Burkert's 1980s study of Greek religion placing hero cult with sections on burial and the cult of the dead.[12] More recently, the derivation of hero cult from the cult of the dead has been rejected by Ekroth, who demonstrates that the rituals do not support this evolutionary model but are, in fact, closer to divine rituals.[13] The word ἐναγίζειν was used for both hero cult and offerings to the dead but the offerings were different. The word θύειν is used for divine and heroic sacrifice. Thus, only heroes receive both ἐναγίζειν and θύειν. This conclusion led Boehringer to argue that a hero is a being between deity and man, and the rituals that he receives can reflect both of these qualities because he receives sacrifices in the same way a deity does but also those suited to a mortal.[14]

Attempts to find the linguistic origin of the word 'hero' have resulted in wide disagreement among scholars, who cannot even concur over an Indo-European or a pre-Hellenic origin. The similarities with the word 'Hera' have been noted, which prompted the pairing of the linguistic origin of the two words. The word 'Hera' has been proposed to derive from the word *iêr*, meaning 'year' or 'spring', making Hera a goddess of seasons and the yearly cycle and 'hero' her consort.[15]

Others find the word *ieE-* as the stem, meaning youth and thus explaining the later use of 'hero' in Homer.[16] Lastly, those who argue for a pre-Hellenic origin note the similarities of ἥρως and Μίνως and therefore see *Hera* and *hero* meaning mistress and lord.[17] These discussions, however, do not provide much evidence around the later use of the word and are not particularly fruitful for our discussion.

1.1.2 The term 'hero' in Homer

The confusion over what constitutes a hero lies primarily with the changing meaning of the term 'hero' from its earliest appearance as an adjective in the Homeric epics to the Hellenistic period when a 'hero' could be used as a term for the recently deceased who were heroized.[18] While 'hero' in the epics merely meant 'lord' or 'noble' its use was not exclusively applied to personalities, such as Agamemnon and Achilles, but was used for everyone including the lower ranks, as well as entire armies.[19] In general, scholars agree that the use of 'hero' in Homer is not religious and the characters of the epics are not regarded as objects of worship.[20] The reason why the characters of the epics are not religious has been a subject of debate in which it is stressed that since 'hero' is used in Mycenaean Greek, sometimes as an epithet as δεσπότης, πότνια, and ἄναξ and is used for both religious and non-religious occasions,[21] the non-religious connotations survived in the epics. West thought that the local origins of the epics played a crucial role: in Ionia, where the epics were developed, the concept of a hero was secular in contrast to the mainland, where the concept of the hero developed independently of the epic and was associated with the honoured dead.[22] Nagy also uses geography as a distinguishing feature and argues that since hero cult is local and the *Iliad* and the *Odyssey* are relatively Panhellenic poems (compared to the *Epic Cycle*), then any allusions to the cult of heroes are shed.[23] Other scholars seek to find explanations within the epics: Hatzisteliou-Price contended that the characters of epic could not be objects of worship because they are part of the living.[24] Currie rather believes that hero cult is absent from the epics because it is suppressed and he blames this on the literary aims, in that for the purpose of the epics death must be tragic and final.[25] We see then that the heroes in the epics do not receive ritual and importantly the term 'hero' does not have religious meaning in works even after the Homeric epics, such as those of Theognis (711), Hesiod (*Works and Days* 159–60), Stesichoros (S137.3; S148.3 Davies, *PMGF*), Ibykos (S151.16, 19 Davies, *PMGF*) and Bakchylides (5.71; 9.56; 11.81; 13.104),[26] which cannot follow the same guidelines as the epics. The most reasonable explanation is probably that the word 'hero' simply was not used as a religious concept until later.[27]

Hesiod, who uses the term as Homer does, for individuals and collectively, should also be considered. The occurrence is most noteworthy in the narrative of the five races of men in *Works and Days*. After the Gold, Silver and Bronze races, Zeus creates a 'divine race of men who were heroes' (159–60). The men of this race are called ἡμίθεοι and encompassed all the men who fought in the Theban and Trojan Wars. The word 'ἡμίθεοι', as West explains, reflects the heroes' divine descent and parentage rather than the semi-divine status that would imply worship.[28] Van Wees, however, argues that the word ἡμίθεοι is only used in the plural and that it refers to characters who surely do not have a divine parent and interprets ἡμίθεοι as a category of superhuman beings somewhere between mortals and gods that existed at some point in the distant past.[29] This definition in turn can be paired with Nagy's claim that when Homer narrates the future events of the Trojan War, including the fallen and those yet to fall, in *Iliad* 12, he refers to the characters of the epics as the race of men who are ἡμίθεοι (12.33).[30] Here, Nagy stresses that Homer steps outside the narrative to talk about these events and only then, when the perspective of the audience is distanced, do the ἡμίθεοι appear because they are viewed as men who died in the distant past. Here, then, Homer has called his heroes ἡμίθεοι in the same sense as Hesiod has, as a generation of great men, now dead, who lived in the distant past.[31]

1.1.3 Hero cult in early literature?

Bremmer suggests that since the word 'hero' does not appear in a religious context until Herakleitos it is not possible to talk about hero cult earlier if we cannot be certain that there was a category of heroes named and conceptualized as distinct from the gods.[32] In general, Bremmer joins a long debate over the existence of hero cult as a religious act within Homer's epics.[33] Rohde perceived that the funeral of Patroclus in the *Iliad* has many features of hero cult, such as the games, the wine libation (*Il.* 23.218–221) and the offering of honey with oil (*Il.* 23.170).[34] Other possible evidence comes from the sacrifices to Erechtheus (*Il.* 2.547–51, *Od.* 7.80–1), the treatment of Sarpedon's corpse (*Il.* 16.674–5), and allusions to the tombs of Aipytos (*Il.* 2.604), Aisytes (*Il.* 2.796–7) and Ilos (*Il.* 10.414–15, 11.166–8).[35] Another incident that has been seen to depict a ritual associated with hero cult is found in the *Odyssey* when Odysseus offers libations and pours the blood of a black sheep into a pit in order to summon the dead (*Od.* 11.23–36; 10.516–29). Even more peculiar is the vow that Odysseus makes to the dead that when he goes back to Ithaka he will sacrifice a barren heifer and pile the altar with gifts for them and that for Teiresias he would sacrifice a black ram (*Od*.11.30–35).[36] Moreover, in the epics, there are a few instances where immortality is implicated because not all characters go to Hades – some go to Olympus, the Isles of the Blessed, or Elysium;[37] still, the mythical allusions to immortality do not necessarily imply hero cult.[38]

It is also worth looking at possible allusions to hero cult in the *Epic Cycle*. Proklos, who has left a summary of the works, gives a number of occasions where characters have gained immortality. In the *Cypria*, Polydeukes (F6 *EGF*) and Iphegenia (*Procl. Cyp. En.*) become immortal. In the *Aithiopis*, Eos gives immortality to her son Memnon (*Procl. Aeth. En.*) and Thetis takes Achilles away from the pyre to the White Island (*Prolc. Aeth. En.*).[39] In the *Telegony*, Kirke gives immortality to Telegonos (her son by Odysseus), Telemachos and Penelope (*Procl. Tel. En.*).[40] These occurrences of immortality have led scholars to contemplate the possible references to hero cult in the *Epic Cycle*.[41] As with the Homeric epics, these references to immortality are not assuming of hero cult.

In Hesiod, too, there is evidence of immortality of men after death. In the *Works and Days*, the men of the Gold race become δαίμονες after their death (122), a term that West and Nagy both observe is used in relation to figures, such as Ganymede and Phaethon, who achieved immortality in the *Theogony*.[42] The Gold race is called φύλακες θνητῶν (guardians of mortals) and live on the earth (ἐπιχθόνιοι, 123) in opposition to the Silver generation who are ὑποχθόνιοι and dwell under the earth. The ὑποχθόνιοι receive sacrifice upon holy altars and are called μακάριοι. Members of the Bronze race go to Hades after death but the Age of Heroes is diverse: some live on the Isles of the Blessed (171) and are called ὄλβιοι ἥρωες (172). The status of the Age of Heroes has prompted Nagy to suggest that Hesiod implies an immortal existence analogous to the one enjoyed by Achilles on the White Island or Menelaus at Elysium (*Od.* 4.561–9).[43] Thus, in the Gold race and the Age of the Heroes in Hesiod we can perceive some kind of immortality as the former live on the earth and some of the latter live on the Island of the Blessed. Posthumous veneration may underlie the sacrifice on altars that is enjoyed by the Silver generation.

The earliest reference to the term 'hero' as a religious may come from Mimnermos (630–600 BC) (fr. 18), preserved from Athenaios (*Deipnosophistae* 4.174A), who mentions that the hero Daites (Feaster) is worshipped by the Trojans.[44] Another suggestion is that the earliest instance of 'hero' in a religious reference is to be found in Draco's law (*c*. 620 BC), which states that the heroes should be honoured according to the ancestral customs (Porphyry, *On Abstinence*

4.22.7).[45] In any case, it appears that the term 'hero' had acquired a religious meaning by the sixth century, if not earlier, and became widespread in the fifth, as is evident from examples of Herakleitos (B 5 DK), Pindar (*P.* 5.95), Aischylos (*Ag.* 516) and others.[46]

Of course, the word 'hero' in its religious sense or even the cults of heroes must have occurred before the proposed date of the late seventh/early sixth century, because by then the religious sense of the word was already fully pronounced in the text of Mimnermos[47] and therefore hero cults must have existed for some time. The possible references to the cult of heroes in the early literary sources, e.g., the cult of Erechtheus on the Acropolis (*Il.* 2.549; *Od.* 7.81), may perhaps allude to early forms of honouring individuals of the distant past although the recipients of cult were not called 'heroes' at first.

It is important to add a few words about the term *heroine*.[48] The earliest attested occurrence comes from Pindar (*P.* 11.2) where the ἡρωΐδων στρατὸν (host of heroines) is called together at the temple of Apollo. This group includes the daughters of Kadmos, Semele and Ino, Alkmene, and Melia the consort of Apollo Ismenios.[49] In Corinna (Page, *PMG* 664b) we find a proclamation of the virtues of the heroines (χείρωάδων).[50] Inscriptions from Attica include the word heroine; the earliest is a fragment of a ritual calendar from the first half of the fifth century BC prescribing sacrifice for the heroine (*IG* I² 840).[51] As with 'hero' one can assume that the term 'heroine' predates its earliest written attestation in the fifth century. Also, as mentioned above, there are *Epic Cycle* instances where Iphigenia and Penelope gain immortality, which may mean that women who lived in the past achieved special status,[52] without assuming heroization.

1.2 Hero cult in the archaeological record

1.2.1 Definition of terms

Considering the problematic evidence in the literary sources, scholars have scrutinized the archaeological record for evidence of early hero cult elsewhere. This task has proven equally challenging and has generated conflicting scholarly opinions. Before our discussion of the early archaeological evidence of hero cult we should add a word about the nomenclature of hero cult places (locations) in ancient literature.

In literature, the term *heroon* appears for the first time in Herodotos (5.47; 67) to indicate a shrine for a hero. However, the literary terminology for hero cult places is diverse with terms, such as *sema, mnema, theke* and *taphos*.[53] In some cases, a cenotaph could be a place of heroic cult and other times we find the terms used for divine cults, such as *temenos, naos, alsos* and *hieron*. Thus, a *heroon* can be anything from a temple type building to a stele. Because a hero is generally a mortal who, now dead, exercises some sort of power over the living and is given cult, often such a cult would be centred around a grave, but not always. Usually, when a grave is present, it is located in the city, sometimes in the agora, a prominent and central place of daily life. The location of a grave in a polis is unlike Greek customs where the dead were considered impure and were buried outside the city walls. The existence of hero cult shrines in the form of graves in a polis demonstrates the special and elevated status of the hero and differentiates him/her from ordinary mortals. Other times, heroic cults would be located within divine sanctuaries, such as Pelops at Olympia.[54] In general, hero shrines are diverse and there is no one model on which we can rely to identify a cult site of a hero. Archaeologists rely instead on votive and epigraphic evidence.

1.2.2 Early archaeological evidence of hero cult

Often refered to as the 'Heroon at Lefkandi', the Toumba burial at Lefkandi on Euboea is worth discussing. Excavations unearthed an apsidal building of about 50 metres in length that dates to the tenth century BC. Within the central room were found two burials, one of a cremated male in a bronze amphora and an inhumed female. Next to them were the remains of four inhumed horses. The burial included rich gifts of weapons and the female was adorned with jewellery of gold, electrum and bronze; the bronze amphora, with the male's remains, was made in Cyprus in the twelfth century BC. The building seems to have been demolished shortly afterwards. Soon after, the area in front of the building (covered by a mound) served as a cemetery.[55]

Because of the elaborate nature of this burial, the excavators interpreted this as a heroic cult site and considered that some features, e.g., the cremation in a bronze vessel, the horses and the mound, recalled Homeric funerals (*Il.* 16.457; 671–5; 23.44–7; 243; 24.795; *Od.* 1.239–40; 14.366–71; 24.73–5), such as that of Patroclus' in the *Iliad*.[56] Similarly, Morris points out the epic similarities but also sees evidence that the burials were part of the elite who connected with the glorious past of the Hesiodic race of heroes.[57] A few scholars have disagreed with this interpretation, particularly because there is no evidence of cult after the construction of the mound above the burials[58] but also because other evidence suggests that rich sub-Mycenaean burials in Cyprus, Knossos,[59] Perati on Crete,[60] and Achaia[61] existed before the Lefkandi burial, demonstrating a tradition of elaborate burials. These are interpreted as the final stages of the LH IIIC, which reached its pinnacle and the transition to the Early Iron Age with the Toumba cemetery at Lefkandi.[62] Elaborate Iron Age burials have also been discovered at Thermon, Nichoria, Eleusis and Eretria.[63] As our knowledge regarding Iron Age Greece and the transition from the Late Helladic period widens, it appears that the Toumba burial probably follows earlier burial traditions and is less likely to be heroic; rather, it demonstrates honours for the deceased because of his elevated social status.[64]

Another type of cult in relation to burials is the one found at Bronze Age tombs. Particularly popular in Messenia, the Argolid and Attica, these cults are evidenced by placing artefacts at Bronze Age tombs, reuse of the area for burials, and in some instances (especially in Messenia), sacrifice and feasting.[65] Evidence of activity of offerings or reuse of Bronze Age tombs for contemporary burials goes back to the eleventh century but peaks in the late eighth.[66] In general, activity is short-lived (with a few exceptions, such as at Menidi in Attica) and sporadic.[67] The quality of offerings at Mycenaean tombs is poor, and metal is very rare.

Because of the intensification of activity at Bronze Age tombs in the eighth century BC, up until the 1970s, the predominant view was that the Homeric epics had an impact on the religious practices of the Greeks, who venerated those in the Bronze Age tombs as the Homeric heroes; however, this claim is now widely disputed.[68] Instead, the two phenomena seem to have been parallel.[69] Some characteristics that we observe in a Homeric burial had already been seen in funerary customs since the tenth century (e.g. the burial at Lefkandi) and predate Homer's text. This is especially true for cremation pyres, burning pits, ornaments and weapons dating to earlier periods. Such elaborate burials may in fact have had an impact on the Homeric epics and inspired the inclusion of elaborate funerals, such as that of Patroclus.[70] Regardless of their relationship to the epics, the Geometric cults that developed at Bronze Age tombs have prompted scholars to suggest that it is a clear indication that for the 'first time, they [the Greeks] began to think of great men of the past as heroes deserving of worship'.[71]

Viewing the recipients of cult at Bronze Age tombs as heroes has not found uniform acceptance.[72] Snodgrass suggested that the Bronze Age tombs were connected with those that Homer referred to as ἡμίθεοι or δαίμονες.[73] Similarly, Morris believes that the Iron Age Greeks deemed the impressive Mycenaean remains as belonging to the ἡμίθεοι and Whitley identifies them as Hesiod's Silver race of men called ὑποχθόνιοι.[74] Antonaccio's important survey of these cults concludes that due to the cults' short duration, the absence of metal and stone dedications, and the lack of inscriptions activity at the Bronze Age tombs, they should be designated rather as ancestor cults.[75] Because of the evidence of Iron Age burials at some Bronze Age tombs, she believes that the cults at the Bronze Age tombs were comparable with burial practices that took place in the eighth century and thus should be interpreted as ancestor cults.[76] But Ekroth finds the categorization of the cult at the Menidi tomb as simply tomb-cult problematic. She argues that due to the rich material and its long duration, it is better understood as tomb cult, which developed into a hero cult.[77] In addition, Boehringer thoroughly rejects the claim of ancestor cult, which Antonaccio defined as the recipients of cult at Bronze Age tombs, on the basis that in Greek religion there is no evidence of ancestor cult (such as the *Lares* in Roman religion), and adopts a wide definition of hero, which includes the cults at Bronze Age sites as places of heroic cult.[78]

Antonaccio recognized the problem in designating these cults as hero cults because of the lack of inscriptions indicating that the individuals honoured were heroes.[79] One possible exception is a black-glazed sherd discovered by Schliemann in the area of Grave Circles A and B in Mycenae with an inscription το hεροος εμ[ι] 'I am of the hero'.[80] However, since this sherd has no context, it is difficult to accept that it originated from one of the grave circles. A more reasonable suggestion is that it may have originally been placed at the fountain-house of Perseus outside the Lion-gate.[81] Another possible example comes from a seventh- or sixth-century fragmentary inscription on a Laconian roof tile found under a pile of stones outside a late Helladic tholos tomb at Georgikon-Xinoneri in Thessaly.[82] The fragmentary inscription may read 'Aiatos', the name of the first legendary king of Thessaly and father of Thessalos. In any case, the argument stipulating written evidence as a chief criterion to reject the Bronze Age tombs as hero cults is not all together valid since the archaeology precedes in time our earliest written evidence. However, even the Menidi tholos tomb in Attica, whose lifespan continued until the fifth century, yielded one example of an inscription but of much later date, the sixth century, and gives no information regarding the recipient of the cult.[83]

As we have seen in the literary evidence, although hero cult was not named and expressed in the same way, from the eighth century BC (if not earlier) there are indications of beliefs in the influential dead. The fact that there was cult activity, even for a short duration (although for some it spanned centuries), at some Bronze Age tombs demonstrates some belief that the long-dead had an effect on the living and therefore were the focus of ritual activity.[84] The early archaeological evidence produces a problem similar to that encountered with the early literary sources: appellation for these cults is absent but there are traces of what later in the Archaic and Classical period would be interpreted as hero cult.[85]

1.2.3 Evidence of cult over Geometric tombs

A somewhat similar situation can be perceived in cult activity that exists over Geometric graves. A number of Early Iron Age burials have been the object of cult in various parts of the Greek world from the seventh century onwards, e.g. the underground shrine in Corinth[86] or the 'Heroon at the Crossroads', also in Corinth, which appear to have been built over Geometric graves.[87] These shrines were not contemporary with the burials but at some later point, the graves were discovered and a shrine built over them.[88] In Athens, the triangular shrine in the agora was located in an area where a significant number of Geometric graves have been discovered within a radius of some 30 metres from the shrine.[89] The Athenian agora has other examples, such as a stone pit north of the altar of Ares amid Mycenaean burials with votives from the seventh century,[90] the shrine near Mycenaean and Proto-Geometric graves at the north-east corner of the agora,[91] and the rectangular shrine also amid Mycenaean graves below the Middle Stoa.[92] Like the cults at the Bronze Age tombs, these shrines yielded no inscriptions, although they are widely accepted as places of hero cult because of their proximity to burials.[93] Of course, the cults mentioned above should not be taken as an interpretative whole as each was formed due to local and various needs. Some of the sites, such as the 'Heroon at the Crossroads' in Corinth and the rectangular shrine below the Middle Stoa at Athens, continued to be the focus of ritual in the Classical period and later, when hero cult is widely attested but the anonymity (at least to us) of the recipient remains throughout their use.[94] These rediscovered burials and others dating from the Bronze Age show that there was a belief that the powerful dead had influence over the lives of the living and were thus the focus of ritual activities.

1.2.4 Cults for the recently deceased

Apart from cults over rediscovered older Bronze Age and Geometric burials, there is also a category of 'true hero cults', as defined by van den Eijnde,[95] of individuals whose graves became the locus of cult after their death, or soon after, in the Proto-Geometric and Geometric periods.[96] In Eretria, a cluster of late eighth and early seventh centuries BC burials at the West Gate saw the erection of a triangular shrine in 680 BC and ritual activity with votive offerings and a *bothros* continuing for over a hundred years.[97] At Paroikia on Paros a Geometric site with two pits was found, one with 40 amphorae and the other with 120 amphorae, containing the cremated remains of men around thirty years of age. In the seventh century, the area was marked by *stele* and offerings and sacrifices continued for at least 200 years.[98] At Grotta on Naxos are a number of enclosures of late Proto-Geometric graves with pyres above and among them. In the Geometric period, platforms were made of pebbles and stones, used for libations and other rituals. This continued until the Late Geometric period, when the area was buried under a tumulus and offerings continued until the sixth century BC.[99] This has been taken to suggest that the site belonged to an ancestor cult that turned into hero cult because of changing circumstances.[100] At Eleusis, a tumulus covered a late-eighth-century burial in front of a house. Sacrificial pyres over the tumulus and the Sacred House at Eleusis, built in the seventh century, have been connected with the burial, whose occupant has been identified as a priest of the Eumolpid family.[101] At the Academy at Athens, a Late Geometric house was established by some contemporary graves and is interpreted as being linked to the cult of the dead by their families.[102]

Recently, Mazarakis Ainian suggested that the growing interest in the epics in the eighth century may have impacted attitudes resulting in prominent individuals honoured after their death.[103] But the burials of the eighth and seventh century more likely followed a centuries-old practice, as we saw in the Lefkandi burial and others, so the funerals in the epics and those attested in the material record were possibly parallel traditions.[104]

These examples presented above and others cannot be taken into an interpretive whole, and there is certainly a distinct difference between the communal burial at Paroikia on Paros and those burials at Naxos or Eleusis. Mazarakis Ainian suggests, nonetheless, that some of these cults were located in elite residential areas and with the rise of the polis they changed into formal cult areas.[105] Indeed, the division between domestic and burial grounds was not distinct in the Iron Age and the majority of the examples may have begun as ancestral cults, meaning they would have been of concern only to family or direct descendants, or perhaps to a group, as with those at Paros.[106] Of course, the boundaries (if definable) between hero cult, ancestor cult and the cult of the dead are unclear.[107] Certainly, it appears that the longevity of the cults should indicate that cult would become more communal, since ancestral cults usually only last a couple of generations.[108] A similar phenomenon is observed at some cults over Geometric graves, as discussed in the previous section, such as that of the 'Heroon at the Crossroads' and the rectangular shrine below the Middle Stoa (both at Corinth), where ritual continued into the Classical period and later: what may have started as an ancestor cult may have turned into hero cult because of changing circumstances.[109]

1.2.5 Evidence of cult to mythical heroes

So far, we have looked at the early evidence of cults whose recipients are unknown to modern scholars. There are, however, some examples where inscriptions give the name of the individual worshipped at the site and thus, can confirm that a hero was the recipient of cult. Much discussed are the Agamemnoneion at Mycenae, the cave to Odysseus at Polis Bay on Ithaka, the cult of Phrontis at Sounion, the Menelaion at Sparta, the cult of Agamemnon and Alexandra/Kassandra at Amyklai (Sparta), and more recently the cult of Herakles by the Elektrai Gates at Thebes.

The roadside shrine at Mycenae known as the 'Agamemnoneion' was active during the Geometric period up to the early fifth century BC. Its activity appears to drop then and possibly stops altogether after Argos' destruction of Mycenae in 468 BC. Activity resumes in the early Hellenistic period, during which identifiable dedications to Agamemnon appear, in the fourth century BC.[110] By contrast, the earlier phase, dating from the Geometric to the early fifth century, has about fifty specimens of terracotta figurines of seated goddesses and some enthroned goddesses among much pottery.[111] This fact is not stressed by the excavator, Cook, who takes the large number of kraters and krateriskoi, as well as three terracotta horse figurines, as indicative of a male recipient of the cult and interprets the site at that of a shrine of Agamemnon dating from the eighth century BC.[112] Assuming the recipient is male because of the horse figurines and the kraters is problematic as such items are also found in female sanctuaries.[113] Therefore, the late date (fourth century BC) of the appearance of Agamemnon in inscriptions has prompted suggestions that the earliest activity at the site was not directed towards Agamemnon but to Hera, whose Heraion on the citadel of Mycenae was nearby.[114] The Hellenistic site dedicated to Agamemnon is seen as part of a romanticism of the past, quite common during the period.[115] Similarly, the cave at Polis on Ithaka was active from the ninth century BC, yielding dedications of tripods, but only reveals dedications to Odysseus from the second century BC. In fact, the earlier dedications, with a sixth-century inscription to Athena Polias and Hera Teleia,[116] masks showing Artemis with a bow and quiver, many female figurines,[117] Nymph reliefs and dedications to Nymphs demonstrate a female presence at the site.[118] Some would like to see an initial use of the cave as a cult site to Odysseus[119] but the latest full publication of the material by Deoudi suggests that there is no evidence of Odysseus' early worship.[120]

The cult of Phrontis, Menelaus' helmsman, at Sounion is another cult whose early date is a subject of debate.[121] A passage from the *Odyssey* 3.278–283, narrates the death of Phrontis by Apollo at Sounion and the funeral rites that Menelaus subsequently gave him. The passage, together with a Proto-Attic plaque depicting a ship of hoplites and a spearman of c. 700 BC, prompted the early excavator, Picard, to identify a heroic cult of Phrontis at Sounion.[122] Considering, however, that the plaque was found in a pit by the temple of Athena, the dedication may belong there.[123] Abramson argues that a cult of Phrontis is found at the small rectangular structure (a *naiskos*) of the late sixth/early fifth century[124] near the temple of Athena but the evidence is inconclusive and no inscription identifies a recipient of cult;[125] the *naiskos* could even be an earlier cult site of Athena since it precedes the temple of Athena.[126] Another site, the Oval Peribolos, perhaps surrounding a tumulus, finds support as the locus of hero cult formed in the Archaic period;[127] this cult may have moved to the *naiskos* in the Classical period.[128] Phrontis may have received cult somewhere near the sanctuary of Athena but it is hard to find concrete evidence for the Late Geometric date proposed by Picard.[129]

The above sites have somewhat doubtful origins in the eighth century but there are examples in the Greek world that show that known mythological heroes indeed received cult in the eighth and seventh centuries: the Menelaion in Sparta, the cult of Agamemnon and Alexandra/Kassandra at Amyklai, and the sanctuary of Herakles by the Elektrai Gates at Thebes. The discovery of the sanctuary of Herakles by the Elektrai Gates confirms the cult of Herakles and his eight sons by his wife Megara known from Pindar (*I.* 4.57–70) at Thebes and suggests that heroic cults to mythological heroes were practised early. The cult was focused round a cenotaph, while votive offerings and an ash altar attest to the cult of Heracles going back to the mid-eighth century.[130] The cult at the Menelaion in Sparta and the material relating to the cult of Agamemnon of Alexandra/Kassandra at Amyklai will be discussed in the following chapters.

1.2.6 *Oikistai*

Lastly, it is important to mention the cults of the *oikistai* (polis-founders), which is argued to provide an impetus for similar cults in the Greek world.[131] As tempting as this theory is, these cults do not exist archaeologically when Greeks intensified colonization in the eighth and seventh centuries;[132] of course colonization and contacts with the East existed for centuries before. The earliest archaeologically attested cult of an *oikist* is that of Battos in Kyrene,[133] which dates from the sixth century BC,[134] which is also the earliest literary reference of an *oikist* cult (Hdt. 5.150; cf. Pind. *P.* 5.93–5; Catull. 7.6; *SEG* XI.72 [fourth century]). Morgan notes that in the Classical and Hellenistic periods there was a tendency to find a *protos heuretes* in everything that may have led to colonies' formation of founding cults.[135] Because of the importance of a polis' identity in the face of an *oikist* other scholars have highlighted that the ritual function of a founder's cult is more important than the historical fact; many of the *oikist* cults then can be seen as a development of the Classical and Hellenistic periods.[136]

1.2.7 Hero cult

As we have seen above, it is particularly difficult to identify a locus of hero cult without inscriptions. Consequently, this has led to wide disagreement regarding the earliest evidence, which spans from the tenth-century Toumba burial (or even the Bronze Age, as Lindblom and Ekroth discuss)[137] to the Archaic cults over Geometric tombs. So it is altogether uncertain if those cults associated with Bronze Age or Geometric graves should be called heroic. It is not until the seventh and sixth centuries when inscriptions become more common that one can confirm that earlier sites of cult were indeed heroic as is the case of the Menelaion at Sparta, the cult of Agamemnon and Alexandra/Kassandra at Amyklai, and the cult of Herakles at Thebes.

The Archaic period sees a boom in heroic cults: a post with an inscription EPOON TON EN ΘHBAIM from Argos dates to the mid-sixth century (*SEG* XIV 565). This post was one of a series, connected with wooden bars to form a fenced enclosure,[138] and has led the excavator to conclude that the inscription was a marker of the temenos of a *heroon* dedicated to the heroes of Thebes. However, early *heroa* are confirmed from other cases even if they are not called such: one of the earliest is the one in the agora of Thasos, where an inscription *c.* 600 BC reads: 'I am the monument (*mnema*) of Glaukos, Leptinos' son. The sons of Brentis dedicated me.'[139] Glaukos, a friend of the poet Archilochos,[140] was a Parian who colonized Thasos in the late seventh century BC.[141] Heroes too in Panhellenic sanctuaries, such as Pelops at Olympia, whose *heroon* was formed over an Early Bronze Age mound, exhibit the earliest evidence of cult in the sixth century BC.[142] The cult of Opheltes at Nemea also commenced in the early sixth century BC around an artificial mound.[143] At Mycenae there is evidence of the cult of Perseus, based on two sixth-century inscriptions.[144] Since these sites are accompanied by inscriptional evidence their heroic status can be established.[145] We will see in Chapter 2 that many heroic cults in Sparta will not be complemented by epigraphic evidence but their origins can be traced back to the early seventh century.

1.3 Conclusion

The early evidence of cult at Bronze Age tombs and Geometric burials suggests that some sort of veneration took place directed to the long or recently dead, probably perceived as powerful figures of the past. These figures, possibly anonymous (to us anyway), often received cults by earlier graves making them of localized nature and mattering only to the local community.

Labelling earlier cult sites as heroic comes from the generalization of the term hero to include any individual who died and later was given honours. The wide application of the term has led to disagreement over the earliest evidence, archaeological or literary, because the contemporary terminology used in the Archaic and Classical periods was applied to the past. As demonstrated above, cults of dead, powerful humans of the distant past were probably not called heroic by their worshippers and had different characteristics from those of later bona fide hero cults.[146] It is important to note that the worship of heroes even in the later Archaic, Classical, and Hellenistic periods was not static: changes included the veneration of the war-dead and the heroization of the recently deceased, especially in the Hellenistic period.[147] It would be reasonable then to suggest that hero cult, or veneration of the dead (or some form of it), also experienced changes but also exhibits variability in the Geometric and early Archaic periods.[148] What seems to have existed is a general perception that powerful humans deserve acknowledgement and veneration, as suggested from the cults at Bronze Age tombs, the cult at the West Gate at Eretria, other cults to the recently or long deceased, and possibly from passages from Homer and Hesiod.[149]

The problem might lie in part with the need to create categories of cult beings, such as divinities and heroes. Scholars, however, have repeatedly stressed that Archaic literature does not group beings into strict categories. Even the mention of the twelve Olympian gods is not attested until the last decades of the sixth century BC with the altar of Peisistratus the Younger in 522/1 BC (Thuk. 6.54.5).[150]

The distinction between gods and heroes is evidenced soon after that: in Pindar (*O*.2) we learn of a tripartite grouping: of divinities, heroes and men. The same scheme is to be found in Antiphon (1.27), Antiphanes (F 204 *PCG*) and Aristotle (*mund*. 400b.22).[151] Plato articulates four groups: divinities, *daimones*, heroes and men (*pol*. 3.392A; 4.427B).[152] Thus, the first testimony of gods and heroes together occurs around 500 BC and thus they are distinctly separate beings, but the 'ontology' of Greek religion is not set: in Plato, the four groups include *daimon* to designate a being between god and man. However, this word is sometimes used for divinities, e.g. in Homer.[153] What the literary evidence shows is the lack of a systematization of Greek religion, even in the fifth century BC.[154] As Boehringer stresses, religious systematization is a modern dogmatic religious concept that we should not apply to Greek religion, which is malleable in its belief systems.[155]

Burkert called the organization of divinities, heroes and men the 'restructuring of spiritual life' that divided the world of divine and semi-mortal. However, this was not always the case.[156] Generally, it is perceived that whoever has not died is a god and is part of an exclusive Olympian group and whoever is left behind is placed under the category of demigods.[157] The large non-divine group helps explain the confusion over the term hero as well as the various *kinds* of heroes. Consequently, some heroes were 'more divine' than others, e.g. Herakles, Asklepios, the Dioskouroi, and Amphiaraos, who are in the category of heroes who become immortals.[158] It also helps explain the confusion over many beings, such as the recipients of cult at Bronze Age tombs. It shows that the kaleidoscope of supernatural beings during the time before the Archaic and Classical periods consisted of many figures who were worshipped in order to cater to the local needs and need not be named *hero*, or *semi-divine*.[159] The term hero in antiquity trespasses the boundaries set by modern scholars who have tried to propose various definitions. The best example of this fluidity perhaps are the sacrificial rituals of heroes and gods, which Ekroth has shown to be very similar.[160]

In explaining the inconsistencies among the hero cults from Greek antiquity, Parker calls heroes 'biographically dead mortals, functionally minor gods'.[161] Indeed, the relationship of a hero with death explains the blurring boundaries and similarities between the cult for the recently deceased, tomb cults at Bronze Age tombs, cults at rediscovered Geometric burials, *oikist* cults, and hero cults of known mythological heroes. We may never know with certainty what the recipients of cults at the Bronze Age tombs were called during the eighth century BC, nor those recently deceased who received posthumous veneration in the Proto-Geometric and Geometric periods, but the evidence demonstrates awareness, respect and veneration of beings of the past – activities that later constitute what we refer to as 'heroes' who receive hero cult. Perhaps, some of the recipients of cult at Bronze Age tombs were thought to be mythical heroes, such as Aiatos at Metropolis in Thessaly.

Indeed, from the Archaic period onwards, when 'hero' is a religious term, the figures who receive this epithet are diverse and include epic characters, *oikistai*, mythological beings and local heroes. Some heroes have cults associated with tombs, while others do not. Others, such as Herakles and the Dioskouroi, demonstrate how a hero can even defy death and achieve immortality. The mortality of the hero is a defining feature since those heroes who achieve immortality are few and are often, though not exclusively, Panhellenic. Their extraordinary achievement to defeat death puts them in an unusual position, and sometimes, such as Herakles, they can be called divine. For the majority of heroes death is definite; yet their power still lingers on in the lives of the living. Thus, a hero in the historical period was a mortal of the distant or recent past who, after his/her death (or apotheosis), was believed to exert power over the living and was therefore venerated. It is worth noting that the earliest possible attestation of cult during someone's lifetime is that of Lysander, who received divine honours while alive as we are told by Duris *FGrH 76 F71* (fourth century BC) quoted by Plutarch (*Lys.* 18.2–4). Apparently, Samos bestowed such honours to Lysander in 404/3 BC by setting up altars and making sacrifices for Lysander as well as singing the paean for him. Perhaps, Sparta's fluid boundaries of mortals and heroes prompted Samos to find lifetime honours suitable for Lysander.[162]

2

Heroic Sites in Sparta: The Archaeological Evidence

Anyone reading Pausanias' description of the city of Sparta of the second century AD cannot help but notice his reference to numerous shrines dedicated to heroes. Nevertheless, we learn little from Pausanias about the architecture, decoration, ritual or votive customs that accompany these shrines. Sometimes, Pausanias will mention a grave, such as that of Kastor, over which is a sanctuary (3.13.1) or a cluster of shrines (3.13.1) or he narrates a myth behind a hero cult (e.g. Astrabacus, 3.16.9). As discussed in the Introduction, the literary evidence predating Pausanias attests to the popularity of heroic cults in Sparta, such as those of the Dioskouroi, Astrabacus, and Helen and Menelaus. This chapter aims to present the archaeological material attributed to hero shrines. The interpretation of a site as heroic depends on a variety of factors, such as typology of votives, inscriptions (though these are rare) and relationship to burials. The material has mostly been discovered in votive deposits that have produced a variety of objects, both votive and architectural. Votive deposits usually accumulate from the process of clearing a temenos of older dedications in order to yield space for new ones. The discarded votives are commonly placed somewhere inside the temenos.[1] Apart from the deposit dedicated to Agamemnon and Alexandra/Kassandra, the other deposits remain little studied. The Menelaion, the temple of Helen and Menelaus, will be examined in Chapter 4 since its material evidence is distinctly different from that found at the sites presented in this chapter.

This chapter is accompanied by a map (0.1) which gives the location of the sites discussed below, to place them in the context of Sparta's topography. Table 3.1 provides an overview and summary of the material found in each of the sites: terracotta reliefs, pottery, terracotta figurines, lead figurines, metal finds, and architectural finds, together with the chronology of each site when known.[2]

2.1 Hero shrines: criteria

Before presenting the archaeological evidence, it is appropriate to specify the criteria that has informed the following selection of sites. Some sites, such as that of the hero shrine on Stauffert Street (no. 8), show clear evidence that a Geometric burial became a locus of a hero cult from the seventh century to the Hellenistic period. Other criteria, such as inscriptions, have been found in some sites but they are generally so fragmentary that, with the exception of the cult of Agamemnon and Alexandra/Kassandra, the cult recipients remain unknown to us. Thus, the identification of a hero shrine based on epigraphic evidence is limited.

Beyond graves and inscriptions, the body of evidence that sets a clearer standard for an identification of a site as heroic are the votives themselves; more specifically, the Spartan custom of dedicating stone and terracotta reliefs to heroes.

Approximately forty stone reliefs dedicated to heroes have been found. They appeared in Laconia during the second half of the sixth century and lasted through the Hellenistic and Roman periods.[3] Unfortunately, only one them, from Chrysapha (*c.* 10 km east of Sparta), was found *in situ*.[4] About half of the known stone reliefs were found in Sparta itself, while the remainder come from various places in Laconia (Chrysapha, Gytheio, Geraki and Areopolis).[5]

The earliest reliefs from the mid-sixth to the early fifth century depict a seated couple.[6] The one from Chrysapha is the earliest and shows a male and female figure seated on the left, side by side on a throne (Figure 2.1).[7] The throne is elaborate with lion feet and anthemion, and under it is a bearded snake that coils upwards behind the seated figures.[8] The male wears a chiton, mantle and sandals, and he holds a kantharos in his hand. He is placed closer to the viewer toward whom he turns his head. The female figure is seated completely in profile and mostly covered by the male. She draws her veil forward in an *anakalypteria* gesture and holds a fruit, probably a pomegranate, in her other hand. Smaller figures of a man and a woman with offerings of a cock, an egg, a flower and pomegranate approach them. Variations of this composition are found on other reliefs, where the couple sits on the right, which results in the man holding both the kantharos and the pomegranate. The smaller figures appear only on the two earliest reliefs so in other examples the reliefs only depict the seated couple (Figure 2.2).[9]

By the early fifth century, the woman is absent and the male sits alone on the reliefs. Other elements, such as a dog or a horse protome, are added to the scene

Figure 2.1 Berlin, Antikenmuseen 731; stone relief of enthroned couple and a diminutive couple bringing offerings; from Chrysapha, Laconia. Photo by Carole Raddato.

(Figure 2.3). The man holds a kantharos or phiale, from which the snake sometimes drinks.[10] Other reliefs depict the man with an attendant, a woman or boy, carrying an oinochoe.[11]

Nine of these reliefs bear some kind of inscription, although it is possible that others had painted texts. Of the inscribed reliefs, only one dates to the Archaic period and has its inscription in retrograde [XI]ΛON (Figure 2.4).[12] Another, of the early fifth century, has the fragmentary inscription HIAT[-. The remaining seven have inscriptions that are either undated or of the fourth century or of Hellenistic and Roman date.[13]

The identification of the figures and the interpretation of the scenes as well as their function have been debated since the time of the reliefs' first publication in 1877.[14] Because of the similarities with the terracotta pinakes from Lokroi Epizephyrioi dedicated to Persephone and the reliefs that decorated the early fifth-century Harpy tomb in Xanthos (Lycia), Furtwängler, in one of the earliest studies on these reliefs, interpreted the iconography as an abstract idea of a

Figure 2.2 Sparta Museum 6517; stone relief of enthroned couple and snake in front; from the Bougadis plot, Sparta. Courtesy of Sparta Museum.

couple known by different names in various places, such as Zeus Chthonios and Ge Chthonia, Zeus Melichios and Meliche, Pluto and Persephone, Trophonios and Herkyra, Neleus and Basile.[15] Others thought of them as grave monuments – a view now disproved but that was at one point supported by many scholars.[16] When Tod and Wace published the *Sparta Museum Catalogue* in 1906, they used the terms 'hero' or 'heroized dead' to describe the figures on the reliefs.[17] Following their interpretation, Andronikos also argued that the reliefs were dedicated to heroes.[18] Since then, the figures have been interpreted as ordinary or heroized dead, as underworld divinities, or as heroes of an established cult.[19] On one rare inscribed relief the word [X]IΛON (Figure 2.4) is written in retrograde under the throne of the seated figure (*I.G.* v.1.244); Chilon, a sixth-century Spartan ephor, was heroized at some point after his death (Paus. 3.16.4), so the relief may refer to him.[20]

In order to comprehend the imagery of the Laconian reliefs, a number of scholars have linked the iconographical motifs with those of votive reliefs elsewhere in the Greek world. For example, Rhomaios compared the Laconian reliefs with the sixth-century Tegea banquet reliefs, which represent a cult scene

Figure 2.3 Sparta Museum 505; stone relief with enthroned man, dog and horse; from near Chrysapha, Laconia. Courtesy of Sparta Museum.

that involved gods or heroes honoured with a meal.[21] Dentzer's thorough iconographical study of banqueting scenes demonstrates that the iconographical motif of the banqueting hero was specifically created for founder-heroes, *archegetai* and ancestors.[22] In her study on the iconography of the Laconian reliefs, Salapata concludes that the imagery shows the hero feasting not at the banquet, where a hero would normally be reclining, but after the banquet during the second phase of festivities, which was devoted to drinking.[23] The reliefs were dedicated to mythological heroes as well as heroes who were recently heroized dead.

Today, the Laconian reliefs are commonly interpreted as dedications to heroes but the discussion is ongoing. Material from the recent excavations at the Archaic–Hellenistic Olive Oil Cemetery located in south-west Sparta, have led

Figure 2.4 Sparta Museum 1005; stone relief of enthroned couple with snake coiling under the throne; inscription in retrograde [X]IΛON (*IG* V.1. 244); from southeast of the acropolis. Courtesy of Sparta Museum.

to funerary connotations in the reliefs.[24] The argument is based on kantharoid vessels with toothed lids that were found in burials at the Olive Oil Cemetery, which the excavator connects to the kantharoi held by the hero in the reliefs. The problem is that the kantharoi depicted on the reliefs are a different shape, with large handles, and are not covered by a toothed lid, such as those found at the cemetery. Here a reverse argument rather, should see an influence from the heroic reliefs to the burials since the kantharoid vessels appear in the Hellenistic period when some ordinary dead received honours similar to old heroes.[25] The appearance of the kantharoid vessels at the Olive Oil Cemetery should not alter the interpretation of the stone reliefs as gifts to heroes.[26] Most noteworthy is the fact that, among the numerous Archaic–Hellenistic graves discovered at the cemetery, not one terracotta or stone relief with heroic iconography has surfaced.

As discussed in Chapter 1, the use of 'hero' is not constant and by the fourth century and later it was common to honour the deceased with the title 'hero'.[27] Such practices were probably reflected in Sparta too. A third-century stone relief carries the inscription 'Choiras son of Choir[as].[28] Another, the Aristokles Relief, dated to the second century BC, and the Timokles Relief, a later copy of a sixth-century relief that bears a later inscription, carry personal names.[29] Some of the stone reliefs dated in the Hellenistic period and later may have been destined for funerary purpose.

Clearer evidence that these stone reliefs are dedications to heroes comes from their iconographical similarities to the Laconian terracotta reliefs, which date from the late sixth to the late fourth century BC.[30] It was customary in various locations in the Greek world to offer terracotta reliefs as votives to heroes.[31] In Sparta, too, the terracotta reliefs are found most commonly associated with hero cults, with very few examples discovered at the sanctuary of Artemis Orthia and the Menelaion.[32] The largest deposit comes from Amyklai and is dedicated to Agamemnon and Alexandra/Kassandra. Furthermore, the iconography of the reliefs resembles that of votives to cults of heroes from other sites throughout the Greek world, such as Corinth, Messenia and Taras. Often, they are found in contexts of rediscovered Bronze Age tombs in Messenia, signifying later veneration, while at Sparta itself, they are also frequently found in connection with areas of earlier Geometric burials (below). None have been found in graves in Sparta, excluding the possibility that these were used for funerary purpose.

The subject matter of the terracotta reliefs is identified as typically heroic and resembles the stone reliefs: an enthroned male is the most commonly depicted individual and appears in the later part of the sixth century. He is shown alone holding a kantharos, a phiale or another item, such as a staff, a pomegranate or a cock (Figure 2.5).[33] Other times, he is accompanied by a standing figure either a woman, a boy, a standing couple or an adorant. In some examples, the woman carries an oinochoe, a phiale, a tray of offerings or a wreath; the boy too in some cases brings an oinochoe.[34] While the seated couple disappears from Laconian stone reliefs by the early fifth century BC, it reappears in the later fifth century on some terracotta reliefs, particularly those from the Amyklai deposit and the Filippopoulou plot.[35] On a rare example, a seated lone woman holds a phiale.[36]

Other reliefs have iconography that does not appear on the stone reliefs:[37] standing figures (triads or dyads) (Figure 2.6);[38] a rider (Figure 2.7), which appears on Laconian terracotta reliefs from the second half of the fourth century BC following iconographical trends for votives to heroes from elsewhere in the Greek world;[39] a warrior (Figure 2.8), seen from the Archaic period onwards, adheres to the Greek ideals of warrior heroes and offers parallels of the striding hero motif found in Attic art of the Classical period.[40] Lastly, the banqueter (Figure 2.9) motif begins in the second half of the fourth century

Figure 2.5 Sparta Museum 3230; terracotta relief of seated man; from the deposit of Agamemnon and Alexandra/Kassandra at Amyklai. Courtesy of Sparta Museum.

and continues into the third century BC. This 'Typus für Heroendarstellungen' became especially popular in fourth-century Attic iconography whence it spread throughout the Greek world.[41] The iconography, which often included a table (*trapeza*) with food offerings, depicts the hero at the *theoxenia*, a meal in honour of the hero.[42] The dedication of terracotta reliefs depicting a banqueter in Sparta is not common before the mid-fourth century, unlike other areas of the Greek world, where the motif existed from the end of the sixth century. The reason behind this difference is because the scene of the seated man with a kantharos, although different, may have assumed a comparable function in Sparta.[43]

Because of the similarities between the stone and terracotta reliefs, it seems certain that the stone reliefs were dedications destined for heroes in Sparta too.

Figure 2.6 Sparta Museum 237-8; terracotta relief with standing triad; from the deposit of Agamemnon and Alexandra/Kassandra at Amyklai. Courtesy of Gina Salapata.

Indeed, often they are found near the area where deposits of terracotta reliefs were unearthed, probably destined for the same hero shrine.

Their appearance in votive deposits in Sparta, together with other dedications, burials and architectural remains, provides a safe indication that the cult recipient would have been a hero or heroine. However, there is a general tendency against using votives to identify the recipient of cult.[44] For example, Hägg argues that there is little difference in the type of votives found in Olympian, chthonian or heroic sanctuaries.[45] He may be largely correct in that some votives are indistinct in their deposition in heroic or divine cults but what he does not consider is the need for a systematic study of sanctuaries within individual poleis or regions where local practices should be borne in mind. Individual poleis may have dedicatory practices that may reflect the nature of the recipient of cult.[46]

Figure 2.7 Sparta Museum 6152-1; terracotta relief with a rider; from the deposit of Agamemnon and Alexandra/Kassandra at Amyklai. Courtesy of Gina Salapata.

2.2 A survey of the sites and deposits

The selection of sites discussed below includes the larger, better-documented sites from Sparta and Amyklai. A grave is present in a number of locations as well as architectural remains, terracotta reliefs and other votives. A list of all the find-spots where terracotta reliefs were found, especially if only one or two are documented, is not attempted here.[47] The sites and votive deposits reported below show evidence that they were related to heroic cults of the Archaic and Classical periods. Since many of them have emerged through excavations of the early twentieth century and more recent rescue excavations by the E' Ephoreia of Prehistoric and Classical antiquities in Greece, they are not fully published. Crucial information, such as date of the finds, stratigraphy, and the relationship of the finds to Proto-Geometric and Geometric burials found in the area, is often missing. Therefore, although the data presented below shows evidence of heroic

Figure 2.8 Sparta Museum 6225-1; terracotta relief with a warrior; from the deposit of Agamemnon and Alexandra/Kassandra at Amyklai. Courtesy of Gina Salapata.

cult, it is impossible to ascertain with confidence that the votives and sites below belonged to heroes only. While terracotta plaques have limited presence in the main sanctuaries of Sparta (Artemis-Orthia, Athena Chalkioikos on the Acropolis, the Amyklaion and even the Menelaion), we cannot exclude the possibility that heroes could have received votives at a shrine that belonged to a deity, hence a 'visiting hero'. The choice of sites below can be methodologically challenging and many localities can be difficult to interpret; nonetheless, they allow us to see some dedicatory patterns, ritual practices, and even architectural observations that will be analysed in Chapter 3.

2.2.1 Agamemnon and Alexandra/Kassandra[48]

The location of the site of worship of Agamemnon and Alexandra/Kassandra is noted by Pausanias (3.19.6). In his description of Laconia, he mentions that there is a temple at Amyklai dedicated to Alexandra, whom the locals call Kassandra, the daughter of Priam,[49] and that nearby is the tomb of Agamemnon and a statue of Clytemnestra.

Figure 2.9 Sparta Museum 6223-1; terracotta relief with banqueter; from the deposit of Agamemnon and Alexandra/Kassandra at Amyklai. Courtesy of Gina Salapata.

Two votive deposits associated with this cult were excavated near the church of Ayia Paraskevi in modern Amyklai. The offerings have been securely identified with the sanctuary of Agamemnon and Alexandra/Kassandra because of the dedicatory vase inscriptions mentioning the names of Alexandra and Agamemnon, the earliest of which dates to 525 BC.[50] Further evidence for the identification of the recipient of the deposit comes from the discovery nearby of two Late Hellenistic works: a marble throne dedicated by the Gerousia to Alexandra and a *stele* inscribed with an honorary decree, which included a provision that the stele should be set up at Alexandra's sanctuary.[51]

The first deposit produced more than 10,000 objects, ranging in date from the early seventh century BC[52] to the Early Hellenistic period, including vases of standard (42 lakainai;[53] 1 miniature lakaina;[54] 1 high stemmed-kylix and 28 of the 'Droop' type;[55] 131 aryballoi including miniatures;[56] 20 cups; 3 bowls[57] at least 45 kraters; 4 oinochoai; 11 hydriai and kyathoi; and 2,000 kylix feet belonging to 'Droop' cups)[58] and miniature size (e.g. 25 krateriskoi), terracotta figurines, two pieces of metal objects, three lead figurines of wreaths, and more than 1,200 terracotta reliefs (Figures 2.5–2.9)[59] Some of the fragments belonging to cups were painted with vines and snakes.[60] One cup depicts a hero holding a kantharos with a snake below, reminiscent of the iconography of the stone and terracotta reliefs.[61] Architectural remains included an Archaic disc acroterion, inscribed fragmentary tiles and gorgoneion antefixes of the second half of the fifth century.[62] The above material was placed neatly stacked and sorted by type of object, clearly the result of the cleaning of a temenos. [63]

The second deposit, also containing material from the Archaic to the Hellenistic periods, encompassed large quantities of terracotta reliefs, pottery, including spherical aryballoi, kylikes, figurines and miniature vases, as well as lead figurines including lead wreaths.[64] Under the deposit were the foundations of two walls for which we are not given any information in terms of size, date or material.[65]

Although the sanctuary reported by Pausanias at Amyklai (3.19.6) eludes us, the two aforementioned deposits, with dedications of Agamemnon and Alexandra/Kassandra, make it likely that it was located near them. Furthermore, the more recent discovery of the two walls under the second deposit[66] may, in fact, belong to a structure associated with the cult site of Agamemnon and Alexandra/Kassandra; further study of the site may help identify the relationship of the two walls to the two deposits.

Salapata, in her study of the heroic cult of Alexandra/Kassandra, concludes that both Agamemnon and Alexandra/Kassandra were worshipped at Amyklai as early as the early seventh century BC.[67] Although Alexandra/Kassandra was a consort of Agamemnon she was by no means subordinate in their worship, as indicated by a number of terracotta reliefs from the later fifth century BC that show a seated couple, as on the stone reliefs, while an attendant holds a tray of offerings before them.[68] On other reliefs, Kassandra appears by herself, which shows that she is also worshipped alone.[69] She is seated, holding a mushroom-shaped sceptre and a phiale, not unlike the male in some of the reliefs.[70] Although some terracotta reliefs depict a seated couple or a single female figure, most depict a seated male. The predominantly male iconography may suggest that Agamemnon was a stronger figure in the cult, at least in the beginning. Agamemnon's popularity in the early fifth century is not only demonstrated by the votives but is also attested by Sparta's response to Gelon (who wanted to lead the expedition against the Persians) that Agamemnon would lament if he heard that Sparta did not command the Hellene troops during the Persian Wars (Hdt. 7.159). By the Hellenistic period, however, Alexandra/Kassandra may have taken a more prominent role in the cult since the

Hellenistic decree dedicated by the Gerousia and the inscribed throne found near the two deposits only mention the temple of Alexandra. Furthermore, Pausanias says that the temple was dedicated to Alexandra/Kassandra and omits Agamemnon. Instead, Agamemnon in the Roman period is connected with the area only by the existence of his tomb (Paus. 3.19.6).

The cult of Agamemnon and Alexandra/Kassandra has been construed as part of Sparta's 'Achaian policy', which saw the appropriation of Achaian heroes in order legitimize its rule in the Peloponnese and show its hegemony against Argos.[71] This interpretation should be viewed with caution, since some literary traditions link Agamemnon with Laconia:[72] in the *Odyssey* (4.514ff.) Agamemnon tells Odysseus the story about how he ran into a storm at Cape Malea;[73] this location is in Laconia near the perioikic town of Boiai and not en route to Mycenae.[74] In the *Iliad* (9.149–56), Agamemnon rules cities in Messenia.[75] Simonides and Stesichoros place him in Sparta (216 Davies *PMGF*; 549 Page, *PMG*),[76] and Pindar locates his kingdom at Amyklai (Pindar *P.* 11.32; *N.* 11.34).[77] Stesichoros names the nurse of Orestes Laodameia, after the daughter of Amyklas king of Lakedaimon (Schol. Aisch. *Choeph.* 733)[78] and gives Agamemnon a different genealogy: the father of Agamemnon was not Atreus but Pleisthenes.[79] Based on the above textual evidence, there was seemingly an alternative tradition that placed Agamemnon in Laconia rather than the Argolid. It is unlikely that the establishment of the cult of Agamemnon was a propaganda tool for Sparta's 'Achaian policy', not only because of the literary tradition, but also based on the archaeological evidence. We know that the cult of Agamemnon and Alexandra/Kassandra commenced in the early seventh century and thus predates any hegemonic aspirations that Sparta may have had in the Peloponnese or against Argos similar to those seen in the sixth century. Moreover, there is overall no evidence that the ethnicity of a hero (Achaian vs Dorian) played any role when Greeks set up heroic cults.[80] Agamemnon was worshipped in Laconia because he was a local hero.

2.2.2 The drainage ditch by the Eurotas Bridge (t.s.[81] 012)

Two deposits were discovered about 50 metres south of the Eurotas Bridge: one with pottery (oinochoai and lekythoi of the fifth and fourth centuries, fragments of kraters, cups, black figure skyphoi; and amphorai; fragments of Archaic pithoi, fragments of Attic black-figure pottery) and figurines dating to the Archaic and Classical period.[82] In the same area were found two fragments of terracotta reliefs (SM 6399) and three bronze snakes, together with other votives in a

Hellenistic context.[83] The area is rich in finds from the Geometric to the Roman period, including what the excavator interprets as a Late Geometric/Early Archaic house, a Hellenistic street, and Geometric, Archaic and Hellenistic tombs. Among them was a pithos burial covered by a heap of stones.[84]

Near this area a third deposit was found containing six large (fragmentary) Archaic terracotta reliefs (Figure 2.10) together with Laconian roof tiles and a fragment of a marble plaque with a partial Archaic inscription.[85] The terracotta reliefs, of which only four are published, are large, *c.* 54 centimetres in height, with traces of paint. They differ to those terracotta plaques discussed above in their iconography: although none survives intact, one depicts pairs of hoplites, two show pairs of riders, while another shows part of a female head turned to her right.[86] Steinhauer interprets the terracotta reliefs as metopes for a hero shrine or a grave monument;[87] these types of terracotta metopes have been discovered elsewhere in Sparta.[88] He explains that each of the reliefs is rendered within a border, leaving some blank space where it would be secured on to a wooden building.[89] His reasoning may be correct considering that Laconian roof tiles were also discovered in the deposit and probably belonged to the same building. The building bearing the metopes is probably a shrine because of the deposit found at the site with pottery and figurines, dating to the Archaic and Classical periods and presumably votive.[90] Among them are a large number of drinking shapes, commonly found in Spartan sanctuaries (Chapter 3).

About 4 metres north from the deposit were found the remains of a paved floor made with five poros slabs forming a corner. Next to it were the foundations

Figure 2.10 Sparta Museum; terracotta metopes with hoplites, riders and a female head; from the drainage ditch near the Eurotas Bridge. Courtesy of Sparta Museum.

of a square structure or a peribolos wall.⁹¹ The excavator dates this layer before the 464 BC earthquake.⁹² It is possible that the metopes and the architectural remains, which belong to the earlier stratigraphic layer, derive from this building.

Another suggestion is that the metopes may belong to the remains of another building found 7 metres north from the deposit and at the same level. Here were found the foundations of a 6-metre wall, embedded in a late seventh-century stratum. Thus, the foundations, tiles and metopes may all be part of the same building.⁹³

The identification on the figures on the metopes remains speculative. Steinhauer suggests that they depict the rescue of Helen by her brothers, the Dioskouroi, after having been abducted by Theseus.⁹⁴ The myth of the abduction of Helen by Theseus is known in Alkman (21*PMGF*; Paus. 1.41.4.) and both Helen and the Dioskouroi were important local heroes who were already the recipients of cult in Archaic Sparta (§ 4.3). The metopes are too fragmentary to allow a confident interpretation but one shows two male warrior figures, one bearded and the other without. Such distinction of facial hair is known in Laconian art from two sixth-century Laconian reliefs that depict the Dioskouroi (Sparta Museum 575, fig. 4.21); cf. Sparta Museum 5380). It is possible, then, that the reliefs show a scene from the adventures of the Dioskouroi, popular heroes in Sparta.

2.2.3 The Heroon by the Eurotas River

An area inside the city walls of Sparta and close to the so-called 'altar of Lycurgus' was excavated in 1905.⁹⁵ The excavators report that the most typical finds are terracotta hero-reliefs (about a hundred specimens) and conclude, on the basis of the iconography, that these belong to the 'well known class of Spartan hero-reliefs'.⁹⁶ The seated male with a kantharos is the most common depiction of the reliefs but other types exist, including a warrior standing before a snake, a rider on horseback and a banqueter. In addition to the terracotta reliefs, there were found a number of Archaic terracotta figurines and pottery: some miniatures, kantharoi, 6 kraters, three-handled vases, 2 lakainai, 10 cups, 13 bowls, 2 cups, 8 kothons (one-handled mugs), 2 kantharoi, 2 oinochoai, 2 amphorai, as well as black-glazed fragments with red dipinti of A and IA.⁹⁷ The terracotta figurines comprise mostly females wearing *poloi*, though many are male nude figurines. Among the vases is a relief krater with a fighting scene that Wace dates to the sixth century on the basis of style⁹⁸ and it too is a votive offering. From the finds, the site appears to be a hero shrine dating from the Early Archaic period.⁹⁹

The excavation did not produce any clear structure but a number of architectural terracottas have been unearthed: two 'late' antefixes of different periods, two fragments of a geison (or cyma) with an acanthus scroll in relief above a painted maeander, a fragment of what the excavators perceived as a black glazed metope or large relief,[100] and a piece of an unpublished terracotta disc acroterion (antefix?) with red glaze only.[101] The architectural finds suggest that a structure was near a street by the city wall, probably a *heroon* associated with the votive material.[102] Although no coherent structure was found the excavators report several walls.[103] Some of the architectural terracottas were also of different periods,[104] suggesting either more than one architectural phase or at least some later repairs. The terracotta geison with the acanthus leaves could be fourth century or later as it is then when such decorative elements become more common.[105]

During the excavation, a *pithos* that lay near a large concentration of vase fragments was also discovered. It was situated near one of the walls that may have belonged to the temenos or to another building. The *pithos* lay on its side, two large slabs enclosed it and it was half full of earth, in which were found calcinated bones, and two mugs. The skeletal remains in the *pithos* prompted the excavators to identify it as a burial and date it to the 'Greek period'.[106] Some *pithos* burials in Sparta date from the Proto-Geometric period but they are most commonly attested in the Geometric,[107] with a number of examples found, including some at Limnai.[108] The relation, if at all, of the burial to the later hero shrine is uncertain. The cult may have formed around an earlier burial, not unlike other examples from Sparta (see below) or it may have been a chance occurrence that a Geometric burial existed. The latter is more probable since in the area within the later kome of Limnai, there was a Geometric necropolis.

The excavator suggested that this shrine may be the heroon of Astrabacus.[109] According to Pausanias, the shrine of Astrabacus was located near the altar dedicated to Lykourgos (Paus. 3.16.6; 3.16; cf. Hdt. 6.69.3.). A long structure found nearby had been identified by the early excavators as the 'altar of Lykourgos',[110] but now long buildings are more commonly interpreted as temples (§ 6.2). Probably the heroon of Astrabacus should be sought further south and closer to the sanctuary of Artemis Orthia since the two are related in myth (Paus. 3.16.9).[111]

2.2.4 O 13[112]

A rich deposit was discovered during excavations in the area of square O 13 located near the Heroon by the Eurotas River (2.2.3). The finds, mostly unpublished, were discovered in the storeroom of the Sparta Museum[113] and include three fragmentary terracotta reliefs, miniature vases and lead figurines. Stibbe reports pottery from all periods (Geometric to Roman) and especially black-glazed pottery of the sixth century BC, including kraters, a fragment of a stamnos, two lakainai and one kylix.[114] Some red-figure fragments (two of which are Attic) are also reported from the same site.[115] The finds, especially of lead-figurines, miniature vases and reliefs, suggest that this material belongs to a cult.[116] Near this deposit, at the Dikaios plot were unearthed the foundations of a square structure which is interpreted now as a courtyard of a Roman villa.[117]

2.2.5 Ergatikes Katoikies (west of town square 101)

A Hellenistic building was discovered on the eastern foot of the Acropolis hill, which appears to have housed a cult that formed around an Early Archaic burial.[118] The Hellenistic structure comprised three very small rooms;[119] in the middle of the southernmost room was an Archaic grave, as indicated by the two small lakainai of Laconian II (610–575 BC) found together with the skeletal remains.[120] The grave was constructed of two erect slabs (0.10 metres) that formed a box-shaped construction (0.75 × 0.60 metres) that rose upright on the floor of the Hellenistic building. The whole expanse of the room around the grave area was covered with 150 terracotta female figurines and handmade animal figurines. Further finds included miniature pottery, lamps, bone knife handles and a statuette of a 'barbarian'.[121] There are two Archaic finds: a bronze protome[122] and a terracotta horse. It is unknown what the other small rooms of the Hellenistic building would have been used for. The central room (2 × 1.80 metres) was paved with stone slaps and had 'benches' in three sides of the room and a drain so perhaps it was used for dining.[123] A smaller Roman-era room (1.50 × 2.20 metres) was constructed over the Hellenistic building and directly over the grave. One fragmentary terracotta relief was found nearby.[124] The phases of construction and the votives show that an Early Archaic burial became a locus of cult; the site was renovated during the Hellenistic period and into the Roman times.

2.2.6 The Stavropoulos plot (N 13) t.s. 101

At this site, a long building (5.10 × 29.20 metres) was discovered atop a marble *krepis*.[125] The excavator reports a south-western side, constructed with blue

Figure 2.11 The Stavropoulos plot, Sparta. Courtesy of Sparta Museum.

Laconian marble in a polygonal Lesbian technique dated to the late sixth/early fifth century BC (based on the masonry style) that survived from an early phase of the building (Figure 2.11).[126] The dimensions of the building from this early phase are not known as the building exhibits constructions, additions, and renovations from later periods all the way to the Late Roman times.[127] The later phases of the walls included a reused Late Archaic heroic stone relief depicting an enthroned couple.[128] There was also an entranceway on the south-east side, which was walled up at some point in antiquity. A deposit dating from the first century BC was found in front of the south-west wall among which were a large number of loom weights, domestic pottery, lamps and two terracotta figurines of Artemis.[129] Under the deposit was a burial constructed of tiles marked with a stone and which contained burned remains and a few gold leaves.[130] Finds reported from the site include terracotta figurines of Artemis, a terracotta figurine of one of the Dioskouroi, and two terracotta comic masks.[131]

During the early part of the twentieth century a 'few small terracotta hero-reliefs … like those from the Heroon on the bank of the river' were found in the same plot.[132] Stibbe reports the finds of a Doric capital (c. 500 BC) and a fragment of an Archaic relief krater like the one found at the Heroon by the Eurotas nearby and commonly found in cult sites in Sparta.[133] Because of these finds, as well as a Late Archaic heroic stone relief found reused in the later wall, we can assume that they belonged to a heroic shrine. The architectural remains of the Lesbian late-sixth/early-fifth-century wall and the Doric capital, could belong to a structure that may have housed the cult. The site was important enough to have gone multiple renovations and constructions during later periods. The building works included the incorporation of architectural elements of the older cult site, such as the wall of Lesbian technique, in front of which was found the Late-Hellenistic burial, and the Archaic heroic stone relief built into the Hellenistic peribolos wall.

2.2.7 The Niarchos plot (t.s. 98)

A votive deposit of large dimensions (3 × 4 metres) containing hundreds of terracotta reliefs, fragments of pottery of the sixth and the fifth centuries BC and lead figurines was found near the remains of a Hellenistic and Roman structure. Below the deposit was a stratum with a large quantity of Geometric pottery.[134]

Just north of the deposit, the ruins of a Roman structure and a circular construction made of slabs (1.72m in diameter and 4.5m in depth) were discovered. An entrance leading by staircase to the interior of the circular structure was found on its eastern side. According to the excavator, Spyropoulos, this circular structure was the deposit area for some form of cult, perhaps contemporary with the aforementioned deposit containing terracotta reliefs found to the south. The excavator speculates that because the circular construction was found under the earth, it may indicate chthonic worship and connects the finds with the cult and sanctuary of Eileithyia, which, according to Pausanias, was located near the sanctuary of Orthia (3.14.6).[135] Salapata offers a different suggestion in that the circular structure bears the resemblance of a tholos tomb, which would have acquired cult at a later time, or it may be related to another cult on Stauffert Street (no. 8), located nearby.[136] If this is a cult at a tholos tomb it would be one of the rare examples of such practice in Laconia; the custom is more commonly seen in neighbouring Messenia.[137] Unfortunately, at this point there is no information on the circular structure's construction, or on whether any finds were collected from its interior. The connection with the heroic votive deposit nearby is tempting but since no publication or further study has been conducted on this site, it remains speculative.

2.2.8 The cult site on Stauffert Street[138] (t.s. 98)

In 1996, a rescue excavation in Limnai at Sparta (town square 98) unearthed a Geometric burial that became the locus of cult.[139] The burial was an inhumation with the body placed in a contracted position. It was protected with a stone slab upon which was a heaped pile of stones, which covered Geometric pottery (Figures 2.12–2.13).[140] A row of stones parallel to the burial marked off the space and the area had numerous Geometric vases.[141] Over the cairn of stones was a votive deposit of the Early Archaic to the Hellenistic periods, including over 2,500 fragments of terracotta reliefs with images – standing figures, the seated male, warriors, riders and banqueters[142] – that correspond to those on the votive reliefs from the deposits dedicated to Agamemnon and Alexandra/Kassandra at Amyklai and those from the Heroon by the Eurotas, as well as 800 terracotta figurines, both male and female, shown standing, enthroned or reclining, among the votives.[143] In addition, a fragment of an Archaic terracotta acroterion, many lead figurines (including wreaths, hoplites, female winged figures, a lead snake);[144] pottery of drinking shapes, such as lakainai, kantharoi, cups and bowls, and

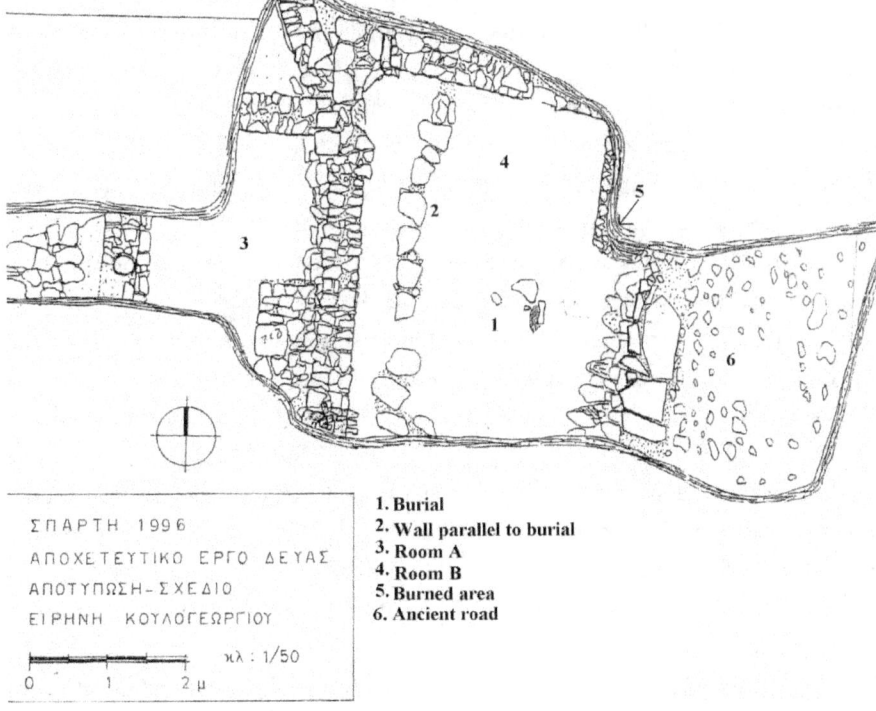

Figure 2.12 Plan of Stauffert Street excavation, Sparta. Courtesy of Christos Flouris.

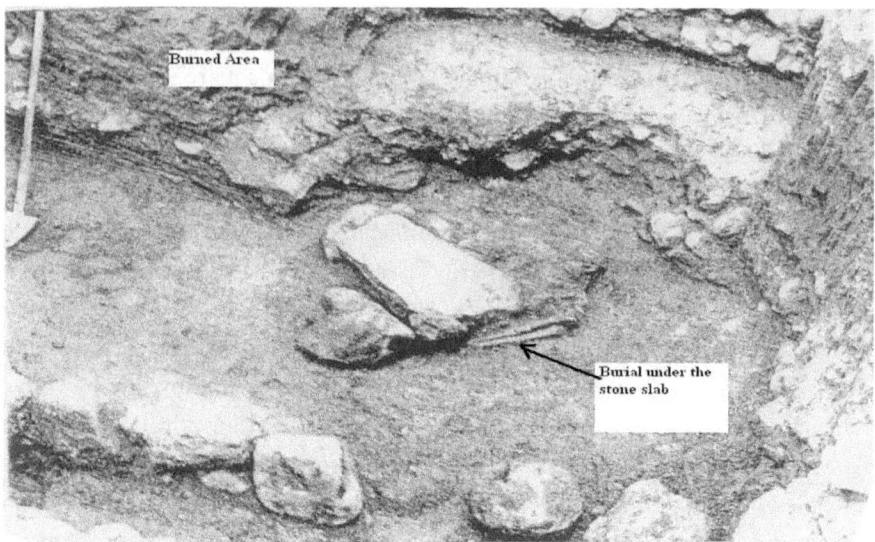

Figure 2.13 Stauffert Street burial, Sparta. Courtesy of Christos Flouris.

around 1,500 miniature vases (including kantharoi and lakainai) were also recovered from the votive deposit.[145] Lastly, the excavator reports the find of a fragmentary stone relief, whose imagery resembles that of the famous Chrysapha relief,[146] which carries the inscription '[...]ΚΕΟΣ', perhaps the ending of a name.[147] The deposit not only lay over the cairn of stones but it actually went through and penetrated into the middle of the cairn of stones in a circular formation about 0.5 metres in depth. The votives were deposited at a single moment, as part of clearing up the temenos.

Near the burial and at the same level was a second deposit composed of a burned area that reached down to the same level as the top of the stone cairn. This burned area contained fragments of animal bones and broken-up material of the same kind as the deposit over the burial (fragmentary terracotta reliefs, figurines and vases).[148] The material dates from the seventh century to the Hellenistic period.[149]

Since a burned area containing fragments of animal bones has been found, there is evidence of sacrifice at the site that would be followed by dining. Among the votive terracotta reliefs, one unusual fragmentary example depicts a woman leading a ram,[150] perhaps illustrative of part of the religious ritual where sacrifice and subsequent dining would occur.

Where the dining would take place is unknown, although the small room (A) next to the burial has been proposed. This room contains three walls (walls

36, 39, 41; room A) that are estimated at 4.1 metres[151] and 3.5 metres. The excavation produced pottery of mostly Archaic and Classical periods from the room's interior.[152] Room A also contained a bench or table running along the southern part of the eastern wall, while one of the walls (36) was later walled up. The interpretation of this room as a dining space lies on the discovery of the bench (or table) and so the room is understood as an *hestiatorion*; on this reading, the building next to the burial is a *lesche*.[153] The identification of a building as a *hestiatorion* cannot lie entirely on the bench. There is no evidence of a paved floor with a raised border, support for couches, drainage, an off-centre doorway, access to water or any other feature that would deem this building a dining space.[154] These features, of course, are not expected to have been fully developed in dining spaces in the pre-Classical Greek world.[155] Still, the interior space of the room is quite small in relation to the bench. The length of the bench is unknown since the excavation did not reach the length of the building but its width is roughly 0.50 metres, quite large for a small room of a width of 2 metres inside. Benches for dining occur in various dining buildings in the Greek world, most famously at Kommos temple B and perhaps temple A but they are not as wide in relation to the room. An internal wall length of *c.* 2 metres is well below the Greek norm for dining rooms of the smaller type, which usually feature a 4.5 metre wall.[156] Smaller dining halls also existed, especially in the private sphere, such as in houses in Delos, but even so, they feature larger sizes.[157] Unless the room was used for seated rather than reclined dining, its size would be impractical.[158]

The bench, rather, is probably for display of votives, much like those benches running along walls in Dreros on Crete,[159] at Kalapodi and at Eloro in Sicily.[160] Two such benches were discovered in Laconia in the seventh-century apsidal building at the sanctuary at Aigies and another just outside the building; they are interpreted to have been used as places to set up votives.[161] Another possibility is that the bench may be associated not with feasting for the mortals but instead for a banquet set up for the hero, the *theoxenia*.[162] Offering tables would be set up, where a hero (or deity) would receive food, such as cheese, fruit, cakes and other foods including some of the sacrificial meat if a sacrifice took place.[163] Such practice is commonly found in various hero cults in the Greek world while the ritual is also depicted on the banquet reliefs.[164] Since the excavation did not fully extend over the area we not have a full picture of the cultic topography of the site. Dining outdoors can also be a possibility, as seems to have been the case at the sanctuary of Apollo and Hyakinthos during the meal of the *Hyakinthia*.[165]

A second phase dates slightly later[166] (wall 35; room B) and encompasses the Geometric burial and the later deposit.[167] It appears to have been built in order to house both deposit and burial since the material is contained within the boundaries of the later wall (room B) (the walls are estimated to over 5.50 metres[168] and 3.75 metres). There was also a road running next to the area of the burial, separated from the burial area by a row of flat stones (wall 37).

Another deposit containing figurines and reliefs was found more recently at the same plot. This deposit was carefully covered with a stone cover of an urn. In the same space was also discovered a section of a wall, remains of a floor and a street.[169] The area also produced figurines from the Archaic and Hellenistic periods and part of a marble figurine. It also produced a stamped tile [Δαμόσιο] ς [-?-] Ἀθάνας Π[---]?.[170]

Nearby, in the same t.s. 98, was found another Geometric or proto-Geometric burial, and three deposits with a lot of Archaic and Classical period pottery. The area produced a large amount of Proto-Geometric to Hellenistic pottery, including further finds of terracotta plaques (SM 15355a-b, 15263), Archaic relief pithoi, a bronze figurine of a lion and a fragment of a terracotta disc acroterion.[171]

2.2.9 The Lykourgos and Karela plot (t.s. 97)

A rectangular building of late Geometric/early Archaic date was unearthed in town square 97 with evidence that the upper parts would have been of mud-brick construction. Three walls survive: of 7.50 metres, 7 metres and (incomplete) 0.80 metres. Among the various finds of pottery, including a significant number of miniature pottery,[172] animal and human terracotta figurines, dating from the Proto-Geometric period to Roman times, was a terracotta relief depicting a seated figure (MS.13712). On the north side of the building was much Late Geometric and Early Archaic pottery and five Geometric burials, one of which was Proto-Geometric.[173]

2.2.10 The Bougadis plot, Gitiada Street (t.s. 104)[174]

The site is located to the north of the Tympanon Hill in Sparta, where two fragments of terracotta reliefs were found (SM 6398), together with other objects, including three bronze snakes and a spindle whorl. Three stone reliefs found in the area are probably related to a cult site.[175] Two date from the last quarter of the sixth century and depict a seated couple, with a male holding a kantharos. The third, which depicts a solitary seated male holding a phiale from which a snake drinks, dates to the end of the fifth/early fourth century. A fragment of an Archaic Doric capital made of poros was also discovered, suggesting that a building was nearby.[176]

Nearby, on Gitiada Street, another deposit, of some fifty terracotta plaques of mostly seated figures and riders, several figurines and miniature pottery, was found under the foundations of a three-room building of Late Hellenistic and Roman times.[177] In the central room of the structure, fragments of statuettes and some lead figurines were found. Nearby was another room (3.07 × 3.20–2.75 metres), which had a small rectangular construction (1 × 1 metre) in which was found a small marble figurine of an enthroned male, miniature vases and terracotta figurines.[178] The rectangular construction is likely part of a household cult for a Late Hellenistic/Roman house[179] and independent of an earlier cult that existed in the area.

2.2.11 The Panagopoulou plot (t.s.112)

A deposit is reported that contained many terracotta reliefs and a stone relief; these are unpublished.[180]

2.2.12 The Karmoiris plot (t.s. 113)

A small 'temple shaped structure' (ναόσχημο)[181] with evidence of use from the Archaic period was discovered in town square 113. Associated with the structure is a votive deposit with terracotta reliefs, miniature vases and normal size pottery recovered from the site as well as a stone relief discovered nearby.[182] Among the remains was a terracotta lion-head, dated to the fifth century BC that formed part of an acroterion.[183]

2.2.13 The Georganta and Petrakou plot (t.s. 113)

By an ancient road were discovered remains of a Hellenistic building. Among the remains were walls, a stamped tile (Δα[μόσιος] Ἀθάν[ας]),[184] an antefix depicting an eagle, other antefixes with plant decoration and an antefix of a woman wearing an himation. Terracotta votive figurines (SM 14463–75, 14486–95) and terracotta reliefs (14476–83), some depicting banqueters and another a rider, of the Archaic–Hellenistic periods, were also unearthed here. Two fragments of less than life-size terracotta statues and a lot of pottery of the Classic, Hellenistic and Roman periods were also found.[185]

2.2.14 The Filippopoulou plot (t.s.116)

The Filippopoulou plot is reported to have an Archaic–Classical deposit with 200 terracotta reliefs, 500 terracotta figurines, 30 fragments of pottery consisting of mostly cups, miniature vases, and sherds inscribed to the 'Hero'.[186] Steinhauer connects this deposit with that of the precinct of the anonymous hero who guided Dionysus to Sparta (Paus. 3.13.7).[187] This identification is speculative as most votive deposits (including this one) lack epigraphic evidence to confirm the identity of the recipient of cult.

The Zaimis plot nearby (t.s. 117) yielded a number of unpublished terracotta reliefs and may be related to the Filippopoulou plot. Another unpublished deposit consisting of thirty-five terracotta reliefs was also unearthed nearby on Tripoleos Street.[188]

2.2.15 The Tseliou plot (t.s. 119)

Three deposits with material ranging in date from the Archaic to Late Hellenistic periods were uncovered amid some Hellenistic and Roman walls. Among other items were a large quantity of votive terracotta reliefs, figurines and pottery including cups, kantharoi, skyphoi, and miniature pottery, such as lakainai, and miniature masks. Most of the terracotta figurines depict a seated female or a standing female wearing a *polos* and date to the Classical and Hellenistic periods.[189] Because of the figurines' gender, the excavator suggests that perhaps a female (deity or heroine) may have been worshipped here.[190]

2.2.16 The Stathopoulos and Argeiti plot (t.s. 120)

A deposit found at this plot consisted of roof tiles, a significant number of lead votive wreaths, miniature vases, pottery from the Archaic and Classical Periods, terracotta reliefs and votive figurines. Among the figurines is one that depicts an enthroned figure, one of a kourotrophic type and a head of the Daedalic type. A fragmentary terracotta plaque bears a representation of a Gorgon. Considering the nature of the deposit, i.e. the terracotta reliefs and figurines, the material probably comes from a shrine in the area. A later Roman-period building was also discovered at the plot.[191]

2.2.17 The Bilida plot

South of the Acropolis Hill was discovered a deposit with many objects dating from the Late Classical and Early Hellenistic periods. Among the finds were some terracotta reliefs and terracotta figurines. The excavator suggests that the deposit belonged to a shrine in the area.[192]

2.2.18 The Kalatzis plot (t.s. 125)

At this site, Steinhauer, in 1973, excavated a shallow pit containing pottery, terracotta reliefs and statuettes (including a Daedalic figurine),[193] fragments of glass and a small marble head of a lion. The finds date from the seventh century BC to the Hellenistic period.[194] The terracotta plaques were not as numerous as in other deposits described above but their iconography was the same as those of the reliefs found in several heroa, such as the Amyklaian deposit.[195] Because of the nature of the finds, we can discern that the deposit was linked to a heroic cult. A stone relief was also unearthed nearby.[196]

Several architectural remains were discovered that enable us to posit a building.[197] The excavation produced the foundations of a wall, 1 metre in width, and another parallel to it, 4 metres away. Remains of a fragment of an Archaic terracotta antefix with incised designs forming a radial crescent (*c.* 650/20–580 BC)[198] and parts of four Hellenistic architectural fragments decorated with a Gorgoneion, riders,[199] and an eagle in relief were also unearthed.[200] There were also parts of a capital, a column base and a drum of a Corinthian column. It appears that a small building was in site with an Archaic phase, as established by the Archaic antefix, but which must have been replaced or underwent repairs during the Hellenistic period.

2.2.19 The Markou plot (t.s. 6)

A deposit of terracotta figurines and terracotta plaques were found here. Most of the reliefs depicted banqueters and some were seated or standing figures.[201]

2.2.20 The Chatzis plot and Arfani plot (t.s. 91)

A rescue excavation unearthed a deposit consisting of tiles, terracotta statuettes, sixteen of which are female (and twelve of these wear a *polos*), and thirty male (most of them nude), twenty-two terracotta reliefs and some miniature vases.

The terracotta reliefs depict the composition of the seated male with a kantharos, banqueters or riders.[202] A wall is also reported (4.80m), which the excavator interprets as a peribolos wall, and some tiles.[203]

Further excavation of square 91 (Arfani plot) revealed further walls of unknown date, but their differing constructions indicate that they belonged to different building phases.[204] The excavators report that they found miniature vessels, Megarian bowls (Hellenistic), 96 loom weights, black-glazed sherds, perfume bottles, lamps, fragments of glass and metal ware, five coins (two are third and first century) and fragments of terracotta statuettes and reliefs. The many terracotta sherds are of the Archaic and Classical times, although most of the deposit is of Hellenistic and Roman date. North of the walls were also found two burials of unknown date without any burial gifts.[205]

Because of the deposit of terracotta reliefs, figurines and miniature vases the deposit was probably linked to a cult site of the Archaic and Classical periods; due to terracotta plaques, the cult was likely dedicated to a hero. The development of the site afterwards remains shrouded.

2.2.21 Thermopylae Street (t.s. 122)

The excavators report of a number of terracotta figurines, miniature vases and terracotta plaques. The terracotta plaques date from the Archaic and Classical periods; one relief depicts a seated male with another figure standing. Among the finds were some dating from the Roman and Hellenistic periods. Given the nature and date of the finds, the deposit probably belongs to a shrine.[206]

2.2.22 The Sourli plot (t.s. 15)

Among the remains of a Roman house (third to fourth century AD) was earlier material of pottery, a loom weight, fragments of sculpture, a poros Doric capital, miniature pottery, fragments of terracotta figurines, parts of terracotta plaques and part of an acroterion.[207]

2.2.23 The Psatha-Iliopoulou plot (t.s.140)

Among the remains of a Roman house was material dating from the Geometric and Archaic periods. These included pottery, a fragment of a terracotta plaque of a woman with a polos, and a terracotta female head wearing a himation on her head and belonging to architectural decoration.[208]

2.2.24 The Zachariadi plot (t.s. 142)

During the excavations of a Roman house was found a deposit containing earlier material from the Geometric-Hellenistic periods, including pottery, terracotta plaques, a marble urn, terracotta animal and human figurines, a large number of pyramidal loom weights, some metal finds, a circular acroterion and an antefix (SM 15623) among others.[209]

2.2.25 The Nikolarou plot

At the area near t.s. 129, by the Sparta-Magoula border were found six unpublished terracotta plaques in a fragmentary condition (SM 6441).[210]

2.2.26 The Valioti plot

This area, with remains dating from the Archaic to the Roman time, produced many terracotta plaques with banqueters and seated figures.[211]

2.2.27 The Stratakou plot, t.s. 47

In this plot were found Hellenistic sherds, miniature vases, fragments of terracotta figurines and terracotta plaques, and a relief *stele* (all unpublished). Among the finds, found built in a Late Roman wall, was a base with a dedicatory inscription to the Mother of the Gods. The excavator suggests that the site is associated with the sanctuary of the Mother of the Gods mentioned by Pausanias (3.12.9).[212]

2.2.28 'A sanctuary at the Megalopolis road' (the 'Achilleion')

On the road leading from Sparta to Megalopolis, just at the outskirts north of the city of Sparta, excavations from the early part of the twentieth century revealed a cult site tentatively called the 'Achilleion'. The early excavators identified it as one of the two cult sites seen by Pausanias in the area (3.20.8; the other was a statue of Athena Parea).[213] The site yielded an array of finds, especially miniature vases, 4,000 whole (of which 700 lakainai, 2,000 skyphoi, 800 aryballoi and kantharoi) and 8,000 fragmentary, 8 terracotta figurines, 49 lead figurines and some miscellaneous objects including some made of iron.[214] Among the finds was a fragmentary terracotta plaque depicting a figure on a *kline* typical of those found at heroic sites.[215] There are a few remains to suggest a military character of votives from among the finds: a bronze lance-head, a bronze spear-head, two bronze arrows and two fragments of shield belts.[216] Other material appears to have been associated with the site, such as bronzes and marble slabs, which would have been of more valuable material but are now lost.[217] A burnt layer found together with charred bones gives evidence of sacrifice.[218]

Nine Proto-Corinthian aryballoi and the miniature pottery that find parallels at the sanctuary of Artemis Orthia provide evidence that the cult site commenced in the seventh century[219] with a peak in the Archaic period.[220] It is unknown when the cult ceased to exist but the terracotta plaque should date to the second half of the fourth century since the iconography shows a figure in a reclining position as a banqueter, indicating that the cult continued into the Classical period.[221] Hellenistic pottery may suggest survival into the third or second century BC.[222] Apart from that, seven bronze mirrors may date to the fourth or third century and could represent an Early Hellenistic period continuity of the cult.[223] However, they have been found north of the walls and outside the main votive deposit, which may suggest that these finds belong to an otherwise undetected cult site nearby,[224] such as that of Athena Parea.

The architectural phases do not shed further light on the chronology. Two building phases are reported: at the burned stratum, an early 18.50-metre-long 'Hellenic wall'[225] of 1.50m in height formed a corner that encompassed a votive deposit of a nucleus of about 4 square metres and contained miniature vases. A second wall that meets the first one is dated later and does not contain any burned material and is of different construction.[226] Laconian black or brown glazed tiles that correspond to those found at the sanctuary of Artemis Orthia were found close to the early wall but it is uncertain whether these indicate a first building construction of a seventh-century date as Stibbe suggests.[227] This is because there is little change in the shape or proportions of the Laconian tiles between the Archaic to the Roman period.[228] Part of a Doric column 'made of coarse stone, originally covered with fine marble stucco' was also found.[229] The dimensions of the column, 0.32m in diameter, with 20 flutes 0.052m in width and 0.047m in height, preserved with 0.005m *entasis*, have prompted the excavator to suggest that this column would be small in its final height and should belong to either an altar or a small building. The Doric column, which was covered in fine stucco, thus imitating marble, indicates a date of 'not before the fifth century'[230] may belong to a later phase of construction. We may then be faced with substantial renovations at a later date and complete construction over the area where earlier votive material was gathered together and placed in the inside of the wall while a new building was erected. Renewed interest in earlier cults is not uncommon in Sparta in the Hellenistic period so the later architectural remains may be connected with expansion of the site to the standards of Hellenistic heroa.

The recipient of the cult is unknown since no inscriptions have been unearthed so the identification of the cult, to Achilles, is uncertain. The material remains from this sanctuary are predominantly composed of miniature pottery of various shapes, which have been found in the thousands. There is nothing unusual about such finds as they are commonly seen in Laconian sanctuaries and also elsewhere in the Greek world. The sheer quantity of miniature pottery at the 'Achilleion' would fit well with a sanctuary that was on the road, where a traveller would deposit a small, easily portable item, such as a miniature votive.[231] The weapons, which could be suitable offering for a warrior hero as Achilles, have been unearthed in other Spartan and Laconian sanctuaries and so cannot provide any further assistance in relation to the recipient of the cult.

2.2.29 Sklavochori (Amyklai), Konidari plot

A number of fragmentary terracotta reliefs (S.M. 1284α–στ and 12844α–θ), fragmentary figurines of the Classical period and a miniature vase were discovered over a Proto-Geometric Grave in Amyklai. The area housed a number of Proto-Geometric burials and is considered a Proto-Geometric cemetery.[232]

3

The Hero Shrines: Votives, Architectural Evidence, Topography

The following chapter examines the votive offerings to heroes, and the architectural remains of heroic shrines based on the available data, as presented in Chapter 2. Because of the limited published material from most sites, the precise quantity, chronology and typology of pottery, terracotta figurines, terracotta reliefs, lead figurines and metal finds remain unknown. Nonetheless, there are some distinct dedicatory patterns and architectural remains that can allow some tentative conclusions about the nature of the cult sites within Spartan religious practice. Taking together the evidence from votive behaviour and architectural remains, at the end of the chapter I offer a discussion on the role of the heroic shrines in the local popular religious tradition of the polis.

3.1 Votives

The study of votive and ritual behaviour examines the ways in which the devotees communicated and expressed their veneration to gods or heroes. The study of votive behaviour can consider various factors regarding the typology of dedications in sanctuaries: economic affordability, occasion, issues of display, gender, and personal vs public dedications etc. Dedicatory practices are an important component in ritual practice not because they can securely reflect the identities of the worshippers, and not because they can always provide the identity of the deity or hero but because they 'may be used by practitioners so as to create as well as subvert categories'.[1] The choice of offering can reflect to some degree differentiation and distinction of cult character within a community. As we will see below, the majority of offerings at hero shrines consist of inexpensive items: terracotta reliefs, terracotta figurines, and pottery (often in miniature). The absence of precious dedications in bronze and ivory displays a distinct difference in patterns of dedication compared to those of the main sanctuaries of the polis.

3.1.1 Stone and terracotta reliefs

As noted earlier, the identification of many sites or deposits as heroic relies primarily on the discovery of terracotta reliefs. The popularity of these votives as gifts to heroes is evident in the numbers offered to Agamemnon and Alexandra/Kassandra (no. 1), the deposit on Stauffert Street (no. 8), the Heroon by the Eurotas (no. 3) and the deposit at the Niarchos plot (no. 7), where hundreds of terracotta reliefs were unearthed. Other sites also yielded terracotta reliefs in significant quantities, such as the twenty reliefs found at the Chatzis plot (no. 20) or the thirty-five at the Zaimis plot (no. 14), and yet more sites may have produced large numbers but remain unpublished. Stone reliefs were found together or nearby some sites, such as at the Stavropoulos plot (no. 6), where a stone relief was found reused in the later long building. At Stauffert Street (no. 8), a fragmentary stone relief bore a partial inscription and at the Bougadis and Gitiada plots (no. 10) three stone reliefs of the Archaic and Classical periods were found nearby. Compared to the large numbers of terracotta reliefs, stone reliefs are not as numerous, probably due to their more expensive nature. In contrast, the terracotta reliefs are cheaper, more portable, mould-made offerings that the general population could afford. As dedications, they are private offerings that portray the importance of offering rather than the value of the gift. Such personal gifts to the hero highlight the intimate relationship between the devotee and the hero (below).

3.1.2 Terracotta figurines

Apart from the terracotta reliefs, another affordable mould-made or hand-made object that appears are the terracotta figurines. The currently available evidence suggests a certain differentiation in sex and in some cases segregation in sex and types of figurines among the deposits. For example, at the Heroon by the Eurotas (no. 3) and the Chatzis plot deposit (no. 20), the figurines are male nudes and females, many of the latter wearing poloi. At the Tseliou plot (no. 15), the figurines are all female, either seated or standing wearing a *polos*. At *Ergatikes Katoikies* (no. 5) the Archaic burial saw offerings of 150 female terracotta figurines and animal figurines of the Hellenistic period. The exclusivity of female figurines illustrates that some sites may have belonged to heroines. Female figurines wearing *poloi* have been discovered at the sanctuary of Artemis-Orthia[2] and at the Menelaion and may represent the heroines themselves, as it is a type of headdress usually worn by goddesses.[3] This is in keeping with Spartan tradition of heroine worship, most famously manifested in the cults of Helen and Alexandra/Kassandra who were worshipped in Sparta, but also others, such as the Leukippidai, the brides of the Dioskouroi (Paus. 3.12.18; 3.16.1).

3.1.3 Pottery and Drinking Shapes

As with the figurines, the pottery recovered from these sites lacks detailed publication. From the material reported, nonetheless, we see that miniature vases, especially of drinking shapes, predominate in several deposits (nos 3, 4, 5, 8, 10, 12, 15, 16, 20, 21).[4] In the example of Stauffert Street (no. 8), the numbers are striking: 1,500 miniatures found. Miniature vessels are not uncommon, being found for instance at other cult sites in Sparta, such as the Menelaion and the sanctuary on the Megalopolis road, the so-called 'Achilleion' (no. 28), where they have been unearthed in the thousands.[5] In general, miniature votives are common in many Peloponnesian sanctuaries, such as that of Athena Alea at Tegea,[6] and at sanctuaries at Corinth,[7] the Argive Heraion, Phlius in the Archaic period and even at Mycenaean sanctuaries.[8] They could have a symbolic value and could be a substitute for more expensive offerings.[9] Their popularity may be explained by their cheap nature and portability.[10] It has also been suggested that the choice to dedicate a small item may have been a way to create a private bond between the dedicator and the dedicatee and may have expressed a more personal dedicate.[11] More recently at Kladas (5 kilometres north of Sparta), near a settlement and an ancient road towards Arcadia, an Archaic to Late Classical votive deposit that probably belongs to a heroic shrine may offer a different picture: within the deposit were many charcoaled seeds of grapes, figs, barley, olives and legumes some of which were found inside the numerous miniature vases.[12] This suggests that the miniature vases were not merely replicas of larger vessels with a symbolic value but could be functional vessels. In other words, miniatures could have a place in the ritual activity of the cult and here they were used to offer seeds and small fruit at the shrine.[13]

Another suggestion is that miniature pottery, such as the drinking cups found at Sparta, may be commemorative items of ritual activity that took place at a sanctuary, such as drinking and dining.[14] In effect, this would deem them 'iconic signs of normal size counterparts.'[15] The proposal that the miniatures would commemorate ritual activity could fit well since regular size drinking shapes have been found at the heroic sites alongside miniatures. For example, in the deposits associated with the cult of Agamemnon and Alexandra/Kassandra (no. 1) were found forty-five kraters together with twenty-five krateriskoi.

Similarly, at the Menelaion were discovered miniature hydriai and oinochoai[16] alongside regular-size pottery.[17] The presence of miniature drinking shapes alongside real-size drinking vases features at other sanctuaries of Sparta, such as that of Orthia, the sanctuary of Athena Chalkioikos, the Eleusinion, and the sanctuary of Zeus Messapeus.[18] Some sites have produced more than others, especially Orthia, the Menelaion and the Acropolis, where lakainai feature in significant numbers.[19] At Orthia, miniature lakainai (50 per cent of miniatures), bowls, skyphoi and cups were found.[20] Thus the miniatures may commemorate and attest to drinking activities that took place at the sites.

Unfortunately, the ratio of miniature versus regular size pottery is overall unknown for the sites presented in Chapter 2, although, regular drinking shapes are widely reported. At site snumbers 1, 2, 3, 4, 8 and 15 the pottery comprises mostly drinking shapes, such as lakainai, kylikes, kantharoi, skyphoi, kraters and oinochoai among others. The cult of Agamemnon and Alexandra/Kassandra (no. 1) is reported to have a significant quantity of regular size drinking shapes (forty-two lakainai, twenty-eight 'Droop' cups, 2,000 kylix feet and the forty-five aforementioned kraters, among others). At the Drainage Ditch (no. 2), a deposit includes predominantly drinking shapes, such as kraters, cups and oinochoai. The Heroon by the Eurotas (no. 3) is also noted for the significant numbers of drinking shapes and especially cups and bowls.[21] At the cult site on Stauffert Street (no. 8), a number of drinking cups were found within the deposit, included lakainai and kantharoi. At the Tseliou plot (no. 15), cups, kantharoi and skyphoi were found.

Although most sites include pottery, the numbers and chronology of vases is not in its majority published or even reported. The commonly found lakainai are shapes usually associated with the Archaic period. The one-handle cup known as the *kothon*, which appears at the Heroon by the Eurotas (no. 3)[22] and probably is the shape of the Laconian red-figure fragment from O 13,[23] is not reported widely.[24] Another drinking shape, the kantharos, is present in a number of deposits (and on the stone and terracotta reliefs), does not appear in red-figure, and it is suggested that it continued to be made in black-glaze in the fifth century, perhaps because of its ritual use.[25]

The considerable presence of drinking shapes and their miniaturized versions suggest that there would be some type of activity involving liquids, either libations or drinking, or both. The wide distribution of drinking vessels and those shapes that would accompany drinking, such as kraters and oinochoai, throughout the sites implies that they were an essential part of an activity that took place. Such shapes, it is suggested, would involve actual use at the sanctuary and thus they are not 'static' votives,[26] i.e. they were not just dedications. At two sites, the one at Stauffert Street (no. 8) and the Sanctuary on the Megalopolis road (no. 25), fragments of animal bones indicate that sacrifice took place. It is expected that after sacrifice there would be dining accompanied by drinking.[27]

Recent research has debunked the impression that Archaic Sparta practised austere forms of commensality whereby drinking was substituted by the *syssition* in that period. Scholars see now that Sparta's more regulated forms of drinking and eating should be pushed to *c.* 500 BC.[28] Drinking at Spartan sanctuaries in the Archaic period is widely reported from *c.* 700 BC onwards, where real-size and miniature drinking shapes such as lakainai, amphorae, kraters and oinochoai have been found at the sanctuaries of Artemis-Orthia, the Amyklaion, the Menelaion and the sanctuary of Zeus Messapeus.[29] These shapes would be used for communal drinking in sanctuary contexts[30] and continue until the early fifth century when simple black-gloss stirrup and bell kraters were produced, perhaps for export.[31]

Ritual drinking in sanctuaries may also be supported by iconographical motifs on sixth-century Laconian vase painting. On a number of vases with images depicting communal drinking in a symposium, small, winged figures bearing wreaths float above the symposiasts.[32] Their presence at a symposium creates a religious setting and has led scholars to propose that the figures are drinking in a sanctuary.[33] Komast scenes may also suggest a religious setting: on one Archaic vase we see a komast dancing in front of a building, probably a temple or a shrine given the presence of a snake. The dancer holds a cup with one hand and slaps his buttock with the other.[34] Since, however, most black-figure pottery has been found in sanctuaries outside of Sparta, such as Samos, Cyrene and Etruria,[35] the iconography of the above vases may not have been indicatory of Laconian tastes but reflected the wishes of the clients abroad.[36]

The drinking shapes – both real-size and miniatures – found at the sites and deposits could have multiple functions and interpretations: they could be appropriate gifts to the hero who is depicted partaking in the activity, especially the kantharos, which is commonly associated with the hero on the stone and terracotta reliefs. Of course, it is uncertain whether *all* the drinking shapes were votives to the heroes or whether they were left behind, some broken, after use following ritual drinking. Thus, they could have been functional vessels, used in drinking at the shrines, and then left behind as token dedications. Beyond drinking, the pottery could also be used for libations. Most of the shapes were associated with wine, which is a common offering of libation in hero cult, although milk, honey and blood could be poured as well.[37] The kantharos, for example, could be used for libations[38] before drinking at a banquet.[39]

The custom of dining and drinking as part of a heroic ritual is famously seen at the heroon at the West Gate at Eretria,[40] Opheltes at Nemea[41] and at Kalydon and Kalaureia among many.[42] Sacrifice and feasting have also been observed in limited cases in the Mycenaean tomb cults[43] and especially in Messenia, where the tombs feature this custom most prominently.[44] In general, scholarship has demonstrated that sacrifice and feasting were activities at hero shrines and were similar to the sacrificial rituals for divine figures.[45] The drinking shapes at the sanctuaries in Sparta demonstrate that Spartans partook in ritual drinking both at divine and heroic sanctuaries.

What remains unknown is the size of the group that participated in ritual drinking at the various sites. At the Menelaion, where more evidence is available, it is suggested that the drinking groups were small since most drinking shapes of the Archaic period were miniatures; larger numbers appear in the Late Classical and Hellenistic periods.[46] The cult site at Stauffert Street (no. 8) produced 1,500 miniatures, the real-size drinking vessels remain unpublished and thus the numbers unknown. The burnt animal bones found together with votive material at the site suggest that dining took place there, perhaps outdoors, as with the festival of Hyakinthia at the Amyklaion.[47] But the evidence from the hero shrine of Agamemnon and Alexandra/Kassandra (no. 1) suggests attendance of significant numbers: 45 kraters and 2,000 kylix feet were reportedly found in one of the deposits. A lot more research and further excavation is needed to examine the drinking rituals at this cult site, which must have been of special significance for the residents of Amyklai. The cult probably was conducive to local Amyklaian identity.

The participation in ritual drinking and dining and sometimes in small groups is supported by literary attestations where, in fact, private sacrifice (and feasting) was one of the exemptions, along with hunting, from attendance at the messes (Plut. *Lyc.* 12.2) – a rule implied in Herodotus (6.57.3).[48] Xenophon, too, mentions that in the Classical period one would entertain strangers staying at Sparta during the Gymnopaidia (Xen. *Mem.* 1.2.61). Religion thus provided an opportunity for private feasts and we also see how private sacrificial meals also existed, which would give the chance for a family to gather together and feast when the occasion came up. Commensality in a group setting, and likely family setting, is also supported by findings at the recent discovery at the organized cemetery on the south-west edge of Sparta. This Archaic-Hellenistic cemetery (otherwise called the Olive Oil cemetery) gives evidence of horse sacrifice, drinking, dining and peribolos walls encompassing family burials. Many drinking vessels indicate that funerary feasts took place, presumably by the family of the deceased.[49] This discovery further supports occasions where a family or group would get together in drinking rituals. The participation of small groups in religious activities within the Spartan polis may occur in relation to heroic shrines within the Spartan *komai* that were attended by people residing nearby, or of hero shrines of family significance[50] and thus frequented by small groups. Evidence from Hellenistic Sparta attests to the dining clubs of the *sitithentes* dedicated to Helen and the Dioskouroi (§6.2). Not all shrines would have had similar numbers for as we see the shrine of Agamemnon and Alexandra/Kassandra attracted larger numbers.

The evidence from the hero shrines of Sparta thus further supports the evidence that religion offered occasion for ritual commensality. This is significant, because studies on Spartan commensality, and especially those regarding commensal practice in Classical Sparta, stress the civic practice of the public messes. The messes introduced sometime at the end of the sixth century were an institution whereby Spartan men dined together daily in groups. In fact, citizenship was highly connected to the messes since for one to be a Spartan *homoios* one would have to make contributions to the messes (Ar. *Pol.* 1271a27–37); this commensal custom, as recent scholarship suggests, provided a seemingly equal meal to all and thus contributed to a seeming equality of Spartan men.[51]

However, as we see from the evidence from the sanctuaries and shrines in Sparta, religion offered another occasion of commensality not structured about the civic units of the polis whereby only Spartan men could participate. The pottery evidence from Archaic Sparta and specifically the Amyklaion and Artemis Orthia shows a popular ritual drinking practice. The Classical material is not so clear. Because of the cessation of production of Laconian black-figure pottery, publications of finds from sanctuary sites in Sparta (most sites lack detail publication of the finds) – for example, from the Sanctuary of Artemis Orthia, or the Spartan Acropolis – focus on the Geometric and Archaic pottery.[52] Most post-Archaic pottery in Sparta is not figurative and is rather predominantly black-glazed or plain pottery, so it is a lot harder to date. What is more, we lack a clear stratigraphic view of the Classical material and thus it is harder to create a chronological sequence.[53]

Still, looking at the material in the deposits and from the main sanctuaries of Sparta we see that in fact Classical material is present. Most published material comes from the sanctuary of Agamemnon and Alexandra/Kassandra at Amyklai.[54] We observe in this sanctuary that the majority of vases are reported to be miniatures or cups and some are decorated with scenes of drinking themes,[55] such as the seated hero with the kantharos (resembling the iconography of the reliefs) or komast scenes.[56] Fifth-century kylikes, black-glazed krateriskoi, a small black-glazed oinochoe (500–480 BC),[57] hydriai of the last-quarter of the sixth century or somewhat later,[58] and small kraters from the fifth century are also reported from the sanctuary.[59] Inscribed rims from large vessels (presumably kraters) are also reported[60] as well as fifth-century kylikes that are also inscribed and more generally vases from the Archaic to the Hellenistic periods.[61] There were over 2,000 feet from drinking cups found at this site; most remain unpublished but from the little that we know it seems that there would be plenty of material continuing into the Classical and Hellenistic periods.[62] Other sites and deposits also offer Classical material and later: fragments of fifth-century kylikes with the iconography of a tippling serpent are known from the Heroon by the Eurotas (no. 3);[63] the Niarchos plot (no. 7) has pottery of the sixth and fifth centuries BC as well the O 13 (no. 4). Many deposits include finds that indicate continuous use from the Archaic to the Hellenistic periods; presumably the pottery would follow this chronology. Archaeological evidence from Spartan sanctuaries shows that it is very likely that commensal activities thus continued into the Classical period and later, as for example at the Menelaion (§ 4.1). Commensal activities at hero shrines therefore offered another occasion of sacrifice, drinking and dining not in accordance with the civic units of the messes.

The sociopolitical implications accompanying the existence of shrines connected with groups who participate in ritual drinking should be further considered. Drinking in Archaic settings is often associated with elite groups within the polis. Such participation marks them off from the rest of the community and defines them as equals with other member of the group to which they belong. The small group of individuals participating in ritual drinking at the hero shrines further supports the evidence discussed by Rabinowitz of elite participation in drinking rituals in Archaic Sparta, similar to other Greek poleis. The evidence for Classical Sparta is poor but as we saw above there is significant evidence that drinking shapes, and thus ritual drinking, continued into the Classical and Hellenistic periods. This is noteworthy because, as Hodkinson has shown, in Classical Sparta public display of wealth was not encouraged, but citizens were able to acquire property and wealth, albeit in a less ostentatious display of affluence (§ 5.1).[64] Lineage and personal connections held great sway in the Classical period, even though on the surface this influence was disguised by a lifestyle that appeared to be restrictive. The hero shrines in Sparta could offer religious occasions at which such elite could meet in ritual drinking.

3.1.4 Lead figurines

Lead figurines appear at sites numbers 1, 4, 7, 8, 10, 16, 25. The iconography, chronology and quantities remain unknown as few are published. Generally, lead figurines are an inexpensive and common Spartan votive and are predominantly found at the sanctuary of Artemis Orthia and the Menelaion where they have been found in their thousands.[65] The chronology of the production of the lead votives remains a difficult question. They appear from the seventh century onwards and their numbers peak in the sixth century. Boardman sees continuity into the fifth century with numbers beginning to decline and continue to fall into the third century.[66] Boss dates the end of the production at ca. 500 BC.[67] For the majority of the sites where lead figurines are reported only a few are found, as is the case of the first deposit associated with the of the cult of Agamemnon and Alexandra/Kassandra (no. 1) where three lead wreaths are reported. At other deposits, the excavators report 'significant' numbers, such as at Stauffert Street (no. 8), the Stathopoulos plot (no. 16) and at the 'Achilleion' (no. 28), where thirty-nine lead figurines have been found.[68] While Cavanagh, in his discussion of the lead figurines from the Menelaion, suggests that they could have been made for a festival occasion, Boss sees them as private dedications that anyone could buy.[69]

3.1.5 Metal objects

Finally, metal objects provide a very different outlook of votive patterns compared to the bronzes unearthed at the sanctuaries of Orthia, the Menelaion, Athena Chalkioikos and the Amyklaion.[70] At the deposit of Agamemnon and Alexandra/Kassandra (no.1) two metal objects are reported. At the sanctuary on the Megalopolis road (no. 25) there are number of bronze arms and armour. At other sites, such as (nos 20, 24, 8), the reported metals are not securely related to the deposits, although the bronze figurine of a lion from no. 8 may belong to the site. At two sites (nos 2, 10) bronze snakes have been unearthed; the former is in Hellenistic context. Compared to the sanctuaries of the Menelaion, Orthia, the Acropolis and the Amyklaion, where bronze vessels, jewellery, figurines and weapons were dedicated in significant quantities, the dedications in relation to the heroic deposits are generally poor in bronzes.[71] The same can be said about the seventh-century ivories and bone finds, which are also expensive items found at the sanctuary of Orthia, Athena Chalkioikos, and the Menelaion in Archaic contexts. At first glance, the votives dedicated at the hero shrines appear to consist predominantly of pottery, both real-size and miniature, figurines in lead and terracotta, and terracotta and stone reliefs.

The inexpensive votives can be a result of a number of reasons: first, either metals did not survive because they were melted down and reused; second, hero shrines did not commonly receive expensive dedications in ivory and bronze; or third, a combination of the above reasons whereby few metal dedications per site made their survival rate even less likely. This is at least possible for most of the Archaic and the Early Classical periods when bronzes were found in Spartan sanctuaries in their greatest numbers.[72] Generally, the end of the Archaic period exhibits a decrease in bronze offerings in Spartan sanctuaries. This decrease is not unique in Sparta and should not be a mark of Spartan austerity (below), as a decrease in bronzes is observed in many sanctuaries in the Greek world.[73] What's more, not only in Sparta but elsewhere in the Greek world we see high numbers of dedicated terracottas in the Classical period.[74] Whatever the implications for the patterns of bronze dedications at the various Spartan and other Greek sanctuaries in the Classical period, the case remains that for the Archaic period at least, the hero shrines present a significant difference in dedicatory patterns to those of the larger sanctuaries of Sparta.

It would be possible to admit that this could be purely based on post-depositional factors and survival rates[75] and that extended excavations at some of the sites, such as that of Agamemnon and Alexandra Kassandra (no. 1), may yield different results. Yet, the consistent absence or meagre quantities of bronzes from the numerous deposits is striking. One hero shrine naturally forms an exception, the Menelaion, whose status is closer to the divine rather to the heroic sanctuaries (§ 4.1). Not only are there numerous bronzes there, but there is also a distinct absence of the terracotta heroic and stone reliefs from the sanctuary. Its votive patterns are closer to those of Orthia rather than to those in relation to other heroic cults. The rest of the deposits or sites related to hero cults, including that of Agamemnon and Alexandra/Kassandra, suggest that heroes received few dedications in precious materials, such as ivory and metal, with the offerings consisting mainly of terracotta reliefs, pottery (including miniatures), and figurines.

Table 3.1 Summary of votives and finds

Site	Terracotta Reliefs	Pottery	Terracotta Figurines	Lead Figurines	Metal	Architecture	Other	Dates
1. Agamemnon Alexandra/ Kassandra	More than 1,200	Miniature vases including krateriskoi; regular size vases; 42 lakainai; 2,000 feet of kylikes; 28 'Droop' cups; 131 aryballoi including miniatures; 20 cups; 3 bowls; 45 craters; 4 oinochoai; 11 hydriai and kyathoi; cups painted with vines and snakes; a cup showing a hero holding a kantharos	√	Wreaths and figurines	Some metal objects; a large iron object	Inscribed fragmentary tiles; Archaic disc acroterion; antefixes; two walls	Hellenistic inscribed throne; honorary decree	Early 7th century to Hellenistic
2. The drainage ditch by the Eurotas Bridge	Two fragments	Oinochoai and lekythoi of the 5th and 4th centuries BC; fragments of craters, cups; black-figure skyphoi; amphorai; fragments of Archaic pithoi; fragments of Attick black-figure pottery	Archaic and Classical figurines		3 bronze snakes	6 Archaic terracotta metopes with traces of paint; Lakonian roof tiles; 4m to the north: paved floor; foundations of square structure; 7m to the north: foundations of 6m wall in a 7th century stratum	Marble plaque with partial Archaic inscription	Archaic- Hellenistic (?)

(*continued*)

Table 3.1 Continued

Site	Terracotta Reliefs	Pottery	Terracotta Figurines	Lead Figurines	Metal	Architecture	Other	Dates
3. The Heroon by the Eurotas	About 100	Some miniatures; kantharoi; 6 kraters; three-handled vases; 2 lakainai; 10 cups; 13 bowls; 2 cups; 8 kothons (one-handled mugs), 2 kantharoi; 2 oinochoai; 2 amphorai; as well as black-glazed fragments with red dipinti of A and IA	Mostly females with *poloi*; nude males			Two 'late antefixes'; two fragments of geison (or cyma); black glazed metope (?); fragment of terracotta disk acroterion (or antefix); several walls	Relief krater with fighting scene; pithos burial	Early 7th century? to ?
4. O 13	three fragmentary	miniatures pottery; black glazed of the 6th century; kraters; a fragment of a stamnos, two lakainai and one kylix; red-figure fragments (two of which are Attic)		√				Archaic-Classical?
5. Ergatikes Katoikies	One fragmentary	Miniature pottery	150 female figurines; handmade animal figurines; terracotta horse (Archaic)			Long Hellenistic Building	Early Archaic burial; bone knife handles; statuette of a 'barbarian'; bronze protome (Archaic);	Archaic-Hellenistic

6. Stavropoulos plot	✓	Domestic pottery	Two terracotta figurines of Artemis	Long building with south-west side of blue Laconian marble in a polygonal Lesbian technique	Archaic stone heroic relief; 1st century BC burial with gold leaves; loom weights; lamps; Archaic relief krater	Archaic; multiple renovations and extensions during later periods to the late Roman times
7. The Niarchos plot	Hundreds	Fragments of the 6th and 5th centuries BC; large quantity of Geometric pottery		✓	Hellenistic/Roman structure made of slabs	Archaic–Classical? Hellenistic/Roman
8. Stauffert Street	Over 2,500 fragments	Geometric pottery; 1,500 miniature vases; lakainai; kantharoi; cups; bowls	800 terracotta figurines, both male and female, shown standing, enthroned or reclining	Wreaths; hoplites; female winged figures; a lead snake	Foundations of two rooms (one with a bench); Archaic terracotta acroterion; stones demarking burial	Geometric burial; burnt area with animal bones; fragment of stone relief with partial inscription	7th century to Hellenistic
9. The Lykourgos and Karela plot	Terracotta relief of a seated figure	✓ including a significant number of miniatures	Human and animal terracotta figurines	✓	Late Geometric/Early Archaic rectangular building	Five Geometric burials nearby	Late Geometric/Archaic to ?

(*continued*)

Table 3.1 Continued

Site	Terracotta Reliefs	Pottery	Terracotta Figurines	Lead Figurines	Metal	Architecture	Other	Dates
10. The Bougadis plot	Two fragments; another deposit with 50 specimens	Miniature vases	√		Three bronze snakes	Late Hellenistic/Roman three-room building with small rectangular construction: evidence of a household cult	Spindle whorl; three stone reliefs; marble figurines with enthroned male	Archaic to ?
11. The Panagopoulou plot	√						Stone reliefs	?
12. The Karmoiris plot	√	√ incuding miniature and normal size				Small 'temple-shaped structure'; a 5th century BC terracotta lion-head (part of an acroterion)		Archaic-Classical?
13. The Georganta and Petrakou plot	√ banqueters; √ rider		√			Hellenistic building; stamped tile; antefix of an eagle; antefixes with plant decoration	Two fragments of less than life-size terracotta statues	Archaic-Roman?

14. The Filippopoulou plot	200 specimens; two more deposits nearby (one with 35 reliefs)	30 fragments of pottery consisting of mostly cups; miniature vases; sherds inscribed to the 'Hero'	500 terracotta figurines		Archaic-Classical
15. The Tseliou plot	√ large quantity	Kantharoi; skyphoi; miniature pottery (lakainai)		√ mostly seated female or a standing female wearing a polos	Miniature terracotta masks	Hellenistic and Roman walls	Archaic-Late Hellenistic
16. The Stathopoulos plot	√	√ miniature vases		√ among the figurines was an enthroned figure, a kourotrophic figure; head of Daedalic type	√ significant numbers of lead votive wreaths	Roof tiles	7th century to Classical?

(*continued*)

Table 3.1 Continued

Site	Terracotta Reliefs	Pottery	Terracotta Figurines	Lead Figurines	Metal	Architecture	Other	Dates
17. The Bilida plot	√		√					Late Classical-Early Hellenistic
18. The Kalatzis plot	√	√	√ including a Daedalic figurine			Foundations of a wall Archaic terracotta antefix; 4 Hellenistic architectural fragments; a capital; a column base; a drum of a Corinthian columns	Fragments of glass; small marble head of a lion; stone relief nearby	7th century to Hellenistic
19. The Markou plot	√		√					?
20. The Chatzis and Arfani plot	22 + reliefs	Miniature vases; Megarian bowls (Hellenistic); black glazed sherds; perfume bottles	16 female of which 12 wear a *polos*; 30 male (most of them nude)			Tiles; various walls	96 loom weights; lamps; fragments of glass and metal ware; 5 coins	Archaic-Roman?
21. Thermopylae Street	√	√	√					Archaic-Roman?

22. The Sourli plot	√		√			Poros Doric capital; parts of an acroterion	Fragments of sculpture	?
23. The Psatha-Iliopoulou plot	A fragment of a terracotta relief	√			√			Geometric-Archaic
24. The Zachariadi plot	√		√			An antefix	Marble urn; pyramidal loom weights	Geometric-Hellenisitc
25. The Nikolarou plot	Six terracotta reliefs							?
26. The Valioti plot	√							?
27. The Stratakou plot	√	Miniature vases	√				Relief stele, base with dedicatory inscription to the Mother of the Gods	

(*continued*)

Table 3.1 Continued

Site	Terracotta Reliefs	Pottery	Terracotta Figurines	Lead Figurines	Metal	Architecture	Other	Dates
28. A Sanctuary at the Megalopolis road	One fragmentary terracotta relief	Miniature vases: 4,000 whole (of which 700 lakainai, 2,000 skyphoi, 800 aryballoi and kantharo); 8,000 fragmentary; 9 Proto-Corinthian aryballoi; Hellenistic pottery	8 terracotta figurines,	49 lead figurines	Some made of iron; a bronze lance-head; a bronze spear-head; 2 bronze arrows; 2 fragments of shield belts; 7 bronze mirrors	Walls; Laconian black or brown glazed tiles; part of a Doric column covered in fine stucco	Marble slabs; burnt layer with charred bones	7th century to ?
29. Sklavochori (Amyklai)	√	√	√				A Proto-Geometric burial	Classical?

3.2 Patterns of dedication

There could be several reasons why this array of dedications adheres to the heroic cults of Sparta. Economic concerns, patterns of consumption, the nature of the cults, and sociopolitical changes could have an effect on dedicatory trends. In the following section, the dedications will be examined within the framework of offerings at the main Spartan sanctuaries and in the context of the dedicatory patterns in Greek sanctuaries in general. It will focus on dedicatory changes between the Archaic and Classical periods in Sparta and elsewhere and will draw in comparative votive offerings from hero cults and non-central cult places from the wider Greek world. A comprehensive picture will hopefully emerge of the dedicatory patterns in relation to various contemporaneous factors that can impact the choice of votive offerings.

It was long thought that Spartan artistic production suffered a decline after 550 BC. This view came about because of the dramatic difference in the material recovered from the sanctuary of Artemis Orthia – remarkable finds from the Early Archaic period but a poor record thereafter. Naturally, the disruption of the quality of finds from the sanctuary of Artemis Orthia was interpreted as a result of the implementation of the Lykourgan institutions and the militarization of the society. More recent studies, however, incorporating material from the Menelaion, Orthia, the Amyklaion and the Acropolis have re-evaluated this position.[76] Indeed, bronzes, such as jewellery, decrease by the mid-sixth century and bronze vessels also declined in sanctuaries – except at the Acropolis, where they continue in the second half of the sixth century but diminish by 500 BC. Other shapes, however, such as animal types, naked girls used as supports for mirrors, and small bronze *kouroi*, which appear at the end of the seventh century, are produced until the last quarter of the sixth century.[77] Indeed, some bronze figurines increase in number in the mid-sixth century and continue into the fifth.[78] The chronological understanding now for the decline of bronze production appears to shift to 500 BC.[79] Hodkinson has shown that Sparta follows a model similar to that of other Greek poleis, where bronzes decrease as dedications in the Classical period. Thus, Sparta's dedicatory patterns should not be interpreted as a result of a path towards Spartan austerity; Spartan bronze dedicatory patterns are no different to those of other Greek poleis.[80]

While bronzes diminish, Sparta's artistic production continues in some forms past the Archaic period, and there are a good few examples in stone sculpture. The reliefs dedicated to the Dioskouroi continue into the Classical and later periods and so do the heroic stone reliefs. Some funerary stone *stelai* are also of

Classical date.[81] Some fragments of an Athena *Promachos* of the early fifth century seem to be the work of an Ionian artist.[82] It appears that rather than an outright decline of Spartan artistic production, as suggested by the patterns of bronze dedications that decline after 500 BC, artistic and dedicatory trends shifted to less emphasis on luxury items and private display of wealth, towards a more public and egalitarian form.[83] The impact of the societal changes on Spartan artistic production is a much-discussed subject. The view that the decline of artistic production was a result of the militarization of Sparta in the sixth century has been challenged;[84] instead, scholars focus on the tension between aristocratic habits and luxury symbols, and an egalitarian ethos[85] of the society that developed by the fifth century.[86] Förtsch has argued for a coexistence of a tendency to luxury and a 'gradually pervading restrictive attitude to visual art'.[87]

An egalitarian and less ostentatious typology of offerings, then, may have found support in post-Archaic Sparta. Returning to the patterns of dedication at the heroic shrines in Sparta, the terracotta reliefs, a cheap mould-made votive, would have been available to the general population and should be considered a private offering. The stone reliefs could be a communal offering or an offering by a wealthier individual.[88] Their similarity, however, to the terracotta reliefs does not allow for an grandiose display of wealth. Rather, due to their religious nature, both the terracotta and stone reliefs embrace a conservative and persisting iconography for hundreds of years.[89] The terracotta reliefs and mould-made repetitive production were suitable for a society adhering to the egalitarian ethos. Together with the terracotta figurines, pottery and miniature pottery, their modest nature may explain their popular appeal and widespread distribution.

The above discussion may contextualize the dedications in Spartan sanctuaries and votive deposits with heroic material at least for the Classical period. However, in the Archaic period (and Early Classical) there appears to be a distinct difference of absence of bronzes and other valuables as offerings to heroes at a time when bronzes and other valuables were dedicated at the main sanctuaries.

The reason for this may be sought elsewhere and would benefit from a brief comparison with other cult places in the Greek world, especially in relation to hero shrines or cults not focused around large central sanctuaries. Strong similarities can be made with material recovered from tomb cults where a similar typology of terracotta votives has been recovered. For example, at Menidi in Attica the votives consisted of terracotta shields, figurines of horses and riders, and oil vessels and *louteria*.[90] Another example is the 'underground shrine' in

Corinth built over Geometric graves. Here, the votives include pottery and lamps.[91] Similarly, the 'Heroon of the Crossroads' in Corinth, which lay over four Geometric graves, had modest votives consisting of terracotta figurines of reclining banqueters, horses and riders, and relief snake *stelai* capped by helmets.[92] A Proto-Attic deposit (640–630) over the ruins of a Geometric oval building on the slopes of the Areopagus in Athens yielded terracotta shields, figurines and vases.[93] Lastly, in Vari, in Attica, terracotta animal figurines, shields and vases were found over seventh-century burials.[94] These sites and many others are often identified as cults to distant ancestors or even mythical heroes and they are often but not exclusively attached to burials.[95] Even the hero shrine of Opheltes at Nemea has yielded primarily pottery and terracotta figurines, although some metals are reported.[96] The hero shrines in Sparta, which commence in the seventh century, feature comparable patterns of dedication to such cult-sites rather than to those of the main sanctuaries of Sparta in which were found numerous valuable dedications of bronze (and ivory).

Beyond cults dedicated to heroes or distant ancestors the hero shrines of Sparta display similar patterns of dedications to smaller shrines within Greek poleis. For example, in Corinth, a type of shrine along the roadway or in an open-air temenos marked sacred areas using statues raised on tall shafts.[97] A well-known one is the Kokkynovrysi shrine where a shaft for a statue base was found together with a pit from which were recovered terracotta votives of a particular kind: dancers around a syrinx player.[98] On the basis of the iconography, Bookidis suggests that a shrine of Pan and the Nymphs may have stood on the spot.[99] There are many examples of such shrines in the Greek world, such as the road shrine of Hera near the Argive Heraion.[100] In Athens, too, a polis famous for its plethora of shrines, archaeological remains reveal that the dedications at many small or roadside shrines consisted mostly of terracotta figurines and pottery.[101] A roadside shrine found west of the Athenian Agora contained material of terracotta figurines and pottery apart from a marble head of a herm.[102] Another roadside shrine, on the south slope of the Athenian acropolis, in a residential district and dedicated to the Nymphs, produced terracotta figurines, masks and thousands of fragments of pottery with the majority belonging to *loutrophoi*.[103] It has been noted, in the context of studying Geometric and Archaic hero cults in Attica and the aforementioned road shrine near the Argive Heraion, that the votive material generally contains few metals, no bronze figurines, no stone-sculpture or inscriptions.[104] Generally, such shrines were small and contained modest dedications of terracotta, such as pottery, figurines and reliefs resembling the votive patterns of the heroic shrines in Sparta.

As is shown on the map, most of the heroic sites and deposits in Sparta were located around the Acropolis and Limnai – two areas that exhibit the greatest activity of habitation from the Geometric period onwards. While many sites were discovered around the area of the Acropolis, none were actually on the Acropolis itself where the central cult of Athena had its place. The distinct absence of hero shrines from the Acropolis may in fact explain the lack of valuable offerings. Central cult places provided the opportunity for the elite and rich to display their wealth and were a unifying part of the polis;[105] thus, dedications of valuable votives in sanctuaries can reflect the status of a cult place. Smaller shrines, by contrast, had a more limited sphere of activity and could be frequented more often by people who lived nearby; literary sources attest to such neighbourhood shrines (Aristoph. *Wasps* 389–394; below).

The locality of many of the heroic deposits in the area of Limnai and around the Acropolis that were inhabited early probably means that they would be near inhabited areas – even if evidence for houses from Archaic and Classical Sparta is elusive (below). Observations of this sort of topographical context and typology of votives resembles the smaller shrines in a Greek polis and even more particularly those of heroic cult. Based on the current excavated finds, the votives associated with most heroic cults in Sparta (excepting the Menelaion) do not differ from offerings discovered in other areas of the Greek world where cult places of less central importance were often given terracotta offerings; small shrines in Athens are a notable comparison.[106]

Rich and poor alike could have dedicated the modest gifts of terracotta reliefs, pottery and figurines. They may have been offered collectively during a specific occasion, such as a festival, as has been suggested for the lead figurines at the Menelaion. Otherwise, a small group of worshippers could also attend the shrine where they would participate in ritual drinking and votive offerings. Alternatively, a passer-by could dedicate an inexpensive object as a token gift and would be a personal gift to the hero. The specialization of some heroes, moreover, especially those of healing cults, would have made them even more important on a personal basis; the shrine to Asklepios near the Booneta may have been one such shrine (Paus. 3.15.10).[107]

The iconographical evidence on some stone and terracotta reliefs of the Archaic period may, in fact, depict the recreation of such ritual envisioned at the Spartan shrines. On two Archaic stone reliefs the diminutive figures bring offerings of a rooster, a flower and possibly an egg, perhaps representing such perishable items to be dedicated at hero shrines.[108] This motif disappears from the Archaic stone reliefs,[109] but a couple of fourth- or third-century examples depict a seated man with adorants:[110] on one example, the seated man faces five adorants (including a child).[111] Another terracotta relief, from Messene, depicts a couple in front of a seated man who pours a libation from a phiale,[112] while a terracotta relief from Stauffert Street (no. 8) conforms more closely to the example of the early stone reliefs: it shows three diminutive figures (an adult male and two children) in front of a seated man.[113] Other examples of terracotta reliefs portray a couple holding wreaths and fruit that they bring as offerings to the hero.[114]

Some standing figures (interpreted as worshippers) on terracotta reliefs have arms raised in adoration while others bring offerings.[115] It is suggested that when placed next to those terracotta reliefs of a seated man they would have had the same effect as those where the worshippers and hero are together on the same relief.[116] The above examples portray a glimpse of the ritual activity that could be performed at the heroic shrines in Sparta. Worshippers bring offerings to the hero, perhaps as passers-by, with their family, including children, either in a festival or in a casual manner. The presence of the hero in the same plane on some examples may further demonstrate the envisioned accessibility of the hero to the life of the worshippers.

Other evidence, namely the anonymity (at least to us) of the heroes, still supports this intimate status of the heroes to the Spartan community. With the exceptions of the deposit to Agamemnon and Alexandra/Kassandra and the Menelaion, no other deposits have produced any complete inscriptions.[117] One Archaic stone-relief mentions Chilon but most inscribed reliefs date from the Hellenistic and Roman periods. The lack of inscriptions on the stone and terracotta reliefs should be unsurprising since heroic reliefs from elsewhere in the Greek world are frequently un-inscribed or simply dedicated 'to the hero'.[118] In fact, in one deposit in Sparta at the Filippopoulou plot (no. 14) sherds are inscribed to the 'Hero'. There are some examples from around the Greek world where the hero receives only an epithet, such as *epikoos*,[119] *eukolos*,[120] *euergetes* or *heros iatros*,[121] indicating his friendly and helpful nature, but remains unnamed.[122] The anonymity of heroes is not unique to the Archaic and Classical periods, but is in fact common within Greek religion in general. We have already seen it in cults at Bronze Age tombs, where the cult may not have been directed to named individuals but possibly to anonymous personalities of interest only to the local community (§ 1.2.2). Even at the cult site at Menidi, which continued in use until the fifth century, the recipient of this cult remained unnamed and perhaps unknown. Anonymity is similarly noticeable at the cults over Geometric tombs at Eretria, Corinth and Athens (§1.2.3). Thus, the Spartan stone and terracotta reliefs follow a tradition in Greek religion where the hero, known only in the local community, may not have to be named because his identity is known and immediately understood by the people who tended the cults; some of these would have belonged to neighbourhood heroes.

The intimate relationship between the hero and the worshippers may be further supported by the iconography on the stone and terracotta reliefs: on a number of terracotta reliefs with seated figures, a smaller individual raises his hand in communication with the hero;[123] a similar gesture is performed by the worshipper on a terracotta relief from Stauffert Street (no. 8).[124] The five worshippers on a third- or fourth-century BC stone relief also have their arms raised in an adoration gesture.[125] Similarly, the seated hero himself, whose free arm is extended or raised with the palm open, also performs a gesture of communication directed towards the worshippers, as, for example, on the famous Chrysapha relief (Figure 2.1). The gestures depicted on the above reliefs imagine an interaction and thus closeness between the worshippers and the heroes who occupied various spaces around the polis (and countryside in the case of the Chrysapha relief).

The offering of a modest gift in a casual manner expresses the closeness between devotee and hero. In essence, a regular visit to a heroic (or divine) shrine and a personal offering of a gift is part of Greek personal religion, which has gained much discussion recently, although scholarly opinion rejects a distinct dichotomy between private versus public sphere of religion.[126] While a personal experience of asking the deity or hero for their own or the family's welfare and depositing a votive can be a private act and one signifying the connection of the individual with the deity/hero at a personal level, the cultic space nonetheless is public and the deity or hero worshipped is one that belongs to the community. Thus, a personal experience can take place in a public cult; the two are not mutually exclusive.[127] The material culture from the heroic shrines in Sparta offers rich evidence for a popular religious practice done at a personal level.

3.3 Architectural evidence

Unfortunately, Roman, Byzantine and modern construction in Sparta has left little architecture associated with hero cults of the Archaic, Classical and Hellenistic periods. Still, the scant architectural remains from the various heroic sites and deposits allow some discussion of certain architectural features and even comparison to those buildings that housed the main sanctuaries of Sparta.

The oddity of Spartan architectural taste is well noted. Excavations from the Menelaion, the Amyklaion, the temple of Athena Chalkioikos and the sanctuary of Artemis Orthia have produced numerous architectural remains that show that Sparta, although aware of architectural trends elsewhere, refrained from producing typical large peripteral temples.[128] Pausanias' (3.18.9–3.19.5) narrative presents an elaborate picture of the architecture of the Amyklaion, designed by Vathykles of Magnesia in the mid-sixth century, which was composed of a striking throne of an armed Apollo and opulent sculptural decoration. Excavations in the nineteenth and early twentieth centuries along with current excavations at the site confirm the elaborate, albeit debated, design of the sanctuary.[129] Likewise, the bronze reliefs decorating the temple of Athena Chalkioikos, designed by Gitiadas, illustrate that the sanctuary of Athena was richly embellished (Paus. 3.17.2–3; cf. Thuk. 1.134) even though little architecture survives.[130] The Menelaion, in ruins by Pausanias' time, is not described in the sources but excavations have shown that the temple consisted of a rectangular monument with a terrace and ramp.[131]

The hero shrines of Sparta are, by contrast, hardly described in the sources, bar the occasional mention that some were associated with tombs. Because no substantial remains have been unearthed, excepting the Menelaion, the architecture of other hero cults remains speculative. Based on the long chronology of the sites, renovations and rebuilding, the architectural forms vary. This is expected, as hero shrines do not have a uniform design. Many different architectural designs could comprise a hero shrine, such as the elaborate architecture of the Menelaion, a long building in the Late Hellenistic/Early Roman period, or a small temple (*naiskos*). Moreover, some heroa were attached to a burial so it is likely that the burial would have to be architecturally incorporated into the shrine, e.g., the tomb of Kastor in Sparta, on top of which was built a sanctuary (Paus. 3.13.1); an elaborate design with an incorporation of a tomb is exhibited in the example of Ergatikes Katoikies (5) or the cult at Stauffert street (8). Others may not have had anything at all apart from a *temenos* that contained an area for sacrifice and votive deposition. The triangular shrine in the agora of Athens attests to the possible simplicity of architectural forms.

From the scant archaeological remains, nonetheless, it is evident that in being embellished with terracotta disc acroteria, antefixes and tiles, certain sites follow some of the main architectural decorative trends of Laconian temples. The Heroon by the Eurotas (no. 3) yielded two antefixes of different periods, a terracotta disc acroterion or antefix (see below), a terracotta geison with the acanthus leaves of the fourth century or later and perhaps part of a black-glazed metope. Many other sites yielded disc acroteria: the cult of Agamemnon and Alexandra/Kassandra (no. 1), Stauffert Street (no. 8), the Kalatzis plot (no. 18), the Sourli plot (no. 22), the Zachariadi plot (no. 24) and the Nikolarou plot.[132] Antefixes have been found also at the cult of Agamemnon and Alexandra/Kassandra (no. 1), at the Heroon by the Eurotas (no. 3), the Georganta and Petrakou plot (no. 13), the Kalatzis plot (no. 18) and the Zachariadi plot (no. 24). Decorative items, such as disc acroteria and antefixes, are strongly associated with Archaic temples in Sparta, Laconia and the Peloponnese.[133] At Sparta, there are multiple examples of disc acroteria and antefixes from the temple of Artemis Orthia, a near-complete example of a disc acroterion found at the Amyklaion, and numerous fragments from the Acropolis and the Menelaion.[134]

Beginning around 650–620 BC, with the earliest examples unearthed at the sanctuary of Artemis Orthia, the terracotta disc acroteria and antefixes (and raking simas) become the only kind of ornamentation of Archaic Spartan temples, which is limited to the edges of the roofs.[135] In their earlier variety (650–620), disc acroteria were monochrome without moulded decoration and a smooth border. Soon, a polychrome type appears (625/620–580 BC) where bright colours of black, purple, red and white along with decorative elements and toothed borders create a focal point at the centre of the building.[136] Their association with the Archaic period is clear and they continue until the late sixth century BC, when marble acroteria appear.[137] Antefixes follow a similar chronological pattern as the acroteria: the earliest, of about 650/20–580 BC, are semi-circular with a radial crescent pattern; some are undecorated (620–550 BC) while others have more ornamental designs (600?–530 BC).

Unfortunately, most of the terracotta architectural members associated with the deposits are unpublished. One fragment, however, of an Archaic terracotta antefix with incised designs forming a radial crescent (650/20–580 BC) found at the Kalatzis plot (no. 18) allows comparison with examples from the temple of Artemis Orthia, the Amyklaion, the temple of Apollo Hyperteleatas at Epidauros-Limera and Apollo Tyritas in Kynouria.[138] Another example, from the Heroon by the Eurotas (no. 3), is red-glazed, which probably makes it an antefix rather than an acroterion, and should date *c.* 570–550 BC; it too has a parallel from the temple of Artemis Orthia.[139] The fragment of a disc acroterion from Stauffert Street (no. 8) exhibits no toothed border, which could allow for an early date of un-toothed disc acroteria. The plethora of terracotta disc acroteria and antefixes are thus probably of Archaic date. This demonstrates not only that hero shrines follow the architectural trends of the main sanctuaries of Sparta (and Laconia), but that some heroic-cults acquired 'elaborate' buildings early in their life. This suggests that although the hero cults, such as those of Agamemnon and Alexandra/Kassandra (no. 1), the heroon at Stauffert Street (no. 8) or the deposit at the Kalatzis plot (no. 18), would naturally be important to the respective inhabitants of the *komai* who housed them, e.g. Amyklai, Limnai, Pitane, the cults would have been incorporated into the religious topography of Sparta. The construction of a building, however large or small, could have taken communal effort and may have been ratified by the state.[140] Subsequent repairs or building also suggest that the cults retained their community importance. Cults that had significance to specific families, however, e.g. the Talthybiads, may have been maintained by the families themselves.

While many sites have produced walls, only a few have produced complete enough examples to allow discussion of the buildings that housed the cults. For example, at the cult site on Stauffert Street, two architectural phases reveal what appears to be one earlier Archaic room (*c.* 4.1 metres x 3.5 metres) and a later one of similar dimensions encompassing the burial and votive deposit. At the Karela plot (no. 9), three walls of 7.50 metres, 7 metres and an incomplete wall of 0.80 metres are the foundations of a mud-brick construction of the Late Geometric/Early Archaic period. At the Karmoiris plot (no. 12), a small temple (ναόσχημο) is reported; the excavation report does not give the length but it is accompanied by a fifth-century acroterion. The Drainage Ditch by the Eurotas (no. 2) has produced metopes and tiles that would have decorated a small building while some walls may belong to it. At the Lykourgos and Karela plot (9), a rectangular building dates to the Archaic period. A column covered with stucco discovered at the sanctuary on the Megalopolis road (no. 25) may also belong to a small Classical period building.

At first glance, the hero shrines appear as quite modest, non-peripteral small buildings embellished with terracottas that may make them stand apart from the main sanctuaries of the polis. In Sparta, however, there was no tradition of large peripteral temples as those found elsewhere in the Greek world.[141] From the remains of the Amyklaion, the Menelaion, the temple of Artemis Orthia and that of Athena Chalkioikos and other Laconian sanctuaries (Apollo Tyritas, Apollo Hyperteleatas, Aigies) it appears that Spartans were aware of the architectural developments of the time but implemented them in rectangular temples, of different design:[142] the remains from the sixth-century temple of Artemis Orthia show a rectangular temple (16 x 7 metres) divided by a cella and a porch with steps at the front[143] while the 'Old Menelaion' is also a rectangular small building of 8.60 x 5.45 metres.[144] Thucydides (1.134) calls the room of the temple of Athena Chalkioikos in which the unfortunate Pausanias sought refuge an οἴκημα οὐ μέγα (small chamber), suggesting that the temple was small.[145] In 1962, a small rectangular naiskos (13 x 8.50 metres) was uncovered in Kalogonia, located at the periphery of Sparta, and it too is non-peripteral.[146] What remains of the several hero shrines shows that the architecture of the hero cults in Sparta followed this tradition but with even less of a grand appearance, as found in the bronze decorations of the temple of Athena Chalkioikos or the throne of Apollo at Amyklai. Thucydides' (1.10.2) famous remark that if Sparta were to become desolate the public buildings would not account for its power shows that most public architecture would not have been of elaborate scale, including the temples.

Some small Archaic clay models interpreted as representations of temples may further enhance our picture of what such temples looked like. There are a number of fragmentary models found in Sparta, two of which come from the temple of Artemis Orthia,[147] three from the Menelaion,[148] one or more from the temple of Athena Chalkioikos[149] as well as a stray find found in the Eurotas.[150] The latter had a tiled roof with black painted tiles decorated with a terracotta disc acroterion and a gorgoneion at the tympanum.[151] The decoration on a fragment from a late seventh/early sixth century model from the temple of Artemis Orthia shows on its upper section triglyphs while the bottom part has what may be timbers reinforcing the frame of the building.[152] These models have been interpreted as temples, rather than houses, and are constructed as simple rectangular buildings with tiled roofs, decorated with disc acroteria, and bearing a Doric entablature.

Admittedly, the remains from the hero shrines at Sparta have not produced much evidence of architectural parts belonging to the entablature of a Doric building, apart from the terracotta metopes from the Drainage Ditch (no. 2). Others include a Doric capital dating to *c.* 500 BC from the Stavropoulos plot (no. 6) that belonged to the first phase of architecture of the cult site, a fragment of an Archaic Doric poros capital from the Bougadis plot (no. 10) and another from the Sourli plot (no. 22), which probably attest to small buildings in *antis*. But the Archaic hero shrines may not differ greatly from other temples in Sparta, since there is not much evidence from Sparta that pedimental sculpture was used to decorate temples as in other parts of the Greek world – apart from acroteria, antefixes and raking cyma (above).[153] The simple terracotta models from the temple of Artemis Orthia and elsewhere that provide a glimpse of Archaic temple architecture in Sparta may give evidence on the appearance of some of the hero shrines in Sparta.

Architectural remains of such small cult buildings, *naiskoi*, have been found in several parts of the Greek world. The mid-fifth-century poros *naiskos* of Athena Nike on the Athenian Acropolis, which preceded the later famous one,[154] had dimensions of 3.65 x 2.47 metres. More recently an Archaic *naiskos* was found at Poulooulou 29, west of the agora and near two ancient roads (3.2 × 3 metres).[155] It would have been a one-room building whose foundations supported an upper mud-brick structure and resembling in form the *naiskos* discovered at the south-east corner of the precinct of the shrine of Dionysus Eleuthereus (2.26 × 2.26 metres),[156] and one by the *Lesche* near the Pnyx (2.08 × 2.27 metres) in Athens.[157] Similarly small buildings in Sparta are evident at the Karmoiris plot (no. 12) where an Archaic 'temple shaped structure' was found and at the Karela plot (no. 9) where a rectangular building would have its upper parts made of mud-brick. Room A from Stauffert Street (no. 8) may also belong to such architectural tradition. Another example comes from Aigies, Laconia where temple B consisted of a small rectangular building, perhaps in *antis*.[158]

The typology of shrines that housed heroic-cults would have held as much variation in Sparta as is observed in the rest of the Greek world. Some would have been of modest appearance, perhaps consisting of only a temenos. Others were decorated with similar architectural elements, such as the architectural terracottas that adorned the temples housing the cults of the predominant deities of the Spartan polis. More notably, the Menelaion occupied a predominant position on the hill of Therapne and had multiple building phases. We also see the construction of the long temples, such as those at Ergatikes Katoikies (no. 5), and the Stavropoulos plot (no. 6). The architectural evidence points that from the Archaic period onwards Spartan hero shrines often adopted and followed the designs of the main sanctuaries of the polis, such as that of Athena Chalkioikos, the sanctuary of Artemis Orthia, the Amyklaion and the Menelaion, but perhaps with less elaborate designs. Although they were not extravagant projects they illustrate how in the Archaic period the community came together to institute and elaborate the heroic cults. Furthermore, their architectural elaboration indicates that these communal projects were taken on from the very early stages of the lives of the cults in Archaic Sparta. Their construction should be contextualized and juxtaposed with the 'monumentalization' of Sparta in the Archaic period that followed the consolidation of the Spartan political community in the eighth and seventh centuries (see Introduction).

The civic importance of the hero shrines is further attested by their duration and building phases. The majority of the sites are not well published, making it impossible to trace the quantity and typology of votives across antiquity. Yet, from the available data, it is evident that hero shrines in Sparta were of long duration that saw the majority of them commencing in the Archaic period and continuing into the Hellenistic and even the Roman periods. Not only is their lifespan of long duration but the finds indicate multiple building phases or repairs. For example, at the Kalatzis plot (no. 18), which has finds from the seventh century to the Hellenistic period, were found the remains of an Archaic terracotta disc acroterion as well as architectural fragments of the Hellenistic period decorated with a Gorgoneion, riders and eagle in relief. Likewise, the Heroon by the Eurotas (no. 3), with activity from the Archaic to the Hellenistic era, had architectural terracottas of different periods including a terracotta geison with acanthus leaves, which should date to the fourth century or later. At the Karmoiris plot (no. 12), an Archaic building acquired a fifth-century lion-head acroterion. At the Chatzis and Arfani plots (no. 20), excavations revealed two walls of different dates and material spanning from the Archaic to the Roman periods. The heroon at Stauffert Street (no. 8) saw the construction of two areas: an earlier one next to the burial and a later one encompassing the burial and deposit. Lastly, the building housing the cult of Agamemnon and Alexandra Kassandra had an Archaic disc acroterion but also gorgoneion plaques for antefixes, which suggests that the sanctuary underwent renovations in the fifth century.[159] Many hero shrines thus had an initial architectural phase that underwent repairs, remodelling, expansions, or that was replaced during later periods. This indicates the importance of these hero cults for the community that had maintained and cared for them.

This view is supported by the literary testimonia: Herodotus (6.69) mentions the hero shrine of the local hero Astrabacus that remained in use and popular for centuries and was also seen by Pausanias (3.16.6) some 700–800 years later. The cult of Talthybios, the herald of Agamemnon, is mentioned by Herodotus (6.69.3) and Pausanias saw a *mnema* dedicated to him (3.12.7; 7.24.1). Orestes' bone transfer and burial mentioned in Hdt. 1.68 was also seen by Pausanias (3.11.10). The cult of ephor Chilon, confirmed by the aforementioned rare inscribed sixth-century stone relief, is also mentioned in Pausanias (3.16.4). It is uncertain how many of the shrines seen by Pausanias go back to the Archaic and Classical periods and how many were founded in the Late Hellenistic and Roman periods as an outcome of the revival of and interest in Spartan antiquity (§ 6.2). Yet, the archaeological evidence, based on votives and architectural phases, attests that many of the hero shrines survived into the Hellenistic and even Roman periods.

The longevity of the cults is noteworthy because shrines receiving votives of one or two generations are usually interpreted as having a family importance:

typical examples are dedications at Bronze Age tombs or the stele shrines located over abandoned houses at the Potters' Quarter in Corinth.[160] By contrast, shrines that last longer have been understood as having acquired state importance as Williams argues for one of the stele shrines in Corinth, that of the South Stoa stele shrine, which received votives from the sixth century until 146 BC.[161] The same can be observed with the cults over Geometric graves, discussed in Chapter 1, where the shrines seem to have originally surrounded cults of ancestors but, because of their longevity and reorganization, they are interpreted to have become more communal, expanded the catchment area, and mattered to a wider audience.

Some of the heroic cults at Sparta may be viewed in the same light. While detailed data is not available for most sites, cults, some cults, such as that of Agamemnon and Alexandra/Kassandra (no. 1), which lasted from the Early Archaic to the Late Hellenistic period, became important enough to be known even in Pausanias' time and acquired state importance since the Gerousia dedicated a marble throne here. The state importance of the Menelaion is undoubted given the discovery of the tiles inscribed 'public property' (see Chapter 5).

The evidence presented above suggests that Spartan hero cults in the Archaic and Classical periods were predominantly housed in modest, small-scale buildings, or perhaps just open temenoi, and commonly received dedications of terracotta reliefs, pottery, figurines and lead figurines – cheap, affordable offerings by the residents of Sparta. Clearly, some of these shrines received more elaborate architectural features, as disc acroteria and other architectural members demonstrate the varied morphology of the buildings, with the most striking example being the Menelaion itself. With the exception of the Menelaion, however, the votive typology of the sites is quite uniform. Regardless of the modest nature of the votives, the heroic cults must have constituted an important component of the religious habits of the people of Sparta because of the abundance of sites, architectural phases, quantity of the votives and their longevity.

3.4 The hero shrines in the context of Spartan topography[162]

In the following section, I explore the topography of some of the sites listed in Chapter 2 and I attempt to contextualize them as much as possible in the layout of Archaic and Classical Sparta. Given that Sparta was built up extensively during the Hellenistic and Roman periods, the relationship of the heroic shrines to the private or public spaces of the Archaic and Classical polis is challenging; nevertheless, some general conclusions can be asserted. Before exploring the topography, I bring in comparative evidence from other Greek poleis where similarly small shrines existed in a city environment.

3.4.1 Small shrines in Greek poleis

The study of Greek religion often centres on the examination of central sanctuaries and cults of a polis that received sizeable temples with a long life and a large number of dedications. Some of these cults belonged to patron deities of a city, most famously that of Athena Polias in Athens, although many other large sacred spaces would coexist in a city. Amid the large temples, civic spaces, by roads, and houses of a Greek polis, many other cults existed. Several studies have highlighted this particular aspect of Greek religion, which may give a glimpse of smaller cults that existed in a Greek polis.[163] Specific types of shrines belonged to Hekate on crossroads, others took the form of Herms, or an aniconic representation of Apollo Agyieus, a protector of roads and houses.[164] Some of these were small, marked only by an altar, accompanied by a stele or a statue and sometimes surrounded by a wall, while others took the form of a small temple *naiskos*;[165] the architectural remains from the votive deposits in Sparta indicate that some hero shrines followed similar features.

Rusten has collected the literary evidence of small shrines, which he perceives as evidence of Greek popular religion[166] – a topic that tended to be omitted from general studies on Greek religion[167] but which has gained much discussion lately (above). Rusten adduces examples from Pindar, who provides us with some of the earliest evidence for shrines set among houses. In N. 7.93–94, written for Sogenes, a boy victor from Aigina who had won the boys' pentathlon, a simile likens the locality of the boy's home, between two precincts dedicated to Herakles, to the yokes of a four-horse chariot. In another ode, an epinician for Hieron of Syracuse, Pindar prays to the Mother and to Pan who 'often sing before my door at night' (*P.* 3.78–79). In fact, Pausanias claims that Pindar had a shrine to Mother and Pan by his house (9.25.3).[168] Inscriptions also provide evidence for such shrines. One of the marble stele recording the sale of the property of Alcibiades in 414 BC, connected possibly with the mutilation of the Herms in 415 BC, specifies that his house was in Kydathenaion, adjacent to the shrine of Artemis Amarysia from Anthomon (*IG* I³ 426).[169] Another inscription, from the fourth century BC, mentions a shrine of Herakles Alexikakos in an area where there was a sale of a confiscated property.[170] Inscriptions attest to shrines in the western part of Athens in the residential district of the demes Melitre and Kollytos on the Hill of the Nymphs, one of which was sacred to the Nymphs.[171] A rupestral inscription on the Hill of the Nymphs reads *horos Dios* (sixth century BC), while another reads *horos* only. It has been presumed that part of the hill was sacred to Zeus.[172]

Small shrines are not limited to cults to divinities, as literary sources attest to cults dedicated to heroes in neighbourhoods and near houses. Herodotus recounts that the hero shrine of Astrabacus in Sparta was near the house of King Ariston (6.69.3).[173] In Aristophanes' *Wasps*, Philokleon prays to Lycus whom he calls γείτων ἥρως, a neighbour hero, indicating a shrine to the hero in the neighbourhood (389–394).[174] In Euripides' *Helen*, a hero shrine was established in front of the palace (1165–68).[175] In Andokides' defence regarding the profanation of the Eleusinan Mysteries, he appears to have been living near the shrine of the hero Phorbas (*On the Mysteries*, 62).[176]

Some evidence provides a varied picture of ritual done at such shrines. In Barbios' fable 63, a man found a hero's grave in his courtyard; he poured libations at the altar and asked the hero for riches and good things.[177] Libations offered to Hermes are also depicted on a number of Athenian vases.[178] We learn that Hekate, who commonly has cult at crossroads, received sacrifices of dogs (Ar. Fragment 608; Eur. *TrGF* frag. 968) and in the fourth epigram of Theocritus, a cow, a goat and a sheep can be offered for sacrifice at a roadside shrine of Priapus. In Theophrastus' *Superstitious Man* (16.5) we learn that libation is offered when passing by a sacred space at a crossroads. The sources thus show how a passer-by could offer libations, place a votive, or may have a more organized ritual of sacrifice, a prayer or a short, casual greeting.[179] The profusion of literary sources in relation to shrines in poleis demonstrates the importance and abundance of such cults.[180] The phenomenon must have been so widely spread in the Greek world that Plato, in the context that no one should own a shrine in their own house, comments on the excessive amount of shrines and altars set up in houses and open spaces that fill homes and villages (*Laws* 10.909d–910a). Pausanias visiting Tanagra compliments the residents of the city because they alone of all the Greeks had their houses and shrines in separate spaces (9.22.2).

While large sanctuaries unified the citizen body, particularly with the celebration of festivals and competitions, other shrines, including hero shrines, presented another aspect of Greek religion.[181] Given their location in different areas of Greek poleis and for our purposes, the Sparta *komai*, they may have had a more limited sphere of activity and would probably be frequented by people living nearby. This would matter little to the average person whose daily life took place in his village or neighbourhood.[182] The worshipper could position the offerings on the ground, hang terracotta reliefs from trees or place them on some base or on the ground.[183] A shrine in close proximity to dwellings means that it could be visited more frequently, if not constantly passed and traversed, thus creating a sacred space close to the operations of the everyday life of the citizens.

Apart from the Spartan villages, the shrines may have had significance for specific families who sought to legitimize themselves through heroic ancestry. The kings themselves were considered priests (Zeus Lakedaimon and Zeus Ouranios; Hdt. 6.56), belonged to a family that had designated burial grounds, and were considered direct descendants of Herakles. Some of them may even have been heroized after their death (Chapter 5). The kings' burial place and heroic status works on two levels: firstly, the burial place would be significant for the royal family and thus a king's burial belonged to a particular group, either the Agidai or the Eurypontidai; on a second level, the buried kings were relevant to the wider citizen body since they belonged and were part of the entire Spartan and Lakedaimonian community. Another family that held hereditary positions was the Talthybiads, the descendants of Talthybios, the herald of Agamemnon (Hdt. 7.134; Paus. 3.12.7; 7.24.1).[184] One would expect that the so-called descendants of Talthybios would have held this sanctuary in special regard.[185] To what extent the shrine of Talthybios constituted an example of a private family worship in Sparta that remained unchanged through antiquity is unknown. Talthybios' cult too may have gradually acquired a more communal aspect.[186] We also hear from Herodotus (4.149) that the clan of the Aigidai, in order to protect their dying children, instituted a temple to Laius and his son Oedipus as instructed by an oracle and thus their children lived; this too, presumably, would have had special significance for the family. The residents who lived nearby to some heroic shrines could have frequented the cults, identifying and feeling closer to their neighbouring hero.

Recent research emphasises the role of smaller groups within a polis, *koinoniai* (Arist. *Nic. Eth.* 8.1160a–29; *Eud. Eth.* 7.1241b25–7; *Pol.* 1.1252b28–32), in which the inhabitants of a polis participated.[187] Such religious habits at a local level are observed intensely in Athenian demes, as shown by the sacrificial calendars of Athens that reveal the relationship of heroes to the topography of the polis. In Athens, cults belonging to gene shared a common ancestor, or a hero,[188] from whom were often derived hereditary priesthoods.[189] At the deme of Thorikos, Thorikos and Kephalos, two heroes connected to the deme by myth, received sacrifices.[190] Smaller groups in Athens would also be associated with some private cult associations, the *orgeones*, where they celebrated sacrificial rites to heroes or minor deities.[191] Hodkinson suggests that beyond the communal life in Sparta, there, too, smaller groups would conduct some pursuits, such as 'modest-scale religious activities'.[192] Private sacrifice (and feasting) is one of the exemptions, along with hunting, from attendance at the *messes* (Plut. *Lyc.* 12.2) – a rule implied in Herodotus (6. 57.3; above).[193] The custom of private feasting is attested during the Gymnopaidia (Xen. *Mem.* 1.2.61; Plut. *Cim.* 10.5). Some of the drinking shapes at the hero shrines may correspond to such small *koinoniai* partaking in ritual activities.

3.4.2 In Sparta

The hero shrines in Sparta are located in a variety of settings within the Spartan *komai*. Based on finds unearthed by the various excavations conducted by the British School at Athens in the earlier part of the twentieth century and the E' Ephoreia in Sparta more recently, it is impossible to overlook that a large concentration of the sites are situated in the area below and around the Acropolis and at the *kome* of Limnai. Other sites are scattered in various locations among the Spartan *komai*. In the following section, I examine the evidence of shrines by houses and roads, and then focus on the area of the Acropolis and Limnai.

Sparta was built over extensively during the Hellenistic and Roman periods and therefore domestic architecture from the Archaic and Classical periods is scarce. Apart from the shrine of Astrabacus, located near the house of King Ariston (Hdt. 6.61),[194] we have no other literary attestations regarding hero shrines and their proximity to houses.[195] Yet, the locality of many hero shrines at Limnai and south of the Acropolis, but also at other spots within the approximate space of the *komai* of ancient Sparta (see Map 0.1), demonstrates that the hero shrines, largely, were situated by areas of habitation. The area south of the Acropolis yielded a significant number of deposits with heroic material, such as numbers 11, 12, 13, 14, 15 north of Gerokomeiou hill and south-west of Toumpano hill,[196] and numbers 16, 17, 18, 19, 21, 22, 23 south of the Acropolis. Apart from these deposits, many other findings of terracotta reliefs have been unearthed in the area, indicating that the space near the Acropolis was rich in heroic cults from the Archaic period onwards.[197] In one example, in the same plot of land of the hero shrine on Stauffert Street (no. 8), ceramic accumulations dating from the Geometric to the Roman times give some evidence of a close topographic relationship to housing facilities since these show that the area was continuously occupied in antiquity.[198] Another shrine also seems to have been located in the area, as evidenced by miniature votives.[199] Gitiada Street nearby offers more evidence for continuous use in antiquity, with the accumulation of Archaic to Roman ceramics and tombs.[200] Likewise, at the Lykourgos and Karela plot (no. 9), the Late Geometric/Early Archaic building was constructed in an area of uninterrupted activity from Geometric to Roman times, including five burials. At the Drainage Ditch (no. 2). the area was also rich in remains that show uninterrupted activity, including a Late Geometric/Early Archaic two-room house and a Hellenistic street. A similar image is presented at the Stavropoulos plot (no. 6), where the excavation yielded remains of houses of the Hellenistic period as well as a road. The Hellenistic period sees houses in the area of Limnai at the Adriopoulos plot (t.s. 104), at the Darmos, Markos and Andriopoulos plot (t.s. 974), and at the Dimitrakopoulos plot (t.s. 98). Parts of houses of the Late Hellenistic period were uncovered at the Sourlis (t.s. 115), Kanellopoulos (t.s 107) and Stathakos plots (t.s. 89) as well as an extensive drainage system (t.s. 98), and roads in the area of Limnai.[201] The south part of the Acropolis and also further to the west and central part of the city also exhibits evidence of intense use during the Hellenistic period, with roads, buildings, tombs and shrines.[202] As Christesen recently demonstrated, in Sparta, there was no clear differentiation of space, and houses, shrines, workshops and burials were all intermixed in many parts of the city, with Limnai a primary example.[203] The other *komai* of Sparta most likely exhibited a similar picture.

Some hero shrines were situated by roads[204] often featuring graves: on the Aphetaid road were the hero shrines of many legendary and historical individuals, such as Maron and Alpheios, who fought at Thermopylai (Paus. 3.12.1–9; below). The connection between roads and shrines is further observed at the northeastern part of the city, by the *kome* of Limnai, where main routes led into the city. There, a fourth-century road was discovered near the site of the 'Drainage Ditch by the Eurotas' (no. 2), where the remains of an Archaic building decorated with metopes was discovered as well as a votive deposit.[205] Christesen speculates that a main road would have run south from the bridge of Eurotas along the east side of the Palaiokastro in the same direction as the modern road today; another road, 66 metres long, connected the area of the Acropolis, running the southern edge of Palaiokastro.[206] In the context of the locality of graves, he suggests that they were located alongside it. In an obvious observation, one would notice that not only are burials located along the likely road on the eastern side of Palaiokastro, but both the eastern side and the area to its south also hosts numerous heroic shrines – perhaps some featuring a burial, as we see with the examples of the site on Stauffert Street (no. 8) and the Stavropoulos (no. 6) plot.

These may be examples of shrines accompanying burials at prominent locations of the city, by a road, and could have been some seen by Pausanias during his visit to Roman Sparta.

As is evident in the survey of sites, no deposits of heroic terracotta or stone reliefs were found on the Acropolis of Sparta. Pausanias talks of the temple of Athena Chalkioikos, Athena Ergane, a shrine to the Muses, a temple of Zeus Kosmetas and one of Aphrodite Areia. Amid the divine cults there was the burial (μνῆμα)[207] of the legendary Spartan king Tyndareus, two statues of General Pausanias and one of a woman, Euryleonis, who won a chariot victory at Olympia (3.17.2–18.9). Statues need not denote cult but Tyndareus' presence on the Acropolis is noteworthy because he is the only mythical hero honoured there. As Kearns explains, the rarity of hero cults is common in the Greek world where the natural position of a protector over a polis belongs to a divinity.[208] Tyndareus' μνῆμα on the Acropolis may correspond to the tradition that he commenced the building of the temple of Athena Chalkioikos (Paus. 3.17.2). His tomb on the Acropolis is also similar to the existence of the grave of Erechtheus, the first king of Athens, on the Athenian acropolis (*Il.* 2.2454–65; *Od.* 7.80–1).[209] Tyndareus too was the king of Sparta after Herakles gave him the throne (Isokr. *Arch*; ps-Apollod. 2.7.3; Paus. 3.15.4–5). This event was important in Spartan legendary history in that it saw the return of the Herakleidai (the ancestors of the kings) and the Dorians – a crucial Spartan cultural memory, which legitimized not only the kings but also Sparta's dominance in the Peloponnese.[210] It is impossible to know with certainty when the cult of Tyndareus was established on the Acropolis since no material remains have secured a site. Still, his sons, the Dioskouroi, are mentioned early in Spartan poetry in Tyrtaeus and Alkman (§ 4.3) so perhaps a monument in his honour existed early.

Although the Acropolis, by the sanctuary of Athena Chalkioikos, seems to be reserved for the veneration of the gods, Pausanias documents Roman Sparta with numerous burials and monuments near the Acropolis and the Palaiokastro hill: going westwards from the agora and near the theatre was the burial of Brasidas. Opposite the theatre were the tombs of Leonidas and that of Pausanias, the general at Plataia (3.14). By these burials, Pausanias also saw a stele naming those who died at Thermopylai (see Chapter 5). The area by the Acropolis at least became a centralized commemoration space on the achievements of the community by giving honours to individuals who demonstrated courage in defence of Sparta and the rest of the Greeks. The antiquity of the above monuments is unknown but the area around the cult place of the Athena Chalkioikos on the Acropolis was already a space for hero cults. Other cults were also housed nearby: the heroon of Chilon (Paus. 3.16.4) was probably on the southern slopes of the Toumpanon hill, given the sixth-century heroic stone relief with the partial inscription [X]IΛON found there.[211] These legendary and historical individuals formed part of the community's cultural memory and thus were of civic significance – their shrines around the central space of the Acropolis reflecting their status.

The Acropolis is not only a place where central cults were housed but is also an area where dedications of athletic commemorations were set up, such as the Damonon stele (*I.G.* V.1.213; 420–400 BC). By placing public burials and cults near the Acropolis, where stood the temple of Athena Poliachos, the protectress of the city, these hero shrines receive a communal importance since they are situated within the context of state religion. Their public importance is also demonstrated by their setting in the context of other public inscriptions.[212] A comparable setting whereby a number of cults are clustered around a central space is mostly noted in Athens, where several smaller cults are situated near the slopes of the Athenian Acropolis.[213] Sparta appears to follow a similar trend.

More than others, the Spartan *kome* of Limnai is noted for its plethora of hero shrines. In Chapter 2, sites numbers 2 to 10 are all located within this *kome* and not far from the important sanctuary of Artemis Orthia. Given the rich archaeological evidence of hero shrines in the area it is unsurprising that Pausanias accounts for a number of hero cults in Limnai at Roman Sparta (3.16.6). Of special importance was the sanctuary of Lykourgos, behind which was the grave of Eukosmos, Lykourgos' son. Across from the sanctuary were situated two tombs: one was that of King Theopompus, a Eurypontid, and the other belonged to Eurybiades, who commanded the Lakedaimonian ships at Artemision and Salamis. Pausanias states the grave of Lathria and Anaxandra, descendants of Herakles, was by the altar of the temple of Lykourgos. The heroon of Astrabacus was also nearby.

Although Pausanias' visit to Sparta is much later than the period examined here, archaeological evidence supports that Limnai was rich in hero cults from an early date. The numerous votive deposits with terracotta reliefs found in the area indicate a wealth of heroic cults from at least the seventh century BC. This tradition continued into the Late Hellenistic/Roman period, with large temples centred around a grave, such as that of Ergatikes Katoikies (no. 5) and Stavropoulos plot (no. 6) (Chapter 6). The *kome* of Limnai, as shown by archaeological and literary evidence, was an area where prominent figures from the Spartan past were venerated.

The area near the Acropolis and Limnai hosted more than settlements, burials and the main sanctuaries of Athena Chalkioikos and Artemis Orthia; it also held the agora, from whence central roads spread and where government and religious buildings were situated. The agora, whose location is disputed, was probably east of the theatre[214] and, as elsewhere in the Greek world, civic and religious functions of the polis would be accommodated here. Among them was the Choros where the Gymnopaidia would take place, one of the main festivals of Apollo (Paus. 3.11.9), and the Persian Stoa funded from the spoils of the Persian Wars (Paus. 3.11.3). It can only be assumed that its development was probably gradual and accompanied the civic growth of Sparta in the area of the Acropolis and Limnai in the Early Archaic period. By the sixth century, it must have been fully developed since it housed the shrine of Orestes, whose bones were transferred from Tegea in the mid-sixth century (Hdt. 1.67.5–68.6).

From the agora, main roads radiated: most notably the Aphetaid road (Paus. 3.12.1–9), which held the procession to Amyklai during the Hyakinthia festival. Public buildings were in the forms of sanctuaries, hero shrines and public meeting places, such as the Booneta, the Hellenion, the hero shrines of Iops, Lelex, Amphiaraus (son of Oicles), Arsinoe (sister of the Leukippides), Talthybios (herald of Agamemnon), the sanctuary of Maron and Alpheios who distinguished themselves at Thermopylai, and at the end of the road the graves of the Eurypontidai kings.[215] Some buildings mentioned by Pausanias may be of some antiquity: at the beginning of the Aphetaid road near the agora was the Booneta, which was once the house of King Polydorus, who along with Theopompus was credited with the conquest of Messenia (Paus. 4.7.8; Ambelius 14.3) and Spartan constitutional reforms.[216] The interpretation of the Booneta as the house of King Polydorus may have been a Hellenistic construct and part of the antiquarianism that overtook Sparta at the time (§ 6.2) but it was probably of some antiquity at the time of Pausanias. The above shrines should be located south of the Acropolis, and roughly follow the modern parallel roads of Gkortsologlou and Palaiologou. As well as a number of heroic deposits located near the axis of the road, such as the Kaltatzi plot (no. 18),[217] burials predominantly of the Archaic, Hellenistic and Roman periods have been unearthed here.[218] It is likely that Pausanias witnessed graves there too, some with elaborate construction, especially those two-storey tombs of the Hellenistic period that have been interpreted as hero shrines.[219] Other hero shrines could have been earlier burials of the Archaic or Classical periods whose recipients were honoured by the community.

The *Skias*, where the Spartan assembly takes place, was situated by another road[220] that exited the agora (Paus. 3.12.10). Theodoros of Samos designed this building around the mid-sixth century. Nearby was a circular building with images of Olympian Zeus and Aphrodite, set up by the Cretan seer Epimenides (Paus. 3.12.11); perhaps this too is a sixth-century construction.[221] Close to the *Skias* and the circular building were numerous cults (dates unknown) of heroes of importance to Sparta's local legendary history: the tomb of Kastor (Paus. 3.13.1), the grave of the Spartan King Kynortas (the son of Amyklas) and those of Idas and Lynkeus (Paus. 3.13.1). The cluster of monuments here pertains to the family of the Tyndaridai and would have reminded the viewer of Sparta's legitimate control of Messenia: Kynortas in some versions of the story was the grandfather of Tyndareus who according to this genealogy is brother to Messenian King Aphareus and Leukippus (Stesichoros *PMG* p 227). In other versions, Kynortas was the great-grandfather of Tyndareus who is brother to Hippokoon (Pseudo-Apollodorus 3.10.4).[222] The former version has been interpreted as manipulation of the legend in order to bring Messenia 'under the genealogical jurisdiction of Sparta'.[223] This image is complemented by the location of the graves of the Messenian Idas and Lynkeus, killed by Dioskouroi. The twins' victory embodies Sparta's control over Messenia (see Chapter 4). The hero shrines described by Pausanias are of unknown date as no archaeological remains have been securely linked to them. Still, their setting near the Skias, the agora and other landmarks of civic and religious importance raises the possibility that other Archaic and Classical buildings, including hero shrines, were located in the area.

The reasons behind the popularity of Limnai and the area around the Acropolis as a 'host' to heroic cults from the early seventh century BC onwards probably vary. The area had long been of particular importance because of the cults of Orthia and Athena Chalkioikos there. Like the Acropolis, where heroic cults were placed near the sanctuary of Athena Chalkioikos, the sanctuary of Artemis Orthia became a centralized divine cult place – an attraction for heroic cults. Moreover, it seems likely that a main road passed through Limnai in a north–south axis on the eastern part of Palaiokastro hill, a location of hero shrines and burials. Beyond that, the space around the Acropolis (including the region south of the Toumpanon Hill) and Limnai has been inhabited since the Geometric period and into the Hellenistic and Roman periods, as evidenced by numerous burials and pottery deposits found there.[224] A slow formation of the Spartan polis as community, especially during the late eighth and early seventh centuries, saw this space gradually become the centre of Archaic Sparta (Introduction). Its relationship to earlier burials will be explored in Chapter 6. The presence of numerous heroic cults in that space, evidenced by archaeological remains and literary attestations, exposes the centrality and standing of the heroes to the developing Spartan community of the seventh century but also later. Since hero cult is a local phenomenon where respective poleis celebrate mythical or historical individuals who represent their polis' past and identity, they commonly belong to the civic sphere. Still, as there is an obvious intersection between grave cults, ancestor cults, tomb cults and hero cults, the private/familial significance of heroes and hero cults should also be considered.

An amalgamation of archaeological, literary and epigraphic sources displays a mixed religious topography in a Greek polis (although most of the evidence come from Athens) and varied religious practices presented to the residents within a society. Some shrines would have been located near main sanctuaries while others were placed by roads and in neighbourhoods.[225] The diversity of the topography and typology of cult sites reveals diverse religious space and occasion available to a community. The hero cults in Sparta provide evidence of a popular religious practice that expressed the connection of the community with those heroes who were omnipresent in the landscape of a polis.[226] Based on the longevity of many hero cults in Sparta, these cults would have been present for generations and were familiar to the locals.

3.5 Conclusion

The topography of many hero shrines near the Acropolis and Limnai, areas that constituted the agora (where Orestes was buried; Hdt 4.67–8; Paus. 3.11.10) and the civic centre of Sparta, together with the architectural designs that often follow those of the main temples of the polis, suggest that the hero cults constituted a component of civic religion that united people in veneration of local heroes. Still, it is logical to assume that some shrines must have been especially important to the respective inhabitants of the five *komai* because of their proximity to each village. Some cults would also be important to certain families who may have established them. The catchment area of the heroic shrines need not be uniform and various numbers (family, group or community) could have attended the cults. The physical accessibility of the hero shrines, the modest but perhaps personal dedication of terracotta reliefs, figurines and miniature pottery need not compete with the main cults of a polis but complement them, offering a diverse occasion for worship.[227]

4

Heroes and Immortality

An essential feature of a hero in the Archaic and Classical periods is that, as a mortal, he/she receives veneration after death. Yet, some heroes in exceptional cases achieve immortality. This chapter presents those heroes in Sparta who transcend their mortal existence: Helen, Hyakinthos and the Dioskouroi. For each hero/heroine, I focus first on the archaeological and textual evidence of their cult before discussing their divine/mortal status in Spartan religious thought. The Menelaion was the centre of cult for the legendary Homeric couple and king and queen of Sparta, Helen and Menelaus, while the Amyklaion held the cult of Apollo and his lover Hyakinthos. These two sanctuaries differ to those discussed in Chapters 2 and 3: firstly, the name of the heroes worshipped is known due to a plethora of epigraphic and literary testimonia. Secondly, the sanctuaries were major cult centres in Sparta (and Laconia) for which both archaeological and literary evidence offer a better-understood biography. Lastly, Helen and Hyakinthos, worshipped at the Menelaion and the Amyklaion, respectively, have seen much scholarly debate over their heroic or divine status. The most famous of Sparta's heroes, the Dioskouroi, who alternate between the world of the living and the dead, are also discussed.

4.1 The Menelaion[1]

4.1.1 The sanctuary[2]

According to Herodotus (6.61.3; cf. Paus. 3.19.9–11), the temple in which Helen was worshipped stood on the hills of Therapne.[3] The hills east of the Eurotas River were explored in the nineteenth and early twentieth centuries when the site of the temple of the Menelaion was discovered and underwent successive excavations (Figure 4.1).[4] Apart from the shrine itself, the investigations also revealed part of a Mycenaean building about 100 metres away, which had been

Figure 4.1 The Menelaion. Photo by George E. Koronaios.

destroyed by fire, as well as parts of Mycenaean debris on the south slope.[5] In 1973–6, Catling explored the Bronze Age site, the Menelaion sanctuary, and the 'Great Pit' (15 metres wide and 2 metres deep),[6] 20 metres north-east from the shrine. In his report, Catling states that due to the large chronological gap in the finds there had been an interval of about 500 years between the disappearance of Mycenaean activity on both the Menelaion Hill and the North Hill[7] and the founding of the later cults.[8]

Among other artefacts unearthed during 1973–6 were two remarkable finds that validated the identification of the site as the temple dedicated to Helen and Menelaus. At the north-east of the monument in a complex of artificial terraces were discovered two bronzes with inscribed dedications to Helen and Menelaus: an aryballos and an unusual object identified by Catling as an *harpax* or *kreagra* (meat-hook).[9] The excavators date the *harpax* to the sixth century BC and the aryballos (Figures 4.3–4.4) to the second quarter of the seventh century but Jeffery thinks that the inscription on the aryballos is later, *c.* 600 BC.[10] Written on the mouth of the vessel in boustrophedon are the words 'Δεῖνι[ς] τάδ ἀνέθεκε Χαρι[·] Fελέναι ΜενελάFo' – 'Deinis has dedicated this in honour of Helen of Menelaus' (*SEG* XXVI 457).[11] On the *harpax* the inscription reads: 'Τᾶι Fελέναι', 'to Helen' (*SEG* XXVI 458).[12] Another inscription of the early sixth century on the rim of a bronze phiale was dedicated to Menelaus (*SEG* XXXV 321)[13] and

Heroes and Immortality

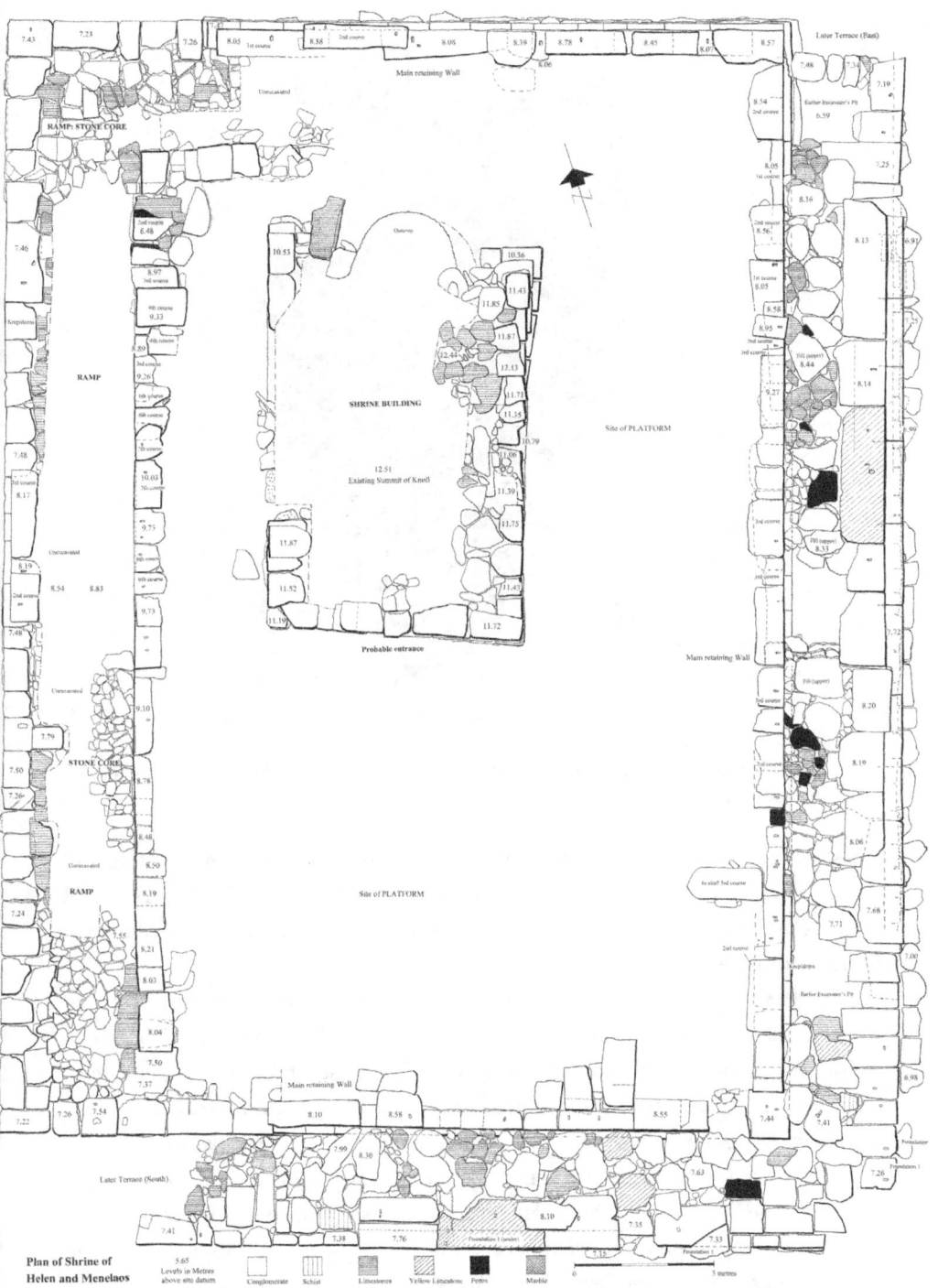

Figure 4.2 Menelaion plan. Courtesy of Richard Catling.

Figure 4.3 Sparta Museum 14742; bronze aryballos from the Menelaion. Courtesy of Sparta Museum.

lastly a stele dating to the fifth century BC (designed to carry a bronze statuette) was dedicated solely to Menelaus (ΕΥΘΥΚΡΕΝΕΣ ΑΝΕΘΕΚΕ ΤΟΙ ΜΕΝΕΛΑΙ; *SEG* XXVI 459).[14] These artefacts secure the site as the temple of Helen and Menelaus.[15]

In 1985, the southern terrace of the Menelaion Hill was further researched where sub-Geometric, Laconian I, some Proto-Corinthian, and early Corinthian pottery was unearthed; among these were Daedalic and Archaic figurines,[16] bronzes and three inscriptions, including an early sixth-century dedication to Menelaus (*SEG* XXXV 319–21). In this area there were also walls and a floor of Late Bronze Age remains. It was not until supplementary trials in 2005 that Late Bronze Age (LBA) remains were uncovered at the site of the standing sanctuary:[17] a LBA structural phase consisting of a wall cut by the Archaic foundations, and a cobbled surface.[18] Overlaying the LBA wall was a layer of burnt soil with LBA pottery, carbonized wood and calcinated burnt bone.

After the 2005 excavations, a revised chronology of the site was established: the cult at the Menelaion starts in the late eighth or early seventh century BC. There is very little evidence of cult before 700 BC apart from a few early Proto-Corinthian and Laconian late-Geometric sherds. A late Geometric shrine, of which no physical remains survive, but perhaps consisting of a temenos and a simple altar, is envisioned. Sub-Geometric pottery discovered at the southern terrace of the Menelaion Hill in 1985[19] and in the trenches around the Menelaion, explored in 2005, indicates this early cult phase. The Bronze Age remains probably inspired the commencement of the cult at the hill of Therapne in the eighth century and were linked with heroes of the local past – a common feature of the eighth-century Greek world. Catling, in reference to the Menelaion, suggested that the shrine's foundation was inspired by a sense of nostalgia for a heroic past – an attitude characteristic of the eighth century – which the excavator correlates to examples of cult at Bronze Age tombs.[20] Unlike the cults at Bronze Age tombs, the cult at the Menelaion was not in connection with a tomb but by Mycenaean remains.[21] The excavator speculates that the structures of the Mycenaean occupation on the Therapne hill were visible in the eighth century, and that the remains were possibly perceived as a hero's home. It is also probable that the knoll whereon the Menelaion was built, and which may have been interpreted as a tomb in antiquity, also inspired the cult.[22] Further, we should note that not only were Bronze Age remains found 100 metres away from the shrine but in 2005 a structural phase of Late Bronze Age remains were discovered on the Menelaion knoll. Also, the LBA pottery, mixed with burned earth, carbonized wood and calcinated bones, bears evidence that some commensal activity took place at the site.[23] More extensive excavations and publication of the material would further illuminate the Menelaion's relationship to the LBA remains.

Helen and Menelaus were prominent personalities in the local 'history' of Sparta and thus were selected to be occupants of the remains. The connection of the LBA material with a heroic world demonstrates how visual and tangible objects are effective in exciting, promoting and keeping cultural memory alive and connecting the past to the present. This past had as an image an age of heroes, aristocracy and individual excellence in warfare among many features. Old relics, remains, oral stories, genealogies constructed to link aristocratic families to the famous heroes, and objects that 'belonged' to heroes were visible to the later Greeks.[24] The hill of Therapne's antiquity inspired the cult and offered legitimization of religious practice.[25]

While there is little material evidence in relation to the cult in the late eighth century, a great deal of pottery is associated with the seventh century BC,[26] such as lakainai, skyphoi, mugs, pyxides, aryballoi, hydriai and a small number of kantharoi and kraters.[27] Other seventh-century votives are Daedalic terracotta figurines, ivories and bronzes. The increase in votives is accompanied by the first phase of construction in the seventh century (650–625 BC), which comprises a monumental terrace surrounding the existing monument. It includes a ramp on the south-west side that doubled around the north and the east sides in order to reach a *naiskos* on top of the knoll, decorated with a terracotta disc acroterion and roofed with terracotta tiles,[28] probably contemporary. The existing building is described by the excavator as a monument on a rectangular foundation surrounded by a broad terrace held in place by a retaining wall creating a structure of 22 × 16 metres.[29] This first phase of construction is a point at which we may assume that by then the cult received state importance.[30]

A second construction phase occurred in the mid-sixth century (*c.* 575–550 BC),[31] during which the area was extended on the east and south side of the retaining wall with the construction of a buttressing conglomerate terrace built in ashlar, increasing the ground plan to 26.5 × 19.5 metres (Figures 4.1–4.2).[32] Architectural members, such as a sixth-century marble triglyph from this phase of construction, may suggest that a triglyph frieze decorated the monument.[33] A

Figure 4.4 Sparta Museum 14742; detail of inscription of bronze aryballos from the Menelaion. Courtesy of Sparta Museum.

sixth-century unpublished roof tile inscribed 'public property' further supports the cult's state importance.³⁴

The two main construction periods, in the seventh century and then in the sixth century, correspond to other major building programmes that took place in Sparta at the time, such as at the Amyklaion and at Artemis Orthia in the late eighth/early seventh century. Another wave of building projects materialized in Sparta in the sixth century that saw the elaboration of state cults with the construction of the temple Athena Chalkioikos by Gitiadas, the second temple of Artemis Orthia, and the elaborate throne of Apollo at the Amyklaion (Introduction). It appears that the Menelaion, in both first and second periods of construction, was part of a general building programme that saw the embellishment of state cults.

Together with the major construction phases, in the Archaic period, deposition of pottery, figurines and bronzes reveal a popular, well-attended cult site. Activity continued in the subsequent centuries as a large number of fifth- and fourth-century pottery shows that the sanctuary remained popular through the Classical period. A homogenous set of tile-stamps with ΔΑ (*Damosion Athanas*) perhaps of the fourth or late fifth century suggests some later construction or repairs on the roof. Inscribed statuette bases of the fourth and third centuries found in the 'Great Pit' infer the continuous importance of the shrine.³⁵ Based on a new Simonides text there is some evidence that the Spartans may have attributed an important role to Menelaus, together with the Dioskouroi, in the victory of Plataia.³⁶ A fragmentary inscription, on a small Doric capital, which reads ΚΥΝΙΣΚΑ [...]ΝΑΙ is of significance because the name may allude to the well-known Spartan princess Kyniska, who won the Olympic chariot games in 396 and 392 BC.³⁷ If so, the dedication indicates that the Menelaion was a place of high standing where royal family members would give offerings and the cult maintained its popularity into the Classical period.

The life of the cult continued into the Hellenistic period, although the votives do not appear in the numbers of previous centuries. The 2005 excavations show a repair to the temple roof was conducted in the third century BC.³⁸ Votives continued into the third³⁹ and until the second century BC, as evidenced by Megarian bowls and two transport amphoras (200–150 BC). Even though the sanctuary fell out of use in the Hellenistic period, the shrine's importance was known and visited later: a second-century AD fibula was f ound in the fill⁴⁰ and of course Pausanias was well aware of the monument (3.19.9–11).

4.1.2 The votives

A full publication of the architecture, bronzes, figurines and pottery is pending, so the typology and chronology of the votives is not well understood yet. The conclusions for most of the votives can thus only be based on the data and chronology of the excavations from the early twentieth century and on general reports from later excavations.

The shrine was clearly of particular importance to the Spartans not only because of its use over a considerable time and building phases, but also because of the many valuable dedications in bronze, such as rings, pins, discs, sheets of bronze belonging to shields, miniature vases, animals (including a crouching mouse and a lion), bronze masks (one female head; one lion head), a female statuette, dice, pendants in the shape of pomegranate, poppy seeds or ox heads, model double axes, fibulae, bowl handles (two with snake heads), statuettes (at least two were male), rosettes, a sickle and bronze vessels.[41] Of special interest is the female bronze statuette found with Laconian 0 and Laconian I pottery.[42] One hundred and sixty-nine bronzes alone were reportedly found at the slope south of the Menelaion by some of the Mycenaean debris.[43] Other expensive objects include items in silver, or gilt silver, such as rings, a bud and a lion-head. Ivory, bone[44] and even a fragment of a sand-core glass bottle were also recovered.[45] Most of the above bronzes should belong to the Archaic period since studies on Laconian material culture show a general decline of bronzes after 500 BC.[46]

Some votives are of military character, especially in bronze, such as remains of shields, an arrow-head,[47] swords and spearheads.[48] Additionally, fragments of a bronze strip preserving the upper parts of four warriors in combat[49] and a Laconian III (575–550 BC) cup fragment with a warrior head on the tondo were also found.[50] It would be tempting to interpret these as offerings to Menelaus but given that Orthia also receives military type dedications at her sanctuary[51] there is no reason to suppose that they were destined for the cult's male figure. In fact, weapon dedications at sanctuaries of goddesses are relatively common.[52] In Sparta, a significant number of weapon votives were found at the temple of Apollo Amyklaios, while the sanctuaries of Apollo Tyritas and particularly Apollo Maleatas in Laconia and that of Apollo Korythos in Messenia are rich in weapons.[53]

Apart from the expensive items, less costly items were also abundant. A large number of terracotta figurines (over 300) such as Daedalic plaques, lions, female figurines, horse and rider, riders seated side-saddle, an ithyphallic figurine, protomai, *hydrophoroi*, and 'bread maker' figurines were discovered.[54] The figurines are largely female, with Daedalic or female figurines predominating within the assemblage in Laconian 0, Laconian I and Laconian II.[55] A hoard of horse-and-rider figurines were found during the early excavations, many of unidentified gender, though Thompson states that the majority are female and reports that they were found with pottery of the later Laconian style, so possibly Laconian III.[56] The terracotta figurines of females standing or as riders have parallels at the Orthia sanctuary. Some of them wear poloi, which may mean that they may represent Helen, while Voyatzis suggests that the riders seated side-saddle also denote Helen.[57] Loom-weights and spindle-whorls may have been appropriate dedications to her by women.

Pottery predominates the votive assemblage from the early seventh century BC onwards including a number of drinking shapes, such as lakainai, kraters, kantharoi, skyphoi, mugs, as well as tripod cooking pots.[58] Also unearthed were fragments of sixth-century panathenaic amphorae won for chariot races.[59] The reports show a large quantity of Archaic and Classical pottery but with examples also continuing into the Hellenistic period.

Lead figurines (approximately 10,000), abundant in the sanctuary of Artemis Orthia, were also unearthed. These are cheap, small items that were found in larger numbers than any of the other objects. The iconography of the lead figurines varies according to the time period.[60] Very few date to the seventh century, and these take the form of jewellery. It not until the end of the seventh century that lead votives become common at the Menelaion: in the Laconian II (610–575 BC) period we see mostly wreaths and twenty-eight figures of other varieties including warriors and women. From Laconian III (575–550 BC) there are mostly wreaths and 149 other varieties, with warriors and females dominating the assemblage; we also see the introduction of the deer. From Laconian IIIB–IV (575–525 BC) we have most varieties seen in Laconian III, but also the beginning of others, particularly deities, such as Poseidon, Hermes, Herakles and the armed goddess (presumably Athena). Horses and deer dominate the numbers of animal figures. From Laconian V–VI (450–300 BC) we see the lead types of Laconian III but with an increase of animal varieties. Cavanagh speculates that the moulds of the lead figurines after 500 BC were in circulation for a while and thus not many new varieties of lead figurines are attested since the same moulds were still in use. Some lead figurines possibly date later, but as these were found in plough soil, it is uncertain that these were made at a later date, i.e. after 200 BC.[61]

The material from the Menelaion belongs to the general repertoire of votives found in the prominent sanctuaries of Sparta, especially Orthia and the Amyklaion.[62] The large numbers of dedications of pottery, figurines, lead figurines, but also precious items in bronze and other metals indicate a widely spread worship in which the figures receiving cult at the Menelaion were important enough to acquire a large number of items from different socio-economic strata. Additionally, the sixth-century panathenaic amphorae, prized objects, demonstrate how the sanctuary was a central cult place for individuals to dedicate objects and display their victories. The only other location in Sparta where panathenaic amphorae were found is the temple of Athena Chalkioikos.[63] Fifth- and fourth-century statue bases show that the shrine continued to attract a wealthier audience in the Classical period and, as the dedicatory inscription from Kyniska may reveal, royalty too.

4.1.3 Ritual

The archaeological and literary evidence can provide some information regarding rituals and festivities at the site. Like many sanctuaries, the Menelaion yielded a large quantity of ceramic drinking vessels, such as kraters, skyphoi and Spartan lakainai, as well as tripod cooking pots.[64] However, the drinking vessels are nearly all miniaturized versions of the regular shape. We have very few kraters, relatively few regular size cups and almost no pouring vessels. Likewise, there is very little cooking ware, and most of that is from the later Classical and Hellenistic levels. These, and the inscribed bronze *harpax* (meat-hook), however, provide some evidence of drinking and dining. The ramp around the Menelaion may offer evidence for sacrifice,[65] further supported by Isokrates' *Enkomion to Helen* (66), which mentions sacrifices to her. The discovery of the cistern, a source of water needed for the participants, probably offers further evidence for feasting.[66] It appears that there was little if any ritual drinking and dining on site – at most, it was restricted to a small group, at least for the Archaic period,[67] while the evidence suggests larger groups in the late Classical and Hellenistic periods.

The presence of large numbers of lead votives may provide evidence for festivities associated with the Menelaion. Cavanagh speculates that the lead votives were made for a festival as a votive occasion, which explains their large numbers at Orthia and the Menelaion and their low occurrence elsewhere.[68] Some of the lead figurines, such as the dancers[69] and flautists, tempt one to suggest that these represent such performances at the site. Since such votives were also found in the sanctuary of Artemis Orthia the same is perhaps true there.

Literary evidence may also help regarding festivities at the Menelaion. Isokrates in his *Enkomion to Helen* (66) talks of processions, sacrifices and festivals in honour of Helen. Hesychios, writing in the fifth century AD, reports that maidens were carried to Helen's place in *kannathra* (wicker carriages), some decorated with images of deer and vultures. Admittedly, Hesychios is late but earlier sources, such as Xenophon (*Ages.* 8.7), also declare that *kannathra* were used for festivals in Sparta to transport maidens to Amyklai for the Hyakinthia.[70] Plutarch also mentions *kannathra* and specifies that young girls ride in them during processions (*Ages.* 19). Hesychios also talks of the Laconian festival the *Eleneia*, which may refer to a festival at Therapne.[71] Based on the literary and archaeological evidence, the Menelaion probably enjoyed a festival with sacrifices and processions.

4.1.4 The literary evidence

The Spartan literary record on the cult place of Helen, who was worshipped in Sparta together with her husband Menelaus at the Menelaion on the hill of Therapne, is early: Alkman[72] talks of a ναὸς ἁγνὸς εὐπύργω Σεράπνας (fr.14, *PMG*) and of Menelaus, Helen and the Dioskouroi receiving immortal rites there (ἀσανάτας τελε[τάς]; fr.7, *PMG*).[73] A fuller reference to Therapne comes later in Herodotus (6.58–61) who tells of an ugly girl transformed when brought to the temple of Helen, where the *goddess* appeared before the girl and changed her. In his *Enkomion to Helen* 63, Isokrates (436–338 BC) elaborates on the cult at Therapne:

> καὶ τούτοις ἔχω τὴν πόλιν τὴν Σπαρτιατῶν τὴν μάλιστα τὰ παλαιὰ διασῴζουσαν ἔργῳ παρασχέσθαι μαρτυροῦσαν: ἔτι γὰρ καὶ νῦν ἐν Θεράπναις τῆς Λακωνικῆς θυσίας αὐτοῖς ἁγίας καὶ πατρίας ἀποτελοῦσιν οὐχ ὡς ἥρωσιν ἀλλ' ὡς θεοῖς ἀμφοτέροις οὖσιν.

> And I can produce the city of the Spartans, which preserves with especial care its ancient traditions, as witness for the fact; for even to the present day at Therapne in Laconia the people offer holy and traditional sacrifices to them both, not as to heroes, but as to gods.

> Trans. Nock 1980

There is more from Isocrates in *Enkomion to Helen* 66:

> Since, then, Helen has power to punish as well as to reward,[74] it is the duty of those who have great wealth to propitiate and to honor her with thank-offerings, sacrifices, and processions, and philosophers should endeavour to speak of her in a manner worthy of her merits; for such are the first-fruits it is fitting that men of cultivation should offer.

> Trans. Nock 1980

Our sources, thus, offer enough evidence to suggest that Helen's status in Sparta was not that of an ordinary heroine and that the cult at the Menelaion at Therapne resembles those of divinities. Herodotus talks of a *goddess* with powers to influence someone's life while Isokrates talks of sacrifices, processions and thank offerings for Helen. He also explains that the sacrifices are done not in the manner conducted for heroes, but in that preserved for the gods.[75]

The Menelaion not only housed Helen's cult but also that of her husband's, Menelaus.[76] Menelaus acquired cult probably because of his prestige as Helen's husband; it is after all because of her that he received immortality: the *Odyssey* tells how, while still a mortal, Menelaus received a prophecy from Proteus, the old man of the sea, that he would not die in Argos but will be sent by the gods to the Elysian plain 'because you have Helen as wife and in their eyes Zeus is your father-in-law' (4.569). In Euripides' *Helen* (697ff.), the eponymous heroine has the power to make Menelaus immortal and he will be her consort. Regardless of Helen's unfaithfulness, we see that the literary tradition presents the couple with a strong husband-wife relationship after Helen returns from Troy.

The inscribed seventh-century bronze aryballos from the Menelaion (*SEG* XXVI 457) 'Deinis dedicated to Helen of Menelaus' attests to Helen's quality as the wife of Menelaus (Figures 4.3, 4.4); of course, we can assume that the story of the Trojan War would have been well known to Sparta.[77] The couple, for example, may be identified on a double-sided pyramid stele (*c.* 600–570 BC) found in Magoula, Sparta.[78] Side A of the stele depicts a man embracing a woman, while the two figures hold a wreath (Figure 4.5). The figures have been interpreted as Paris and Helen or Zeus and Alkmene, among others.[79] On side B, a man threatens as woman with a sword (Figure 4.6). The most generally accepted interpretation, especially for side B, is that it depicts Menelaus recovering Helen and threatening her with a sword as told in the *Ilioupersis* (*EGF*) and the *Little Ilias* (F 19 *EGF*).[80] Helen and Menelaus are likely featured on side B since a similar scene is attested and interpreted as such on a number of seventh-century Cycladic relief amphorae.[81] The stele also depicts snakes on each of its slimmer sides, which may allude to Helen's hero brothers, the Dioskouroi.[82]

The cult at the Menelaion indeed appears to favour the image of Helen as a wife of Menelaus, rather than her portrayal as an adulteress who fled to Troy.[83] The royal couple as rulers of Sparta offers a more positive image to that of the unfaithful wife and the discontent husband. Perhaps the impression one perceives is of the royal couple after Helen's return from Troy when life resumed to normal in the royal household (*Od.* 4. 260–65). Additionally, unlike the *Odyssey*, where Menelaus had a son by a slave-woman (*Od.* 4.10–12), the couple,

Figure 4.5 Sparta Museum 1; pyramidal stele (side A) from Magoula, Sparta. Courtesy of Sparta Museum.

according to the Spartan poet Kinaithon,[84] had two sons, Nikostratos and Aithiolas, who were honoured in Sparta: Κιναίθων δέ, φησι Νικόστρατος, καὶ Αἰθιόλας, παρὰ Λακεδαιμονίοις Ἑλένης δύο παῖδες τιμῶνται (*Scholia In Homerum, Scholia in Iliadem* 3. 175). Hence, the honours to Nikostratos and Aithiolas follow perhaps the local Spartan tradition that enhanced the image of the royal couple; these sons are also attested in Hesiod (*Cat.* fr. 175 M–W).

Further literary evidence portrays a more complex picture of Helen's role in Sparta.[85] In the late-sixth century, Helen is portrayed on the sculptural programme of the throne of Apollo at Amyklai being abducted by Theseus (Paus. 3.18.15); this myth of the young Helen was also recounted in Alkman (fr. 21

Figure 4.6 Sparta Museum 1; pyramidal stele (side B) from Magoula, Sparta. Courtesy of Sparta Museum.

Davies/Page). In Euripides' *Helen* (1465–78) and Aristophanes' *Lysistrata* (1296ff), Helen leads a chorus of young girls in local Spartan festivals. Theocritus (third century BC) in his *Idyll* 18 talks of Helen as formerly an adolescent who participated in races with girls but is now a wife, and girls put a garland and pour libations for her at a Plane tree. Calame associates the Plane tree in Theocritus with another cult of Helen at Platanistas, in Sparta, which is also mentioned in Pausanias (3.15.3).[86] He suggests that she has two aspects: Helen as an adolescent at Platanistas and Helen as a wife at the Menelaion, where she is worshipped with her husband. Because of the two cults (the adolescent and the wife), she is associated with rituals that focus on the transition from adolescent to adulthood,[87] marriage and fertility.[88] More than anything, Helen would have been important to girls of marriageable age. Still, as Parker emphasises, there are dedications by men at the Menelaion and so the cult catered not only to women.[89]

4.1.5 Discussion

Scholars devoted much discussion to Helen and her position in the Spartan pantheon. Larson considers that Helen and Menelaus exemplify a heroic couple worshipped in the Peloponnese, such as Alexandra and Agamemnon. She finds the cult relationship of husband and wife at the Menelaion to be a characteristic of chthonian cults rather than Olympian and sees Helen as an example of a 'faded goddess' who is connected with fertility.[90] Others trace Helen's origin and background in Indo-European mythology and regard her as the daughter of the Vedic sky god Dyaus, therefore the Dawn goddess.[91] But as Parker explains, there is no evidence that when the cult at the Menelaion began, Helen was a fertility goddess downgraded to the status of heroine. Indeed Helen was the legendary wife of Menelaus and associated with marriage in Sparta – as the earliest inscription attests (*SEG* XXVI 457; Figures 4.3–4.4). In Herodotus (3.61 6), Helen makes a girl the most beautiful in Sparta and so desirable that when she grows up King Ariston steals her from her husband and marries her himself. The evidence from Euripides' *Helen* (1465–78) and Aristophanes' *Lysistrata* (1296ff) as well as Isocrates' *Idyll* 18 shows a close relationship of Helen to girls in Sparta; we can even speculate that girls who were about to marry presented some of the votives found at the Menelaion.[92] As Parker stresses, Helen's mythology where she is recurrently 'raped', i.e. carried off – it is her nature to disappear recurrently – has no effects on the dying and the rebirth of the earth and seasons which would make her a fertility goddess (unlike Kore).[93] Edmunds moreover, finds that the only evidence in relation to Helen as a fertility or nature goddess is in Theocritus' *Idyll* 18, linked to the cult at the Platanistas, and this is problematic since an unparalleled ritual is performed.[94] In the case of Helen, her cult was established in connection to myths that *pre-existed* the cults. Thus, any ritual came after and is in relation to those cults; there are no rituals or myths linked that reveal an original nature goddess in Helen's cults.[95]

Parker suggests that Helen and Menelaus should be viewed as belonging to the class of mortals who do not die but became immortals, such as Herakles, the Dioskouroi, Asklepios and Amphiaraos.[96] Helen's status being elevated[97] may be because she is the only mortal daughter of Zeus.[98] The other daughters of Zeus, such as Athena, Aphrodite and Persephone, had two parents who were immortal and so were themselves divine.⁹⁹ Accordingly, it is possible that Helen would have assumed her divine position as a goddess, particularly since Menelaus' immortality is implied early (*Od.* 4.561–9). Parker's thesis is convincing. Yet, the definition of what constitutes a divinity is worth considering, since as Edmunds advocates, there are other characters in Greek myth who receive immortality but their status is not divine e.g. Ganymedes and Tithonus.¹⁰⁰ Edmunds' protest appears sound but, without Zeus as their father, Ganymedes and Tithonus should not be put in the same category as Helen; Helen more closely resembles Herakles and the Dioskouroi.

What about the cult at the Menelaion? There are several features relating to her cult that have been posited as evidence for Helen's divinity. Herodotus (6.61.3) attests that Helen has an ἄγαλμα (cult statue) at Therapne, a characteristic that is suggested to be more common in divine rather than heroic cult – but the division is not strict and so not indicatory of divine cult.¹⁰¹ Another aspect of the cult pertains to dedicatory patterns: the votive material from the Menelaion was part of the general Spartan votive repertoire common to Spartan sanctuaries but not hero shrines. In particular, the votive assemblage from the Menelaion lacks typical Spartan heroic stone and terracotta reliefs, most famously known from the deposit dedicated to Agamemnon and Alexandra/Kassandra, the Heroon by the Eurotas, and many others discussed in Chapters 2 and 3. These reliefs have been identified as typically heroic and are not found in any of the divine cult places in Sparta. The contrast between the votive assemblages of the two heroic couples worshipped in Sparta is significant. Both the cults at the Menelaion and that of Agamemnon and Alexandra/Kassandra (Chapter 2) were in place by the early seventh century BC; other hero cults presented in Chapter 2 also commenced in the seventh century. However, it seems that the cult at the Menelaion followed a different route: while the cult of Agamemnon and Alexandra/Kassandra acquired a votive depositional character according to the customs of heroic cult, the cult at the Menelaion was *expressed* in the same way as the divine cults of Sparta.

Parker uses the votive material as evidence to argue for Helen's divine status,¹⁰² while Edmunds considers Parker's argument from absence unconvincing.¹⁰³ But the absence of stone and terracotta reliefs *is* important and should be considered. If anything, the nonexistence of these votives should signify that the cult at the Menelaion differed greatly to those of the other hero shrines. Why did Helen and Menelaus not receive these popular votives that were in use for hundreds of years? In fact, the earliest heroic stone reliefs depict an enthroned couple, which, if anything, carry appropriate iconography for the couple's cult at the Menelaion;

and yet none have been found at the Menelaion. The Menelaion, instead, has a rich dedicatory pattern of bronzes (together with other material of pottery, and terracotta and lead figurines), which is uncommon at other heroic shrines (Chapter 3). As we saw in the discussion on the votive patterns at the heroic sanctuaries in Sparta, the votive deposits associated with heroes in Sparta generally consist of inexpensive items, such as vases and terracottas, while bronzes are rare.

When I wrote my PhD, I argued that Helen and Menelaus could still have been considered heroes at the Menelaion but their cult was *expressed* in a divine way. Since then, Edmunds has presented a similar idea in a further developed way, namely that *ritual* at the Menelaion resembled that of a divine cult.[104] Greek religion allowed this to occur because heroes are heterogeneous and so are the rituals performed for them. Broadly speaking, as Parker explains, on a biographical level heroes are dead mortals, 'functionally minor gods',[105] and thus there are variations in how the cult to heroes is expressed. Cults and rituals to dead mortals, whether grave cults, tomb cults, ancestor cults, hero cults, ruler cults or even divine cults (if one can actually clearly define all the terms), were not fixed but very fluid and worked on a spectrum of religious expression: some rituals were closer to the human sphere and others to the divine sphere with many layers in between. There is no unchanging and uniform set of rituals in Greek religion that belongs only to divinities and likewise only for heroes – although there are some common patterns observed for heroes.[106]

If ritual is what expresses the character of the cult then let us allow the Spartans themselves to 'tell us' what the cult of the Menelaion was for them. Edmunds, quoting Burkert, states that the Greeks were less concerned with theology[107] than with ritual.[108] By all means, then, for the Spartans Helen was *treated* as a goddess – at least based on votive practice since there is a clear differentiation between the votive patterns in the Menelaion and other heroic cults in Sparta. Helen though can still be a heroine; an immortal heroine, such as the Dioskouroi. Regarding other rituals, e.g. sacrifice or festivals, it is hard to know with certainty due to the paucity of comparative evidence with other heroic sites in Sparta. A full excavation of the site of the two deposits dedicated to Agamemnon and Alexandra/Kassandra may shed some light on the rituals performed for them and give us a fuller picture of heroic rituals in Sparta.

Lastly, it is important to note that the cult was not static. It probably began as heroic cult, associated with Late Bronze Age remains out of nostalgia for a heroic past, as Catling explained. But its character, prestige and popularity grew – so much so that in the eyes of the Spartans Helen was treated as a divinity. By the time Pausanias visited the area, the Menelaion was the place where Helen and

Menelaus were allegedly buried (3.19.9). Since heroic cults were commonly associated with graves, as evident from the Hellenistic and Roman *heroa*,[109] Helen and Menelaus also acquired a 'grave' at the place of their temple.[110]

4.2 The Amyklaion

The sanctuary of Apollo and Hyakinthos located at the fifth *kome* of Sparta, Amyklai, was considered one of the most important sanctuaries in Sparta and possibly Laconia. Polybius calls it the ἐπιφανέστατον sanctuary for the Laconians (5.19.3). The Hyakinthia festival,[111] celebrated there in honour of Hyakinthos who was accidentally killed by his lover Apollo,[112] was a joyful community affair where Spartans, perioikoi and slaves were entertained (Polykrates *FGrH* 588 F1).[113] The sanctuary was famous for the architectural construction of the 'throne of Apollo', whose base was the grave of Hyakinthos (Paus. 3.19.2). The antiquity of the cult is evident since a cult existed at the site from the thirteenth to the eleventh centuries BC and continued into the Iron Age and later periods. Because of this continuity between the Bronze Age and the Geometric and later periods, the hero Hyakinthos has been viewed as a Mycenaean deity who was demoted in status in the historical period.[114] This suggestion is problematic as it is impossible to trace Hyakinthos' presence within the remains of the Bronze Age cult. Hyakinthos certainly is a hero who has a symbiotic relationship with the god who killed him. The Hyakinthia festival, a communal celebration of the Spartans from all five *komai*, illuminates aspects of this hero and his place in Sparta's religious system.

4.2.1 The sanctuary

The site of the sanctuary of Apollo and Hyakinthos, the Amyklaion, was discovered at the area of the Agia Kyriaki hill, about 600 metres from the village of Sklavochori-Amykles and 5 kilometres from Sparta.[115] The area was explored in the late nineteenth and early twentieth centuries[116] and is also currently undergoing excavations (2006–23) under the directorship of Stavros Vlizos.[117] The investigation of the site established that Early and Middle Helladic settlements were present on the hillside, followed by a reorganization of the space in the late Helladic LHIII B–C period when the site became a locus of cult. This is evident by the large number of wheel-made animal terracotta figurines, female Psi figurines, fragments of large wheel-made terracotta statuettes, rhytons used for libations, and two fragments of large anthropomorphic figurines.[118]

Although there is substantial reduction to the material remains from the mid/late eleventh century to the early tenth century, ritual activity at the site continued into subsequent centuries (1050–700 BC) with evidence of intensification of the cult from the tenth century onwards. During this time, pottery numbers increased substantially and the pottery shapes indicate that rituals of commensality with drinking and dining occurred at the sanctuary.[119] Moreover, metal finds (swords, tripods and pins) from the Early Iron Age show a distinct change in votive practice. Metal finds from the middle of the eighth century attest to the high artistic quality bronzes.[120] This rich material reveals aspects of competitive display by the local elite.[121] Two large anthropomorphic clay heads dated to the end of the eighth century BC depict a female with a polos and a male with a helmet and have been interpreted as cult figures.[122] Lastly, where the later altar was, there probably existed an earlier ash altar as the evidence of pottery, votives, bones and black fatty earth indicates.[123] The archaeological evidence confirms Polybius' remark on the importance of the cult for the Laconians as cult activity continued into the Archaic, Classical, Hellenistic and Roman eras.

The excavators assume that the cult site before the sixth century must have been an open-air temenos. It is during the late Geometric/early Archaic period (c. 700 BC) that there was a monumentalization of the site with the construction of a precinct wall discovered recently.[124] The wall appears to go through the length of the south side of the hill and east of the so-called late-sixth-century Π-shaped 'South-Building'. The excavators concluded that due to the typology of material and traces of burning, the area must have been the focus of ritual activity.[125] A monumental late-seventh-century wooden statue seems to have preceded the sixth-century elaborate construction of the throne of Apollo. Architectural members indicate that this *xoanon* would have stood on a base that may have served as the grave of Hyakinthos in a similar manner to that of the famous sixth-century statue.[126]

The increase of ritual activity and number of worshippers resulted in a second monumentalization of the site in the late sixth century BC. Part of this project was the famous throne of Apollo that Pausanias (3.18.9) tells us was designed by Vathykles of Magnesia.[127] Without having reached a consensus, scholars have proposed different reconstructions regarding the design of the temple (i.e. the throne) aided by literary and archaeological evidence.[128] It is generally accepted that the temple was planned as a large throne on which stood a pillar-like image of an armed Apollo. Probably this was the one that pre-existed the late-sixth-century construction by Vathykles;[129] the architectural parts of the seventh-century base for the statue were incorporated into the sixth-century construction.[130] The pedestal was designed as a very large altar within which Hyakinthos was purportedly buried (Paus. 3.19.2–3). The sixth century also saw the construction of an extensive Archaic peribolos wall (116 metres long, 2 metres high and 2.50 metres wide) whose 'intentional and emphatic configuration is probably directly related to the procession that took place at Hyakinthia' (Figure 4.7).[131] The late sixth century saw further construction at the site: a stepped altar, whose location was confirmed and was partly restored in 2009,[132] and the Π-shaped 'South Building' (probably quadrilateral or rectangular; one wall is missing) unearthed in 2017.[133]

What is particularly remarkable is the 'fate' of the older Geometric precinct wall during the sixth-century extensive monumentalization of the sanctuary. Recent excavations (2018–20) show that in the sixth century, cult activity moved outside the Geometric wall and that this older wall became a locus of cult. Along the outer face of the south section of the Geometric wall and on top of it were found about 2,000 miniature pottery, such as kantharoi, lakainai, amphorae, as

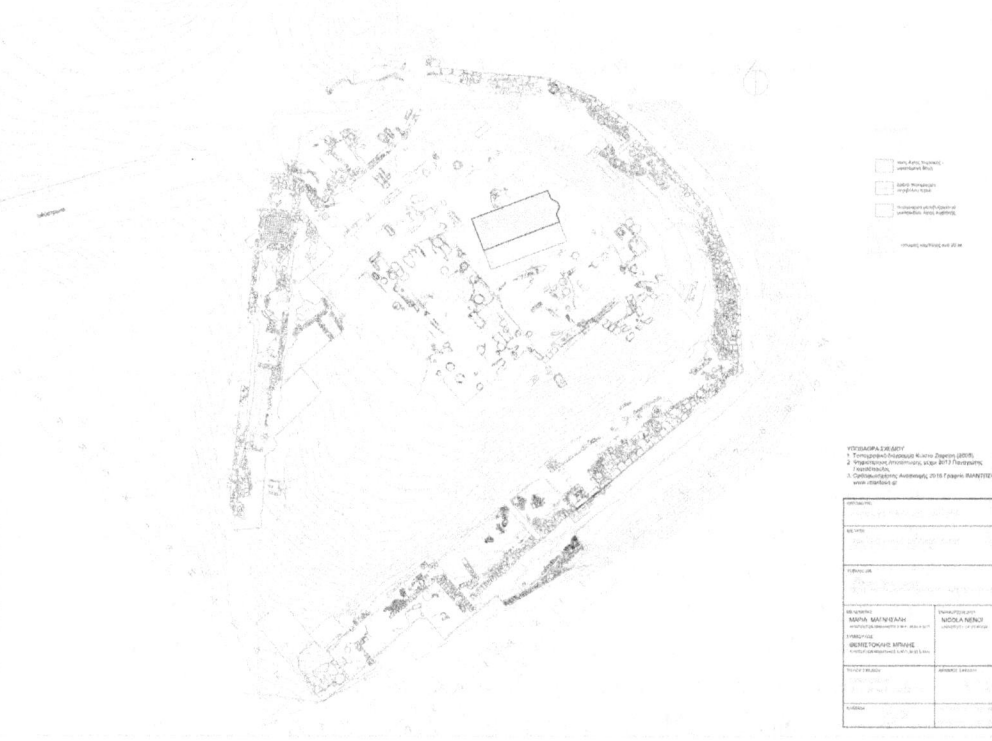

Figure 4.7 Plan of the Amyklaion. Courtesy of Amykles Research Project, Th. Mpilis, M. Magnisali and N. Nenci.

well as aryballoi, thymiateria, bone artefacts, metal finds (e.g. iron spits, part of a bronze helmet and the eyelids of a bronze statue), animal bones, a roof tile with an inscription with the name ΗΟΡΜΙΠΠΟΣ, a fragmentary figurine of an owl, and traces of burning; the material dated from the seventh and sixth centuries BC.[134] These finds, and a dark layer of earth, suggest that the area became a dumping ground after the destruction of the Geometric wall in the mid-sixth century BC.

Building and ritual activity continued into the Classical period and later, into the fourth century AD, as evidenced by votives, inscriptions and architectural fragments;[135] destruction began at the sanctuary in the fifth century AD.[136]

4.2.2 From the Bronze Age to the Iron Age

Apollo's presence in the Late Bronze Age Greek world is uncertain, while it is commonly considered that the deity must have 'arrived' in Greece at some point in the Early Iron Age.[137] Therefore, the change in the nature of finds, from the LHIIIC animal terracotta figurines to the metal dedications in the Early Iron Age (which show a change in the social conditions), together with the epigraphic and literary evidence for a cult of Apollo,[138] has led scholars to believe that there were newcomers in the area.[139] It is also argued that during the LHIIIB–C period the sanctuary was dedicated to a different native deity, the vegetation deity Hyakinthos, whom Apollo then superseded. In this line of thought, Hyakinthos was a Mycenaean deity whose myth in which he is killed by Apollo with a discus may function as an allegory for the establishment of the new cult of Apollo superseding the older 'pre-Dorian' religion.[140] Indeed, the name Hyakinthos, with the suffix –νθ, indicates a pre-Greek origin (not only pre-Dorian), perhaps alluding to the antiquity of his existence.[141]

However, the association of Hyakinthos with a pre-Dorian native vegetation deity is hard to prove. The month Hyakinthos exists in Dorian-speaking areas and is part of a Dorian calendar, making his existence and continuity from the Bronze Age problematic;[142] this is especially true since Hyakinthos is exclusively associated with Dorian-speaking areas.[143]

It is difficult to substantiate that the Bronze Age cult was dedicated to a divinity called Hyakinthos whose cult was then taken over by Apollo. The site certainly attests to changes between the Bronze Age and the Iron Age: the LHIII B–C material consists mostly of small or large terracotta statuettes; during the Early Iron Age, the artefacts, bar the Proto-Geometric pottery, are mostly metal, such as jewellery and weapons.[144] At the Amyklaion, unlike other sanctuaries, in which the divinity shared the sanctuary with a hero, e.g. Pelops at Olympia, there was never a shrine dedicated to Hyakinthos separately; rather, Hyakinthos' grave was at the base of the throne of Apollo. So it is impossible to determine the cult's date of foundation. One suggestion is that the Hyakinthia festival and the athletic competitions that took place may be 'visible' in the discovery of thousands of aryballoi found at the site. This is because the aryballoi would be indicatory of athletic events of the Hyakinthia festival and thus Hyakinthos was present at the site by then.[145] If Hyakinthos was worshipped at the sanctuary in the Bronze Age, his cult is altogether elusive.

I will not join the ongoing debate on the identity of the recipient of the cult in the Bronze Age. What is certain is that the cult at the Amyklaion was old; its antiquity would have contributed to the site's status, perhaps prompted by cultural memories lost to us. There is no trace of architectural remains from the Bronze Age that would suggest a certain *lieu de memoire* for the community in the manner that Cosmopoulos has argued for the cult at Eleusis in Attica.[146] Other material, such as visible older dedications, cult images, and of course oral histories could have kept the sacredness of the site alive and into the Early Iron Age. Importantly, compared to other Spartan sanctuaries (Athena Chalkioikos Acropolis, Orthia, the Heroon by the Eurotas, and Zeus Messapeus at Anthochori), which have produced few Proto-Geometric sherds, the Amyklaion yielded abundant Early Iron Age material,[147] revealing the status of the sanctuary for those who lived nearby. The regional standing of Amyklai is further attested as it is mentioned in Homer (*Il.* 2.584) in the catalogue of ships.[148] Thus, its distinction, centrality and antiquity may explain not only how the sanctuary retained its prominent status in later periods, but also why Amyklai, 5 kilometres from Sparta, became the geographically 'awkward' fifth *kome* of the Spartan polis.

Traditionally, the takeover of Amyklai is thought to have taken place in the mid-eighth century BC[149] when it joined the other four central Spartan *komai*, Limnai, Pitane, Kynosoura and Mesoa.[150] The conquest of Amyklai, with its renowned sanctuary, would have given 'an important symbolic and cultic status in the definition of the Spartan territory'.[151] Notably, a section of the Hyakinthia festival consisted of the display of the breastplate of Timomachos (the Aigeid who supposedly conquered Amyklai for the Lakedaimonians) to those participating (Pindar *I.* 7.13–15; Aristotle *Lac. Pol.* fr.532 Rose; Schol. Pind. *I.*7.18a).[152] This tradition could not make more obvious how the sanctuary was linked to the cultural memory of the conquest of Amyklai regardless of whether Hyakinthos was an older deity or a newcomer with Apollo.

4.2.3 Hyakinthos, the Hyakinthia and his Apotheosis

As it is hard to detect the worship of Hyakinthos in the material record, literary references to the festival of the Hyakinthia should also be considered. While Euripides' *Helen* (1469–73; below) gives us the first solid mention to the famous Hyakinthia festival, earlier texts may attest to it from the late eighth or seventh centuries BC. The first evidence comes from a couple of lines from a second-century AD papyrus that Calame attributes to Alkman. The lines are preceded by a reference to the Spartan origin of Alkman and to his *Hyakinthia* and may allude to a girls' chorus at the Hyakinthia.[153] The second piece of evidence derives from Antiochus of Syracuse (*c*. 425 BC), quoted by Strabo (6.3.2). In his narrative of the foundation of Taras, traditionally dated 706 BC, Strabo states that the Partheniai were plotting an attack during the festival of the Hyakinthia.[154] These sources are controversial, but if accepted, can establish an early date for the celebration of the Hyakinthia at Amyklai. The rich votive bronzes that commence in the mid-eighth century BC and the first monumentalization of the site, with the first peribolos wall *c*. 700 BC, allow us to accept that not only was the sanctuary a place of elite competitive display, but also that a community came together to organize the cultic space. Plausibly, the festival of the Hyakinthia was already celebrated in some form by the late eighth century by the community that sought the first monumentalization of the sanctuary to organize the festival space.

While we have to wait until Euripides to get a secure confirmation of the celebration of the Hyakinthia, the aetiological myth, which explains the cult of Hyakinthos and Apollo in which Hyakinthos is killed by Apollo with a discus, may be 'detected' by the presence of several disc-related dedications. The earliest is the inscribed bronze disc dated to the sixth century BC that reads 'ἄε<θ>λον Ἀμυκ{ι}αίοι'[155] and a bronze figurine of a discus thrower *c*. 520–500 BC.[156] Most impressive, however, is the famous fragmentary inscribed and sculpted stone stele dated to *c*. 475 BC bearing a life-size frontal relief of a discus thrower.[157] The inscription reads: ---ας δέκα κα(ὶ). hένατον | --κε --. Massow has identified this stele with that of Ainetos, an Olympic victor whose stele was seen at Amyklai by Pausanias (3.18.7).[158] It is likely that these dedications were in reference to the athletic competitions during the Hyakinthia; the discus event would have alluded to the aetiological myth in connection to the cult at Amyklai.

Before continuing on with the sources that relate to the Hyakinthia let us digress to Hyakinthos' most famous appearance in Sparta, his tomb, which also served as the pedestal of the statue of Apollo.[159] Pausanias describes the sculptured altar of Apollo as designed by Vathykles of Magnesia:

> The pedestal of the statue is fashioned into the shape of an altar and they say that Hyacinthus is buried in it, and at the Hyacinthia, before the sacrifice to Apollo, they devote offerings to Hyacinthus as to a hero into this altar through a bronze door, which is on the left of the altar. On the altar are wrought in relief ... Demeter, the Maid, Pluto, next to them Fates and Seasons, and with them Aphrodite, Athena, Artemis. They carry Hyakinthos and Polyboea, the sister, they say, of Hyakinthos who died a maid, to Olympus. Now this statue of Hyacinthus represents him as bearded[160] but Nicias,[161] son of Nicomedes, has painted him in the very prime of youthful beauty, hinting at the love of Apollo for Hyakinthos of which legend tells. Wrought on the altar is also Herakles; he too is being led to Olympus by Athena and the other gods ... As for the West Wind, how Apollo unintentionally killed Hyacinthus, and the story of the flower, we must be content with the legends, although perhaps they are not true history.
>
> Paus. 3.19.3–5; trans. Jones and Ormerod 1926[162]

Hyakinthos thus according to the iconography on the altar becomes immortal. His status is juxtaposed with that of Herakles (3.19.5) and Dionysus (3.18.11), who are also shown on the altar on their way to Olympus.[163]

This theme is essential in viewing the local Spartan perception of Hyakinthos – his mortality and then immortality. In the earliest literary evidence in the Hesiodic *Catalogue of Women* (fr.171 M/W), he was a local hero, son of Amyklas and the Lapith Diomede.[164] The fragment is badly damaged and thus sections that appear to narrate the myth are missing. In Euripides (*Hel.* 1465–75), Hyakinthos is a young man, loved by Apollo but accidentally killed by him with a discus. The god then orders commemorations of the death of Hyakinthos with sacrifices. We also hear of the dances and revels in a night long joy of a festival for Hyakinthos; presumambly in celebration of the Hyakinthia festival. In the work of the Hellenistic bucolic poet Bion, Apollo is desperate to save Hyakinthos, who cannot escape the fate of death:

> When he beheld thy agony Phoebus was dumb. He sought every remedy, he had recourse to cunning arts, he anointed all the wound, anointed it with ambrosia and with nectar; but all remedies are powerless to heal the wounds of Fate ...
>
> Bion 11 *Of Hyakinthus*; trans. Edmonds 1928

This myth has some essential differences to that of the iconographical programme of the altar of the throne of Apollo.[165] On the altar, Hyakinthos is a mature man and is not perceived as having died; in parallel to Herakles and Dionysus, and also Ino and Semele,[166] he ascends to Olympus.[167] Thus, like Herakles, his status is closer to the divine, or rather to immortality, than to a dead hero. By contrast, in the works of Euripides and Bion, Hyakinthos dies. Apollo does not save him, but the celebrants of the Hyakinthia enjoy a night-long dance and a sacrifice of oxen (βούθυτος), as prescribed by Apollo to honour Hyakinthos (Eur. *Hel.* 1470). Unlike the stories that portray Hyakinthos as dying, Hyakinthos' ascent to Olympus does not survive in the literary sources. Still, the story must have been old, since not only does it appear on the late-sixth-century reliefs of the throne of Apollo at Amyklai, it was also celebrated at the Hyakinthia:[168]

The festival, according to the fragments of Polykrates (*FGrH* 588 F1) from Athenaeus (4.137d–139f),[169] commenced with a mournful period devoted to Hyakinthos' death when certain prohibitions existed, such as wearing wreaths, eating bread and singing the paean. The participants offered sacrificial cakes and foods and ate in an orderly fashion before departing. In the middle of the third day the mood changed when there was a great spectacle, including boys playing the lyre, singing and dancing by young men, and the attendance of unmarried girls in *kannathra* (carriages ornamented with wicker) or horse-racing chariots. Archaeological and epigraphic evidence attest to athletic contents, e.g. the discus (above).[170] The festival concluded on the third day in a joyful manner with a sacrifice of many victims and a ritual meal in which everyone participated, including the servants (Athen. 4.138f). The festival indeed reflects the myth of Hyakinthos – its schedule presumably imitating the mournful lament for the hero, followed by the joyful celebration of Hyakinthos' ascent to Olympus.[171] The Hyakinthia festival echoes the iconographical programme on the temple of Apollo where he receives apotheosis.[172]

Pausanias also gives information on Hyakinthos: 'at the Hyakinthia, before the sacrifices (θυσίας) to Apollo, they devote offerings to Hyakinthos as to a hero (ἐναγίζουσιν) into the altar [in which Hyakinthos is buried] through a bronze door' (Trans. Jones and Ormerod 1926). In Euripides' *Hel.* (1470) and Athenaios (4.139c), however, no such rite is attested, only θυσίαι. It seems that by the time of Pausanias, while Apollo receives a θυσία, the worshippers ἐναγίζουσιν to Hyakinthos. As this verb is reserved for heroes and the dead, by the Roman period Hyakinthos' heroic/dead attributes were apparently accentuated.[173]

Hyakinthos' emphasized mortality is indeed supported by his burial inside the pedestal.[174] We do not hear of this feature of the cult before Pausanias. We do not know, for example, if the pedestal that held the statue of Apollo, at its late-sixth-century construction, was considered the tomb of Hyakinthos. Since the famous throne of Apollo appears to have been preceded by the seventh-century xoanon that also had a pedestal, we may wonder if Vathykles reworked an earlier construction that was also believed to hold the tomb. In practical terms, the Archaic pedestal where Hyakinthos was 'buried', was very large and one could offer *enagismos* or sacrifice inside.[175] Naturally, the existence of Hyakinthos' tomb inside the throne of Apollo contradicts the iconographical programme where Hyakinthos receives apotheosis. How can Hyakinthos be both dead, entombed in the altar/pedestal of Apollo, and also be received at Olympus as shown on the reliefs?

The contrasting depiction of the status of Hyakinthos' mortality need not pose a problem. Research in cognitive science explains how thought process has a dualistic nature in intuitive and reflective cognition.[176] Intuitive cognition[177] is non-conscious, quick and implicit and is affiliated with emotions and automacy, while reflective cognition[178] is explicit, slow and includes deliberative thinking. Like most domains of thought, religious thought typically exhibits a mixture of the two. The relief representation of the apotheosis of Hyakinthos is a product of highly reflective cognition because it is the product of stories, and mythmaking. A visit to the grave of the dead Hyakinthos at the statue of Apollo is an example from the real world. Real-world practice favours intuitive cognition because the dead are in a specific physical location that humans can perceive and see. The practice of *enagismos* through an opening of the door to the tomb of Hyakinthos complements this intuitive belief.

The distinction between intuitive and reflective cognition explains the mechanism that allowed the Greeks to hold mental representations of Hyakinthos as being entombed and simultaneously as being at Olympus. Although reflectively Hyakinthos received apotheosis, a belief that was celebrated at the Hyakinthia festival and depicted on the iconographical programme of the throne of Apollo, Hyakinthos was also buried in the pedestal and received sacrifice or *enagismos*. Whenever they wished, the visitors at the sanctuary could shift thought to an intuitive mode, which saw the pedestal as Hyakinthos' tomb. Thus, as cognitive research explains, '"intuitive dualism" could override ... reflective beliefs'.[179]

Spartan local tradition must have therefore conceived Hyakinthos in a somewhat different light to those traditions that considered his death final. Both the Hyakinthia festival and the reliefs on the throne of Apollo demonstrate that Hyakinthos was not thought of as having died but rather as having gone to Olympus and become immortal. The coexistence of an iconographical representation of the apotheosis, the grave and the ritual of *enagismos* is indeed possible since humans can hold both a belief in Hyakinthos' immortality and still consider the tomb his place of burial.

4.3 The Dioskouroi

Although the Dioskouroi were worshipped in multiple locations in the Greek and Roman world, they are quintessential Spartan heroes of attested Spartan origin. In the *Iliad* (3.238), they come from Lakedaimon, where Pindar (*P.* 11.61–2) tells us that they dwell on alternating days at Therapne and at Olympus (cf. Alkman fr. 7.14 *PMG*). Their early local importance is shown in the poetry of Alkman, where they frequently appear in a number of surviving fragments (frs. 5.1; 8; 10; 12 Page, *PMG*). Their mother is Leda married to the legendary Spartan King Tyndareus and thus they are also known as Tyndaridai while Helen is their famous sister. The Dioskouroi appear intertwined in their mythology and cultic topography with other local heroes who formed the religious landscape of the Spartan mythic world.

While some of the earliest evidence, e.g. *Hesiodic Catalogue of Women* (fr. 66 Schol. Pind. 10.150) and *Homeric Hymn* 17 give a divine parentage to both twins (Kastor and Polydeukes) as sons of Zeus (cf. Pseudo-Hyginus, *Fab.*14), other narratives tell how Zeus, in the form of a swan, visited Leda who then bore children of mixed parentage: Polydeukes and Helen were the children of Zeus, while Kastor and Clytemnestra were the children of Tyndareus (Pseudo-Hyginus, *Fabulae* 77; cf. *Cypria* fr. 7 Clem. Al. *Protrept* 2.30.5; pseud. Apollod. 3.137). The different fathers also explain how Polydeukes was considered immortal but Kastor was doomed to die (*Cypria* fr. 7 Clem. Al. *Protrept* 2.30.5).

Various stories circulated relating to the adventures of the Dioskouroi, such as joining the Argonauts (Diod. 4. 43. 1; 4. 48. 6; 6.6; Valerius Flaccus, *Argonautica* 5. 366) or partaking in the Kalydonian boar-hunt (Ovid *Metamorphoses* 8. 370), but certain legends were of Spartan significance and some even took place locally. The Dioskouroi were involved in rescuing Helen from Theseus – depicted in the iconographical programme of the throne of Apollo at Amyklai (Paus. 3.18.15; cf. Alkman fr. 21 Davies/Page). In the stories that interweave local mythological characters, the twins steal the Leukippidai, who were engaged to their Messenian cousins and counterparts Idas and Lynkaeus (the Apharidai; sons of Aphareus the Messenian king) and proceed to make them their brides (Ovid *Fasti* 5. 697 ff. cf. Apollod. 3.10.3; Paus. 1.18.1).[180] Most famously, the twins share their immortality: when the Dioskouroi stole the cattle of the Apharidai, a fight ensued that resulted in the death of Kastor. Polydeukes proceeded to kill the Apharidai and when Zeus came to take him to Olympus he refused to part from his brother and thus chose to share his immortality. The twins, hence, alternate their days between the underworld and Olympus (*Cypria* fr. 1 Proclus Chres. 1; Pind. *P.* 11.61–2; *N.* 10.50-90; pseudo-Apollod. *Bibl.* 3.136–7).[181] The

Figure 4.8 Sparta Museum 575; stone relief with Dioskouroi and two amphorae. Courtesy of Sparta Museum.

Dioskouroi and their brotherly love were widely celebrated in Sparta in their role as protectors of Spartan youths, as overseers of athletics and warfare, and in their connection to the Spartan kings. Numerous dedications to the Dioskouroi and the literary sources attest to their widespread worship.

The antiquity of their cult (or cults) is supported by the discovery of about fifty reliefs offered to the twins, ten of which date to the Archaic and Classical periods.[182] The twins are usually represented on the reliefs together, often holding spears (Figure 4.8).[183] Two amphorae sometimes stand between them; sometimes the amphorae stand alone and so represent the twins *in absentia*.[184] On other occasions, the peculiar *dokana* (two wooden beams connected together at the top) are present in the iconography of the twins but other times, as with the amphorae, the *dokana* represent the twins.[185] Furthermore, a re-reading of the Archaic 'Thiokles relief' by Lanéres interprets it as a dedication by Namartes to the Dioskouroi.[186] Both the literary and the archaeological evidence suggest that the Dioskouroi held a prominent position in the religious life of the Spartans from the Archaic period onwards.

While no archaeological sites associated with the cult of the Dioskouroi have been unearthed, Pausanias (3.13.1) informs that they were venerated as gods forty years after their death and records six places where they were worshipped (3.13.1, 13.6, 14.6, 20.1–2).[187]

The first place is the tomb of Kastor, which was also a sanctuary (3.13.1). As Kastor is the twin who has a mortal father and dies, he gets a grave in Sparta unlike Polydeukes who was the son of Zeus. His tomb and sanctuary is also near the burials of the twins' Messenian enemies, the Apharidai – although Pausanias suggests that they were actually buried in Messenia (3.13.1). In fact, it was because of this fight that Lynkeus killed Kastor and the twins came to famously share their immortality (*Cypria* fr. 1; Pindar *N.* 10. 55-95; pseudo-Apollodorus 3. 136-7; Ovid *Fasti* 5. 697).

The Dioskouroi also had an altar as Dioskouroi Amboulioi near the old market (Paus. 3.13.6). There, they were not worshipped alone but were joined by altars to Zeus Amboulios and Athena Amboulia. These titles were similar to those held in Athens by Zeus Boulaios, Athena Boulaia and Hestia Boulaia, who were patrons of the Athenian Boule (Council). This suggests that the Dioskouroi, together with Zeus and Athena, were patrons of the Spartan Council.[188] The grave of Kastor near the Skias (Canopy) where the Spartan assembly takes place may complement their function as protectors of the Spartan government bodies and the Spartan kings.

The twins also had a sanctuary near the Dromos (racecourse), shared with the Graces, Eileithyia, Apollo Karneios and Artemis Hegemone (Leader) (Paus. 3.14.6);[189] another one at the Dromos itself counterparts this sanctuary, where the Dioskouroi are called Apheterioi (Starters) (Paus. 3.14.7). It is unsurprising that the twins were worshipped near the Dromos, where athletic competitions would take place, since the Dioskouroi were considered patrons of athletics, as Pindar explains in his *Olympian* 3.70–73 and *Nemean* 10.52–53.

The other cult places dedicated to the Dioskouroi are located in relation to the hill of Therapne in proximity to the Menelaion, where their sister Helen had her temple. Pausanias (3.20.1) informs us that on his way to Therapne he came across the roadside sanctuary of Polydeukes where he is worshipped alone. By the sanctuary, the traveller also saw a fountain called 'Polydeukaia'. It is the Phoibaion at Therapne, nonetheless, that seems to be the best-known sanctuary of the twin heroes (Paus. 3.20.2; cf. Hdt. 6.61.3). This is where the Dioskouroi were thought to dwell when not at Olympus. At the Phoibaion, the Spartan youths sacrifice a black puppy to the war god Enyalios before their fight at the Platanistas;[190] thus, scholars have linked this cult to rituals in relation to adolescents (Paus. 3.20.2; cf. 19.4).[191] The above-described cults have not been confirmed archaeologically but a brief mention of the Phoibaion in Herodotus (6.61.3) attests to the antiquity of some of the cults.

The cultic topography of Sparta held monuments and cults of other individuals connected to the Dioskouroi by myth: their father, Tyndareus had a *mnema* on the Acropolis (Paus. 3.17.2), their sister Helen had cults at Therapne and at Platanistas as we saw above, and the Apharidai were buried near the tomb of Kastor (Paus. 3.13.1). The Leukippidai (Hilaeira and Phoebe), the brides of the Dioskouroi, also enjoyed a cult at Sparta (Paus. 3.16.1–2; 3.13.7; Plut. *Moralia, the Greek Questions*, 48), as shown by an inscription dating to AD 200 (*IG* V.1.305) that mentions a priest of both the Tyndaridai and the Leukippidai. The priestesses themselves were named after the heroines 'Leukippidai' (Paus. 3.16.1) and were linked to a group of girls, the Dionysiadai, who ran a race for Dionysus Kolonatas (Paus. 3.13.7).[192] The Leukippidai appear again when Pausanias informs us that they weave the tunic for Apollo at Amyklai (Paus. 3.18.3), presumably for the Hyakinthia.[193] Although the above relate to Roman Sparta, the 'Leukippidai' are connected with ritual festivities in Classical Sparta too. In Euripides' *Helen* (1465–75), Helen will join the Leukippidai 'by the river or before the temple of Pallas, at long last having joined in the dances or revels for Hyakinthos for nightlong festivity'. Spartan girls and women partook in choral singing and dancing in various religious festivals and here we see how they were linked to the cult of the Leukippidai.[194] Their sister Arsinoe also had a cult in Roman Sparta (Paus. 3.12.8). The Dioskouroi, their family, brides and enemies coloured the religious landscape of Sparta, at least in the Roman period. The antiquity of some of the sites cannot be confirmed archaeologically but the reference to the Leukippidai in Euripides offers support for the cult's antiquity.

In Roman Sparta, the twins are worshipped at multiple locations in varied roles within Sparta's religious life. In Archaic and Classical Sparta, they feature prominently as protectors of Spartan military affairs. As Herodotus (5.75.2) explains, the Spartan kings went into battle accompanied by the images of the Dioskouroi who helped them. When the rules changed whereby one of kings remained at home while the other went into battle, one of the Tyndaridai also remained (Hdt. 5.75.2). The double kingship would find easy parallels with the twin Dioskouroi, each accompanying one king.[195] On one occasion, the Spartans, when asked by the Locrians for military help, gave them the Dioskouroi (Diod. 8.32).[196] This refers presumably to images of the Dioskouroi. Furthermore, these local heroes offered protection to Sparta from Aristomenes of Messene (Paus. 4.16.9), and according to the New Simonides (fr. 11.30 W²), the Dioskouroi and Menelaus accompanied the Spartans when they left to fight the Persians at Plataea. In Plutarch (*Lys.* 12.1; cf. ML 95) we hear that the Dioskouroi appeared as stars at the battle of Aegospotamoi. Such stories may echo in a sword-dance in honour of the Dioskouroi performed in Classical Sparta (Plato *Laws* 796b; cf. Paus. 4.27.1–2; Polyainos 2.31–4; *IG* V. 559, second century BC).[197] It was invented by the Dioskouroi themselves and performed when Athena played the flute for them (Epicharmus *Mousai* fr. 92 *PCG*).[198] This dance is seen as a ritual that celebrated the martial and protective aspects of the Dioskouroi.[199]

The martial qualities of the twin heroes complemented the military ethos of Spartan society, the training of the youth in the *agoge*, and the Dioskouroi could serve as exemplary figures for men. Their shared immortality, after all, was achieved after fighting with the Messenian Idas and Lynkeus. The encounter with their Messenian counterparts and their subsequent victory can thus be seen to symbolize Sparta's subjection of Messenia.[200] The Dioskouroi were apparently hostile towards Messenia, moreover, because two Messenian men, Panormus and Gonippus of Andania, disrespected a festival of the Dioskouroi that was held in Sparta (Paus. 4.27.1–3). The Dioskouroi's hostility can serve as a complement to the hostile relationship between Sparta and its neighbour that pre-dated the Messenian Wars.[201] The burials of Idas and Lynkeus, close to the grave and sanctuary of Kastor, would remind the viewer of the fight between the Dioskouroi and the Apharidai, which resulted in the death of Kastor and the twins' immortality.

The dual mortal and divine nature of the twins is indeed extraordinary even by the imaginative standards of Greek myth. No one else, not even heroes, such as Herakles, Theseus, Orpheus or Odysseus who visited the underworld, can regularly come and go between the two spheres.[202] Aside from the queen of the underworld, Persephone, only the Dioskouroi have a dual existence where they alternate between these worlds (Pind. *N.* 10.5; *P.* 11.62–4). Their status once in the underworld is uncertain: are they dead when they dwell under the earth at Therapne? Do they retain their immortal nature? Ancient authors offer various views: in the *Cypria* (fr. 1 Evelyn-White), they get immortality every other day, implying that the other day they have a mortal nature. In Lykophron's *Alexandra* (564) they are 'undying and dead'; thus, when under the earth, they forgo their divinity. But for the Spartan Alkman the Dioskouroi are never dead (fr. 2 Campbell) since when they dwell underneath at Therapne they are ἀειζώοι 'always alive', highlighting their immortal nature. This view is supported by later authors who consider the Dioskouroi immortal (Diod. 4.48; Cicero, *De Natura Deorum* 2. 24; 3.15). This inconsistency need not pose a problem. As heroes who dwell under the earth at Therapne it would be intuitive for people to think of them as dead while at the same time still accepting a divine nature, especially in Sparta, where the twins were worshipped at multiple locations. The cognitive explanation is similar to that of Hyakinthos, who can be buried in the altar of Apollo and also receive apotheosis.

4.5 Conclusion

From the discussion on early hero cult in Sparta, we see that both the Menelaion and the Amyklaion carry evidence of a local treatment of heroes, which reflect differing religious needs of the community. The expression of cult at the Menelaion resembles that of divinities, as articulated by both the votive and literary evidence. The Amyklaion is a complex case in which Hyakinthos shows how diverse hero cult can be. Hyakinthos may have been an older deity whose cult was superseded by that of Apollo; alternatively, Hyakinthos and Apollo may have been introduced together at the site later.

The above examples from the Menelaion and the Amyklaion demonstrate the ways in which the local religious requirements create not only different kinds of heroes, but how the nature of those heroes depends on and responds to the community as it changes over time. The Menelaion should probably not be taken to imply divine cult during the late eighth/early seventh century BC because it formed one of several heroic cults that appeared around Sparta during the early seventh century. However, the votives at the Menelaion indicate that the local heroes (Helen and Menelaus) could be treated as gods and still retain the heroic identity. By the time Pausanias visited the Menelaion, local tradition had made Therapne the burial place of Menelaus and Helen. Although Hyakinthos dies in other traditions, at Amyklai he receives apotheosis. Hyakinthos acquires a burial inside the base of the statue of Apollo in accordance with the pronouncement of the funerary aspects of hero cult. The two cults – that of the Menelaion and the Amyklaion – are therefore distinct Spartan peculiarities; their standing in terms of Greek hero cult in general remains difficult to define, but they reflect the heterogeneity of hero cult itself. The Dioskouroi, who can dwell both in the world of the gods and the dead, also show the fluidity of the post-mortem status of heroes in Greek thought: the permeable boundaries of mortality, immortality and divinity.

5

Honouring the Dead

Examples of heroization of historical personalities in Sparta vary: Xenophon famously remarks that Spartan kings were honoured as heroes after death (*Lak. Pol.* 15.9); archaeological evidence points to the heroization of public figures, such as the ephor Chilon; and literary evidence highlights the commemoration of the exceptional war-dead, such as Leonidas.[1] The heroization of the recently deceased is not unique to Archaic and Classical Sparta. As discussed in Chapter 1, cults to the recently deceased occurred in the Greek world in an array of contexts: over Geometric burials, for *oikistai*, and in Hellenistic Greece, families would heroize their own dead to elevate their status. As heroization would take place after the burial, the realm of grave ritual and hero cult intersect here. Within this, we see that since burial rites traditionally belong to the family, the spheres of family ritual and polis ritual meet in the heroization of exceptional individuals. Certainly, the posthumous heroization of a person elevates them to an extreme degree. The circumstances that prompted their heroization vary, but often, personal excellence and achievements that matter to the community, such as warfare, politics or athletics, will deem a person worthy of posthumous veneration. Other times, the local elite heroized their ancestors to gain prestige in the community.

Here, I present the evidence of heroic cults associated with the recently dead in Sparta. The material is based on both archaeological evidence and literary testimonies. Before discussing the heroization of the historical figures, I examine how an individual could gain prominence and excellence in Spartan society in order to follow the reasons behind the heroization of certain figures. Since heroization would take place after the death, I present an overview of Sparta's burial customs from the seventh to the fifth centuries BC. Examination of the burial customs will help to establish a comparative context in relation to the treatment of the dead.

5.1 The prominence of the individual in Archaic and Classical Sparta

Recent research has succeeded in unfolding a new image of Sparta that refutes its reputation, presented by ancient authors, as an austere society in relation to wealth, art and architecture, luxury goods, and a community composed of strictly equal citizens (Thuk. 1.10.1; Xen. *Lak. Pol.* 5,-7.14; Isok. *Panathenaikos* 225). Rather, Sparta in the Archaic to early Classical periods experienced highly regarded artistic production, especially of ivories, pottery and bronze-work, and embellished its city with ornate temples.[2] It is not until the end of the sixth and early fifth century that artistic production declines and only then did some reforms probably take place that introduced a seemingly regulated lifestyle of citizens as that of a society of equals.[3] Even then, the Spartan community formed a more complex picture than that of citizens of equal status or *homoioi* – a term that implies that wealth and personal standing was the same for all. The active involvement of the citizens in the *messes*, the *agoge* and military training shows that some public institutions encouraged certain communal features in its citizens.[4] Yet, Classical Sparta is now understood as a society that enjoyed luxury items, property and personal wealth; concurrently, public display of wealth was not always encouraged.[5]

Apart from the ability to acquire property and wealth, albeit in a less ostensible display of affluence, personal prominence was a reality. Lineage and personal connections held great sway in the Classical period, even though on the surface this influence was disguised by a lifestyle that appeared restrictive (Thuk. 1.6).[6] In Classical Sparta, someone could be called 'θεῖος ἀνέρ' (god-like man) to express their great virtue (Plato *Min.* 99d8-9; Aristot. *eth. Nic.* 1145a18-30),[7] and Sparta gave honours to men who excelled, such as Themistokles (τιμηθῆναι, Hdt. 8.124.2-3) and Brasidas (ἐπῃνέθη, Thuk. 2.25.2).[8] One can undergo the vigorous selection process and join the distinguished *hippeis* (the kings' bodyguards) and hold special responsibilities (Hdt. 8.124; Xen. *Lac.Pol.* 4.1-6).[9] Military commanders were chosen for their skills but also due to friendships and familial connections with the Spartan elite (e.g. Xen. *Hell.* 2.4.28; 4.8.32).[10] Individuals who showed valour, such as Eurybiades, the Spartan commander at Salamis, also received official honours – an olive wreath (Hdt. 8.124) and a tomb (*mnema*) in a public space (Paus. 3.16.6). It is likely that the pre-eminence of, and honours to, the individual were compatible with Spartan ideals of excellence because the individual's victories and achievements were achieved for Sparta, not for him alone.[11] A perfect example is

Pausanias, who added his name to the tripod dedicated collectively by the Greeks at Delphi and on which were inscribed the names of all Greek states that fought against the Persians (Thuk. 1.32.2). Such personal glorification would go against Spartan customs and so the Spartans had Pausanias' epigram erased (Thuk. 1.132.3).

Social hierarchies existed, not only in the hereditary position of the kings, which came with certain privileges, but also with other institutions: the Gerousia (council of the elders) and the ephors. The Gerousia was open to twenty-eight men over sixty, was a lifetime appointment, and gave its members judicial and legislative powers (Arist. *Pol.* 1275b 9–10; Xen. *Lak. Pol.* 10.2). It also had a probouleutic function for the Spartan assembly (Plut. *Lyk* . 6) and its members could offer advice to the king (Hdt. 5.40; Xen. *Hell.* 3.3.8); election to the post would be prestigious and presumably sought after by the elite.[12] Given the limited availability of membership at the Gerousia, the ephorship was a more realistic political prospect for Spartans with political aspirations aged 30 to 60. The five ephors held their position for only one year and could only hold the position twice. They had an array of executive powers, including powers of oversight, even for the kings (Thuk. 1.131).[13]

Inasmuch as Sparta encouraged a seeming equality, Spartans in the Classical period were able to distinguish themselves not only in military and political affairs, but at athletic events too. At Olympia, a series of victories in the four-horse chariot race produced commissioned victory monuments abroad.[14] Olympic victors not only gained prestige abroad, but had the opportunity to advance into military and political roles in Sparta.[15] With the exception of the late fifth-century Damonon stele (*IG* V 1.213), where Damonon records numerous victories by himself and his son in Laconia and Messenia over a period of at least twelve years, monuments for chariot competitions are absent in Sparta.[16] A recent suggestion sees the absence of monuments of equestrian victories in Sparta as a sign of less tolerance of victories based on hereditary wealth.[17] Other athletic commemorations, however, were celebrated: at Sparta, Pausanias (3.18.7) saw the stele of Ainetos in the Amyklaion that commemorated his *pentathlon* victory at Olympia; Jeffery includes an early fifth-century fragment, possibly identified with the stele.[18] Athletic victory lists consisted of the inscription on a stele of a victor's achievements commemorating victories in local festivals in Laconia and Messenia, such as the Damonon *stele*. As a number of these *stelai* have been discovered in Spartan sanctuaries, it is evident that the custom of dedicating inscribed victory lists may have started as early as the late sixth century and was certainly popular in the fifth.[19] Naturally, the *stelai* indicate public recognition of athletic success but they are not ostentatious.[20] Nonetheless, the placement of the *stelai* in public space illustrates that as much as the collective and communal elements were valued in Sparta, so was personal excellence. Lastly, Spartans commissioned not only visible monuments but *epinicians* too in order to celebrate victories abroad, as presented in the fragments of Ibykos (fr. S 166) and Simonides (fr. 34 Poltera).[21]

The importance of athletic victories is further demonstrated by the erection of statues not for contemporary athletes but for those of long ago. Hipposthenes, a seventh-century athlete, was given honours like those for Poseidon (Paus. 3.15.7; 5.8.9). Chionis, another seventh-century athlete, received a statue made by the Classical sculptor Myron, at Olympia, together with a stele recording his victories (Paus. 6.13.2). A stele listing Chionis' victories was also set up in Sparta (Paus. 3.14.3).

From the above evidence, Sparta's social institutions in the late Archaic and Classical periods clearly held a degree of influence over the flaunting of personal wealth. But as Hodkinson puts it, 'private influence of wealthy citizens conditioned all levels of public activity, from the operation of the small-group *koinoniai* in which Spartiates led their everyday lives through the highest levels of official policy making'.[22]

By the late fifth and fourth centuries, Spartan socio-economic relations had changed. During this time, we see the introduction of currency, the decline of Sparta's public institutions, the engaging of Spartan mercenaries abroad, and the *oliganthropia* (decline in numbers). The concentration of wealth seems to have moved into the hands of a few, and thus the numbers of Spartan citizens fell (because for one to be a citizen and an *homoios* one had to contribute to the Spartan state in funds).[23] The concentration of wealth in the hands of few prompted the personal promotion of historical figures, such as Spartan princess Kyniska, who won the Olympic chariot race in 396 and 392 BC.[24] Kyniska had a bronze horse and statue group set up at Olympia with an inscription declaring her the first female to win the wreath in the chariot events at the Olympic Games (Thuk. 4.55; Xen. *Ages.* 9.6; Paus. 5.12; 6.1.6; *IG* V 1.1564a). Lysander, a celebrated Spartan general during the Peloponnesian War, had a statue group at Delphi commemorating his victories (Plut. *Lys.* 18.1; Paus.10.9.7–10) and he dedicated two eagles upon which were two victories on the Spartan acropolis (Paus. 3.17.4).[25]

With this in mind, let us return to the topic of hero cult. The heroization of a person is a differentiation of treatment of the individual after death that elevates them to an extreme degree. How might the ideals presented above affect the choice of heroization of the recently dead? Before proceeding, let us examine the funerary customs of Sparta.[26]

5.2 Burial and commemoration of the individual in Archaic and Classical Sparta

5.2.1 The war-dead

In her discussion of the honours for the Athenian war-dead, Loraux stresses that:

> between the funeral and the cult there is ... both a tight link and a gap, and there is no doubt that the Athens of the fifth and fourth centuries had nothing comparable to the beautiful, coherent ceremonial of the Hellenistic Epitaphia. So it is hardly surprising that the question of the status conferred on the dead by the official ceremony has been the object of endless dispute ... How are we to resist the temptation to confuse heroization and immortal glory?[27]

The above excerpt expresses the problem when scholars consider honours given to the war-dead. The topic has proven particularly elusive for two reasons: first, the relationship between literal versus metaphorical interpretations of texts with references to immortality, altars, precincts and offerings to the war-dead; and second, the possible early date of such customs when evidence of heroic honours for the war-dead is later, particularly Hellenistic. In the case of Sparta, Tyrtaeus and Simonides, writing for the dead of the second Messenian War and those of the Persian wars, respectively, are critical to this discussion because of the language they use to honour the war-dead in song. The language used in the poems prompted an interpretation of heroic honours for the war-dead.[28] Others argue that poets use metaphorical allusions, not literal ones, and deny that Sparta sacrificed to its war-dead.[29] The dispute over the interpretation of the honours given to the Spartan war-dead reminds us of Loraux's comments relating to the Athenian war-dead, in that it can be difficult to differentiate between heroic honours and immortal glory.

Evidence for the commemoration of the war-dead in the Archaic period comes to us primarily from Tyrtaeus, who recounts the honours given to a man who had died fighting in battle (fr.12 West 27–34):

αὐτὸς δ' ἐν προμάχοισι πεσὼν φίλον ὤλεσε θυμόν,
ἄστυ τε καὶ λαοὺς καὶ πατέρ' εὐκλεΐσας,
πολλὰ διὰ στέρνοιο καὶ ἀσπίδος ὀμφαλοέσσης

καὶ διὰ θώρηκος πρόσθεν ἐληλάμενος.
τὸν δ' ὀλοφύρονται μὲν ὁμῶς νέοι ἠδὲ γέροντες,
ἀργαλέωι δὲ πόθωι πᾶσα κέκηδε πόλις,
καὶ τύμβος καὶ παῖδες ἐν ἀνθρώποις ἀρίσημοι
καὶ παίδων παῖδες καὶ γένος ἐξοπίσω·
οὐδέ ποτε κλέος ἐσθλὸν ἀπόλλυται οὐδ' ὄνομ' αὐτοῦ,
ἀλλ' ὑπὸ γῆς περ ἐὼν γίνεται ἀθάνατος,
ὅντιν' ἀριστεύοντα μένοντά τε μαρνάμενόν τε
γῆς πέρι καὶ παίδων θοῦρος Ἄρης ὀλέσηι.

And if he falls among the front ranks, pierced many times through his breast and bossed shield and corselet from the front, he loses his own dear life but brings glory to his city, to his people and his father. Young and old alike mourn him, all the city is distressed by the painful loss, and his tomb and children are pointed out among the people, and his children's children and his line after them. Never does his name perish, but even though he is beneath the earth he is immortal, whoever it is that furious Ares slays as he displays his prowess by standing fast and fighting for land and children.

Trans. Gerber 1999

The fragment discusses the death of a Spartan during the second Messenian war and demonstrates the community's posthumous regard for the individual and his family. Tyrtaeus' description of those honours led Fuqua to interpret the words γίνεται ἀθάνατος (line 32) as evidence for Spartan heroization of the war-dead as early as the seventh century BC.[30] The problem with this interpretation is that it does not consider the traditional poetic language of praise. Tyrtaeus probably speaks of immortality only metaphorically.[31] Moreover, the stanzas (31–4) used as evidence for heroic honours for the Messenian War dead may not belong to the original seventh-century composition of Tyrtaeus but may have been added later in the fifth century.[32] Tyrtaeus' poem should probably be viewed as a celebration of *kleos*, which is acquired by death in war.[33]

With this in mind, we would expect Spartan burials from Archaic Sparta to reveal the honouring of the dead, probably with rich burial goods or weapons. From the archaeological evidence, however, we have nothing comparable to the richer burials of the Proto-Geometric and Geometric periods. One two-storey grave found at the Zaimis plot gives evidence of a grave ritual meal consisting of twenty vases and of a later attempt to preserve the burial. Other Archaic burials, such as those found at the Olive Oil cemetery are either pit, cist or tile graves; some have periboloi and contain either no gifts or modest gifts of pottery.[34]

Other examples come from sanctuary settings: two ivory fibulae, from the third quarter of the seventh century found at the sanctuary of Artemis Orthia, depicting *prothesis* scenes.[35] Being expensive, the dedications would have derived from wealthier families.[36] Some have interpreted a number of terracotta relief kraters, which commence *c.* 625 BC and are found primarily in sanctuaries in Sparta, as funerary monuments but there is no concrete evidence for this since they do not have a clear association with burials.[37]

The archaeological record, therefore, does not exhibit burials fit for heroic immortality as lauded in Tyrtaeus' fragment. The Spartan poet explains that the death of a warrior in battle would have been a communal event impacting the entire polis and his grave would be remembered in posterity. This remembrance will take place with no burial markers or elaborate burials with ostentatious display of offerings.[38] We may assume that the immortality would be achieved by the collective remembrance of the community, through oral histories.

Other evidence regarding the pre-fifth-century war-dead comes indirectly from festivals celebrating battles: for example, there was the festival of the Parparonia,[39] which celebrated the battle of Thyrea with Argos (*c.* 546 BC).[40] Although there is no evidence that the Parparonia festival dealt with the war-dead directly, the commemoration of the battle demonstrates a remembrance of those who died at the battle. According to Sosibios, at another festival, the Gymnopaidia, garlands were worn and choruses sang songs of Thaletas and Alkman and paeans of Dionysodotos in celebration of the Spartan victory over the Argives (Sosibios *FGrH* 595 fr.5=Athen. 15.678b–c).[41] Sosibios talks of a celebration of the victory and of paeans, presumably connected with Apollo, which would not be out of context with the god's military character in Laconia.[42] Because later sources refer to the festival as one in honour of those who *fell in the battle of Thyrea*,[43] the Gymnopaideia festival has been taken to imply hero cult for the war-dead.[44] Considering the late date of the evidence, I would suggest that the festival in its earliest form probably celebrated the battle with particular emphasis on Apollo and not the war-dead, who assumed prominence later on.

The aforementioned fragment of Tyrtaeus is the last reference to Spartan burial practices until Aristotle's *Lakedaimonian Constitution*, which claims that 'graves are modest and the same for all' (*Lak. Pol.* 611.13 Rose). Aristotle's comment and the virtual disappearance of rich burial gifts after the Geometric period brings to mind Plutarch's statements that the Spartan statesman Lykourgos abolished the pollutions associated with death and burial (*Lyc.* 27.2; *Mor.* 238b). He permitted the people to bury nothing with their dead, but only to enfold the body in a red robe and olive leaves and to treat all their dead alike. He also abolished inscriptions on memorials, except for the war-dead and the *hierai* 'priestesses' (see 5.2.2).

The archaeological evidence confirms such assertions with the discovery of a series of inscriptions inscribed ἐν πολέμωι. Approximately twenty-five *stelai* from the mid-fifth century BC through to the first century BC commemorate men who died in war. The *stelai* were made of local stone and were modest, plain memorials with only a plain inscription. The inscriptions record only the individual's name and that he died in war (the victory of Olympic winners was also added), omitting a patronymic or ethnic.[45] Because about half of the inscriptions were found in Sparta, it is likely that they refer to Spartan hoplites; the ten discovered in perioikic territories (e.g. *IG* v.1.1124: 'in war at Mantineia' found at *Geraki*) probably belong to perioikoi, an important component of the Lakedaimonian army.[46]

While the connection of the *stelai* with the war-dead is certain, the occasion of the inscriptions is inexact since none were found in situ. Because Spartans who fell in war were buried on the battlefield,[47] these *stelai* could be cenotaphs for the dead hoplite who was buried elsewhere, or represent the actual graves of hoplites who were wounded in war and died in Sparta.[48] In either case, the *stelai* remain the largest body of evidence for the posthumous commemoration of anyone in Sparta.[49] There were no ostentatious monuments, such as sphinxes, or *kouroi* to mark burials as in other areas, and when *stelai* appear, they are quite modest.[50]

5.2.2 Priests and priestesses

In the previously discussed passage in Plutarch (*Lyc.* 27.2; *Mor.* 238b), which considers the Spartan funerary customs implemented by Lycurgus, we learn that the legendary statesman eliminated inscribed memorials for all but for the war-dead and the *hierai*. A previous emendation to Plutarch's text (*Lyc.* 27.2) led to the translation of *hierai* as women who died in childbirth based on Hellenistic and later date inscriptions from Laconia.[51] The inscribed memorials of women who died in childbirth were thought to reveal that Spartan women were valued for childbirth, particularly for producing men whose duty would be to become warriors (Aristoph. *Lys.* 77–82; Xen. *Lak. Pol.* 1.3–4; Plut. *Lyc.* 14.1–4; 16.1–2);[52] a fact that would match the romanticized Spartan ethos of military value expressed in Plutarch (*Apoph. Lak.*).[53] Death in childbirth was viewed as a contribution to the state, a sentiment reflected in other poleis, such as Athens (Aristoph. *Lys.* 651).[54] However, the Laconian inscriptions used to emend

Plutarch's text are all Hellenistic or later and some come from perioikic poleis (*IG* V 1.713, 714, 1128, 1177).[55] Their late date and place of origin are an argument against the choice to emend Plutarch's text and would, therefore, make it more difficult to consider this emendation as evidence for Spartan burial customs of the Archaic and Classical periods. More recent studies reject the emendation and defend Plutarch's original text. This is supported by Richer's discussion of five epitaphs from Laconia describing women as *hierai* (ἱιαρά or ἱιερά; *IG* V 1.1221; 1283; 1127; 1129; *SEG* XXII 306).[56] This body of evidence is accompanied by a number of inscribed *stelai*,[57] many found in Laconia and Messenia. *IG* V.1. 1214, 1356, 1329, 1337-8, 1367 presumably refer to epitaphs of male religious personnel.[58] *IG* V 1.1337-8 (from Gerenia, Messenia) date from the fifth century and while *IG* V 1.1337 includes only a name, *IG* V1.1338 mentions the term *ἱιαρός*, which possibly belonged to a tomb of someone of the same status as *hierai* 'holy ones' or priests.[59] Another example, *IG* V 1.1329 (from Leuktra, Laconia), of the fifth or sixth century BC mentions an ἱιαρεύς and preserves the fragmentary name of a man.[60] Similarly, *IG* V 1.711 (from Sparta), an allegedly second-century AD copy of an earlier epitaph, bears the title ἱιαρεύς.[61] Recent suggestions compare the text in Plutarch (*Lyc.* 27.2) *hierai* with the male equivalent *hieros* and read it as 'holy ones' signifying their special merit or priestess status.[62]

The term also appears as a category of dead whom the Spartans buried after the Battle of Plataia (Hdt. 9.85). Here, the term (*h*)*irees* in Herodotus has been taken to mean either 'those who fought heroically', priests or (*e*)*irenes*, an age group that appears in Hellenistic Sparta.[63] Recently, Christesen offered a more radical solution by athetizing the text and giving a reading of 'priests'.[64] If his view is accepted, then Plutarch's text (*Lyc.* 27.2) concerning women finds further support that it refers to priestesses. The texts, together with the inscriptions of *hiereus* or *hiera* from Sparta, Laconia and Messenia, probably attest that religious personnel likely enjoyed a somewhat different treatment after death.

Given the rich attestations for priests in the Roman period, it is likely that important cults of Apollo, Orthia, Athena Chalkioikos and the Dioskouroi had their own priests in the Archaic and Classical periods.[65] The kings themselves were priests (see 5.3.1) and the ephors also had religious responsibilities.[66] There is also evidence for *manteis*, hereditary positions of heralds, the Talthybiadai, descended from Agamemnon's herald Talthybios (Hdt. 7.134.1), and the hereditary caste of the *mageiroi*, who were present at both public sacrifices and those offered by the king on campaign (Hdt. 6.60).[67] Moreover, Pausanias (3.12.8), when visiting Sparta, saw the tombs of the Iamidai seers from Elis towards the end of the Aphetaid road. Indeed, Sparta was known for its piety and religiosity, with sources frequently mentioning its delays in going to battle because of festivals or the Spartan tendency to attribute misfortune to the divine (Hdt. 5.63; 6.106, 120; 7.206, 220; 9.33–5; Thuk. 5.54.2; 7.18.2).[68] The religious mentality of Sparta can, therefore, be offered as an explanation for the posthumous commemoration of priests and priestesses.

5.3 Heroization of the recently dead

5.3.1 The Spartan kings

In a passage from Xenophon's *Constitution of the Lakedaimonians*, the author controversially states that the kings' funeral rites revealed that they were honoured 'not as men but as heroes' (15.9, οὐχ ὡς ἀνθρώπους ἀλλ' ὡς ἥρωας τοὺς Λακεδαιμονίων βασιλεῖς προτετιμήκασι).[69] This text has been the subject of debate: is it literal or metaphorical? Cartledge and Nafissi read it literally and cite it as proof of the heroization of the Spartan kings.[70] Parker interprets it metaphorically and argues that Spartan kings simply enjoyed great funeral rites, but not heroization with continuous cult,[71] while Lipka likes to see only exceptional kings, such as Leonidas, heroized.[72] In the following section, I examine the religious position of the kings in Sparta and argue that it is unfruitful to create a specific ontological category for the Spartan kings by denying or affirming their heroic status.

Undeniably, the Spartan kings enjoyed significant privileges – social, military and religious (Hdt. 6.56–7).[73] From Tyrtaeus we learn that the kings were divinely honoured, θεοτιμήτους βασιλῆας (fr.4 West). They also held priesthoods of Zeus Ouranios and Zeus Lakedaimon, and they could sacrifice as many sheep and goats as they wished at the start of expeditions (Hdt. 6.56). The kings also held the oracular Delphic responses and could use them when needed (Hdt. 6.56)[74] and had messengers (called Pythians) whom they chose and with whom they ate at public expense (Hdt. 6.57; Xen. *Lak. Pol.* 15.5).[75] Aristotle claims that the kings were hereditary military commanders who also had been assigned the matters relating to the gods (*Pol.* 3.1285a3–10). Lastly, Xenophon says that Lykourgos granted to the king rights to all the public sacrifices on behalf of the city, since he was descended from a god, and to lead an army whenever the city sends him (Xen. *Lak. Pol.*15.2; 13.11).

The religious position of the Spartan kings is indeed pronounced as kings are thought to have divine descent.[76] In a poem written by the fifth-century Ion of

Chios (fr.27 West) for a Spartan symposium, the poet calls for libations to be poured to the kings' ancestors, who include Herakles, Alkmene and Prokles, after a first offering to Zeus.[77] During the Peloponnesian War, the Pythia told the Spartans to restore the exiled King Pleistoanax by calling him 'the semi-divine son of Zeus' (Thuk. 5.16.2).[78] When Pleistoanax was restored to the throne the Spartans, they received him with dances and sacrifices as those that occurred when the kings were first enthroned at the foundation of Lakedaimon (Thuk. 5.16.2). Xenophon brings forth three examples where the divine descent of the Spartan kings is noted (*Kyr.* 4.1.24; 7.2.24; *Lak. Pol.* 15.2). The kings' divine descent was also used when needed by the kings themselves, such as in Isokrates' *Archidamos* (366 BC),[79] where Archidamos III states that he is descended from Herakles, asserting the apparent belief that Spartan kings were of that line (8ff.). As Malkin emphasises, the Herakleidai were regarded not only as having brought the Spartans to their land but also were thought to rule Sparta.[80]

From Pausanias we hear about the sacred topography related to the kings in Sparta since they have their assigned burial places. At the end of the Aphetaid road at the southern part of the city are buried the Eurypontidai (3.12.8),[81] while the burial grounds of the Agidai were located in the north-western part of the city in an area called Theomelida (3.14.2); we even learn about a temple of Asklepios near the Theomelida called the ἐν Ἀγιαδῶν (Paus. 3.14.2).

The divine descent and the sacred space in Sparta demonstrate the closeness of the king to the divine even while alive (without supposing a cult of the living).[82] As Greek custom saw heroes as dead and did not normally heroize the living during the Archaic and Classical periods, the burial of the king would be a prerequisite for heroic treatment.

Of course, with royal funerals, the Spartans displayed none of the modesty of their burial rites. As Herodotus attests, the burial was a grand event (6.58):

The kings are granted these rights from the Spartan commonwealth while they live; when they die, their rights are as follows: horsemen proclaim their death in all parts of Laconia, and in the city women go about beating on cauldrons. When this happens, two free persons from each house, a man and a woman, are required to wear mourning, or incur heavy penalties if they fail to do so. The Lakedaimonians have the same custom at the deaths of their kings as the foreigners in Asia; most foreigners use the same custom at their kings' deaths. When a king of the Lakedaimonians dies, a fixed number of their subject neighbours must come to the funeral from all of Lakedaimon, besides the Spartans. When these and the helots and the Spartans themselves have assembled in one place to the number of many thousands, together with the women, they zealously beat their foreheads and make long and loud lamentation, calling that king that is most recently dead the best of all their kings. Whenever a king dies in war, they make an image of him and carry it out on a well-spread bier. For ten days after the burial there are no assemblies or elections, and they mourn during these days.

Trans. Godley 1920

From this passage we learn that the special treatment of the dead kings was a pan-Laconian consideration, not just a Spartan one, as perioikoi and helots – two from each household – also had to attend. It was so ostentatious that Herodotus compares it to the burials of the barbarian kings.[83] The pan-Laconian mourning of the death of a king can also be alluded in the oracle from Herodotus before the Battle of Thermopylai (Hdt. 7.220.4) when the Λακεδαίμονος οὖρος (the boundary of Lakedaimon) must mourn the dead king in order that Persia does not destroy Sparta.[84]

Other sources (Xen. *Hell.* 3.3.19; 5.3.19; 6.4.13; Diod. 15.93.6; Plut. *Ages.* 40; Paus. 9.13.10) attest that among the kings' privileges was the transfer of the body of the king who died abroad (preserved in honey or wax) back to Sparta – which also protected it from falling into enemy hands.[85] By contrast, Spartan men who died abroad in battle were buried on the battlefield.[86] For Leonidas, whose body was mutilated and head impaled after the Battle of Thermopylai in 480 BC, an effigy took his place until his body was transferred to Sparta, some forty years later (see 5.3.2). The necessity for the bodies of kings to be returned to Sparta is important because it shows how these became relics, which, as with other bone transferrals (Orestes), required transport to Sparta.[87] The funeral then becomes a public rite and supports belief in the divine descent of the kings from the Herakleidai and Herakles (and subsequently from Zeus).[88] Further, it also reinforces support for the Spartan state because the Herakleidai were founders of the community. In a way, the rites for Spartan kings are comparable to those for *oikistai*, who enjoyed public burial (Pind. *P.* 5.99–100; Thuk. 5.11.1).[89] The Spartan kings indeed received special honours both during their lifetime and during their funeral.

Let us now examine more closely the views that Spartan kings were not heroized. The first argument concerns Xenophon's *Lak. Pol.* 15.9 δηλοῦν οἱ Λυκούργου νόμοι ὅτι οὐχ ὡς ἀνθρώπους ἀλλ' ὡς ἥρωας τοὺς Λακεδαιμονίων βασιλεῖς προτετιμήκασι, which is taken by Lipka to mean that Spartan kings were honoured not *as* heroes but *like* heroes.[90] Lipka bases his argument on the use of ὡς in Hellenistic inscriptions, which I do not think should be applied in the current text. Lipka concludes that Thucydides' use of the same expression (ὡς ἥρωι ἐντεμνουσι, Thuk. 5.11.1) for the honours for Brasidas do not indicate heroic honours and instead interprets the sacrifices and honours for Brasidas to be *like* those given to a hero and *oikist*. First, unlike the evidence regarding the Spartan kings, Brasidas was clearly heroized because other authors attest to sacrifices in his honour (Aristot. *eth. Nic.* 1134b).[91] Second, Ekroth demonstrates that, based on contemporary literary sources, the expression ὡς ἥρωας indicates the religious status of the recipient, who should be considered a hero.[92] She also illustrates that ὡς ἥρωας is often used to clarify the status of the recipient.[93] The use of ὡς ἥρωας as a description of the burial of the Spartan king is suitable because it is during/after burial that heroization would have taken place.[94]

The second argument against the heroization of the Spartan kings is based on the fact that Xenophon does not refer to cultic honours post-burial.[95] Evidence concerning the kings' treatment after burial is indeed limited since neither Xenophon nor Herodotus mention anything. Our only knowledge comes from Pausanias who, during his visit to Sparta, viewed the designated burial areas, one for each of the royal houses, of the Agidai and the Eurypontidai. From Pausanias' description we can assume that the land was demarked yet it remains unknown what forms the burials had and how or if they differed from those of other Spartans. Did they host any monumental tombs? Were there inscriptions identifying specific kings? Not a single shred of evidence is linked with a Spartan royal tomb, nor have the burial grounds been identified. What is important to highlight here is that *unlike* heroes, Spartan kings were not buried in central areas, such as the agora, near central cult places, or roads.

The crucial question here is whether the Spartans *believed* that the kings could exercise a form of influence over the lives of the living after they died. This in itself would indicate that the kings were considerate heroes on an ontological level and that they could influence the lives of the living – for which we have no evidence of any sort. The kings did not have unlimited powers while alive and could be removed from office.[96]

I propose that the post-mortem treatment of the Spartan kings should be viewed within the blurred parameters of the heroization and commemoration of the dead as expressed by ritual behaviour. On one end of the spectrum of ritual expression we may place heroes, such as Helen and Menelaus, whose status was close to the divine. On the other end, we may position ordinary mortals who receive burial rites at their grave. In between these two there is a large area that contains a variety of individuals who were given rituals. The boundaries of these rituals were not strict – they could move from grave ritual to ancestor cult to hero cult, as we saw with examples in Chapter 1. Nor was the status of the individuals fixed, such as Herakles, who could receive both divine and heroic cults. The boundaries are even more blurred for the historical personalities whose cult at the grave and heroization can be indistinct. Lycurgus was given a temple and sacrifices; Chilon was a mortal statesman who was heroized (see 5.3.3). The brief survey of grave cults, ancestor cults and hero cults in Chapter 1 shows that the boundaries are fluid and so are the rituals; not all post-mortal honours would fit nicely and easily in these categories.[97]

Let us look at Xenophon's (*Lak. Pol.* 15.9) passage again, which is taken as evidence for royal honours; it has not been interpreted within the context of Spartan (and Greek) hero cult. Since the passage concerns the funerals of Spartan kings, the honours mentioned are first honours for the recently dead. Xenophon then juxtaposes the honours offered to dead kings with those offered to heroes and suggests that both parties, as dead mortals, were honoured in similar ways. Xenophon's comment is of particular importance because it is reflective of the corporeal nature of heroes. Indeed, the honours for the Spartan kings belong first of all within the spectrum of post-mortem rituals.

Denying or confirming the heroization of the Spartan kings with the limited available evidence is thus unfruitful. They were clearly given distinct post-mortem treatment once they had died. Their funerals constituted an elaborate and public event that included Spartans and all Lakedaimonians. The kings and their funerals were thus of central importance to a large community that united in a ritual context. As kings of Sparta and Lakedaimon, they are of symbolic value to the people and just like heroes they belong to the civic institution of the polis (and Lakedaimon) that bonds the population. Nevertheless, they were not given burials within the civic space of the polis as heroes were but had their own designated grounds. It is highly doubtful that the Spartans believed that kings could *influence* the living after their death. We may conclude that in the view of Herodotus the Spartan kings were honoured with the same post-mortem rituals that heroes receive; the ontological level and religious belief, however, remains elusive.

5.3.2 Leonidas and the Thermopylai War dead

Unlike the heroization the Spartan kings, solid evidence that the Spartan King Leonidas was heroized exists from Roman Sparta. Pausanias, visiting Sparta, saw near the acropolis an area commemorating the Battle of Thermopylai: there was the tomb of Leonidas (next to that of Pausanias, general at the Battle of Plataia) where 'every year they deliver speeches over them, and hold a contest in which none may compete except Spartans' and a stele inscribed with the names of those who died at Thermopylai (3.14.1). Roman date inscriptions from Sparta confirm Pausanias' narrative: *IG* V.1.19 dates from the reign of Trajan and mentions the festival, while *IG* V.1.659 dates from sometime before Nerva, cites the Leonidea and adds that it included the athletic events of the *pankration* and wrestling.[98] The above offer confirmation for a Roman-period festival that honours Leonidas at the site of his grave that would have become the locus of cult and also those who died at Thermopylai; its existence in the preceding centuries remains uncertain. Herodotus (7.224.1) remarks that he learned the names of all 300 who fought at Thermopylai, perhaps because there was already a stele with their names. A stele naming the men in the Classical period, such as that seen by Pausanias, is argued to be unlike Spartan custom, and thus it is likely that Herodotus encountered the names from oral traditions attesting to the bravery of the men.[99] The list of the 300 that Pausanias mentions may be an outcome of Hellenistic or Roman-period antiquarianism.[100] Still, the battle was exceptional, and as we have seen above, there are occasions in Classical Sparta where personal excellence (e.g. athletic or military victories) was praised. The setting of names need not denote cult but commemoration. The festival may have only occurred in the late fourth century or the Hellenistic period, as was the honouring of the dead at Marathon[101] and Plataia.[102]

Honours given to Leonidas and the Thermopylai dead followed the immediate aftermath of the battle. The bravery of the Spartans was noted on the epigram composed by Simonides and placed at the site of Thermopylai where the Spartans buried their dead: 'Foreigner, go tell the Spartans that we lie here obedient to their commands'; two other epigrams were composed, one for the rest of the Greeks and another one for the seer Megeistias who was a guest-friend of Simonides (Hdt. 7.228).[103] There is nothing remarkable about the treatment of the Spartan dead who are buried at the battlefield.[104] A stone lion in honour of Leonidas was set up on the hill at the mouth of the pass at Thermopylai where the Spartans fought the Persians after being encircled (Hdt. 7.225.2). This monument may have been commissioned by the Amphiktyons since, as Herodotus (7.228.4) explains, it is they who honour the Thermopylai dead with the erection of the inscriptions and pillars. The above was not a commemoration set up by Sparta nor did it take place in Sparta itself, but rather at Thermopylai with a more Panhellenic audience in mind.

A brief comparison with the Plataia war-dead would give a greater perspective: Thucydides (3.58.4) recounts that, while pleading with the Spartans not to destroy their city, the Plataians emphasize the existence of the graves of the Spartans who died during the Persian Wars there, where they honour them every year with offerings. Because of the annual honours mentioned, the text has been interpreted to refer to local hero cult of the war-dead at Plataia.[105] It is debated whether the annual offerings allude to heroization or just honouring of the war-dead.[106] In any case, the text mentions nothing about the Spartans granting honours to their war-dead; in fact, the Spartans seem to care little about the Plataian custom and proceeded with the destruction of Plataia (Thuk. 2.75–8). There is no evidence that Sparta offered any special treatment to the Persian War dead in the immediate aftermath of the battle; the war-dead of Thermopylai and Plataia were honoured respectively by the Amphiktyons and the Plataians.

Other evidence on the commemoration of the Battle of Thermopylai yet comes from a fragment of Simonides 531 Page, *PMG*=Diod. 11.11.6:

τῶν ἐν Θερμοπύλαις θανόντων
εὐκλεὴς μὲν ἁ τύχα, καλὸς δ' ὁ πότμος,
βωμὸς δ' ὁ τάφος, πρὸ γόων δὲ μνᾶστις,ὁ δ' οἶκτος ἔπαινος
ἐντάφιον δὲ τοιοῦτον οὔτ'εὐρώς
οὔθ' ὁ πανδαμάτωρ ἀμαυρώσει χρόνος.
ἀνδρῶν ἀγαθῶν ὅδε σηκὸς οἰκέταν εὐδοξίαν
Ἑλλάδος εἵλετο μαρτυρεῖ δὲ καὶ Λεωνίδας,
Σπάρτας βασιλεύς, ἀρετᾶς μέγαν λελοιπὼς
κόσμον ἀέναόν τε κλέος.

Of those who died at Thermopylai
renown is the fortune, noble the fate:
Their grave's an altar, their memorial our mourning,
their fate our praise.
Such a shroud neither decay
nor all-conquering time shall destroy.
This sepulchre of great men has taken the high
renown for Hellas for its fellow occupant, as witness
Leonidas, Sparta's king who left behind a great
memorial of valour, everlasting renown.

Trans. Green 2006

The above fragment has caused a great deal of discussion regarding the occasion and the meaning of its composition. For Bowra, it was a song sung as part of cult enacted on behalf of the fallen warriors.[107] Indeed, the language used by the poet reminds us of that used for hero cult, particularly expressions such as ἀνδρῶν ἀγαθῶν alluding to the cult of the war-dead[108] and βωμός δ'ὁ τάφος.[109] Such expressions, however, need not be taken literally because, as with Tyrtaeus, Simonides' poetry derives from a long tradition traced back to

Homer (and the Homeric elements in Simonides have been noted)[110] in which the metaphorical use of words to praise and elevate someone's status is common. For example, one can cite the undying renown (*kleos*) that a person having died in war achieves (metaphorical immortality) through song (Pind. *P.* 3.115; *P.* 11.55–61; Isokr. *Panath.* 260).[111] The poet probably implies that their achievements will be forever immortalized, not that they themselves are immortal heroes.

Other interpretations are offered for the composition of this poem. Some scholars suggest that the fragment was written not as a celebration of the war-dead of Thermopylai but rather as a commemoration of Leonidas, whose name is withheld until the end.[112] Podlecki proposes that the song was commissioned by Sparta to be sung at private occasions, such as the messes (which in fact are public occasions).[113] However, there is no concrete evidence for this suggestion, and in particular that it was sung *only* for the Spartan war-dead; instead, the language of the poem points to it being in honour for *those who fell at Thermopylai* – especially if it had been commissioned by the Amphiktyons who authorized the three epigrams at the site of Thermopylai (Hdt. 7.228).[114] Another suggestion considers that the song is meant not only as a way for memorializing the dead but also to inspire and praise the living.[115]

The perplexity over the honours for the dead of the Persian Wars can be explained through the similarities of rituals for fallen heroes and the ordinary dead. Currie argues for the heroization of the Persian War dead and other individuals by claiming that all those who receive public burials and praise are thus given heroic honours; this, however, is to confuse two distinct types of honour: cultic honours for the heroic dead and those honours bestowed upon the un-heroized individual after his death, sometimes in public areas.[116] Rather, it is possible that the treatment of extraordinary dead individuals resembled that of heroes because this was the way the Greeks customarily treated the special dead; this may explain the annual offerings described by the Plataians in Simonides and Thucydides. As Parker states:

> What could be readily done, of course, was to pay the war-dead honours indistinguishable from those of heroes, since no sharp divide separated funerary from heroic cult. They might then grow fully into the heroic mould; and later ages at a greater cultural remove duly applied the term 'hero' to the dead of the Persian Wars.[117]

Here, we see gradual heroization of the war-dead initially treated with great honours because of the way they died. In this context were composed the works of Simonides.

Even if the festival 'Leonidea' may be a Hellenistic or Roman construct, I see no reason to dismiss a heroic cult for Leonidas himself. The Spartan kings, as discussed, were considered to be descendants of Herakles and were thought of as close to divine. Burial of Spartan kings was an exceptional pan-Lakedaimonian occasion and those kings who died abroad had their bodies returned home. Leonidas was not only a king who died in battle abroad; his death was a nessesity: before the battle, a consultation at Delphi declared that Lakedaimon would be saved with the death of a king (Hdt. 7.220.3-4). Leonidas' body was not transferred to Sparta until after the Persian Wars, which by then, had ended with a Greek victory. The victory thus would have validated the claim of the oracle and made Leonidas' death all the more important to the eyes of the Spartans since with his death he *saved* and protected Sparta.

Heroes are often associated with aiding in battle, even appearing in epiphanies to fight in battles themselves, and offering protection to their respective cities.[118] Leonidas' fight at Thermopylai can be paralleled with those mythical local heroes who fought to aid their own poleis. But instead of assisting the protection of the city posthumously, he fought while alive and his death granted the safety of Lakedaimon. The sacredness of his death is further supported by the involvement and 'backing' of the Delphic oracle. Because of his position as a Spartan king and his achievement in battle, Leonidas was a perfect candidate for heroization. If the cult of Leonidas is to be dated in the Classical period, then it may have been instituted after the transfer of his bones to Sparta.[119] By then, the legend of the battle and the subsequent Greek victory over the Persians had been glorified in the perceptions of the Greeks. We can imagine that the arrival of the bones of Leonidas in Sparta would have resembled the description of the coming of the bones of Theseus in Athens: with processions and sacrifices in celebration of the return of the local king (Plut. *Thes.* 36.2; *Cim.* 8.6).

Leonidas was not buried in the designated burial grounds of the Agiad kings at Pitane – his bones were placed by the acropolis, opposite the later Hellenistic theatre. The location of Leonidas' burial (and that of Pausanias) is noteworthy: the Spartan acropolis is where central cults were housed and an area for athletic commemorations, such as the Damonon stele (*IG* V 1.213). By placing the tomb of Leonidas (and Pausanias) beneath the temple of Athena Poliachos, the protectress of the city, the grave attests to his communal importance for Sparta and Lakedaimon; after all he was buried within an area of state religion. The burial, moreover, was situated at a public space in accordance with the tradition of burial of heroes, such as *oikistai*, but also others, such as Orestes, whose burial was located in the Spartan Agora (Hdt. 1.67-8).

Leonidas and his heroic sacrifice must have lived in the communicative memory of the people. It would not be hard to see how his legendary sacrifice became assimilated to the local heroes of Sparta who protected the city.

5.3.3 Chilon

Many sources attest to the wisdom of the sixth century Spartan ephor Chilon (Hdt. 1.59, 7.235; Plat. *Prot.* 343 A; Paus. 10.24; Diog. Laert. 1.68-73).[120] He was a politician, credited with the institution of the ephorship (Diog. Laert. 1.68).[121] He is thought to be behind Sparta's foreign policy in the deposition of tyrants (*FGrH* 105 F 1) and Sparta's hegemonial success in the Peloponnese during the sixth century.[122] Chilon's reputation in antiquity saw him as one of the Seven Sages (Plat. *Prot.* 343 A; Diog. Laert. 1.68–72) and many aphorisms were attributed to him, including Delphic maxims (Diog. Laert. 1.73; Arist. *Rhet.*1389b1-12; Schol. Eur. *Hipp.* 264–6).

It is thus not surprising that Pausanias (3.16.4) saw the heroon of Chilon in Sparta during his tour of the city in the second century AD. Unlike other heroa of historical and mythical individuals that Pausanias mentions, Chilon's heroization is confirmed by the Archaic hero relief, inscribed [X]IΛON in retrograde (*IG* V 1.244) (Figure 2.4).[123] Interpreted as a votive or grave relief, its existence offers probable evidence that Chilon was heroized after his death.[124] The heroon of Chilon was possibly located on the southern slopes of the Toumpanon hill since the aforementioned heroic stone relief was found reused as a cover of a Christian grave.[125]

The relief itself is exceptional because it carries an Archaic inscription with the name of Chilon, unprecedented on other Archaic hero reliefs in Laconia. The inscription is a single name in the nominative. A number of dedications from Archaic Sparta, especially from the Orthia sanctuary but also from elsewhere, carry single names in the nominative that refer not to the deity but to the dedicant.[126] If the dedication were *to* Chilon, then the inscription perhaps would be expected to be in the dative case as is the usual for the recipient of cult[127] and as we see in dedications to Athena, Apollo and the Dioskouroi (*IG* V 1.919; *SEG* XI 652).[128] Nonetheless, the use of the dative for the name of the recipient of the cult is not absolute and it is grammatically possible that the name of the cult recipient is in the nominative; Chilon can certainly be the recipient of cult.[129]

The heroization of the Spartan statesman Chilon would benefit from a brief comparison with the most famous Spartan lawgiver, the quasi-historical

Lykourgos,[130] who had a temple and received sacrifices in Sparta. Herodotus says that when Lykourgos visited Delphi the priestess said:

> You have come to my rich temple, Lykourgos, a man dear to Zeus and to all who have Olympian homes. I am in doubt whether to pronounce you man or god. But I think rather you are a god, Lykourgos .... Thus they [the Spartans] changed their bad laws to good ones, and when Lycurgus died they built him a temple and now worship him greatly.
>
> Hdt. 1.65.3-66.1; Trans. Godley 1920

Lykourgos thus was worshiped in Classical Sparta where he had a temple. The same reference to a temple is found in Ephorus (*FGrH* 70 F 118=Strabo 8.5.5), who also adds annual sacrifices, while Aristotle (fr.534, Rose=Plutarch *Lyc*. 31) is quoted to have said that Lykourgos had a shrine and that they sacrifice to him as a god.[131]

In the collective memory of Sparta, Lykourgos was credited for reforming the laws and bringing *eunomia* to Sparta (Hdt. 1.65.2; Aristot. *Ath. pol.*1313a 26f; Plut. *Lyc*. 8.3). The Delphic oracle (Hdt. 1.65) validated his cult, as it did Sparta's laws.[132] Lykourgos was a statesman who contributed to the laws and civic institutions (either historically or legendarily) that subsequently formed part of the distinct Spartan social structure.[133] His status can be paralleled to those of the *oikistai*, hero-founders whose achievements mattered to the community. Lykourgos and his so-called 'Lykourgian institutions' were so famous in antiquity that they came to embody Sparta itself and its unique lifestyle. As a 'symbol of the past' Lykourgos became part of the Sparta's local identity.

Chilon's status in Sparta should consequently be viewed as that of a communal individual who also received heroization immediately or soon after his death; perhaps in the same manner as the dead from the Geometric burial in Limnai (Chapter 2, n. 8). The heroon of Chilon was an important communal and civic intuition that was seen some 700 to 800 hundred years later by Pausanias (3.16.4). As a personality, he became part of the collective memory of Sparta whose achievements were celebrated by future generations. Chilon and Lycurgus' cults show that Spartan cultural norms allowed for the cult of exceptional personalities.

5.3.3 Other distinguished Spartans

Apart from Leonidas, the only testimony to the heroization of other Thermopylai dead is Pausanias' later record of the existence of shrines of Maron and Alpheios, who fought with exceptional bravery (3.12.8; cf. Hdt. 7.223). A late source, Aelian (*V. H.* 6.6), states that 'those fighting nobly and dying are crowned/bound with olive and other branches and carried (off) with praises; those who were supremely brave were wrapped in their *phoinikis* and buried with special honours' (trans. Hodkinson 2000, 245), suggesting that the Spartans would identify and give special burial to those who distinguished themselves.[134]

When might their shrines have been placed in Sparta and by whom? Did the descendants decide on a shrine to honour the two men? Were the bodies of Maron and Alpheios collected from the battlefield in an unlikely Spartan custom to be buried in Sparta? Was this an outcome of a state decision soon after the battle or was the set-up of the shrine an outcome of cultural memory in the centuries to come? If this was a family affair then the shrines would have had a familiar importance for the descendants in the way that Tyrtaeus (Fr. 12 West) described the tomb as a site of remembrance for the dead and their family. In a similar fashion, Pausanias saw the tomb of Eurybiades, the commander of the Lakedaimonian ships at Artemision and Salamis, opposite the tomb of the statesman Lycurgus and by the tomb of the legendary Spartan King Theopompus (Paus. 3.16.6). After the Battle of Salamis, Eurybiades was rewarded with an olive wreath by the Spartan state, so his shrine was likely a state decision to honour his exceptional military qualities (Hdt. 8.124). His tomb was placed near that of other exceptional individuals, Lycurgus and King Theopompus, who mattered to the state. Of course, these hero shrines may not have been associated with a cult at the entombment of the dead. Perhaps the graves may have gradually become the locus of cult as the cultural memory of the Persian Wars and especially Thermopylai came to embody the Spartan military ethos.[135] Their commencement date is uncertain and it may indeed be Hellenistic or Roman as with the many other cults of the historic dead in Sparta attested by Pausanias.[136]

Indeed, Pausanias' description of Roman Sparta makes clear the large number of hero shrines of historical figures in Sparta. The problem is to what extent the shrines dedicated to the recently dead, such as Dorieus (*c*. 510 BC) or Kyniska, were instituted immediately after death (Paus. 6.1.6).[137] In some instances, such as the seventh-century athlete Hipposthenes, who was given honours like those for Poseidon (Paus. 3.15.7; 5.8.9), it is proposed that the cult was instituted in the fifth century BC.[138] Another seventh-century athlete, Chionis, was honoured at Olympia with a statue made by Myron (470–440 BC)[139] and a stele recording his victories, commissioned by Sparta (Paus. 6.13.2), although a statue does not denote heroization.[140] The aforementioned examples are only known from Pausanias, so with our current knowledge, uncertainty projects over the institution of the cults of many of the shrines and tombs of the historic dead. Yet, as evidenced by the heroization of Chilon and the divinization of Lycurgus, it seems that cult to historical personalities was within the parameters of Sparta's religious tradition. Thus, it would not be unreasonable if other exceptional individuals, such as Kyniska (and Sparta had a long tradition of female heroines) were heroized after their death.

5.4 Conclusion

The heroization of the recently deceased here follows the picture of a hero as a symbol of a polis and further complements hero cult and its localized nature. The individuals who received heroic cult in Sparta in the Archaic and Classical periods fall into this category since their achievements were extraordinary and belonged to Sparta as a whole. Although it is uncertain that the Spartan kings were heroized, their communal importance and collective position are apparent both when alive and during their burials. Statesmen and exceptional war-dead who contributed to Sparta and its fame in the Greek world were also deemed worthy of bestowment of the highest post-mortem treatment in their heroization.

In Xenophon's (*Lak. Pol.* 15.9) famous passage on the burial of Spartan kings, where the author emphasises that they are honoured not as humans but as heroes, we see a clear connection between grave and heroic ritual. The realization that heroes were understood to be dead mortals and honoured as such helps explain how grave ritual overspills into heroic ritual and results in the heroization of not only the Spartan kings, but also the ephor Chilon and other Spartan heroes unknown to the modern audience. The overlap between mortuary and cultic practice in Sparta will be explored further in the next chapter, focused on the archaeological evidence of burials and heroic cults.

Sparta's fluid boundaries between mortals, heroes and gods manifested in a multifarious cultic landscape: Helen and Menelaus were worshiped in the same manner as divinities, Hyakinthos received apotheosis, Lykourgos was divinized, and Chilon's heroization came after death. Sparta's cultural norms thus allowed for the permeability of ritual boundaries and thus the heroization of an array of exceptional individuals from lawgivers to kings, exceptional war-dead and even perhaps the first woman to win the Olympic Games.

6

Burials and Hero Cult: Three Case Studies

Because the post-Homeric hero is generally considered to be a deceased mortal who exercises a certain amount of influence over the living and is deemed worthy of veneration, his cult was often (but not exclusively) concentrated around a tomb, thus contributing to his localized nature. This is such an important component of heroic nature that even heroes who achieved immortality had a burial: Helen and Menelaus were allegedly buried in Therapne (Paus. 3.19.9), Hyakinthos had a tomb at the base of the statue of Apollo (Paus. 3.19.2) and Kastor had a temple in Sparta over his grave (Paus. 3.13.1). It is therefore not surprising that some of the sites and deposits associated with hero cults in Sparta are found by, near or incorporate burials. The relationship between hero cult and burials is a complex topic. A cult surrounding a grave could be instigated right after a burial or it may develop later upon the rediscovery of an older burial. Heroic bone transfers, such as that of Orestes (Hdt. 1.68), demonstrate how heroic bones feature as relics and can empower the possessing city.[1] In the Hellenistic period, extravagant tombs belonged to those recently deceased who were heroized. The existence of graves and bones shows that heroes lived not only in the imagination of the population with the quality of a dead person from the distant past. It illustrates how tangible and real the heroes were and how the physical remains could evoke feelings of reverence. Here, I present three case studies from the Survey of Sites in Chapter 2 where burials become the focus of ritual and building activities. For each, I give a discussion that contextualises the archaeological evidence in its contemporary context. Material evidence from the area of Limnai offers further support that the mortuary and the sacred world in Sparta overlapped.

The heroization of the dead in the Greek world exhibits a variability of contexts from cults at the grave of *oikistai* or ancestors to tomb cults at Bronze Age tombs dedicated to those long-dead (Chapter 1). Although Sparta did not have a tradition of veneration over Bronze Age tombs, a number of cults are situated near earlier Proto-Geometric or Geometric graves. In Chapter 2 it is noted that apart from the burial on Stauffert Street (no. 8), other cults are also located in relation to burials. A Geometric *pithos* burial was unearthed at the Heroon by the Eurotas (no. 3),[2] a Geometric burial with a cairn of stones was discovered at the Drainage Ditch (no. 2),[3] and at the Lykourgos and Karellas plot (no. 9) were found five Geometric burials, one of which was Proto-Geometric.[4] Near the Kalatazis plot (no. 18) was also unearthed a Geometric burial.[5] Various excavations report of Archaic burials, such as that by the Ergatikes Katoikies (no. 5)[6] and the late-Hellenistic burial incorporated in the long building at the Stavropoulos plot (no. 6), discussed in section 2.2. The relationship, if any, of the burials to the heroic cults that formed later is not always clear. At Stauffert Street (no. 8), Ergatikes Katoikies (no. 5) and the Stavropoulos plot (no. 6), the graves appear to have been known by the community that erected the structures that included the burials architecturally in later buildings. In another example, from Sklavochori, Amyklai (no. 29), a number of terracotta reliefs and figurines were discovered over a Proto-Geometric burial. Other times, it is unclear whether the burials were chance findings unknown to the local community or if the existence of earlier burials influenced the setting of later cults.

The close spatial proximity of hero shrines and burials may echo Plutarch's comment on Sparta's burial practices that Lykourgos permitted the burial of the dead within the city and the location of the tombs near the shrines (*Lyc.* 27.1).[7] Due to its late date, Plutarch's testimony could only questionably be applied to the Archaic and Classical periods, but the archaeological association of the burials and the deposits confirms that the spatial boundaries of the sacred and the mortuary appear to cross here.[8]

The cults that either incorporate a burial or have a burial near the site are mostly located in the *kome* of Limnai. The tradition of the area as a 'host' to heroic cults is apparent since it not only produced hero cults, dating from the early Archaic period, but also shows continuity of cults, such as that of the Heroon by the Eurotas (no. 2) and the cult on Stauffert Street (no. 8); Limnai already held an important position in the religious life of Sparta with the sanctuary of (Artemis) Orthia located there – a central cult place that attracted smaller cults. Concurrently, the topography of Limnai is more complex than the locality of a main sanctuary. Limnai, as evidenced by burials and pottery, was among the earliest settled areas and thus provides an obvious locality where figures connected with the region's past should be found.

Excavations at Limnai have shown that the area was partly a Proto-Geometric and Geometric necropolis.[9] A Geometric grave was excavated by some Late Archaic walls,[10] and further Geometric burials were discovered in the area near the burial at Stauffert Street.[11] Nearby, other Geometric or Proto-Geometric burials[12] were found at Konstantakis (t.s. 98), Dimitrakopoulos (t.s. 98), Sotiriou (t.s. 97A) and Bouchalis plots (t.s. 102).[13] A little further south at Sourli plot (t.s. 92) a Proto-Geometric infant burial was discovered.[14] Christesen lists twenty-two Geometric burials in Sparta; ten are located in Limnai.[15] An Archaic burial was found at Ergatikes Katoikies,[16] a number of Hellenistic burials have been found at Limnai, such at the Demetrakopoulos plot (t.s. 98),[17] and a two-storey tomb was found in the same area.[18]

Clearly, then, Limnai had a long tradition as a burial area. As the discussion of the Bronze Age tombs and the Geometric cults in Chapter 1 showed, burial areas were often deemed sacred and frequently gave rise to later cults. It is, therefore, of particular importance that the area of Limnai, rich in hero cults, is also rich in earlier burials, some of them located at the cult sites. Often, when burials were found in an inhabited area, such as the examples in Corinth and Athens, we know that this area was protected and incorporated into the urban context out of fear and respect for the dead. That the dead would be outraged if their graves are disturbed is evident in Euripides' *Medea*. Medea articulates to Jason that she will bury their children herself, 'taking them to the sanctuary of Hera Akraia, so that none of my enemies may outrage them by tearing up their graves' (1378–81; Trans. Kovacs 1994). Limnai's use as an old burial ground could have contributed to a particular 'sacredness' to the area.

The interpretation of cult sites in connection with burials varies: as with those cults formed over Bronze Age and Geometric graves elsewhere in the Greek world, the cults attached to burials in Sparta have been interpreted as having particular familial links, hence ancestor cults; they have also been understood as hero cults and grave cults. Another point is whether there were lost local histories attached to the space. In this context, some of the burials would be understood as belonging to known heroes upon their rediscovery; some of those hero cults attached to tombs presented in Pausanias' narrative of Roman Sparta may be in relation to rediscovered burials. For example, Pausanias narrates that near the temple of Lykourgos was located the tomb of Eukosmos (son of Lykourgos) and the graves of Lathria and Alexandra, descendants of Herakles (Paus. 3.16.6). These individuals were not historical personalities whose graves were also nearby; the graves of Eukosmos, Lathria and Alexandra were of legendary individuals who dwelled in Sparta in the distant past and were in connection with local histories that formed a cultural memory for the local population. The two females, as descendants of Herakles, are reminiscent of the early settling of Sparta by the Dorians. An individual such as Eukosmos characterises the time of the 'political' formation of Sparta, however unhistorical his father Lykourgos may be. It is likely that the graves attributed to them were either cenotaphs or rediscovered burials. A rediscovered burial near the temple of Lycurgus may well have been interpreted as the famous lawgiver's son.

Cults, with or without a burial that honour individuals who lived in the past, exhibit a want to connect the present to an older era. The very existence of an older burial provided a physical link to the past as, in essence, a burial was a tangible manifestation of this older time. Additionally, the cults in relation to graves offered a connection with the previous occupants of the space where the Spartans lived. There could have been a certain cultural memory of the area as a place of 'old' where the population's older inhabitants dwelled.

6.1 The cult at Stauffert Street

One of the most notable examples among the heroic cults from Limnai is that on Stauffert Street (no. 8; Figures 2.12–2.13). A Geometric-period burial became the locus of cult that formed during the seventh century and lasted at least until the Hellenistic period.[19] The thousands of offerings of terracotta reliefs, figurines, pottery and lead figurines attest to the popularity and longevity of the cult. Fragments of bones and drinking shapes present evidence of sacrifice and drinking rituals at the site. There have been different interpretations of the meaning of the ritual activity here. It has been suggested that the site is indicatory of grave cult and is an example of an elaborate grave ritual.[20] Another proposal is that the cult is connected to a private cult or a family cemetery,[21] or that the dead was given heroic honours and belonged to the civic community of Sparta.[22] Neither of these suggestions is easily comprehensible before expanding further into what constitutes grave cult or ancestor cult and how they can relate to hero cult.

The distinction between hero cult and ancestor cult is often hard, if at all possible, to differentiate.[23] It is even trickier to differentiate, detect and understand in early periods. The problem arises partly because there is a common quality shared by both hero and ancestor cult, in that they both surround the cult of an individual (mythological or historical) who, now dead, is venerated with cult. The definition of ancestor cult is not even agreed upon: to begin with, the existence of ancestor worship in Greek religion has been questioned since there is little evidence of such practice as the Roman *Lares*.[24] In this view, an ancestor cult would have its primary location in the domestic arena and the focus on the dead would be from his descendants alone.[25] In general, ancestor cult in this view was not a community event but a family one, which constitutes one of the greater differences between hero cult and rituals for the dead.

Others see that the distinction should lie between grave cult and ancestor cult. Grave cult would constitute funerary rites over a grave that continue by the family for some time afterwards and are addressed towards a particular deceased person.[26] Ancestor cult on the other hand would be established much later – so definition of 'ancestor' in this case should be seen more broadly.[27] In this view, Antonaccio has argued that the veneration of the dead at rediscovered Bronze Age tombs is not a sign of hero worship but rather ancestor worship.[28]

There are a number of examples of what one may call ancestor worship in the Greek world in the form of cults often by or near earlier burials, especially observed in the Geometric period but also later periods where a group would claim ancestry from burials. At Naxos, a grave cult over late-Proto-Geometric burials underwent changes that saw the formation of a more communal ancestor or even hero cult.[29] At the North Cemetery at Vari in Attica, we see the formation of grave cult for an individual in the seventh century following his death. The cult continued into the mid-sixth century and it too has been interpreted as a cult that became more communal, with a wider audience, thus hero-cult.[30]

The circumstances, chronology and geographical range are diverse and no single explanation would suffice in explaining the occurrence of cult forming over burials.[31] There is enough evidence to suggest that in some cases such cults would not be static and the 'catchment area' could change. What may have originated as cult for a family or group claiming ancestry from a burial/burials, may gradually change to a larger more communal cult. Generally, an ancestor cult is often linked with a burial where a hero cult may or may not have a burial attached. The distinction between the two is often not made.[32]

The cult on Stauffert Street is a Geometric burial (*c.* 750–650 BC)[33] that appears to have received cult from the early seventh century onwards. But without a precise date it is hard to appreciate its relationship to the votive material. Did the grave receive cult immediately? In other words, was there continuity of cult from the time of burial all the way to the Hellenistic time or was this a rediscovered burial? The publication of the Geometric pottery found with the burial is pending and so is the precise chronology of the burial. However, it has been suggested to me recently (with caution) that here we have a late-Geometric burial with most likely continuity of cult.[34]

There is evidence now of burials in Sparta that exhibit elaborate ritual activity following burial, such as drinking and dining, as shown at the Zaimis plot. There, at an Archaic two-storey tomb, a whole dining set was found for a ritual meal; the set was subsequently pierced and deposited with no further evidence of ritual activity.[35] The Archaic grave had a series of channels built around it to collect rainwater. In the late Classical period, a conduit to control the flow of water in the area was constructed (perhaps to protect the site) but there is no evidence of cult formation at a later date. More recently the discovery of an Archaic–Hellenistic cemetery (the Olive Oil Cemetery) at the edge of southwest Sparta gives evidence of horse sacrifice, drinking, dining and peribolos walls encompassing family burials.[36] While this discovery is significant in rethinking the treatment of the dead in Sparta, there is no concrete evidence (yet) of subsequent cult at the graves here.[37] Further publication of the excavation will give a clearer picture.

In contrast, the cult at Stauffert street is an example of a cult formed over a burial, (if we accept continuity of cult from the Geometric to the Archaic period) – a common enough phenomenon in the Greek world. The institution of a cult over a burial shows fundamentally that the dead individual was considered to hold power over the living and with ritual and offerings the living could gain benefits.

Was the buried individual thought an ancestor to a group or family who resided at Limnai? There has been a fair amount of discussion over the connection between the worship of heroes and certain families or groups in the Greek world. In order to legitimize political and social positions families and groups often claim a hero as an ancestor. Such interpretations have been proposed for the votive offerings placed at those rediscovered Bronze Age tombs in Messenia as well as the Argolid and Attica[38] and the Geometric and seventh-century tombs in Naxos and elsewhere.

Moreover, recent discoveries from the excavation of the Olive Oil Cemetery support ancestral connections with burials. There, two large Classical-period periboloi walls (A and B) have been unearthed of which peribolos A is fully excavated.[39] Peribolos A contains a group of six graves in the lower level and eight burials in the upper level centred around a horse burial. This horse burial was carefully preserved when later burials were deposited – an indicator, as the excavator suggests, that the horse burial served as a centre for the family tombs.[40] This burial, as with others in the cemetery, was not marked, bar the encompassing wall. The discovery of this typology of burials not only enriches our understanding of burial customs in Sparta it also shows that burials took place with families in mind. The cemetery finds can offer enough evidence to show that the Spartans in Archaic and Classical Sparta connected the dead with the world of the living in familial contexts. It illustrates that burial areas were demarked for particular families that related themselves to their direct ancestors.

It may be the case, as in other Greek poleis, that the cult at Stauffert Street may have founded initially by a family in order to celebrate their dead and elevate their societal status. The late eighth century, from when this late-Geometric burial dates, was a time of internal and externall unrest (Introduction). Moreover, if we are to take the comments of Tyrtaeus, seventh-century Sparta had been marked by severe inequalities in wealth (fr. 1 West; cf. Alkaios fr. 360).[41] Dedications in sanctuaries exhibit a plethora of votives to suggest a display of personal riches. In the climate of late eighth- and seventh-century Sparta, a family could celebrate an ancestor with a cult at the grave.

The cult at Stauffert Street may have begun by the local inhabitants of Limnai (perhaps a specific family) who lived nearby. Still, the site and finds carry certain features that can give clues as to the status of the site beyond its initial instigation. The two architectural phases and its longevity into the Hellenistic period are characteristics usually associated with state cults (Chapter 3). The discovery of a terracotta disc acroterion of a type found commonly on Archaic Spartan and Peloponnesian temples indicates a project in line with the main sanctuaries of the polis, such as those of Orthia, the Amyklaion and the Menelaion (Chapter 3). Likewise, the location of the cult at Limnai is also noteworthy since the concentration of finds from the Acropolis and Limnai shows that this area was developing in the Archaic period into the civic and residential centre of Sparta.[42] Intensification of votive offerings from the seventh century onwards at the nearby sanctuary of Artemis Orthia and the setting up of other contemporary cults in the area, such that of the Heroon by the Eurotas (no. 3), O 13 (no. 4), the Niarchos plot (no. 7) and Lycourgos and Karella plot (no. 9), shows that the Spartan community united, among other ways, in a cultic context. Other cults, including those of epic heroes at the Menelaion and at Amyklai, with the cult of Agamemnon and Alexandra/Kassandra (no. 1), had also commenced by the early seventh century. The dead at the cult of Stauffert street was eventually treated with the same votive gifts of terracotta reliefs as those given to Agamemnon and Alexandra/Kassandra at their shrine at Amyklai – gifts suitable for heroes in Sparta.

The cult at Stauffert Street therefore belongs within the framework of setting up cults at graves; these may be thought of as ancestral cults initiated and maintained by families or groups, often seen in the Greek world, especially in the Geometric period (Chapter 1). Yet, the cult was not static: seemingly, the development of the polis saw the absorption of these cults into the civic sphere and the cult became a more communal heroic cult with a wider catchment area. This is evidenced by: its longevity since family cults are usually tended by only one or two generations; the building works that adhere to the architectural trends of Spartan temples and show community venture; and the votives of terracotta plaques (and one stone relief) that are strongly associated with heroic cults and not grave cults. As explained in the Introduction, hero cults were a symbol of identity and the polis' past. In Sparta, they developed alongside the consolidation of Spartan territory and monumentalization of Sparta itself.

Upon the set-up of the cults and the monumentalization of the site, the burial became then part of the cultic 'urban' topography of Sparta. Unlike the Menelaion, its location within the settled *kome* of Limnai would provide a frequent visual reminder to the Spartan inhabitants of the hero and any local or polis histories associated with him/her. Daily passing by this heroic cult and others offered a perpetual dialogue with the local past and enhanced the cultural memory of the population. Repeated ritual activity of votive offerings, prayers, sacrifices and other rituals heighten this memory.

Thus, the cult at Stauffert Street expresses an interest in the past as part of the civic and communal investment of the people. What the burial and subsequent heroic cult contributed was a memory that is localized in objects and places, a crucial component of Halbwachs' thesis on remembering: 'But if a truth is to be settled in the memory of a group it needs to be presented in the concrete form of an event, of a personality, or of a locality.'[43] The 'past' has been preserved because it has not vanished fully, some sort of evidence has been left behind;[44] in this case, the old burials. The numerous heroic cults in Limnai thus created the physical manifestation of the past and a reference point for its memories. These sites evoked the collective memory of the Spartan community and the Geometric burial at Stauffert Street provides an example where this past was embraced. The rich Geometric burial ground at Limnai offers ground where local beliefs and funerary tradition saw the area become a locus for heroic cults that linked the present to the past.

6.2 Hellenistic and Roman Sparta

Pausanias' Roman Sparta, visited in the second century AD, is a city with numerous monuments, cenotaphs and tombs belonging to mythical and historical individuals. Although these monuments are preserved in the literary record, given the lack of epigraphic evidence, it has been impossible to match most archaeological remains of the Roman period to Pausanias' description of heroic sites. This section will not focus on those sites mentioned in Pausanias, and it will only briefly mention the ways prominent families found genealogical links to heroes.[45] Instead, it will examine two sites of late Hellenistic/Early Roman Sparta: Ergatikes Katoikies and the Stavropoulos plot. These sites are noted for two reasons: first, because they incorporate burials; second, because they had an initial Archaic period phase. Each site offers an opportunity to look at an example of a type of monument that Pausanias saw when he wrote about heroic cult sites associated with a grave.

The sites will be contextualized against the backdrop of the antiquarian tendencies of Sparta that saw heroes and hero cult as avenues to connect the present to the past. The Hellenistic period in Sparta, but also elsewhere, witnessed a resurgence of interest in and intensification of the local past.[46] Perhaps because of the new world order stemming from the rise of Macedon, poleis exhibited renewed attention in local self-definition.[47] Heroes and hero cults found a place in this revived awareness of the mythological and recent histories of their respective poleis, which generated the reorganization of older cults, the institution of new heroic cults and the genealogical connection to heroes.

In Sparta too the Hellenistic period offered a time of searching for the local past. Aspirations by Agis (reigned 244–241 BC) to bring back the lifestyle of his forefathers failed (Plut. *Agis* 8) but the reforms were later implemented by Kleomenes, enthroned in 235 BC. Kleomenes introduced various reforms including the institution of the public messes and *agoge* (Plut. *Cleom*. 11.2) looking back to the Lykourgan lifestyle of Sparta.[48] Kleomenes also probably rebuilt the temple of Artemis Orthia and placed her image in a series of silver tetradrachms as part of the 'Lykourgan revival'.[49] But it is the decades after 146 BC that was a time of 'intense antiquarian activity at Sparta'[50] including, again, the revival of the *agoge*,[51] which flourished under Roman patronage.

Aristocratic families took greater responsibilities as εὐεργέται that brought new structural stresses within the society and especially saw tension in the relationship of wealthy benefactors to civic ideology. In Sparta, the first century BC was characterized by the prominence of the Spartan Eurykles, whose patronage was famous within Sparta and Laconia.[52] It also included the revival of a number of civic cults for which there is inscriptional evidence (*I.G.* v.1. 141–2; 206–9; 210–12), such as the heroic cult of the Dioskouroi and Helen at the Phoibaion (whose priests were related to Eurykles) and of Poseidon Tainaros in Sparta.[53] Some of these cults were not necessarily new but intensification of cults is attested with rebuilding and expansion of pre-existing cults.[54]

Such sentiments will become even more prominent during the second sophistic of the late first century AD.[55] The rhetorical style that sought to revive the style of the Archaic and Classical periods 'was paralleled in the civic culture of the time, when urban elites, especially in Greek-speaking areas, embraced an insistent and pervasive sense of the past, using local histories as a means of legitimizing their own positions and, more generally framing the world around them'.[56] Sparta was not exempt from this movement that saw the institution of the Leonidaia (*IG* V.1 18–19; late first century AD). The cultural memory of Roman Sparta[57] was conveyed in the city's topography decorated in buildings and monuments that evoked heroes pertaining to local legends, such as Herakles and the Hippokontidai, the Dioskouroi, Helen and Menelaus, Lycurgus and historical personalities, such as Brasidas and Lysander.[58] Moreover, the Persian Wars were roused in the cultural memory of Roman Sparta not only through the Leonidaia but through the tombs of Leonidas, Pausanias, Maron and Alpheios, and Eurybiades.[59]

Furthermore, in the Hellenistic and Roman periods, notable families recorded their descent from heroes, such as Herakles, to the exact number of generations, in order to mark their inherent right to dominate public life through magistracies and hereditary priesthoods. In a Hadrianic inscription (*I.G.* v.1.471), Herakles and Rhadamanthys are the ancestors of a Publius Memmius Spartiatikos and on another inscription from the reign of Trajan (*I.G.* v.1.477) Herakles and Perseus are linked genealogically with a Lucios Ololoussios Aristocrates.[60]

Tyndareus and his sons, Kastor and Polydeukes, were also popular ancestors (e.g. *IG* V.1 529, 536, 559, 562), as part of the legendary Spartan royal family and since they fought beside Herakles against the Hippokoontidai. Evidence from late Hellenistic Sparta links certain groups and families with the family of Tyndareus. *IG* v.1. 209 (first century BC) is a list of σιτηθέντες (dinners) associated with the cult of Helen and the Dioskouroi, presumably at the Phoibaion. Members of the same family (Sidekta or Pratola) are listed, suggesting a family affiliation, and even kinship with the priestess (Eurybanassa Sidekta).[61] One member even has a name stemming from the prominent heroic Spartan family of the Tyndaridai, e.g. Tyndares Sidekta. On another stele of the same series (*I.G.* v.1. 206; first century BC), only the first few lines survive, but they mention Deximachos Sidekta, further linking the family with the cult of Helen and the Dioskouroi. Spawforth suggests that the Erybanassa Sidekta was a hereditary priestess whose family claimed descent from the Tyndarai, thus Tyndareus Sidekta.[62] Presumably, the *sitithentes* (dinners) would have gathered and dined in a ritual setting as members of the cult of Helen and the Dioskouroi.

Linking heroes to prominent families is not a phenomenon restricted to the Hellenistic and Roman periods, where mythical figures share ancestry with prominent families and even Lycurgus himself.[63] The merging of the recent and distant past, the historical with the mythological, is common in Greek thought. Schachermeyr demonstrated that often genealogies in Greek aristocracy comprise ten to fifteen generations. They begin with historical figures for two to four generations and, as they go back, merge with mythological characters.[64]

The two sites that will be presented below flourished in this context. They were associated with long buildings from the Hellenistic/Roman periods and offer evidence of a conscious connection of the present to the past.

6.2.1 Ergatikes Katoikies

The first example is the site of Ergatikes Katoikies (no. 5) where the remains of a long Hellenistic structure were discovered on the eastern foot of the Spartan acropolis. This three-room late Hellenistic building is particularly noted because it encompassed a burial in the middle of the south room. The burial was not contemporary with the construction of the long building since it dates to the early Archaic period, based on two lakainai of Laconian II style (610–575 BC). The focus and centrality of the later building around the burial is apparent, however, since the grave was not only housed in the building but the burial actually rose over the paved floor of the later room.

The erection of the building to encompass the burial and the deposition of votives are indicative of a cult formation over an earlier burial. The deceased was probably thought of as a hero, perhaps even a heroine, judging by the predominately female figurines.[65] The site retained its importance into the Roman period when further renovations resulted in the erection of a small room directly over the burial.

The conditions of the formation of cult around this grave are vague because of the incomplete publication of the site. There is no clear evidence that the burial received posthumous cult right after its deposition since there is no apparent continuity of activity after the burial; only two artefacts are of Archaic date. There are many questions that are unanswered: why and when did cult commence? Was the burial rediscovered in the late Hellenistic period, prompting the erection of a building and the accumulation of a plethora of votives, including 150 terracotta female and animal figurines? Or was there an earlier cult there that received renovations and revival in the Hellenistic period? Was the individual buried connected to a specific family that claimed ancestry?

Both Steinhauer and Stibbe propose that this may be a family shrine because of its small dimensions.[66] A local elite family in pursuit of familial links with heroes of the past could have claimed the burial. Such assertions are recognized in Sparta and elsewhere during the Hellenistic and Roman periods, as evidenced by inscriptions that attest to the alleged genealogical links between families and prominent heroes.[67] We cannot exclude the possibility that an elite family in order to promote itself asserted a familiar link to the buried hero or heroine.

The construction of the late Hellenistic long building at Ergatikes Katoikies (5) was not an isolated incident in the topography of late Hellenistic Sparta. It is during the same period that other hero shrines exhibit expansion or complete rebuilding. One such shrine, at the Kalatzis plot (no. 18), has produced an Archaic disc acroterion but also substantial Hellenistic architectural fragments, such as gorgoneia, an eagle and riders, which may have been acroteria or antefixes, and a Corinthian column, which suggests either expansion or rebuilding at the site. At another, the Georganta-Petrakou plot (no. 13), the votive remains date from the Archaic period but it is during the Hellenistic period that the cult may have acquired a more substantial building, as evidenced by the stamped tile, and the many antefixes. Similarly, the burial at Ergatikes Katoikies (no. 5) may have received cult long before the Hellenistic period. The veneration of the dead would not be unusual for Sparta as we have other cults near or at burials, such as that of Stauffert Street (no. 8), but also support for the heroization of Chilon. Ergatikes Katoikies may be another example, therefore, where the dead received veneration in Sparta and then received building and renewed interested in the Hellenistic period. A clearer publication of the finds, their stratigraphy and the activity at the site between the early Archaic and the Late Hellenistic period would shed further light on the site.

6.2.2 The Stavropoulos plot

The second example is notably different. At the Stavropoulos plot (no. 6), an earlier late-sixth/early-fifth-century building that housed a heroic cult (as shown by a remaining polygonal wall, an Archaic Doric capital, and the stone and terracotta reliefs) was extended to a long building built atop a marble *krepis* (Figure 2.11). The long building, by the first century BC also housed a burial, which was placed by the earlier late-sixth-/early-fifth-century wall. Therefore, the remains of the earlier heroic cult were incorporated into the later building that also served as a space of an elaborate late Hellenistic burial. Here, the heroic cult offers a *model* for an ostentatious Hellenistic/Early Roman burial where the deceased was buried 'like a hero' (if we are to follow Herodotus' words regarding the kings' burials). Such treatment of the dead is in line with the flexibility of the term 'hero' in the Hellenistic period and the increase of heroization of the dead.

The architectural typology of these long buildings finds other parallels in Sparta, e.g. Ergatikes Katoikies (no. 5). Other examples are those of the Laskaris plot and the so-called 'Altar of Lykourgos' near the Eurotas.[68] All these buildings have been interpreted as temples.[69] The contemporary and preceding tradition of heroes and hero cult thus impacted burial practices of the local elite. So much so, that this first-century BC burial is given a long building following the model of temples as seen in some cults sites.

The Stavropoulos plot (no. 6) burial is also representative of a number of extravagant graves discovered in various locations in Sparta, some of which had elaborate doors made of *rosso antico* while others were situated at prominent public locations.[70] Indeed, the aforementioned burial was positioned by an ancient road and near Hellenistic houses.[71] Other monumental graves of the Hellenistic period that commanded roads or public space have been unearthed in Sparta.[72] The Hellenistic burials are probably inspired by Macedonian burial customs, not uncommon in the Hellenistic Greek world, and were signs of aristocratic spectacle.[73] Roman Sparta too sees such customs with an example found in the heroon of the benefactor Caius Iulius Eurykles Herculanus, whose monument dates to the years after his death (136/7 AD). A number of architectural pieces were found reused in the Roman fortification wall of the Spartan Acropolis (*I.G.* V.1. 489; 575) but the original monument may have stood in the agora or near the theatre.[74] These late Hellenistic and Roman burials display the effort of the Spartan aristocracy to flaunt a wealthy burial in a prominent location – a common custom in the Greek world at the time.[75] During the Hellenistic period and later, moreover some recently deceased were given elaborate burials and were more freely bestowed with the term 'hero'; consequently, their burials were influenced by contemporary and preceding practices of hero cult. The treatment of the dead like heroes in the Hellenistic period is also seen on the stone reliefs, where the heroic motif is adopted now for mortals.

6.3 Conclusion

The three burials presented above display different contexts where the sphere of burial ritual and heroic ritual cross over. In the first example at Stauffert Street (no.8), what may have begun as an elaborate grave ritual soon took new dimensions as a heroic cult that lasted for hundreds of years, becoming incorporated into the religious landscape of the polis. The other two examples belong in the context of Hellenistic Sparta when it exhibited a resurgence of interest in the local past. The Archaic burial of Ergatikes Katoikies (no. 5) was given an elaborate temple construction in the first century BC and hundreds of votives, with further building in the Roman period. Another first-century BC burial at the Stavropoulos plot (no. 6) was granted a similar treatment. Unlike the first example, however, the building did not surround an earlier burial but a contemporary tomb that was housed in a long building. In the three examples, we see that since a hero is considered a mortal who dies and receives veneration, it is thus relatively easy to cross the boundaries between grave ritual and hero cult, resulting in a variability of contexts in which we can encounter this intersection.

Conclusion

Hero cult in Sparta had a long tradition, from the late eighth/early seventh centuries BC to the Roman period. The Menelaion, the cult of Agamemnon and Alexandra/Kassandra, and other cults to heroes who remain unknown to us were an integral part of the religious tradition of the city. The heterogeneity of hero cult in Greek religion is encapsulated in the variety of individuals worshipped in Sparta: heroes of epic, local heroes, Panhellenic heroes, and the heroized dead among many. Within this heterogeneity we see how heroes catered to the various needs of the people: self-definition as a community, elite promotion and personal needs in everyday life.

The appearance of hero cult in Sparta at the end of the eighth/early seventh century is of importance. Sparta at the time faced internal and external unrest, as we see from the expansion into Messenia and the socio-political inequalities that necessitated the foundation of Taras. Religion offered delineation for the community with building projects that elaborated its state cults at the Amyklaion and the temple of Artemis Orthia. Roughly contemporary to these building projects were the commencement of the cults at the Menelaion, Zeus at Tsakona and the Eleusinion by the Taygetos. The emergence of hero cult in Sparta during this time offers another mode whereby religion served to the local needs of self-definition both spatially and conceptually. Some hero cults, such as those of the cult of Agamemnon and Alexandra/Kassandra at Amyklai or the Heroon by the Eurotas at Limnai, may have been started by groups who lived locally in the respective areas. Hero cults founded near or at a number of Geometric burials at Limnai and from one example from Amyklai (Sklavochori, no. 29) may show that certain families could have claimed ancestry from earlier burials – a common phenomenon in various places in the Greek world. Internal and external instability stimulated a need for people to reach out to the past in order to find common ground and contextualize their world. Heroes who lived locally in the remote past offered a frame of reference, grounding and structure to the contemporary world and became omnipresent in the religious system of Sparta over subsequent centuries.

By the sixth century, we truly see the growth and extent of the religious tradition of hero cult in Sparta. Some that commenced in the early seventh century acquired buildings, some with elaborate terracottas in line with the architecture of the main sanctuaries of the polis. Certain typologies of votives destined for hero cults also arose at the time: the stone reliefs appear in the middle of the sixth century and the terracotta reliefs by the end of the sixth century, both with distinct iconography appropriate for heroes. The Dioskouroi receive their own dedications with a series of stone reliefs that appear in the sixth century onwards. The transfer of the bones of Orestes in Sparta and burial in the agora reveal the communal and civic significance of the cult. The heroization of the ephor Chilon offers ground for discussion that Sparta would heroize exceptional personalities early.

The longevity of the cults for hundreds of years, some continuing from the early seventh century into the Roman period, demonstrates that some, perhaps instigated by families or groups, would have gradually gained civic significance. Epigraphic evidence, such as the Hellenistic inscription from the cult of Agamemnon and Alexandra/Kassandra by the Gerousia and the tiles from the Menelaion, confirm their civic status. Architectural elaborations, such as terracotta disc acroteria and antefixes of the same typology as those used on the building projects of the main temples of Sparta (and Laconia), exhibit the standing that hero cults acquired during the Archaic period. Multiple building phases reveal the permanence of these structures within the community that cared for them for hundreds of years. Indeed, the longevity of the cults of Orestes, Chilon and Talthybios is supported by literary testimonia from Pausanias' Roman Sparta.

The heroic cults in Sparta and within the four central *komai*, although not lavished with the architecture and the expensive votives of the Menelaion, the temple of Artemis Orthia or the Amyklaion, were a popular aspect of the religious life of Sparta. The votive deposits discovered throughout the modern city show that the most common offerings were modest dedications of terracotta reliefs, terracotta figurines, lead figurines, miniature vases and pottery. Expensive dedications in bronze and ivory are rare to non-existent. This typology of votives need not demote the standing of these cults within the religious system. Rather, the modest votives would be predominantly private gifts offered personally and show the intimate relationship between the worshippers and the hero; the stone reliefs could be offered at a group level or by wealthier individuals.

The typology of votives (where bronzes are infrequent) is paralleled to cults to heroes from elsewhere in the Greek world, and more importantly to smaller cults (both heroic and divine) sometimes, but not exclusively, within settled areas, by neighbourhoods and streets. The find spots of most deposits and sites associated with hero cults in Sparta were within the area of Limnai and south of the Acropolis, which was inhabited continuously from Geometric to Roman times and where ceramic accumulations, shrines, tombs, roads, walls and even remains of a late Geometric/early Archaic house were found. Literary attestations from Pausanias offer a glimpse that in Roman Sparta numerous hero cults were located in the centre comprising the area by the theatre below the Acropolis, the Spartan agora, along the Aphetaid road, and Limnai. Chance findings of other sites and deposits within the areas of the Spartan *komai* give further support that the hero shrines would be located in many locations within the settled areas of Kynosoura, Limnai, Mesoa and Pitane. The topography of the finds illustrates that in Sparta too the hero shrines were part of the everyday life of the people and in locations where individuals would frequently pass and live close to. From the uniformity of the iconography of the reliefs, the anonymity of the receiver of the cults, and the inexpensive nature of the terracotta reliefs and other votives, it can be concluded that they were personal votives offered in an intimate gesture to the local heroes with whom they resided in the city. Heroes could have been linked to specific families, some may have catered more frequently to those who lived close by, while others would surely have had a more communal catchment area.

By examining the heroic cults of Sparta I emphasized the need for a local perspective on the religious habits of the polis. I hope to have shown that the study of small shrines, neighbourhood shrines, shrines associated with groups or families offer a viewpoint where daily life and daily concerns could take place. Without denying the overarching religious customs of the polis, by examining the activity at such cults sites we see a bottom-up approach from the participants' point of view. The surviving archaeological evidence of this more 'popular' aspect of Greek religion, namely the smaller sanctuaries and shrines, their inclusion in the religious habits of a polis or a region offers another neglected but essential view of Greek religion.

The book has explored both the variability of hero cult in Sparta as well as the form this variability took. As mortality is a defining feature of hero cult, we see how it becomes a focal point of discussion around the hero cults. Indeed, hero cults show the flexibility of Greek religious thought, where a hero, although a mortal, can achieve immortality. They also show how seemingly 'irrational'

Greek religious belief can be when both immortality and burial can coexist: Helen and Menelaus received an elaborate cult in line with the divine sanctuaries of the polis and were thought to be immortal; by the time of Pausanias they were presumed buried there. Hyakinthos, whose cult is viewed by some as that of a pre-Dorian deity, had a tomb at the base of the statue of Apollo on which he is pictured during his apotheosis. The Hyakinthia festival celebrated the death and apotheosis of the hero. The Dioskouroi reveal just how fluid heroic nature can be by spending alternate days in the underworld and on Olympus but Kastor too had a grave in Sparta over which was a temple. During the Hellenistic and Roman times, the mortality of heroes was especially accentuated when hero cults were often associated with graves, as we see from Pausanias' Roman Sparta. From the Hellenistic period onwards it became more common to heroize the recently dead elite, offering prestige and extreme honours to the deceased and his family.

Indeed, a common prerequisite for heroization in the Archaic and Classical periods was the individual's death. Thus, the parameters between burial ritual and hero cult become blurred with the heroization of historical personalities and with cults over graves. Sparta's religious tradition accepted the heroization of the exceptional dead in the Archaic and Classical periods, as we see from the heroization of Chilon and most likely King Leonidas. These two, and others such as the statesman Lycurgus, who attained special post-mortal status, were communal individuals who mattered to the people in a collective sense and achieved extraordinary deeds when alive. The Spartan kings, however, did not all receive this level of post-mortal treatment but obtained burial ritual in line to heroization. A spectrum of post-mortal rituals allowed for extreme honours after death and need not be viewed in the same light as those hero cults commonly found in Sparta. Apart from a select few, such as Maron and Alpheios, who fought most bravely at the Battle of Thermopylai, or Eurybiades the commander of the Lakedaimonian ships at the naval battles of Artemision and Salamis, Sparta did not heroize its war-dead. It is unknown if the state or families instituted the cults at the time of burial of Maron and Alpheios, or if cults grew gradually over the course of time when the feats of the Persian Wars flourished in the cultural memory of Sparta and the Greek world.

Further evidence of the permeability of boundaries between rituals for the dead and heroic cults arises from cults formed by graves as supported by archaeological evidence: rituals were performed at rediscovered Bronze Age and Geometric burials. In Geometric Greece, we see ancestor cults formed over burials following the death of the individual that may later assimilate into civic cults; and cities offered cults to *oikistai*. Sparta did not have a tradition of cults at Bronze Age tombs but a number of hero cults were located in the area of Limnai, which housed Proto-Geometric and Geometric burials. The intersection between burial ritual and hero cult met in a variability of contexts there: with the veneration of earlier Geometric burials, which may have begun as ancestor cults but gained civic importance, with the rediscovery and elaboration of an Archaic burial in line with Sparta's antiquarianism and interest in the local past in the Hellenistic period, and the burial of an elite dead with an ostentatious building also of the late Hellenistic period.

Notes

Introduction

1 Antonaccio 1994: 390; 1999, 120; Currie 2005, 100.
2 Dressel and Milchhöfer 1877; Fürtwangler 1883–7; Andronikos 1956; Stibbe 1991; Salapata 1993; 1997; 2006; 2009; 2014.
3 Sanders 1992b.
4 Stibbe 1991, 12, fig. 6, no. A3; Kaltsas 2006, 100; Salapata 2014, 347 R10.
5 This view has now been challenged and scholars see Sparta more in line with the rest of the Greek poleis. The bibliography is immense; see for example Kennell (2010) and various chapters in Powell (2018).
6 Salapata 2014, 232.
7 See argument against Sparta's 'Achaian Policy' and previous scholarship on the topic in Pavlides 2021.
8 Bowra 1933; 2001, 345; Fuqua 1981; Boedeker 1998; 2001.
9 See for example Cartledge (1987, 339–41; 1988); Nafissi (1991, 290); Parker (1988); and Lipka (2002, 248–51).
10 Regarding ancient Spartan religion, Cartledge remarks that Pausanias' evidence is 'simply indispensable'; Cartledge 2001b, 170; cf. Hutton 2005, 19–20). Still, Pausanias' preference for describing Archaic and fifth-century monuments and his depreciation of Hellenistic and Roman artefacts has been noted (Arafat 1996, 36–42, 44–5; Bowie 1996, 210–11, 229; Porter 2001, 67; Hutton 2005, 64).
11 Parker 1989, 147–8; Richer 2007, 249–52; Jones, C. P. 2010, 14–15.
12 Dawkins, *Orthia*; Carter 1987; Parker 1989, 148, 151; Kennell 1995, 136–8; Richer 2007, 237–8; Kopanias 2009.
13 Pettersson 1992; Parker 1989, 144, 146, 149; Richer 2007, 238.
14 Dickins 1906–7a, 142–56; Stibbe 2006, 127–33.
15 Some heroic burials could exist in more than one place – most famously Agamemnon, who is reported buried in both Sparta and Mycenae. This is quite distinct from the worship of deities who travelled and visited different places and did not always stay in one sanctuary. Gods must be summoned to come to a land or sanctuary as evidenced by the *Hymnoi Kletikoi* (Menander *Peri Epideiktikon*; Wallach 1980, 317–18).
16 Some Panhellenic heroes existed, such as Herakles, Asklepios and the Dioskouroi, but these often transgressed the boundaries of a hero and were often considered

divine. For example Herakles is called a hero-god (Pind. *N*. 3. 22) or god (Xen. *An*. 6.2.15). Herakles: Lévêque and Verbanck-Piérard (1992, 85–106), Georgoudi (1998b) and Stafford (2005); Asklepios: Verbanck-Piérard (2000, esp. 301–28) and *LIMC* I. II, 863–6; Dioskouroi: Farnell 1921, 175–228; Hermary 1978; Walker 2015; *LIMC* III. I, 567–93; here § 4.3.
17 Pavlides 2011; cf. Hall 2000, 88.
18 Dickins 1906–7a; 1907–8; Spallino 2016. The temple interior was decorated with bronze sheets, hence the name 'Chalkioikos'. Thucydides is the earliest writer to use the name Chalkioikos (1.134). On the Damonon stele (*I.G.* v. 1.213) Athena is called Poliachos, which is given by Pausanias (3.17.2) as an alternative name.
19 Dawkins *Orthia*. The name Artemis does not appear until *c.* AD 50 in inscriptions, Dawkins *Orthia*, 308–74.
20 For Geometric burials, see Raftopoulou 1988, 133–4; 1996, 273–6; Kourinou 2000, 216; *ArchDelt* (1996) vol. 51 (B1), 129–31; Zavvou and Themos 2009, 111; Tsouli 2013, 151–2, n.6; Christesen 2018, 320.
21 Kennell 2010, 9; Rusch 2011, 3.
22 Kennell 2010, 9.
23 Coulson 1985. Latest research suggests continuity of cult at the sanctuary of Apollo at Amyklai between the Late Bronze Age and the Early Iron Age, 2009a; 2011–12; Vlachou 2011–12; cf. *Amykles Research Project,* 2011 Report: http://www.amyklaion.gr/?page_id=818; *infra* § 4.2.
24 Malkin 1994, 111–13, n.211; Cartledge 2002, 92; Kennell 2010, 9, 31.
25 The existence of a community, as argued by Cohen (1985, 98), is in the 'minds of its members' and not in geographic boundaries.
26 R. Catling 2002, 155. Sparta was not unique in its transformations: the seventh century saw a plethora of changes in Greek arts and society, such as the monumentalization of temples and sculpture, narrative imagery, written laws and, at the end of the century, coinage, among other changes (Étienne 2017); see Brisart (2011) and various chapters in Charalampidou and Morgan 2017.
27 Cartledge 2002, 88.
28 The dates of the Messenian Wars are debated. Different proposals support dates of 735 to 715, 668 to 625 or 660 to 600 BC; V. Parker 1991; Figueira 1999, 225–9; Luraghi 2008, 141–2; Kennell and Luraghi 2009, 250
29 Luraghi 2008, 141–2; Kennell and Luraghi 2009, 250.
30 Ephorus (*FGrH* 555); Nafissi 1999, 254–5; Kennell 2010, 35–6.
31 Kennell 2010, 35–8.
32 van Wees 1999, 2–6.
33 R. Catling 2002, 154, 156–7, 160, 174. There is however fair evidence of cult activity in various sites in Laconia from the PG period onwards. See catalogue of cult sites in Laconia in Pavlides 2018b.

34 Nafissi 2009, 129.
35 The term *homoioi* ('the similars') appears first in Xenophon (*Lak. Pol.*13.7; *Hell.* 3.35; *Anab.* 4.6.14), but the idea is implied by earlier authors (Hdt. 234.2; Thuc. 4.40.2; 126.5); Cartledge 2001a, 66–75; Wees 2018a, 226–7.
36 Nafissi 2009, 130.
37 The discussion nowadays tends towards the tradition of Lykourgos in antiquity rather than his historicity; Nafissi 2018 for the history of scholarship and debate.
38 Plut. *Lyc.* 6.4; Ogden 1994; Kennell 2010, 46. I owe this point to Paul Christesen.
39 Hodkinson 2005, 223–38.
40 Kennell 2010, 77–88.
41 Vlachou 2017b, 41; cf. Amykles Research Project 2019 excavation report: https://amyklaion.gr/en/research/reports/54/
42 For the chronology of Artemis Orthia see Boardman 1963.
43 Cartledge 1998, 44; R. Catling 2002, 220–1.
44 Shipley 2006, 62.
45 Shipley 2004, 593.
46 Hodkinson 1998a, 1998b; Förtsch 1998; 2000, 87–103; Coudin 2009a, 51–64; Kopanias 2009; for Artemis Orthia see Léger 2015, 11–14, 55–90.
47 Polignac 2009, 427.
48 Snodgrass 2006, 258.
49 Morgan 1993, 19; cf. Mazarakis Ainian 2017b, 183–4; Vlachou 2017a, 261.
50 Snodgrass 1980, 33–4, 52–63; 2006 258–66; Morgan 1993; Osborne 2009, 88–98, esp. table 4.
51 Morris 1996, 35.
52 Snodgrass 2006, 265–6.
53 I thank Paul Christesen for this point.
54 Cohen 1985, 102; cf. Assmann 2011, 250. The heroization of the seventh-century Spartan athlete Chionis in 470 is seen as a use of the past: this heroization was promoted, according to Christesen (2010, 49–52, 60), by the Agiad family with the aim of restoring their standing in Sparta after their position was damaged by Pausanias.
55 Nora 1989, 7.
56 Nora 1989; cf. Confino 1997. For space, localization and memory, the seminal work has been published by Nora in three volumes (1984, 1986, 1992).
57 Assmann 2011, 37.
58 Papakonstantinou 2018, 72.
59 Zaitman and Pantel 1994, 9. See Christesen (2009, 20–1) for a discussion of the use of 'cult' in Classical studies.
60 Renfrew 1994, 51.
61 See Renfrew 1985, 24.

62 As a definition for ritual, I use Zaitman and Pantel 1992, 27: 'A ritual is a complex of actions effected by, or in the name of, an individual or a community. These actions serve to organise space and time, to define relations between men and gods, and to set in their proper place the different categories of mankind and the links that bind them together.'
63 Salapata 2014; see also her various articles on the terracotta reliefs (1993; 1997; 2000b; 2006; 2009).
64 Bonias 1998.
65 Wace and Husluck 1904–5.
66 Catling R. 2002, 218–24.
67 Shipley 1996.
68 *ArchDelt* (2013) vol. 68 (B1), 165.
69 Antonaccio 1995, 69–70.
70 Ekroth 1999, 157–8; Pirenne-Delforge 2006, 112–14, 127; 2008, 97, 284, 286–7. For the use of the past in Pausanias, see eadem, 2008, 41–3.

Chapter 1

1 Herakleitos here attacks the false understanding of gods and heroes that people have because they pray to statues; Kahn 1979, 266–7, no. cxvii with commentary.
2 Kron 1976, 22, 28, 54; Kearns, 1989, 64ff.
3 Boehringer 2001, 360ff.
4 Coulanges (1991, 227–8; first edition 1864) thought that heroes were in same category as the Lares, Genii, Penates and Daimones.
5 Rohde 2000, 118 (first edition 1894).
6 Rohde 2000, 118–20.
7 Farnell 1921, 280–3.
8 Brelich 1958.
9 Burkert 1985, 203.
10 Henrichs 2010, 31; cf. Ekroth 2015, 384.
11 Nilsson (1967, 715) argued for an evolutionary model.
12 Burkert 1985, 190–9. See also Seaford 1994, 114–23 and Parker 1996, 34–5 who follows Seaford.
13 Ekroth 1999 151–4; 2002, 140–69; 2009, 131 n.68; This is unlike earlier theories regarding sacrifice for hero, which relied on Roman and Byzantine literary sources and claimed that there was a holocaust sacrifice of the victim without dining afterwards. On the topic see also Parker (2005b, 43) and Sourvinou-Inwood (2005, 330, n.5) who agree that there were similarities with divine cults, which may have differentiated over the course of time but there was still differentiation; e.g.

14 Boehringer 2001, 39ff.
15 O'Brien 1993, 114–15, n.1.
16 Adams 1987, 177.
17 O'Brien 1993, 114 for further discussion.
18 Kearns 1989, 5, 132–3; Sourvinou-Inwood 1995, 199–216, 205–6; Parker 1996, 276; Wypustek 2013, 65–95; 2014; Fröhlich 2013. A practice that may have started early in Boiotia; see Plato *Comicus* fr. 77 (Lyons 1997, 23, n.84).
19 Used for leaders: *Il.* 1.102; 6.61; 2.708; 15.121; 23.824. For armies: *Il.* 15.219, 230, 261, 702; 20. 326; *Od.* 1.100–1; Kearns 1989, 2; Barrigón 2000, 2; Van Wees 2006, 368 n.15.
20 Kearns 1989, 2; Barrigón 2000, 2; *contra* Van Wees 2006, 366–70.
21 There are two Linear B tablets from Pylos that feature the figure *ti-ri-se-ro-e*, who is the receiver of an offering from the central palace. On one of the tablets, PY Tn316, which mentions the records of offerings to various deities whose shrines seem to be in the district of *pa-ki-ja-ne*, *ti-ri-se-ro-e* receives a gold vessel in his shrine, which also appears to be in the district. On the other tablet, PY Fr1204, is recorded the sending of rose-oil to *ti-ri-se-ro-e*; the reading of the name is not certain; Bennett and Olivier 1973, 155; Van Wees, 2006, 367–8. *ti-ri-se-ro-e* has been interpreted as *trisheros* meaning thrice hero; Antonaccio 2006, 383. Antonaccio (2006) notes a similarity between the *trisheros* and the Tritopatores whose cult is attested in Athens and elsewhere in the historical period and who represent the collective ancestors. For a view that hero cult was in practice during the Mycenaean times, see Lindblom and Ekroth 2016.
22 West 1978, 370–3.
23 Nagy 1979, 116; 2012, 33–4.
24 Hatzisteliou-Price 1973, 134.
25 Currie 2005, 56–7.
26 Bremmer 2006, 18 and n.30, 31.
27 cf. Parker 1996, 33–9.
28 West 1978, 191.
29 Van Wees 2006, 364–6. There is no evidence of ἡμίθεοι as having one divine parent before Isokrates (3.42; 9.39); Bremmer 2006, 24–5.
30 Nagy 1979, 159–61.
31 Bravo 2009, 15.
32 Bremmer (2006, 18) cites Herakleitos as the source for the earliest religious use of hero but it may be Mimnermos (fr. 18) in Athenaios (4.174A).
33 Bremmer 2006.
34 Rohde 2000, 116–17; Hatzisteliou-Price 1973, 143.

35 For the evidence of hero cult in Homer see Hatzisteliou-Price 1973; Kearns 1989, 131; Van Wees 2006, 367–8; Burgess 2001, 168; Currie 2005, 48–57; Nagy 1979; 2012; 2015.
36 Ekroth (1998, 218–21) thoroughly rejects this as an act of hero cult.
37 Hatzisteliou-Price 1973, 133–5; Nagy 1979, 190–7; Van Wees 2006, 372.
38 Burgess 2009, 114; Naggy 1999, 151–73. See also how in the *Iliad* 8.538–41 Hektor wishes to become a god.
39 For the cults of Achilles see Burgess 2009, 111–31.
40 Burgess 2001, 164–5; Nagy 2005, 81.
41 Burgess (2001, 168) is not certain. Nagy (1979, 152–4; 2012) argues that these references indicate hero cult.
42 West 1978, 182–3; Nagy 1979, 154.
43 Nagy 1979, 167–8; 189–90.
44 In West 1972, no. 18. See Barrigón 2000, 4. On Mimnermos' fragment see Allen 1993, 128.
45 Burkert 1985, 205. However, the law in regards to heroes may date to the Hellenistic period; Ekroth 2002, 179 n.212.
46 Barrigón 2000, 1–14; Bremmer 2006, 18.
47 Boehringer 2001, 30.
48 For a fuller discussion see Larson 1995, 21–5; Lyons 1997, 13–16; Barrigón 2000, 12–13.
49 Larson 1995, 21.
50 Lyons 1997, 14; Barrigón 2000, 13. The date for Corinna is disputed: although it is traditionally taken to be the fifth century; Davies 1988b. West (1970; 1990) supports a third-century date.
51 Larson 1995, 22; Barrigón 2000, 13.
52 Bravo 2009, 17.
53 Abramson 1978, 168; Kearns 1992, 65–7; Larson 1995, 9–13; Mikkola 2008, 17; Ekroth 2009, 122–4.
54 Kearns 1992, 77–93.
55 Popham *et al.* 1993; Antonaccio 1995, 236–40; Morris 2000, 218–19.
56 Popham *et al.* 1993, 100.
57 Morris 2000, 231–2.
58 Antonaccio 2006, 393; Bravo 2009, 19.
59 Antonaccio 2002; Whitley 2002; Crielaard 2002.
60 Deger-Jalkotzy 2006, 154–7; Antonaccio 2006, 389–94.
61 Deger-Jalkotzy 2006, 157–60.
62 Kilian-Dirlmeier 1998, 328–9.
63 Mazarakis Ainian 1999, 25–33; Morris 2000, 222–8.
64 Antonaccio (2006, 393) proposes that he was seen as an *archegetes*.

65 Boehringer 2001, 301–11, tables 13–14.
66 It is important to note that there is no evidence of continuation of either tomb-cult or hero cult from the late Helladic to the historical times (Hatzisteliou-Price 1973, 131), in contradiction to previous claims by Nilsson (1967, 378 ff.). On later cult at Bronze Age tombs see Antonaccio 1995; Boehringer (2001), who studies the social function of the cults in Attica, Argos and Messenia; Deoudi (1999, 12–15), who separates early archaeological evidence of hero cult into houses, stone platforms for ritual meals, Bronze Age tombs, and sanctuaries.
67 Antonaccio 1995, 245–6. For other examples of continuation of cults at Bronze Age tombs, such as that at Thorikos, see Devillers (1988) and Alcock (1991, 451–67).
68 Nagy, 1979, 114; Bérard 1982, 91–4; Calligas 1988, 233; Morris 1988, 754–5; Whitley 1988, 174; Kearns 1989, 129–31; Crielaard 1995, 268–73; de Polignac 1995, 138–9; Antonaccio 1995, 5–6; Parker 1996, 36–42. Snodgrass (1988) saw problems in the matter of burial practices in Homer as opposed to the Mycenaean tholos and chamber tombs. Snodgrass (1998) and Ahlberg-Cornell (1992, 179–88) have demonstrated that vase-painting scenes seldom depict incidents from the Homeric epics but instead the artists favour a non-Homeric version of an episode, specifically from the *Epic Cycle*. Seaford (1994, 145–6), Snodgrass (1998, 164) and Taplin (2000, 34) do not see a demonstrable influence of the epics over Greek poetry and art before 600 BC. Moreover, another problem is that there might be some references of hero cult in the epics, which means that 'the poet cannot cause a phenomenon which he also reflects'; Parker 1996, 36.
69 Crielaard 2002, 245.
70 Crielaard, 1995; Antonaccio 1995.
71 Van Wees (2006, 376); he actually calls them epic heroes.
72 Antonaccio 1995; Whitley 1995; Bremmer 2006.
73 Snodgrass 1979, 123–4; 1982: 114–16.
74 Whitley 1995, 58.
75 Antonaccio (1995, 246) who cites the exception of the Menidi Tholos and the Thorikos tomb I in Attica. 'Ancestor cult' is defined as 'the formal attention afforded a group of past members of the community' (Lindblom and Ekroth 2016, 236).
76 Antonaccio 1995, 248ff.
77 Parker 1996, 34–5; Ekroth 1997–8, 162.
78 See Boehringer (2001, 42–5) for a definition and discussion of ancestor cult whose primary location should be the domestic area of the social life and the focus of the dead by his descendants and not by the entire community.
79 Antonaccio 1995, 247.
80 *IG* IV 495; *IGA* 29; Jefferey (*LSAG*², 173, no. 6. pl. 31.6) dates it to 475 BC.
81 *LSAG*², 173, no. 6.
82 Intzesiloglou 2002, 289–95; Mili 2015, 226–7, 255, 334.

83 *ABV* 40.21, 42.36; *Para* 18; *Add*² 11. The inscription was by the painter Sophilos (Kilmer and Develin 2001, 23–5).
84 There are many opinions regarding the reason behind the phenomenon of cults at Bronze Age tombs. Land competition and population growth have been proposed by Snodgrass (1988). He argues that cult at local tombs may have helped the communities establish themselves in the area – gave them the right to the place by claiming the tombs as those of their ancestors. Still, scholars do not accept a universal explanation but rather different stimuli in each region and even within regions: De Polignac (1995, 138–45) sees the Argolid as a place where cult at Bronze Age tombs was a result of competing early poleis and politics in cult, while Boehringer (2001, 132–241) saw a change of focus of the cults, such as those near the Argive Heraion, which he interprets to be of interest to the aristocracy of the eighth century in order to display wealth the same way they used the nearby Heraion. Whitley (1988) saw the cults at the Athenian countryside as reactions of the pre-existing communities to new settlers, thus a claim to their land. Boehringer (2001, 47–131) points out the differences between the various cults within Attica and argues that at the Menidi tholos the aristocratic families worshipped a common ancestor while the Thorikos tomb is linked with agricultural cult, of interest to the rural populations. Messenia has been viewed usually in the context of the Spartan occupation. There was eighth-century activity at tombs at Volimidia (Boehringer 2001, 249–58), Kopanaki (id. 284–6), Karpophora (Antonaccio 1995, 89 and Boehringer 2001, 269–70) and Koukounara tomb 6 (Boehringer 2001, 265–6, 310–11, n.4), which ceased to exist after the Spartan domination, possibly around the end of the eighth or early seventh century (Alcock 2002, 142ff). This, argued Morris (1988, 756), would be expected if the cults 'were simply as expression of the Messenians now extinct claims to the land'. However, during the period of Spartan conquest, until 371 BC, new cults sprang up at Papoulia (Boehringer 2001, 259–60), Koukounara (idem 261–5), Vasiliko (id. 267–70, 282–6) and Voilimidia (idem 268–9), which may have been a way of perpetuating traditions in the face of Spartan occupation. Boehringer (2001, 242–371) again links the eighth-century cults with local elites and attributes the short cult duration to the Spartan occupation. He finds the fifth-century cults to be a reawakening of the Messenian self-identity.
85 Boehringer 2001, 33.
86 Williams and Fisher 1973, 10–12, no. 12; Williams, MacIntosh and Fisher 1974, 3–4, no.1 pl.1; Pfaff 2003, 127.
87 Williams and Fisher (1973, 6–12, fig. 2, 3, pl. 1–5; 1974, 1–6, fig. 1, pl. 1) commend that the shrine could have been built to propitiate the person found at the grave who may have been seen as a hero or ancestor. See also Pfaff 2003, 128.
88 Broneer 1942, 141–4.
89 Wycherley 1970, 289, 291; 1978, 192–4; Lalonde 1980, 97–8.

90 Thompson 1958, 148–53, esp. 152–3; Thompson and Wycherley 1972, 119.
91 Shear 1973, 360–9; Camp 1986, 78–82. Proposed as the Leokorion but so is the small enclosure in front of the Stoa Basileus (Thompson and Wycherley 1972, 123; Wycherley 1978, 63–4). See Wycherley (1957, 109–12) for ancient testimonia and Kron (1999, 80–81, fig. 10) with bibliography on the location and function of the Leokorion.
92 Thompson 1966, 48–9; Lalonde 1980, 98–105, fig.1, pls. 15–16.
93 Lalonde 1980, 104; Kearns 1989, 11; Bookidis 2003, 252; Papadopoulos 2003, 275.
94 Many heroes were anonymous in antiquity and they would just be referred to as *heroes*.
95 van den Eijnde 2010, 397.
96 Mazarakis Ainian 1999, 18–25; 2007–8; 2017a, 102–3; *ThesCRA* II, 131–40.
97 Bérard 1970, 31, 69–71; 1982; Blandin 1998; Ducrey *et al.* 2004, 172–6. In the area was found a pit filled with ritual debris, the remains of two buildings associated with ritual dining, and a possible altar.
98 Zapheiropoulou 1999; 2006.
99 Lambrinoudakis 1988; Zapheiropoulou 1983; Kourou 2002. Other examples of a cult consisting of libation and funerary meals on pebble platforms have been discovered at Xombourgo on Tenos and Euboea; *ThesCRA* VI, 372.
100 Parker 1996, 37; Bravo 2009, 22.
101 Boehringer 2001, 111–12; *ThesCRA* II, 136.
102 An early Helladic apsidal building has also been suggested as being the focus of the cult; see Mazarakis Ainian 1999, 16–7, 21, fig.4. For other Geometric burials where family may have paid honours to the dead, see idem, 21–3.
103 Mazarakis Ainian 2017a, 110.
104 Crielaard 2002, 245.
105 See *infra* § 6.1.
106 Mazarakis Ainian 1999, 18–25.
107 See Mazarakis Ainian (2017a, 103) who lists other examples at Oropos and the Areopagus in Athens.
108 *Infra* § 3.2 and § 6.1 for further discussion on the topic.
109 cf. Parker 1996, 37; Bravo 2009, 22.
110 Cook 1953; Hägg 1987, 97–8; Antonaccio 1995, 147–52; Boehringer 2001, 173–8; 200–3.
111 Cook 1953, 62–3, fig. 36.
112 Cook 1953, 33.
113 Morgan and Whitelaw 1991, 89, n.50; Hall 1995, 603.
114 Whitley 1995, 54; Hall 1995; 1999, 58–9; Ratinaud-Lachkar 2000, 254–7. This is further supported by another shrine assumed to be dedicated to Hera on the road to the Argive Heraion; Hall 1995, 603. Still, Salapata (2011, 40–1) notes that the

absence of inscriptions during the early phase of the shrine does not exclude the possibility that it belonged to Agamemnon.
115 Hall 1995, 601–3.
116 *IG* IX 1.653; *SDGI* 1669; Jefferey (*LSAG*² 231, n.3) dates it to *c.* 550–525 BC.
117 Benton 1938–9, 39–43, nos 62–4, 56.
118 Benton 1938–9, 45.
119 Coldstream 1976, 17; Malkin 1998, 94–109; Mazarakis Ainian 1999, 12. Upon his arrival at Ithaka, Odysseus has to hide a treasure in a cave in order that he could travel incognito and keep it safe from the suitors (*Od.* 13.364).
120 Deoudi 2008.
121 See recent discussion in Theodoropoulou-Polychroniadis 2015, 107–8; Barletta 2017, 81–2.
122 Picard (1940, 19–24) had then identified the bastion near the temple of Poseidon as the hero cult shrine. For the plaque, see Abramson 1979, pl. I. I.
123 Abramson (1979, 9–12) bases his argument on the type of votives found in the pit together with the plaque, but these votives (swords, tripods, shields, painted plaques and horses), mostly dating from the late eighth and early seventh century to the mid-fifth century, have been found in various areas of Attica and elsewhere and cannot be used as evidence for hero cult.
124 For the date see Barletta 2017, 71–3.
125 Abramson 1979.
126 Barletta 2017, 82.
127 Barletta 2017, 82 citing the comments of Thompson and Dismoor in their manuscript in the archives of the Blegen Library, American School of Classical Studies at Athens.
128 Goette 2000, 36–7, 40.
129 For various opinions on the cult see Kearns (1989, 41–2), Antonaccio (1995, 169), Mazarakis Ainian (1999, 13, n.23), and Parker (2005a, 410).
130 Aravantinos 2014a; 2014b.
131 Malkin 1987, 263. See the discovery of an archaic grave with a peribolos wall found in the agora at Selinous as a possible example of a burial of an *oikist*; Mertens 2006, 178.
132 Antonaccio 1999, 119–21.
133 Malkin 1987, 212.
134 Antonaccio 1999, 120.
135 Morgan 1990, 173; see also Malkin 1987, 256ff.
136 Dougherty 1993, 26; a possibility that Antonaccio (1999, 119–20) and Malkin (1987, 201) also speculate.
137 Lindblom and Ekroth 2016.
138 Pariente 1992. In the fourth century AD these posts were reused to surround a large pit filled with ashes and calcinated logs, which may have belonged to a

cult, possibly a hero cult, which Pausanias (2.19.2) called the 'Fire of Phoroneus'; idem 196.
139 Picard 1921, 95–7; Grandjean and Salviat 2000, 69.
140 Pouilloux (1955, 78–9) quotes Archilochos (fr. 15, 48 Gerber 1999a) in which Glaukos the son of Leptinos is mentioned as the poet's friend; cf. Martin 1978, 189.
141 Graham 2001, 228. For the monument see Pouilloux (1955, 82), (1979, 136 fig. 7), Grandjean and Salviat (2000, 69–70).
142 Pelops: Kyrieleis 2002, 219–18; 2006, 55–7; Pache 2004, 91–3; Ekroth 2012.
143 Bravo 2006.
144 Jameson 1990, 214–15.
145 There is plenty of other evidence of heroic cults from the Archaic period onwards. Ptoios: Antonaccio 1995, 177–8 with references. Melikertes-Palaimon at the Isthmian sanctuary where the earliest archaeological evidence for his cult dates to the Roman times; Gebhard and Dickie 1999, 159, n.1; Pache 2004, 135 ff. Gebhard and Dickie (1999) argue for an earlier date due to the evidence in a fragment from Pindar (fr. 6.5 [1] Snell).
146 Hatzisteliou-Price 1973, 133.
147 cf. Ekroth 2015, 393.
148 Lindblom and Ekroth 2016.
149 Boehringer (2001, 30) following Rohde, argues that the *naming* of cult beings 'heroes' is due to the popularity of the Homeric epics because one would conceive the heroes of the epics as men of an earlier time.
150 The remains of the altar together with an inscription have been identified in the Athenian Agora; Parker 2005a, 73; Georgoudi 1998b, 73–83; Bremmer 2006, 19–21, n.48.
151 Bremmer 2006, 19. Isokrates' (9.39) tripartite scheme does not mention heroes but men, demi-gods and gods.
152 For the *daimon* see Gasparro 2015.
153 Boehringer (2001, 31) for a discussion on δαίμων and its occurrence in literature.
154 The fluidity of some concepts and terms is seen in the cult-song of women from Elis to Dionysus (sixth century BC) where the word hero is used in ἥρω Διόνυσε, (Plut. *Mor.* 299B); Bremmer 2006, 18). For this cult see Mitsopoulos-Leon 1984, 278–80, n.25.
155 Boehringer 2001, 31; Kindt 2009, 12.
156 Burkert (1985, 205) saw the influence of the Homeric epics as the catalyst of this restructuring. I agree with Bremmer (2006, 19) that Burkert may have dated this 'restructuring' slightly early and would like to see it, following Bremmer's suggestion, to have taken place in the sixth century BC. Parker (2011, 291) also suggests that 'a reconfiguration of the supernatural world occurred' but was not carried out very effectively, which explains the inconsistencies in Greek religion.

157 Burkert 1985, 205.
158 For the kind of heroes who were mortals and became immortals see Pausanias 8.2.4; Currie 2005, 41–6; Sourvinou-Inwood 2005, 329–45. Sourvinou-Inwood (2005, 340) explains that although many of these heroes were of Panhellenic importance, e.g. Herakles and Asklepios, others were in fact local, such as Hylas or Lampsake.
159 See the Classical and Hellenistic shrine of Glaukos at Knossos, whose cult was insinuated into an existing house. The excavators assume that there was hero cult before 500 BC; Callaghan 1978, 3.
160 Ekroth 2002; see also Parker 2005b, 37–45.
161 Parker 2011, 110.
162 Boehringer 2001, 29–36; Ekroth 2007, 101–6; Bravo 2009, 9–17. But see Currie (2005, 164–71), who argues for cultic honours for the living in the fifth century. The evidence, however, regarding the lifetime heroization of Hagnon, (the *oikist* of Amphipolis) based on Thuc. 5.11.1, is vague. Thucydides mentions the buildings of Hagnon, which Currie interprets as buildings that have to do with the lifetime cult of Hagnon, but these buildings need not be religious. The same goes for the honours (τιμάς) for Hagnon that are also not necessarily religious. The honours for the athlete Euthymos at Lokroi (early-fifth century) are altogether uncertain because the date of our evidence is Callimachos (in Pliny *nat.* 7.152) who dates from the third century BC. Currie's argument for lifetime honours for Brasidas is again uncertain because the evidence given only refers to public praise not cult (idem, 169). Lysander see Flower 2018, 447.

Chapter 2

1 Simon 1986, 172; Osborne 2004, 4; Patera 2012, 193–9; Bradley 1990, 14, table 1.
2 The primary sources are the excavation reports published in the *Archaiologikon Deltion* or *Praktika*. However, other sites – as yet unpublished – came to my attention through contacting the E' Ephoreia of Prehistoric and Classical Antiquities in Greece.
3 Salapata 1993, 189.
4 Berlin, Pergamonmuseum 731; Stibbe 1991, fig. 5; Salapata 2006, fig. 3.
5 In some cases, reliefs were discovered in a general area, such as three at the Bougadis plot (*infra* no. 10), three near Chrysapha, and two at Geraki (Salapata 2014, 345–56).
6 About twenty reliefs, almost all of them of the sixth century, depict a seated couple; three or four date to the early fifth century; Salapata 1993, 189.
7 Salapata 1993, 189.
8 The Greek perception of the closeness of snakes with the earth and with death is attested in ancient literature and iconography (Hdt. 1.78.3; Pliny *Nat. Hist.*10.188;

16.85). On snakes in a funeral context see Wide (1909, 221–3), (Harrison 1912, 269–70), Küster (1913, 47–9), Bremmer (1983, 80–7) and *Ogden* (2013, 249–50). For the snake in Laconian art see Salapata 2014, 100–15; 136–8.
9   Stibbe 1991, 11; Hibler 1993, 201.
10 For the meaning and iconographical tradition of the drinking snake, see Salapata 2006, esp. 546–7.
11 Salapata 1993, 191. There is only one example of a Laconian stone relief where a woman holds an oinochoe and pours in the kantharos; other examples are found on terracotta reliefs (eadem, 191).
12 For the heroization of Chilon, see § 5.3.
13 Salapata 2014, 107.
14 Dressel and Milchhöfer 1877.
15 Furtwängler 1883–7, 23–5.
16 Dressel and Milchhöfer 1877, 460, 473; Johansen 1951, 82; Neumann 1979, 17, 21.
17 Todd and Wace 1906, 101.
18 Andronikos 1956, 296–8.
19 Dionysus: Stibbe 1991; see Salapata 1993, 189, n.6–9 for further references.
20 Wace (1937) dates it to *c*. 520 BC; Stibbe 1991, 12, fig. 6, no. A3 dates it to *c*. 550; Kaltsas 2006, 100; Salapata 2014, 347 R10.
21 Rhomaios 1914, 225–6.
22 See Dentzer 1982, 51–60, figs 89–91; cf. Effenberger 1972, 143–4.
23 Salapata 1993, 194, n.67. Compare the motif also to a group of late fifth/early fourth century BC votive reliefs from Attica interpreted to be dedications to heroes, which depict a woman pouring a libation for an armed warrior; Shapiro 2012.
24 Tsouli 2016, 377.
25 I thank Gina Salapata for this suggestion.
26 Tsouli 2016.
27 Hibler 1993, 201; Salapata 2006, 546. On the topic see Hughes 1999.
28 Stibbe 1991, 11, no. D3, fig. 18; Hibler 1993, 201, figs 4–5; Salapata 2006, 545–6, fig. 7.
29 Aristokles Relief (*IG* v.1. 746): Dressel and Milchhöfer 1877, 418, no. 258; Stibbe 1991, no. D7 fig. 20; Salapata 2014, 352 no. R23, pl. 7.27 (Roman period?). Timokles Relief (*IG* v.1.747): Milchhöfer 1879, 127, no. 5, pl. 8; Stibbe 1991, 11, no. E2, fig. 23; Salapata 2014, 346–7 no. R7, pl. 7.3
30 See Salapata 2014, 61–2 on dating and problems of dating repetitive moulds. Terracotta reliefs were common offerings in Greek sanctuaries. Some terracotta reliefs have holes in them for hanging or a part in the back to place standing (like photo-frames); Salapata 2002b, 28–9 and discussion in Salapata 2014, 56–8.
31 For deposits at a hero shrine in Corinth, see Salapata 1997. For deposits in Messene, see Themelis (1988, 157–86) and Peppa-Papaioannou (2012) and for the Hellenistic deposits at Messenia where such terracotta relief reliefs were dedicated at Bronze

Age tombs, see Korres (1981–2; 1988), and Luraghi (2008, 239–45). Deposits of Archaic date were also found in Messenian tombs (Luraghi 2008, 125–6, with bibliography). Rider reliefs at the shrine of Glaukos at Knossos: Callaghan 1978, 21–2, pl. 9. At Troy: Barr 1996; Lawall 2003, 97–9.

32 Artemis Orthia: eight fragments, one of which is described as a piece of relief vase, are dated c. 740 BC, with four fragments from c. 700 BC and one from the fifth century BC. Their iconography consists of a standing couple holding a wreath, a man mounting a chariot, sphinxes, and a warrior (Dawkins, *Orthia,* 154–5; Salapata 2014, 333). Menelaion: one early Archaic example shows three standing draped females and recalls the style of many female figurines found at the site; Thompson, M. S. 1908–9, 121 fig. 3.32; Salapata 2014, 340.
33 Salapata 2014, 63–8.
34 Salapata 2014, 69–95.
35 Salapata 2014, 95–6.
36 Salapata 2014, 96–7 with examples from Amyklai and Messene.
37 There are other miscellaneous subjects, such as a gorgoneion; Salapata 2014, 214–16.
38 The standing triads, whether similar or dissimilar, have been interpreted as worshippers who may appear with attributes, such as wreaths or snakes; Salapata 2014, 176–83. The reliefs bearing dyads in other contexts are usually identified as two closely related deities, such as Demeter and Kore, but in the Spartan examples they lack attributes so their identification is uncertain and they could be worshippers; Salapata 2014, 183–4.
39 From the late sixth century and Classical period onwards, the rider is a common iconographic motif for heroes, often found depicted on heroic votive reliefs of a banquet. By the fourth century, the rider reliefs became common votives to heroes, particularly at Crete and Troy; Salapata 2014, 186–94. For Boiotia see Fossey 2014. The connection of a rider with heroic iconography is evident from Aineias Taktikos (31.15), who describes a wooden votive tablet painted with a horseman that was destined for a hero shrine (πινάκιον ἡρωϊκὸν); Salapata 2014, 201. By the third century BC a horse was represented on the grave *stelai* of the heroized dead in order to define them as heroes; Dentzer 1982, 429–52; Larson 1995, 43–53; Palagia 2003, 144, 146.
40 Salapata 1997.
41 *ThesCRA* I, 143; Lawton 2016. During the fourth century, funerary *stelai* with a banqueter also appear. The difference between the votive and the funerary *stelai*, however, lies in the design of the stele. The funerary ones were long and slim as opposed to the votive ones, which were wider. Moreover, there are no adorants, snake or horse protome on the funerary *stelai* and inscriptions are always provided; Rhomaios 1914, 211; Thönges-Stringaris 1965, 58–62; Dentzer 1982, 529–40; Salapata 2014, 211–13.

42 The *theoxenia* were not exclusive to heroes; a number of divinities also enjoyed this offering; Verbanck-Piérard 1992, 91–2, 96; Jameson 1994, 38, 42; van Straten 1995, 94; Ekroth 2002, 177–9, 280–6.
43 Salapata 2014, 214.
44 Morgan and Whitelaw 1991, 89.
45 Hägg 1987, 99.
46 The specialization of votives among sanctuaries in Sparta is noticeable, primarily with the terracotta and stone reliefs, but also other items, such as the lead figurines (Orthia and Menelaion) and the terracotta masks (at the sanctuary of Orthia but now found in a deposit elsewhere in the city of Sparta from a rescue excavation [personal communication with the E'Ephoreia]). Apollo Maleatas in Laconia was a predominant recipient of offensive weapons (Pavlides 2018). For the multiple interpretations behind the meaning and status of votives see *ThesCRA* I. 269–326; van Straten 1981; Osborne 2004; Kindt 2012, 64–7, 125–30; Patera 2012.
47 There are more deposits or lone findings of terracotta reliefs discovered every year, which appear in the *Archaiologikon Deltion*.
48 For a full discussion of the site, cult, and deposit see Salapata 2014.
49 In literature, the identification of Alexandra with Kassandra appears first in Lykophron's *Alexandra*, written in the early third century BC; Momigliano 1945, 49; Hornblower 2015, 5–7.
50 *Praktika* 1960 230, pl. 171β- γ; *LSAG*^{2}, 447, n.21b; Salapata 2014, 18–19.
51 Salapata 2014, 19. Honorary decree: Sparta Museum 441; *IG* V 1.26; *SIG*^{3} 932; Tod and Wace 1906, 5, 65–6, 177, fig. 54, no. 441; Salapata 2002a, 131–3. Marble throne: *SEG* XXIV 281; *AAA* (1), 44–5, fig. 8; Salapata 2002a, 143, fig. 159.
52 The earliest pottery dates to the first quarter of the seventh century BC; Margreiter 1988, 17, 57; Salapata 2014, 61.
53 See examples in Stibbe 1972, 209, pl. 8.4; 228, no. 109, pl. 34.2; 1994a, 2, 33, 122; 2004, 251, nos 4–5. For the shape see Stibbe 1992.
54 Stibbe 1994, 34, pl. 3.2.
55 See examples in Stibbe 1994a, 2, 87, 212, no. C42, pl. 17.5; 18.1; 2004, 71, 222, no. 44.
56 Stibbe 1972, 228, no. 108, pl. 34; 2000, 20–52; 212, groups A–H, K–P.
57 Stibbe 1972, 257, no. 276, pl. 91.3–4.
58 Stibbe 1972, 225, no. 84, pl. 30.1; 1994, 17, 19; 2004, 207, nos 51–2; Coudin 2009a, 52–3; 'kyathoi': Salapata 2014, 18 n.32.
59 Salapata 2014, 18. Cups: Stibbe 1972, pl. 132, 7. On one example (Sparta Museum 6106), a warrior stands before a seated male. Kraters and krateriskoi: idem 1989b, 19, 21, 48–50, nos F28–30, figs 61–3, G21, G23, H1–2, H6, I1–13, I17–18, 120–25, L14.
60 Stibbe 1976, pl. 5.6; 1991, 36.
61 Stibbe 1994b, 77, fig. 1.
62 Salapata 2014, 16, 217.

63 Salapata 2014, 18.
64 *ArchDelt* (1998) vol. 53 (B1), 173; *AR* 2004–5, 30; Salapata 2014, 18, 20. The identification of the second deposit with the cult of Agamemnon and Alexandra/Kassandra is based on a shard inscribed to Agamemnon; Sparta Museum 14662; *ArchDelt* (1998) vol. 53 (B1), 173. An unidentified large iron object is also reported; *ArchDelt* (1998) vol. 53 (B1), 173.
65 *ArchDelt* (1998) vol. 53 (B1), 173.
66 ibid.
67 Salapata 2002a.
68 Sparta Museum 6231/2; Salapata 1993, 190; 2014, 22–45.
69 Sparta Museum 6233/1+6149/1; Salapata 1993, 192; 2002a, 142, fig. 4 2014, 96–7, pl. 16b–c.
70 On the topic see further: Salapata 2002a, 142–3 n.65.
71 For an Achaian policy in Sparta, see Huxley 1962, 68–71; 1983, 6–8; Kardara 1975; Forrest 1980, 74–6; Calame 1987, 177; Thommen 2000, 47, 52; Cartledge 2002, 137–9, 247–8; Ste Croix 2002, 219; Asheri 2007, 129; Pretzler 2007, 4 (calls it non-Dorian); Cavanagh 2018, 69. Parker 2011, 118 and Nafissi 2016 have raised caution. Phillips 2003 and Pavlides 2021 argue against it.
72 See Salapata 2014, 33–4 and Pavlides 2021, 20–8 on the two different traditions of Agamemnon's kingdom.
73 Finglass 2014, 489.
74 Kunst 1924–5, 22–3; Ferrari 1938, 8, n.1; Podlecki 1971, 315; Malkin 1994, 82; Robertson 1996, 45; West 2013, 265–6, 565–6.
75 Robertson 1996, 459. For the seven Messenian cities see Shipley 2004, 549.
76 Finglass 2014, fr. 177.
77 Finglass 2007, 86, 102–3.
78 Bowra 2001, 114; *contra* Finglass 2014, 28, 489.
79 Hall 1997, 90–1; Bowra 2001, p. 254; *contra* Finglass 2014, 28. We find the same in the *Catalogue of Women* fr. 194 M/W; Hall 1997, 90–1. Other authors also show knowledge of this tradition but sometimes it is inconsistent within authors: Bacchyl. *Dithyramb* 1.48; Ibyc. fr. 1.21 Page, *PMG*; Aisch. *Ag.* 1569, 1602; Gantz 1993, 552–6.
80 Pavlides 2021.
81 t.s. here and thereafter is in reference to 'town square', the modern building blocks of the town of Sparta.
82 *ArchDelt* (1972) vol. 27 (B1), 245, pl. 181α-στ.
83 Salapata 2014, 330.
84 *ArchDelt* (1972) vol. 27 (B1), 242–6. Unfortunately, the material is not fully published and no more information is known of the architectural remains of what is interpreted as a late Geometric/early Archaic house.

85 *ArchDelt* (1972) vol. 27 (B1), 245–6. The inscription, discovered amidst the reliefs, reads 'HE', which makes it impossible to attribute any meaning to it, but perhaps it could be ΗΕΡΟΣ. The material of this plaque is marble and its width is the same as that of the reliefs, prompting the excavators to suggest that the inscriptions and the reliefs may be part of a funeral monument. For the monument and reliefs, see Stibbe 1989a 92–3; Junker 1993, 128–9; Förtsch 2001, 123–4, pls. 96–100.
86 *ArchDelt* (1972) vol. 27 (B1), 240; Steinhauer 1982, 329–41.
87 Steinhauer 1982, 329–41; Förtsch 2001, 123–4.
88 A fragment of a sixth-century terracotta metope was found at Kladas (5 kilometres north of Sparta), *ArchDelt* (2013) vol. 68 (B1), 170, fig. 93; a fragment of a terracotta relief krater from Sparta, published in *ArchDelt* (1964) vol. 19 (A), 174, pl. 85a, is interpreted by Steinhauer (1982, 330) as part of a metope but he gives no explanation for his interpretation. He may be correct because the particular fragment is rendered in much higher relief than the terracotta relief kraters and has traces of red slip; another metope of similar type was discovered recently at the Theophilakos plot (t.s. 113) with a depiction of a hoplite; Vasilogamvrou, Tsouli, and Maltezou 2018, 331, fig. 91d.
89 Barletta (2001, 68) explains that terracotta metopes are relatively thin and require an addition of backer blocks to support the upper structure of the temple.
90 The pottery begins in the Laconian III period (575–550 BC) and ends in the fourth century BC; Steinhauer 1982, 340.
91 *ArchDelt* (1972), vol. 27 (B1), 243, pl. 178στ.
92 *ArchDelt* (1972), vol. 27 (B1), 243.
93 Steinhauer 1982, 329.
94 Steinhauer (1982, 340) compares the scene with that on a proto-Corinthian aryballos (Paris, Musée du Louvre, CA617; *CVA* III 13, pl. (483) 14.1–4.14).
95 Wace 1905–6a, 288.
96 Wace 1905–6a, 288–9.
97 Wace 1905–6a, 291, 292; Stibbe 1994a, 19, 23, 42, 45, 58; Coudin 2009a, 52–3, 59–60.
98 The relief vessels have been called *pithoi*, amphorae and kraters; *ArchDelt* (1964) vol.19 (A), 170–1, 241, 243–4, 246, 259; *ArchDelt* (1972) vol. 27 (B1), 244; Hodkinson 2000, 240–3. I accept Stibbe's (1989b, 65–7; 2004, 240, n.7) designation as kraters because they have wide mouths, wide bellies and, in some cases, volute handles and a narrow foot. Their profile is similar to that of the kraters depicted in sixth-century Laconian vase paintings. The fragments of relief kraters from Sparta with known provenance have been found in religious contexts: six fragments from the Heroon by the Eurotas, five fragments from of the area of a the 'Altar of Lykourgos', three fragments from the area of the theatre, two fragments for the sanctuary of Orthia, one fragment from t.s. 113 and two fragments from t.s. 112–14; Andersen 1977, 66ff.; Förtsch 2001, 100, n.879; the above list is not complete.

99 In his chronology, Wace (1905–6a, 294) specifies that objects are Greek or Hellenistic, indicating that this is the general chronology that he uses sometimes to express dates. Stibbe (2002, 207) also speculates the same regarding Wace's chronology.
100 Wace 1905–6a, 293, fig. 4.
101 Dawkins *Orthia*, 118; Lauter-Bufé 1974, 21.
102 Wace 1905–6a, 288–9.
103 Wace 1905–6a, 293; Stibbe (1994b, 73–4, fig. 12) reports an encircling wall.
104 Wace 1905–6a, 294.
105 Winter 2006, 7 with n.19.
106 Wace 1905–6a, 288–9.
107 See Coldstream (1968, 213) and Coulson (1985, 30) for the Proto-Geometric pottery also found in the area.
108 Raftopoulou 1998, 133; 1996–7, 277–8; Christesen 2018, 319–21 and *infra* § 6.
109 Wace 1905–6a, 288–9.
110 Dickins 1905–6, 295–302.
111 Kourinou-Pikoula 2000, 152.
112 The name of this site 'O 13' is in reference to the British grid system.
113 Stibbe 1989a, 87, n.115.
114 Stibbe 1989a 87, n.115; 1994, 19. Kraters: Stibbe (1989b, 91, fig. 2, no A2); fragment from a stamnos: Stibbe (1984, 10 no. 17).
115 McPhee 1986, 154, fragments 5, A1 (Attic) and A5 (Attic).
116 Since there is no excavation report it is uncertain if all material from the Geometric–Roman times is related.
117 *ArchDelt* (1967), vol. 22 (B1), 201–2; Stibbe 1989, 86–9, figs 15–17; Giannakaki 2008, 7; https://eurotas.wordpress.com/2015/09/29/1794/ (accessed 15/02/2022).
118 *ArchDelt* (1972) vol. 27 (B1), 246–8; Stibbe 1989a, 92–3; Alcock 1991, 463.
119 *ArchDelt* (1972) vol. 27 (B1), 246–8.
120 *ArchDelt* (1972) vol. 27 (B1), 248, pl. 184β.
121 *ArchDelt* (1972) vol. 27 (B1), pls. 184α, γ, δ; 185α–δ; 186α; Stibbe 1989a, 92.
122 Similar bronze protomai have been discovered at the acropolis, the Menelaion and Artemis Orthia; Lamb 1926–7a, 92–3, pl. X.
123 The dimensions would be unusually small for a dining space. See *infra* Stauffert St. (no. 8).
124 Salapata 2014, 331.
125 *ArchDelt* (1968) vol. 23 (B1), 151–2; *ArchDelt* (1969) vol. 24 (B1), 134–5; *AAA* 1, 41–2, pl. 103.
126 *ArchDelt* (1968) vol. 23 (B1), 151; *ArchDelt* (1969) vol. 24 (B1), 134–5. See another such wall from recent excavations at the Oikonomopoulos plot (t.s. 58); Vasilogamvrou, Tsouli, and Maltezou 2018, 33, fig. 11a.

127 Giannakaki 2008, 11.
128 Only the bottom right corner survives, which depicts part of a throne and the legs of a seated couple; *ArchDelt* (1969) vol. 24 (B1), 134–5, pl. 132a; Stibbe 1989a, 89–92, figs 21–6; Salapata 2014, 346, R6.
129 *ArchDelt* (1968) vol. 23 (B1), 152, pl. 103d; *ArchDelt* (1969) vol. 24 (B1), 134–5.
130 As is true elsewhere in Greece, gold leaves as grave goods are rare and indicative of wealth. Other examples were discovered in Sparta for which see *AR* 2002-3, 29; *ArchDelt* (2006) vol. 61, (B1), 186; *ArchDelt* (2004–5) vols 56–9, (B1) 197; *ArchDelt* (2013) vol. 68 (B1), 1223.
131 Giannakaki 2008, 11.
132 Dawkins 1908-9, 3.
133 Stibbe 1989a, 92, figs 25–6; Förtsch 2001, 100.
134 The site and finds remain unpublished. I owe this information to Flouris (2000, 14), who reports having heard this from the excavator Spyropoulos. The site is mentioned also in Zavvou and Themos 2009, 116. One of the terracotta reliefs depicts a hoplite mounting a chariot, which is rare among the terracotta reliefs; Kaltsas 2006, 208, n.102.
135 Flouris (2000, 14) agrees with the cultic nature of the subterranean structure.
136 Salapata 2014, 331–2.
137 § 1.2.
138 I am grateful to Christos Flouris for giving me access to his unpublished dissertation on the terracotta reliefs found at the site.
139 *ArchDelt* (1996), vol. 51 (B1), 123–5.
140 For Geometric burials in Sparta see *ArchDelt* (1972) vol. 27 (B1), 242, 244–5; Raftopoulou 1996, 280; Flouris 2000, 4–5; Christesen 2018, 320–1.
141 Flouris 2000, 16.
142 *ArchDelt* (1996), vol. 51(B1), 123–5; Flouris 2000, 33–129. See also a possible example of a standing woman holding a kantharos (idem 130, no. 13465, pl. 120).
143 Flouris 2000, 17.
144 Flouris 2000, 18, pl. 17.
145 Flouris 2000, 17, pls. 12–16, 19.
146 Flouris 2000, 18.
147 Flouris 2000, 69, n.146; Salapata 2014, 355, no. R47. The inscription is too fragmentary to make out a name.
148 Votive material mixed together with ash and bone is commonly found in sanctuaries. Alroth (1988, 203) speculates that the votives could have been displayed on the altar or near it and then deposited together during cleaning of a sanctuary.
149 Flouris 2000, 17.
150 Flouris 2000, 130, no. 13470, pl. 120.

151 The excavation did not reach the whole length of the wall.
152 Flouris 2000, 16, pl. 10.
153 Tosti 2011, 102–3. For the *lesche* see § 6.1 n. 68.
154 Bergquist 1990, 38 for the common characteristics of dining rooms in the Greek world.
155 Nevett 2012, 50–7.
156 Bergquist 1990, 38, 44–5, and see table I.
157 Bergquist 1990, 44; Dunbabin 1998, 88. At the sanctuary of Demeter and Kore at Corinth rooms measure between 3.60 metres and 4.60 metres with a few as much as 5 metres per side; Bookidis and Stroud 1997, 396. See also the eighth-century house from Thorikos in Attika where a room features with three benches on its sides. Nevett (2012, 51–2) remarks on the small dimensions, which would pose difficulty for reclined dining. She suggests that the raised areas may be used for storage rather than benches (eadem).
158 For a possible example of seated dining see Nevett 2012, 52. On dining postures and their social significance see Roller 2006.
159 Marinatos 1936, 257–8.
160 Alroth 1988, 199–201.
161 Bonias 1998, 28–9, figs 2–3. Benches can sometimes be used for both display of offerings and sitting; Alroth 1988, 196 n.7
162 Jameson 1994.
163 Ekroth 2009, 132–4.
164 *Theoxenia* for the Dioskouroi may be attested in an incident described by Pausanias (3.16.3) when the Spartan Phormion is punished for not being as hospitable to the twin heroes.
165 Vlachou 2018, 111.
166 *ArchDelt* 1996) vol. 51(B1), 123–5. No further information regarding the date of the second room is reported.
167 The length of the walls in the room have similar dimensions to those of room A. Wall 36 belongs to both rooms and the excavation did not reach its full length.
168 The excavation did not reach the whole length of the wall.
169 *ArchDelt* (2001–4) vols 56–9 (B1), 179.
170 *ArchDelt* (2001–4) vols 56–9 (B1), 179–80. This type of tile is commonly found in various locations is Sparta (e.g., at the sanctuary of Artemis Orthia, the Heroon by the Eurotas, the sanctuary by the Megalopolis road) and does not mean that the shrine belongs to Athena. The name Athena is in connection with the factory attached to the shrine of Athena Alea, which produced the tiles; Wace 1905–6b, 346–7; 1906–7, 28–31.
171 *ArchDelt* (2006) vol. 61 (B1), 275.

172 *ArchDelt* (1996) vol. 51 (B1), 101–3, 103, pl. 41α–β.
173 *ArchDelt* (1996) vol. 51 (B1), 101–3; *ArchDelt* 52, 160–2; Raftopoulou 1998, 133, fig. 12.14. The area also produced two later burials, one of which contained a marble urn; Poupaki 2009, 248.
174 Due to the proximity of the two deposits it is likely that the votives at the Bougadis plot and Gitiada Street belong to the same cult site; cf. Salapata 2014, 339.
175 *ArchDelt* (1973) vol. 28 (B1), 166–7, pls.145–6; Salapata 2014, 346, nos R4–5, 350 no. R26.
176 *ArchDelt* (1973) vol. 28 (B1), 166.
177 Flouris 2000, 133–4; *ArchDelt* (1997) vol. 52 (B1), 177.
178 Raftopoulou 1998, 127, fig. 12.4.
179 Tsouli 2014, 145. See another such Roman period household cult to Dionysus found at t.s. 115; eadem 2014.
180 Salapata 2014, 333.
181 Kourinou-Pikoula 1987–8, 477.
182 Salapata 2014, 333, R50.
183 Salapata 2014, 333; The terracotta lion-head is published by Kourinou-Pikoula (1987–8, 477–8, pl. ΞH, 2).
184 See *supra* n. 173.
185 *ArchDelt* (2001–4) vols 56–59 (B1), 262; Zavvou and Themos 2009, 116, 118, fig. 11.29; Salapata 2014, 334.
186 Korres 1988, 322 n.45; cf. Salapata 2014, 334, 339; Steinhauer 2020, 263.
187 Steinhaer 2020, 272–3.
188 Stibbe 1991, 38, 43, fig. 39, no. A12; Salapata 2014, 334 n.29.
189 *ArchDelt* (1997) vol. 52 (B1), 179, pl. 79β–γ.
190 *ArchDelt* (1997) vol. 52 (B1), 178–9.
191 *ArchDelt* (1999) vol. 54 (B1), 159–60, fig.4; Zavvou and Themos 2009, 116, fig. 11.22; kourotrophic figurine: Sparta Museum 13430–13449; Daedalic figurine: Sparta Museum 13406; terracotta plaque: Sparta Museum 13397.
192 *ArchDelt* (1982) vol. 37 (B1) 112, pl. 59γ.
193 *ArchDelt* (1973–4) vol. 29 (B2), pl. 185γ.
194 *ArchDelt* (1973–4) vol. 29 (B2), 286–7.
195 *ArchDelt* (1973–4) vol. 29 (B2), pl. 185β.
196 Salapata 2014, 338, R42.
197 *ArchDelt* (1973–4) vol. 29 (B2), 286–7.
198 Compare with Winter 1993, 106 I, Ia, pl. 31.
199 *ArchDelt* (1973–4) vol. 29 (B2), 287. Acroteria depicting the Dioskouroi as riders are not uncommon, especially in South Italy (in Taras and Lokroi) and Sicily (in Akragas, Gela and Syracuse); Szeliga 1981; Eaverly 1995, 59–61.

200 *ArchDelt* (1973–4) vol. 29 (B2), pl. 185στ.
201 The finds are unpublished; see note in Salapata 2014, 337 no. 40 n.41.
202 *ArchDelt* (1973–4) vol. 29 (B2), 291–2, pl. 188a–b.
203 *ArchDelt* (1973–4) vol. 29 (B2), 291–2, pl. 188α–β.
204 *ArchDelt* (1996) vol. 51 (B1), 118–19.
205 *ArchDelt* (1996) vol. 51 (B1), 119–20.
206 *ArchDelt* (1996) vol. 51 (B1), 185.
207 *ArchDelt* (2001–4) vols 56–9 (B1), 196.
208 *ArchDelt* (2001–4) vols 56–9 (B1), 265–8.
209 *ArchDelt* (2001-4) vols 56–9 (B1), 275.
210 Salapata 2014, 337 no. 38.
211 *ArchDelt* (1997) vol. 52 (B1), 181–3, pl. 81α.
212 Zavvou and Themos 2009, 116, 118–19; *ArchDelt* (2001-4) vols 56–9 (B1), 237–40.
213 Dickins 1906–7b, 169–73; Cook, 1950, 273, n. 29; Stibbe 1991, 20 n. 57, 38, 43; 2002; Salapata 2014, 329.
214 Aryballoi: Stibbe 2000, B40–41; C33, G15, M12; Krateriskos: Stibbe 1989b, 119 no. I19, fig. 115.
215 Stibbe 1991, 38, fig. 40, no. a13.
216 Stibbe 2002, 218–19, nos 40–1, figs 43–4, 47.
217 Dickins 1906–7b, 169.
218 Dickins 1906–7b, 170; Stibbe 2002, 219 fig. 48.
219 Stibbe 2002, 212–13, nos 4–17.
220 There are three reported Mycenaean pottery fragments, which Stibbe (1989, 96, fig. 31; 2002, 211–12, cat. nos 1–3) sees as evidence that the cult originated in Mycenaean times.
221 Cf. Salapata 2014, 209, 214.
222 Dickins 1906–7b, 172.
223 Stibbe (2002, 210, cat. nos 33–9, figs 36–41) suggests Hellenistic. For a fourth or third century date see Rolley 1976, 112–13, nos B 33–4.
224 Stibbe 2002, 2010 n.25.
225 Usually taken to mean pre-Hellenistic.
226 The early excavator does not see a connection between the earlier and later wall (Dickins 1906–7b, 171) although Stibbe (2002, 209) suggests otherwise.
227 Stibbe 2002, 208.
228 Winter 1993, 108.
229 Dickins 1906–7b, 171–2.
230 Stibbe 2002, 209 n.16.
231 Dickins 1906–7b, 172.
232 *ArchDelt* (1996) vol. (51) B1, 130.

Chapter 3

1. Antonaccio 2005, 100.
2. Orthia: Dawkins *Orthia* 146, pl. XXX, XXX, 2. Menelaion: Thompson 1908–9, 121–2, pl. 3.33 and § 4.1.
3. Müller 1915, 45–6; Romano 1995, 24, 26–8; cf. Merker 2000, 133; Ammerman 2002, 23, 36, 78–86, 135.
4. Miniature vessels are often an indicator of cult activity; Hammond 2009, 143.
5. Dickins 1906–7b, 173.
6. Voyatzis 1990, 80–1; Hammond 1998.
7. Williams 1989, 65; Bookidis 1993, 54.
8. Hammond 2009, 141–4; Barfoed 2015
9. Biers 1971, 397–8, 414–15.
10. The miniature vases could be a substitute for more expensive offerings; Hammond 2009, 144.
11. Ekroth 2003, 36.
12. Introduction n.65.
13. The dedication of perishable items, such as fruit or cakes is well documented in Greek sanctuaries and supported epigraphically, e.g., on the deme calendar from Marathon (*IG*² 1358 column II 4, 30); Kopestonsky 2018, 245–7. Greeks also dedicated 'first fruits' (*aparchai*); Jim 2014.
14. Barfoed 2015.
15. Pilz 2011, 17.
16. Catling 1992, nos 55–7.
17. Catling, R. 1992, 58–70.
18. See Stibbe (1989b; 1994) for Laconian kraters and other drinking vessels from the sanctuaries of Sparta and abroad. The absence of such forms from residential contexts in Sparta can be explained by the fact that there is little archaeological evidence surviving from houses of Archaic and Classical Sparta. For drinking in Sparta in general, see Nafissi 1991, 175–7, 215–24; Powell 1998; Hodkinson 2000, 216–17; and Rabinowitz 2009.
19. Coudin 2009a, 52–3, 54–5, 58ff.
20. Dawkins *Orthia* 106–7.
21. Coudin 2009a, 59–60.
22. Stroszeck 2014, 138, 143.
23. cf. McPhee 1986, 155; Stroszeck 2014, 142.
24. For the *kothon* as an outdoor and military use item, see van Wees 2018b, 243 with sources. This may explain why it is not found in the heroic shrines. The *kothon* is also not seen on symposium scenes of Laconian vase painting; idem, 250.
25. Stroszeck 2014, 144.

26 Rabinowitz 2009, 170, n.25; cf. Stroszeck 2014, 138.
27 For the majority of sites, however, we lack the evidence of sacrifice and subsequent dining since no animal bones are reported. It could be that the remains of meals are collected and disposed elsewhere and were not found within the buried votive deposits. See similarly at the shrine of Opheltes at Nemea; Bravo 2018, 182.
28 Rabinowitz 2009, 114; van Wees 2018b, 236, 251. Literary evidence attests to restraints in drinking practice in Sparta in the Classical period, e.g. Critias, while contrasting the Athenian symposium to the Spartan drinking practices at the *syssition*, mentions that the Spartans drank from the own cup and did not offer toasts (fr. 6 West =Athen. *Deipn.*10.432d; cf. 11. 4633; cf. Xen. *Lak. Pol.* 5.6).
29 Rabinowitz 2009, 124–8.
30 There is also evidence of ritual banquets in funerary contexts in Sparta; Tsouli 2016. Catling (2002, 193–4) reports of drinking shapes in residential contexts in rural Laconia after 550 BC.
31 Rabinowitz 2009, 126–7; cf. Nafissi 1991, 239–53.
32 Paris, Musée du Louvre E 667 by the Naukratis Painter: Pipili 1987, 71, fig. 103, no. 194; Stibbe 1972, no. 13, pl. 6.1. Samos Archaeological Museum K 1445: Stibbe 1972, no. 19; Pipili 1987, no. 202. Samos Archaeological Museum K 1203, K 1541, K 2404: Stibbe 1972, no. 191, pl. 58; Pipili 1987, 72–3, nos 196, 204b. Samos Archaeological Museum K 2073: Stibbe 1972 no. 215, pl. 71. Museo Nazionale di Taranto 20909: Stibbe 1972, no. 312, pl. 110). The same winged figures are also seen around riders or divinities on Laconian vases (Pipili 1987, 76). The rider has been interpreted as part of a religious procession for a festival (eadem). For the winged creatures around a divinity, see Pipili 1987, 41; 1998, 87–9, figs 8.5–8.
33 Pipili 1987, 75; 1998, 83; Smith 1998, 78; Powell 1998, 126; Rabinowitz 2009, 123.
34 Pipili 1987, fig. 107, no. 208; Smith 1998, 76, fig. 7.1; 2010, 130, pl. 26C.
35 Coudin 2009a; 2009b; Pipili 2018, 139–42.
36 Pipili 2018, 146.
37 Henrichs 1983, 98–9; Ekroth 2002, 67, 75, 109. For blood libations see Ekroth (2002, 265–8; 2012 104–5).
38 Hoffmann 1989.
39 Fuchs 1961, 179.
40 Bérard 1969, 74–6.
41 Bravo 2018, 32, 41–2 figs 68–9.
42 Kalydon: Dyggve, Poulsen, and Romaios 1934, 31–2, 70–1, 94; Kalaureia: Welter 1941, 51–2, pl. 44. For dining at Greek temples see Mazarakis Ainian (2017b, 178–80) with examples and bibliography.
43 Antonaccio 1995, 249.
44 See Boehringer 2001, 311–18.
45 Ekroth 2012.

46 Personal communication with R. Catling.
47 Vlachou 2018.
48 Hodkinson 2009, 488–9.
49 Tsouli 2016, 371–7.
50 cf. Tosti 2011.
51 In Classical Sparta, communal dining at the messes was mandatory and part of an *homoios*' lifestyle. It was so important that if one could not afford the contributions of food and wine, he would lose his status as an *homoios* (Ar. *Pol*. 1271a27–37). Each man belonged to a group with he dined as a public mess hall (Plut. *Lyc.*12.2); van Wees 2018, 236–8.
52 See for example Dawkins 1929, figs 77, 80, 81. Publications by Stibbe (1986, 1989, 1994, 2000) offer more but there is still very little material belonging to the fifth century. See also McPhee 1986, 153 n.3 for bibliography.
53 There is little discussion on the shapes and uses of pottery from Laconian sanctuaries in the Classical period. Thus, the history of Laconian pottery has been misleading and, as Prost (2018, 170–1) remarks, there should be a distinction between 'Laconian craftsmanship and Laconian art'.
54 See for example the fifth-century vases in Stibbe (1994, 75–85).
55 Stibbe 1994, 75.
56 Stibbe 1989, figs 1, 3.
57 Stibbe 2000, 64 no. F13 fig. 137, pl. 11.2
58 Stibbe 2000, 78.
59 See Stibbe 1986, 87, pl.50.1–50.2; 1989, 41, 44–5, 58–9, 127, no. L for fifth-century kraters from Amyklai (one with graffito dedication to Agamemnon); cf. Förtsch 2001, 188. Fifth-century kraters are reported in Sparta and are also exported; Förtsch 2001, 188.
60 These carry the names of Agamemnon and Alexandra in graffiti and dipinti (see Salapata 2014, p X for references).
61 Zavvou *et al.* 1998, 173 (e.g., ΑΓΑΜΕΜΝ[ΟΝΙ]: SM 14662).
62 Stibbe 1972, 43, pl. 132.6–7 (kylikes, aryballoi, lakainai, kyathoi).
63 Salapata 2006, 547 n.21.
64 Hodkinson 2000, 216–56; 2018, 43.
65 Boardman 1963; Cavanagh and Laxton 1984; Cavanagh *forthcoming*; Boss 2000; Gill and Vickers 2001. They have been found also in other areas in the Peloponnese, such as Perachora, the Argive Heraion, and Apollo Maleatas at Epidaurus. See Boss (2000, 218–23) for find-spots outside Sparta.
66 Boardman 1963.
67 Boss 2000, 146–77, 232.
68 The difference of the dedicatory patters of the lead figurines among the hero cults may be pure chance of survival. Another possibility is that there was specialisation

among the votives dedicated at specific sites. This dedicatory pattern is observed among the main Spartan sanctuaries where the sanctuary of Artemis Orthia and the Menelaion were appropriate places for lead figurines but the Amyklaion and the sanctuary of Athena Chalkioikos did not receive them in large numbers.

69 Cavanagh *forthcoming*; Boss 2000, 197.
70 Hodkinson 1998.
71 For the Menelaion and the Amyklaion § 4.1 and 4.2.
72 Hodkinson 1998, 59 table 5.3. The patterns of bronze dedications are not consistent for all Spartan sanctuaries – while Orthia and the Menelaion show a decrease of metal votives after 550, the Amyklaion and the Akropolis exhibit an increase. There is also variation in typology, e.g. jewellery types appear to decrease by the mid-sixth century, while statuettes and figurines exhibit an increase. The bronzes, specifically of bells, moreover, are maintained on the Acropolis into the fifth century and even into the later fifth century; Hodkinson 1998, 57–8.
73 Hodkinson 1998, 60. Snodgrass 2006, 260–1. See idem (262–7) for a discussion behind the possible reasons for the change of pattern of dedications.
74 Whitley 2001, 311–13.
75 For example, many of the Archaic bronzes from Orthia have survived because the layer of sand placed ocer them in the early sixth century aided the survival of earlier bronzes.
76 Hodkinson 1998; Förtsch 1998; 2001.
77 Herfort-Koch 1986.
78 Herfort-Koch 1986, 19–47, 50–4, 54–9; Hodkinson 1998 59 table 3; Förtsch 1998, 53 table 4.1; 2001, 221–4.
79 Förtsch 1998.
80 Hodkinson 1998.
81 Stibbe 1996.
82 Palagia 1993.
83 However, some ostentatious votive offerings were placed in Spartan sanctuaries and abroad, as for example the statues of Pausanias in Sparta by the altar of Athena Chalkioikos (Förtsch 1998, 54; Prost 2018, 73), the dedications of Lysander at the sanctuary of Athena Ergane on the Spartan Acropolis (Paus. 3.17.4) or the Spartan dedication at Delphi honouring Lysander's victory at Aegospotamoi (Scott 2010, 105–7).
84 Prost 2018, 172.
85 Hodkinson (2018, 44–50) discusses the persisting evidence of wealthier individuals in Spartan society in the fifth and fourth centuries and their ability to influence various aspects of the public sphere.
86 Nafissi 1991; Förtsch 2001; on the topic see also the recent discussion in Prost 2018, 172–3.

87 Förtsch 1998, 54.
88 Salapata 2014, 231.
89 Salapata 2014, 231.
90 Antonaccio 1995, 104–9; Boehringer 2001, 53, table 1.
91 Broneer 1942, 144; Williams and Fisher 1972, 149; Pfaff 2003, 128. For other Corinthian examples, see the stele-shrines built over earlier houses (Stillwell 1952, 22–8; 31–2; 41–2; 49–53; Williams 1978, 2–12; 1981, 411–12). One particular example is the South Stoa stele-shrine, which was given numerous terracotta figurines of horses and riders, standing korai, birds and banqueters, as well as votive pottery; Williams 1978, 5–12; 1981; Pfaff 2003, 128. See also a third century BC deposit, which contained a number of terracotta figurines, lamps and terracotta miniature shields, discovered at the eastern end of the South Stoa in Corinth. Broneer interpreted the material as heroic offerings.
92 Williams and Fisher 1973, 10–12, no. 12; Williams, MacIntosh and Fisher 1974, 3–4, no. 1 pl.1.
93 Antonaccio 1995, 121–6; Boehringer 2001, 68–72.
94 Alexandridou 2017, 284–6.
95 Antonaccio 1995, 102–26; Boehringer 2001, 47–131.
96 Bravo 2018, 183–296.
97 Depictions of such shrines are commonly found on Hellenistic reliefs; Williams 1981, 408 n.4 with references.
98 Williams 1981, 409ff.; Bookidis 2003, 253; Merker 2003, 237, fig. 14.8.
99 Bookidis 2003, 253.
100 Hall 1995, 601–3.
101 Vikela 2011, 167. For roadside shrines in Athens see also Costaki (2008); Best (2015).
102 Best 2015, 103.
103 Best 2015, 100–2, figs 10.2–3; cf. Lalonde 2006, 23, 67. See also the altar of Zeus Herkeios, Hermes and Akamas inside the Dipylon Gate; Best 2015, 104.
104 Hägg 1987, 99.
105 Pedley 2005, 121.
106 Vikela 2011, 167 and n.232.
107 For the possible identification of the shrine see Kourinou (2000, 167–84). Among the finds were eighteen Hellenistic marble reliefs, some of anatomical parts, and inscriptions to Kyparissia. But see also Salapata (2001), who has reservations that all the material belongs to the same cult; cf. Pavlides 2018 299, n.112.
108 For the relief, see Salapata (2014, R1 and R2); they are almost identical. The rooster, the egg and the flower as dedications may have multiple meanings. Often associated with fertility, youth, chthonic deities, and symbols of life, they can be offered to the dead, heroes or gods and not one meaning is sufficient; Salapata

2014, 139–41. The rooster appears also on a number of terracotta reliefs (Salapata 2014, 141, nos SEA 1/16 and 1/19).

109 The motif is unusual in Greek Archaic art as normally worshippers and deities do not to appear in the same space, nor are the worshippers diminutive; Salapata 2014, 131–2. See for example the famous pinax from Pitsa, c. 530 BC; Berger 1970, 104 and Neumann 1979, 27, fig. 12a. On the iconography of the donors, see *ThesCRA*, I 284–7; van Straten 2000, 216–23. There is only one known example that dates earlier than the Laconian reliefs, a stele from Prinias (Lembessi 1976, 93–4, A5 pl. 6–7; Neumann 1979: 19, pl. 5A; Edelmann 1999, 14, A1, fig.1) on which a small figure stands next to a warrior, gesturing and offering him a flower. Since the Prinias reliefs are funerary, this relief is sometimes seen to be a predecessor of the Classical grave reliefs. It is only in the Classical period that depictions of adorants and divinities are shown together, as in an Attic relief with Athena which dates from the early fifth century (c. 490–480 BC); Berger 1970, 109, fig. 129; Comella 2002, 19, fig. 11.

110 Salapata 2014, 351–2, nos R31, R32 with bibliography.

111 *ArchDelt* (1962) vol. 17 (B1), 85, pl. 94γ.

112 Themelis 2000, 21–2, fig. 17; Salapata 2014, 130, pl. 8.6.

113 Flouris 2000, 55, 84, 105, pl.86; cf. Salapata 2014, 131.

114 Salapata 2014, 100, no. SEA 1/164

115 Salapata 2014, 181–3.

116 Salapata 2009, 333–4; 2014, 182.

117 The terracotta reliefs themselves were not awarded distinct identifiable characteristic of heroes. An exception is a relief from the votives to Agamemnon and Alexandra/Kassandra, where a seated male holds a staff, possibly an attribute of Agamemnon as king and possibly representing him; Salapata 1993, 194. On another from the same deposit, a female sits alone, and this figure is probably Alexandra/Kassandra; Salapata 2014, 96–7. The lack of inscriptions on the terracotta reliefs is due to their inexpensive nature. Created from moulds, like terracotta figurines, these votives were not produced as individual commissions; Salapata 2002b, 22–3. Any inscription would have to be done before firing and would have to be commissioned.

118 Dentzer 1982, 453–4; van Straten 1995, 96; Shapiro 2012, 118.

119 van Straten 1995, 95, n.289. The inscription is from Olbia.

120 For example, there is a fourth-century inscription from Attica where the hero is called *eukolos* (Thönges-Stringaris 1965, 81, no. 92) and another also of the fourth century (Thönges-Stringaris 1965, 95, no. 174) and Asklepios is called *eukolos* on a first- or second-century AD inscription from Epidauros (*IG* IV^2 I, 469; van Straten 1995, 95, n.291).

121 This inscription is from Athens, van Straten 1995, 96, n.296.

122 See Thönges-Stringaris (1965, 56–8), van Straten (1995, 95) with references and other examples.
123 Salapata 2014, 130, no. S 1/162.
124 Salapata 2014, 131.
125 *ArchDelt* (1961–2) vol. 17 (B1), 85, pl. 94γ.
126 Schmitt Pantel 2012, 1–7; Parker 2015; Kindt 2015.
127 Parker 2015, 72.
128 Tomlinson 1992, 253.
129 Tsountas 1892; Fiechter 1918; Buschor and von Masssow 1927 figs 22–3; Tomlinson 2008; see also excavation reports at the *Amykles Research Project*: www.amyklaion.gr.
130 Dickins 1906–7a, 142–6; cf. Tomlinson 1992, 247.
131 Catling 1976–7, 37.
132 The material from the Nikolarou plot is unpublished. The plot (in t.s. 113) produced a few fragmentary reliefs and what may be either a terracotta acroterion or an antefix depicting a gorgoneion; Salapata 2014, 333 and n.25.
133 Winter 1993, 101–4, 138. See also Kästner (1990, 251–4) and Förtsch (2001, 210–14) for a full list and discussion of the acroteria.
134 Dawkins *Orthia*, 118–26; Winter 1993, 101–4,138.
135 Winter 1993, 97.
136 Winter 1993 97, 101–3.
137 Kästner 1990, 256, C7; Winter 1993, 101; Förtsch 1998, 51.
138 Winter 1993, 107.
139 Dawkins *Orthia* 139, no. 29 G; Winter 1993, 107, type I, variant ib.
140 cf. Salapata 2014, 219.
141 Simple rectangular shrines existed in Arcadia too but were replaced in the sixth century by peripteral Doric temples; Østby 2005; cr. Tomlinson 2008, 323.
142 Tomlinson 1992, 253; 2008, 323.
143 Dawkins *Orthia*; Tomlinson 1992, 248; Cavanagh 2018, 67.
144 *AR* 1976–7, 34, fig. 21. Catling 1995, 323.
145 Dickins 1906–7a, 142–3.
146 The excavation generated considerable archaic material, among which were a large number of miniature vases; *Praktika* 1962, 115–16; *ArchDelt* (1963) vol. 18 (B1), 86; *AR* 1962–3, 18; Cavanagh *et al.* 1996, 289, 78).
147 Schattner 1990, 92, no. 40, fig. 44, pl. 27.3–4, 50.
148 Catling 1994, 274.
149 Catling 1995, 317.
150 Catling (1994, 274; 1995, 317 n.2) mentions the existence of nine models from Sparta.
151 Catling 1995.

152 Catling 1994, 271–2. See also another fragments (now lost) in Dawkins *Orthia* (159, no 10, pl. 42.8). An unfinished model from the Menelaion (*c.* 570/60) also has a Doric entablature; Schattner 1990, 92–4, no. 50, fig. 44, pls. 27, 3–4, 28.
153 Fragments of poros sculpture depicting lions decorated the sixth-century temple of Artemis Orthia; Dawkins *Orthia* 387, nos 1–2, pl. 5.
154 Travlos 1971, 148, 151; Mark 1993, 42–52.
155 Best 2015, 102–3.
156 Travlos 1971, 151; Costaki 2008, 158; Greco 2010, 166.
157 Travlos 1971, 151; Greco 2010, 255–6; Wycherley 1970, 291.
158 Bonias 1998, 30–1.
159 Salapata 2014, 217.
160 On the topic see further discussion in § 6.1.
161 Williams 1981, 418.
162 For the location of cult sites see Zaidman and Pantel (1992, 55) and for heroes specifically Kearns (1992, 71–2). Some heroa can be associated with a cult of a divinity with whom they may be tied in myth, as for example the grave of Hyakinthos at the throne of Apollo at Amyklai. Other times, heroa are located in a space that signifies their importance in the civic and religious unity of the polis, such as the agora, a major road of the city, or around a centralized cult place, such as a major sanctuary.
163 Costaki 2008 and Vikela 2011 on the archaeological evidence from Athens. Kearns (2010, 152–61) collects and comments on some texts that deal with shrines in households and in neighbourhoods.
164 Vikela 2011, 146.
165 Zaitman and Pantel 1992, 55; Vikela 2011, 141–6. For the variety of cult places associated with hero cults see Ekroth 2009, 126–30.
166 Rusten 1983.
167 Burkert 1985, 276 wrote that 'Greek religion, bound to the polis, is public religion to an extreme degree'. The omission of small shrines and the personal relationship of people and the divine is evident in scholarship, e.g. Buxton 2000 and Ogden 2007 although van Straten (2000, 216–22) discusses the relationship between the worshippers and the recipients of cult. Instone (2009) collects literary sources that deal with the way gods and individuals interacted and the ways that individuals thought they could make 'contact' with the divine. Purvis (2003) explores the foundation of private cults in the Greek world. On this topic, see also Rask 2016.
168 See also Pindar's *P.* 8.56–60; and Sophocles' *Oid. t.* 919; Rusten 1983. There are other many examples of small shrines, such as Herms, or shrines to Hekate at crossroads, near houses or by streets.
169 Pritchett 1953, 272 (stele 6, lines 78–9); Wycherley 1970, 286; Costaki 2008, 152–3.
170 Meritt 1936, 400; Wycherley 1970, 286.

171 Wycherley, 1970, 287, n.12.
172 Wycherley 1959, 67.
173 Astrabacus was also close to the temple of Artemis Orthia (Paus. 3.16.6), perhaps because of his relationship with the divinity. According to myth, he and his brother Alopekos lost their sanity when they found the xoanon of Artemis Orthia, which had been brought to Sparta by Orestes (Paus. 3.16.9).
174 For cults dedicated to the domestic sphere in Sparta, see Zeus Herkeios (Hdt. 6.68.1); Poseidon Domatites (Paus. 3.14.7). A Roman date inscription (*IG* v. 1.497) mentions Karneios Oiketas and Poseidon Domateitas. Priesthoods of the cult were hereditary κατὰ γένος (*IG* v. 1. 589, 487).
175 See Rusten (1983, 293–5); and Rohde (2000, 155, n.136) for a discussion of shrines in front of gates, e.g. Euripides' *Heraclid* 609.
176 Wycherley 1970, 286.
177 This fable may be an example of a discovery of an older grave that was given heroic honours by later generations. For another case explaining the reason for setting up a shrine, see Theophrastos (*Char.* 16.4), in which we are told that if anyone sees a red snake in his house, he should call on Sabazius but if he sees a snake of the sacred kind, he should build a shrine then and there (Rusten 1983, 294; Kearns 2010, 153).
178 Best 2015, 105.
179 See Athenian examples for stones given to Hermes and monthly food offerings to Hekate in Best (2015, 105).
180 Other examples include Aesop's fab. 112, where a hero's shrine near the house did not help the man with his offerings. In Artemidoros' *Oneirocrites* 4.78 he advises that the appearance of a dejected hero in a dream means that the hero's shrine has been neglected (cf. Costaki 2008, 152).
181 Dodds 1973, 153; Rusten 1983, 295; Zaidman and Pantel 1992, 80–1. Of course, not all small sanctuaries were located in habitation areas; many, were located near religious centres, such as the Athenian Acropolis; see Wycherley 1970.
182 Dodds 1973, 150.
183 Salapata 2002b, 31; 2014, 58.
184 Parker 1989, 144; Taita 2001, 69–70.
185 From Herodotus we also hear that the heralds, the musicians and the sacrifices also inherit their trade (Hdt. 6.60).
186 Taita 2001, 69–70.
187 Jones 1999; Vlassopoulos 2007, 69–99; 143–55; Gabrielsen and Thomsen 2015.
188 Kearns 1989, 65–72. There were also gene without a heroic ancestor; Kearns 1989, 71.
189 Parker 1996, 58.
190 Daux 1983, 153–4; Parker 1986, 38; Ekroth 2002, 138.

191 Ferguson and Nock 1944; Kearns 1989, 73–7; Parker 1996, 109–11, 337–40; Arnaotouglou 2015.
192 Smaller-group activities could co-exist in Sparta beyond the communal lifestyle of messes, military training and the *agoge* in the form of team ball games, chorus, attendance at the *gymnasium* and hunting (Plut. *Lyc.* 12.2; Hodkinson 2018, 45–6).
193 Hodkinson 2009, 488–9.
194 Astrabacus is also famously credited as being the father of King Demaratus (Hdt. 6.69.3).
195 Better documented evidence of shrines by houses, or actually inside houses, comes from Analipsis-Vourvoura, identified as ancient Iasos, by the Laconian border with the Argolid; McPhee 1986, 154, n.9. In an ancient settlement with both public and private buildings, in the interior of the houses were found triangular, semi-circular or rectangular constructions for household cults. Within these were unearthed vases with many red-figure examples of the late fifth and early fourth centuries; Karouzou 1985; Stroszeck 2014, 138, 141–9, nos 1–6, 12, 14, 16, 17.
196 The area produced even more unpublished terracotta reliefs. See the Nikolarou plot, Nikolopoulou plot, and Loumou plot in Salapata 2014, 333–4, nos 17, 18, 20.
197 See Salapata 2014, 125, Map 1.
198 *ArchDelt* (1992) vol. 47 (B1), 105.
199 *ArchDelt* 1999) vol. 54 (B1), 168–71, pl. 14, figs 15–17; Zavvou and Themos 2009, 113.
200 *ArchDelt* (1992) vol. 47 (B1), 105; *ArchDelt* (1996) vol. 51 (B1), 123.
201 Zavvou and Themos 2009, 117–18.
202 Zavvou and Themos 2009, 118–19.
203 Christesen 2018, 337–8.
204 A roadside shrine was unearthed at t.s. 256 on the south of Sparta where a votive deposit of Classical and Hellenistic material was found by the remains of a road; *ArchDelt* (1995) vol. 50 (B1), 124.
205 *ArchDelt* (1972) vol. 27 (B1), 245.
206 Christesen 2018, 333; *ArchDelt* (2011) vol. 66 (B1), 163–5; *ArchDelt* (2014) vol. 69 (B1a), 453–7.
207 For μνῆμα in relation to burials in Pausanias see Larson 1995, 12–13; Ekroth 2002, 94 n.297.
208 Kearns 1992, 72.
209 Parker 1996, 19–20.
210 On the Herakleidai and the Dorian identity of the Spartans see Pettersson 1992, 108; Malkin 1994, 15–45; Hall 2000, 60–3.
211 Wace 1937; Stibbe 1991, 12; Kourinou 2000, 148–9.
212 See a similar setting around the Athenian acropolis, Wycherley 1970.

213 Wycherley 1970.
214 Most scholars agree that it is located east of the theatre, on the eastern part of the Palaiokastro hill because Pausanias walked west from the agora to the direction of the theatre (3.14.1) and because of architectural remains interpreted as those of the Persian Stoa and the Skias. For the debate and bibliography of the location of the Spartan Agora see Stibbe 1989a, 65–6; Kourinou 2000, 99–129; Greco 2011; Baudini 2006, Fouquet 2019, 207–15.
215 The cult of Poseidon Tainaros located on the Aphetaid road has been identified by Kourinou (185–99) at t. s. 36; there are three late-first-century-BC inscriptions associated with the cult (*I.G.* V. 1.210-212). The possible identification of the Aphetaid road itself comes with the discovery of a road with a NE–SW orientation at t.s. 39 on the southern part of Sparta. By the road was found a burial monument of Hellenistic times, graves of Roman and late Roman date, but also traces of an Archaic shrine (Zavvou and Themos 2009, 119, n.85). On this topic, see also Santa 2014, 89–90.
216 King Polydorus together with Theopompus is noted to have made an addition to the *Great Rhetra* (as instituted in Sparta by Lycourgus) called the 'Rider'; Plut. *Lyc.* 6.4; Ogden 1994; Kennell 2010, 46.
217 Note numerous reported finds of terracotta reliefs in Salapata 2014, 336–7, nos 30, 31, 32, 36
218 Christesen 2018, 333–4, fig 13.
219 On the two-level elaborate Spartan tombs most common in the Hellenistic period but with some earlier examples, see Raftopoulou 1998, 134–6 and Christesen 2018, 322, 330–2, table 6. A striking similarity comes from the description of the tomb of Minos from Crete (Diod. 4.79.1–3). The body of Minos, after an elaborate ceremony, was buried in a two-storey tomb; in the underground part, they placed the bones and in the upper part they constructed a shrine to Aphrodite.
220 This road is commonly thought to be north of the agora; Kourinou 2000, 139–46.
221 Mattusch 1988, 49–50; Stibbe 1989, 7. Greco and Voza (2016) identify the remains of the Round Building as those of the *Skias*. The remains of the Round Building may also be associated with the Circular Building of Epimenides the Cretan; for Epimenides, see Levaniouk 2012, 384–5; 392.
222 Other sources for the genealogy is the Scholia to Euripides *Orestes* 457.
223 Calame 1987, 168.
224 Raftopoulou 1996; Zavvou and Themos 2009, 111, fig. 11.10. Settlement and habitation are identified not because there are many remains of houses from the Geometric–Classical periods but based on burials and pottery discovered (idem 112 n.35 and 116). One building forms an exception in Limnai where a late Geometric/early Archaic two-room house has been discovered; *ArchDelt* (1972)

vol. 27 (B1), 243. The area of Limnai by the Drainage Ditch, as presented in the excavation report by Steinhauer (*ArchDelt* [1972] vol. 27 [B1], 242–5), is a good example that shows the continued habitation of the area from the Geometric period into the Byzantine times.
225 For roadside shrines in Athens, see Costaki (2008); Vikela (2011); Best (2015).
226 cf. Kindt 2012, 1–2.
227 Costaki 2008, 152 n.32; Best 2015, 106.

Chapter 4

1 The name Menelaion is attested first in Polybius (5.18.4)
2 For a synthesis of the archaeological evidence see the recent publication by Stelow 2020, 265–75.
3 The cult, located on the Hill of Therapne, is positioned in the rural area in the immediate vicinity of Sparta rather than within the Spartan *komai*. The sanctuary demarked Spartan territory and formed part of a ring of sanctuaries around Sparta (see Introduction).
4 For the early excavations see Ross 1855, 6; 1861, 342; Kastriotis in *Praktika* 1900, 74–87; Wace, Droop and Thompson 1908–9, 108–57.
5 Catling 1976–7, 24–34; Catling R. 1986, 208–10, fig. 215.
6 For more on the 'Great Pit' see Catling 1976–7, 38–41, fig. 33. There is also a large sample of late-fourth/early-third-century pottery reported in the 2005 excavations.
7 The excavations from 1973–6 also revealed a second cult site on the North Hill near Late Bronze Age remains where sixth-century miniature vases and horse and rider figurines were unearthed; Catling 1976–7, 33–4; 2009, 143–68.
8 Catling 1976–7, 34.
9 Catling 1976–7, 37, figs 26–7; Catling and Cavanagh 1976, figs 1–3, pls. I–II. The *harpax* is identified as a meat hook. For a discussion regarding the function and other examples, including an Attic stamnos (*c.* 500–450 BC) depicting Medea using such an instrument (Berlin, Antikensammlung 2188; ARV^2 297, no. 1), see idem, 153.
10 Catling and Cavanagh 1976, 148–56, figs 1–2, pl. I–II; $LSAG^2$, 446, n.3a, pl. 75.2. The date is based on a comparison with Corinthian aryballoi that were imitated by Laconian potters.
11 Catling and Cavanagh 1976, 151.
12 Catling and Cavanagh 1976, 153.
13 Catling, R. 1986, 212.
14 Catling 1976–7, 36, fig. 28.

15 There are other as yet unpublished inscriptions, including some on pottery and an inscribed rim on a marble perirrhanterion (Catling, R. 1986, 212, n.1).
16 For the Daedalic figurines from Laconia, see Jenkins 1932–3.
17 This information is based on an unpublished report by H. Catling from the 2005 excavations. I would like to thank Richard Catling for giving me access to the report. In 2005, the areas north, south, east and west of the Menelaion were investigated, as well as the Great Pit and an intermediate area between.
18 *AR* 2005–6, 37.
19 Deposition of votives continued occasionally in this area as a sixth century bronze bowl fragment dedicated to Menelaus (*SEG* XXXV 321; R. Catling 1986, 212) and a spherical pierced stone dedicated by Ankaidas indicate (*AR* 1985–6, 29).
20 Catling 1976–7, 34.
21 In a similar fashion, Crete also did not have a tradition of cults at Bronze Age tombs. Comparatively to the Menelaion, there were sanctuaries in relation to remains of Minoan structures (Prent 2003).
22 Tomlinson 1992, 249.
23 *AR* 2005–6, 37.
24 Boardman 2002; Grethlein 2010, 132.
25 cf. Bommas 2012, xxix.
26 Personal communication with R. Catling.
27 Catling, R. 1986, 211; 1992, 58–70.
28 Catling 1976–7, 37, figs 21, 30–1. The total height of the monument is estimated at 8 metres; the standing monument today is at 6 metres, op. cit.
29 Catling 1976–7, 37.
30 Alkman mentions a temple at Therapne in fr.14 Page, *PMG*. It is possible that the poet would praise the patronage (by Spartan royalty) of the temple, a not uncommon poetic feature. See also West 1992, 3–5 (for *POxy* 2390) and Hinge (2009, 219–21) on the possible patronage as well as references to members of the Spartan royal family in Alkman's fr.5 Page, *PMG*.
31 Catling (1976–7, 37) had dated the monument then to the fifth century BC. Now, the date has been revised to the mid-sixth century BC (H. Catling 2005, unpublished report).
32 Catling 1976–7, 37.
33 A fragmentary terracotta model found at the site may indicate the architecture of the building surmounted by triglyphs (Tomlinson 1992, 249 n.13).
34 No. B3 of the *forthcoming* Menelaion publication. The information is based on Parker (*forthcoming*) who cites Spawforth's forthcoming publication on the inscriptions of the Menelaion.
35 Catling 1976–7, 41.
36 Cartledge 2002, 120–1. For the text see Chapter 5.

37 Woodward 1908–9, 87.
38 H. Catling unpublished provisional chronology of the Menelaion. There was no further construction on the building until the abandonment of the cult in the second century BC.
39 A significant number of fourth- and third-century pottery is reported from the excavations of the 'Great Pit' in 2005.
40 Catling 1976–7, 41, fig. 52.
41 Droop 1908–9, 144–8; Catling 1976–7, 38; Catling R. 1986, 211.
42 Wace 1908–9, 146, pl. x.
43 Catling, R. 1986, 211.
44 Silver: Thompson, M. S. 1908–9, 142, fig. 12, pl. viii 5–9. Ivory and bone: idem 143–4, pl. viii 11–21.
45 Catling 1976–7, 38.
46 See Förtsch 1988 and Chapter 3 for a discussion of the dedicatory patterns in shrines in Sparta.
47 Droop 1908–9, 148.
48 Catling 1976–7, 38. See parallels at Olympia, Bol 1989, 21–3, pls. 2–1.
49 Catling R. 1986, 211, fig. 5.
50 Catling 1976–7, 41, fig. 48; 1977, 415, fig. 15.
51 Dawkins *Orthia*, LXXXo, LXXXVIIh, LXXXVIIId, i.
52 Larson 2009.
53 See Pavlides 2020.
54 Thomson 1908–9, 116–26, figs 2–5, pl. vi.
55 This is based on the 1908–9 report so the dating is tentative.
56 Thompson M. S. 1908–9, 124 fig. 3.35–6, 41–2, 46–7. The female gender of the figurines was also observed by Catling (1976–7, 38, fig. 42).
57 Voyatzis 1992, 275.
58 Droop 1908–9, 150–7, pls. iii–iv; Catling 1976–7, 38–41, figs 44–51; Catling, R. 1992, 58–64.
59 Wace, Thompson and Droop 1908–9, 114; Catling 1976–7, 41; Bentz 1998, 129, no. 6.067; Hodkinson 2000, 308.
60 The same series of lead figurines is found at the sanctuary of Artemis Orthia, see Dawkins, *Orthia*, 249–84; Boardman 1963, 1–7.
61 The material is discussed in Cavanagh (*forthcoming*).
62 Lamb 1926–7a; 1926–7b.
63 At least seven vases were identified, mostly in fragments (Dickins 1906–7a, 150–3, pls. iv–v; Bentz 1998, 132, 6.097, 6.098; 6.099; 6.100, 6. 101, 6.102, 6.106, pl. 32).
64 Catling, R. 1992, 71.
65 Edmunds (2016, 357–8, n.112), quoting personal communication with Antonaccio in 2006.
66 Catling 1976–7, 37. For water in Greek sanctuaries, see Cole (1988).

67 Personal communication with R. Catling.
68 Cavanagh *forthcoming*; *contra* Boss (2000, 197), who argues that they were made in workshops away from the sanctuaries and that anyone could buy them for a private occasion.
69 Smith (2010, 143–5, fig. 3) interprets some of the dancers from the lead figurines from the Menelaion as komasts.
70 s.v. κάνναθρα
71 s.v. Ἑλένεια
72 Cambell 1988, 268.
73 Σεράπνα is also mentioned in Alkman fr.8 Page, *PMG*. Pindar (*P.* 11.61–2), and Polybios (5.18.21) say that Therapne was the burial place of the Dioskouroi. Herodotus (6.61.3) mentions that the shrine of Helen (i.e. the Menelaion) at Therapne was above the Phoibaion, in which, according to Pausanias, (3.20.2) was a temple of the Dioskouroi.
74 There are other literary sources that recount Helen's extraordinary powers: in the *Odyssey* Helen slips a potion into the drinks of Menelaus and Telemachos in order to bring forgetfulness (4.219–30). In Plato's *Phaidros* (243A) she deprives the poet Stesichoros of his sight when he composed a poem in which he spoke negatively of her. After he realized the cause of his misfortune, he wrote the *Palinodia*, of which we have a small fragment preserved in the *Phaidros*, and Helen restored his sight. Isokrates also claims that Helen appeared in front of Homer at night and asked him to compose a poem on the topic of those who went to Troy 'because she wished to make the death more to be envied than the life of the rest of mankind, because of her the poem has such charm and it became so famous' (*Enkomion to Helen* 65; Trans. Van Hook 1944).
75 For this passage see discussion in Edmunds 2016, 179–82.
76 Stelow 2020, 259–64, 275–84.
77 For Homeric elements in the poetry of Tyrtaeus and Alkman: Fowler 1987, 30–3.
78 Pipili 1987, 30–1, no. 87, fig. 45; Ahlberg-Cornell, 1992: 80; Edmonds 2016, 110–14; *LIMC* IV.I. 539, no. 230. For the possible find-spots see Pipili 1987, 93, n.274.
79 Pipili 1987, 30–1.
80 For the iconographic motif see Stelow 2020, 207–23.
81 Mykonos Museum 2240; Ahlberg-Cornell 1992, 78, figs 120–1.
82 Snakes are commonly associated with heroes. They feature on the *stelai* dedicated to the Dioskouroi but also on other stone and terracotta reliefs dedicated to heroes.
83 Calame 2001, 193–4; Parker *forthcoming* 21.
84 For Kinaithon see Huxley 1969, 87; Burkert 1987, 46; Tsagalis 2017, 177–96.
85 Elsewhere, Helen was considered to be a mortal heroine and worshipped as such, specifically in association with her brothers the Dioskouroi. In Athenian vase painting beginning from the last third of the fifth century she is depicted as born from the egg of Leda (*LIMC* IV. I. 503–4), and in the aftermath of the Persian Wars

she is depicted on the base of the statue of Nemesis at Rhamnous (Shapiro-Lapatin 1992, 107, 111–19). For Helen's cult in Attica, shared by her and her brothers the Dioskouroi, see Euripides' *Helen* (1666–9) and *Orestes* (1625–40) and the calendar at Thorikos, where she is worshipped together with her brothers (*SEG* XXXIII 147). Pindar begins a victory ode (*Ol.* 3.39–40) for Theron of Acragas and his kin, whom he says 'receive the Dioskouroi with hospitable tables more than any other mortals ... in honouring famous Acragas I pray to please the hospitable Tyndaridai and Helen of the lovely locks'. At the end of Euripides' *Helen*, the Dioskouroi tell Helen that when she dies 'you will be called a goddess, and you will share in libations along with the Dioskouroi. And you will receive entertainment (*xenia*) from men with us. Such is the wish of Zeus (1666–9).' *Xenia* here refers to the rite of *theoxenia*. It is not until the Roman period that there is evidence outside of Sparta for the cult of Helen herself, without the Dioskouroi. A cult of Helen Dendritis existed at Rhodes (Paus. 3.19.9–10) and a miniature gold cup from Egypt bears a dedication, dated 9 January 58 AD to 'Helen the sister of Aphrodite' (Perdrizet 1936, 5–10), which perhaps alludes to the legend in Euripides' *Helen* that she was never at Troy but went instead to Egypt (Parker *forthcoming*). For the cults of Helen outside Sparta, see Wide (1893, 340–6), Clader (1976, 63ff.), and Edmunds (2007, 26–9; 2016, 162–86).

86 Calame 2001, 191–202, esp. 193–4; Edmunds 2016, 164–8. No archaeological evidence is known for this cult.
87 Calame 2001, 193–4; Edmunds 2016, 168. Calame refers to the term 'initiation ritual' but this expression has come under a fair amount of criticism because it is not attested in Greek literature; see Graf (2003, 8–15) and *ThesCRA* II (91–2) for discussion.
88 Helen is also viewed as a fertility symbol because of her amorous liaisons; see Clader (1976, 71) with references.
89 Parker *forthcoming* 21–2.
90 Larson 1995, 78–9. The opposition of Olympian vs chthonian is disputed; see Schlesier 1991–2; van Straten 1995, 165–7; Verbank-Piérard 2000, 283–4; Ekroth 2002, 310–25 *contra* Scullion 1994; 2000.
91 West 1975, 8–10; Jackson 2006, 56–72. This point is also stressed in Bowra (2001, 52) who sees the reference to Ἀῶτις (from Doric dawn) in Alkman's *Partheneion* as an allusion to Helen. On the *Partheneion* see Jackson (2006, 48–56). For the etymology of her name, see the recent presentation of the scholarship in Edmunds (2016, 87–90).
92 Pausanias (3.13.9) says that it was to 'Aphrodite Hera' that Spartan women made offerings at the time of their daughters' marriage, so this must remain hypothetical. Naturally, Pausanias' Roman Sparta may have had different customs than Archaic and Classical Sparta when Helen may have assumed that role.

93 Parker *forthcoming*; cf. Edmunds 2016, 187–8.
94 In fact Edmunds 2016, 164–8 finds the entire context of the poem problematic.
95 Edmunds 2016, 186–8.
96 Parker *forthcoming* 3. In the Homeric epics, Helen is considered mortal but it is noteworthy that Helen's character has epithets, such as κούρη Διός, commonly used for Hera and Aphrodite. Clader (1976, 41–4) lists Helen's epithets and their occurrence in Homer.
97 Helen and Menelaus may not be the only heroes whose cult started as heroic and then turned divine: Herakles dies in the *Odyssey* (11. 602–4), but in later stories becomes immortal (*Theogony* 950–5; *Catalogue of Women* F 25. 26-33; West 1985, 112, 130; Sourvinou-Inwood 1995, 85–7; Stafford 2005, 393).
98 Her mother was the mortal Leda and her father was Zeus (Eur. *Helen* 16–23). Alternatively, in the *Cypria* (fr.7, in Athenaios 8.334B), she was the daughter of Nemesis and Zeus (Shapiro-Lapatin 1992, 117).
99 Parker (*forthcoming*) proposes that Helen should be compared to the sons of Zeus, who were born of mortal women, rather than his daughters.
100 Edmunds 2016, 178.
101 Ekroth 2002, 149, n.108; 2009, 125; cf. Parker *forthcoming* 3. Cult statues are, however, found in some hero cult sites but these are major heroes who had large precincts, such as Amphiaraos at Oropos or Heros Ptoios at Akraphiai (eadem). Other heroes too had cult statues, e.g. Alexandra/Kassandra and Clytemnestra at Amyklai (Paus. 3.19.6).
102 Parker *forthcoming*, 2–3.
103 Edmunds 2016, 183–4.
104 Edmunds 2016, 184.
105 Parker 2011, 110.
106 See for example the evidence from Attic cult calendars where heroes received lesser offerings than gods and often act as minor partners to gods. Parker (2011, 110–12, 114–16) also discusses the typology of votive of a banqueting hero.
107 Literary evidence concerning apotheosis is found in Paus. 8.2.4: 'For the men of those days, because of their righteousness and piety, were guests of the gods, eating at the same board; the good were openly honored by the gods, and sinners were openly visited with their wrath. Nay, in those days men were changed to gods, who down to the present day have honors paid to them – Aristaeus, Britomartis of Crete, Heracles the son of Alcmena, Amphiaraus the son of Oicles, and besides these Polydeuces and Kastor.' (Trans. Jones and Ormerod 1918). On the topic see also Cicero *On the Nature of the Gods* 2. 24; 3.15.
108 Edmunds 2016, 184.
109 When Pausanias visited Laconia most of the hero shrines he describes were also tombs: 3.11.9; 11.11; 12.7; 12.11; 13.1; 14.1–3; 14.6; 15.2; 15.6; 16.6.

110 Note that there is no earlier reference to the Menelaion as the burial place of Helen and Menelaus although the Dioskouroi were thought to dwell there.
111 For the festival see Hdt. 9.9; 9.11; Thuc. 5.23.4–5; Xen. *Ages.* 2.17; *Hell.* 4.5.11; Arist. frg. 532 (Rose); Paus. 3.10.1; 4.19.4; Athen. *Deipn.* 4.139c–f. Philostr. *VA*, 6.20; Ovid. *Met.* 10. 217–19; Pettersson 1992; Richer 2004; Sourvinou-Inwood 2005, 122–3; Ehrenheim 2015; Petropoulou 2015. It was incredibly important for the Spartans who delayed battles and returned home to attend the festival.
112 For the myth, see a possible reference in the Hesiodic *Catalogue of Women* fr. 171 M/W), Eur. *Hel.* 1469–75; ps-Apollod. *Bibl.* 1.3.3; 3.10.3; Lucian *d. deor.* 14.2; 15.2; 16.2; Richer 2004, 89 n.12; Petropoulou 2011–12, 153. There were other versions of the myth in which Hyakinthos is not killed by Apollo but by the west wind Zephyros (Philostr. *im.* 1.24; Ov. *fast.* 5.223; Nonn. *Dion.* 10.253; Mellink 1943, 170–2). Sourvinou-Inwood (2005, 122–4) places Hyakinthos in the category of heroes who die young and receive public lamentation, such as Adonis.
113 Ehrenheim 2015, 358–62.
114 Dietrich 1975, 134, 137–40; Burkert 1985, 351; Cartledge 2002, 80; Vlizos 2009, 22.
115 The identification of the site has been confirmed by stamped tiles, inscribed pottery and inscribed metal finds (*IG* V 1.145, 511; Tsountas 1892, 3, 19–31; Buschor and Massow 1927, 61–4; *SEG* XI. 689–97).
116 See Vlizos (2009, 12–13) and Demakopoulou (2009a, 95) for the history of the excavations, with bibliography.
117 Amykles Research Project: https://amyklaion.gr/en/.
118 Terracottas: Demakopoulou 1982, 43ff.; 2009a; 2015; metal objects: eadem 73–8; 2009a, 103. No architectural remains were found. Demakopoulou (2009a, 102) suggests that it was an open-air shrine. The Mycenaean wheel-made terracotta animal figurines leave no doubt that the site of the later Amyklaion was previously a Bronze Age cult place; Demakopoulou 2009a, 95–6, 102.
119 Vlachou 2011–12; 2018; Vlizos 2017b, 33.
120 For the chronology of the site, see Buschor and von Massow 1927, 32–3; Calligas 1992, 34–5; Cartledge 2002, 81–2; Demakopoulou 1982, 74; 2009, 103; https://amyklaion.gr/en/sanctuary/chronology/.
121 cf. Vlachou 2017b, 40.
122 Kaltsas 2006, 59–60, nos 10–11; Demakopoulou (2011–12, 109) compares them to other cult figures in Mycenaean centres; Vlachou (2017b, 26, figs 15–16) interprets them as Hyakinthos and his sister Polybia.
123 Vlachou 2018, 98.
124 For the late Geometric/early Archaic peribolos wall: https://amyklaion.gr/en/monuments/precinct-walls/; 2019 Report: https://amyklaion.gr/en/research/reports/54/. The reorganization and expansion of the cult site corresponds to other building programmes that took place in Sparta at the time with projects, such as the Menelaion, the temple of Artemis Orthia, and others (Introduction).

125 2018 Report: https://amyklaion.gr/en/research/reports/50/; 2019 Report: https://amyklaion.gr/en/research/reports/54/
126 On the precinct walls https://amyklaion.gr/en/sanctuary/precinct-walls/; On the early statue: Romano 1980, 104; Vlizos 2017, 35–6; https://amyklaion.gr/en/monuments/throne/.
127 The date is based on the architectural fragments; Faustoferri 1996, 227; Tomlinson 2008, 324. See also https://amyklaion.gr/en/monuments/throne/. Iconographic evidence from bronze coins dating from the reign of Commodus and Gallenius shows the statue as a pillar standing on a base; Grunauer-Von Hoerschelmann, 1978, pl. 32.12. A third-century BC relief stele from the Amyklaion shows similar iconography; Schroder 1904, fig. 2. For an Ionian influence see Svenson-Evers (1996, 460) and Ohnesorg (2005, 248). Not much is known about Vathykles as our only source is Pausanias but it is possible that Samos provided a link between Sparta and Ionian artists (Hdt. 3.47). On the relations of Sparta and Samos: Cartledge 1982, 243–65. The large number of Laconian vases found on Samos at the Heraion and Artemision demonstrate the closeness of the two areas (Pipili 1998, 85–6; 2000; 2001; Coudin 2009b, 236–7).
128 For the throne: Fiechter 1918, 166–245; Bushor and Massow 1927, 15–23; *AAA* 1 (1968), 42–5; Delivorrias 2009; Bilis and Magnisali 2011–12; Korres 2011–12; Amykles Research Project https://amyklaion.gr/en/monuments/throne/. Reconstructions in Fiechter 1918, 169–71, figs 40–2, 245, fig. 39; Martin 1976, 215, 217; Faustoferri 1996, figs 1–4, 6, 9–15.
129 Romano 1980, 103–4.
130 Personal communication with the director of the excavations, Stavros Vlizos.
131 Amykles Research Project: https://amyklaion.gr/en/monuments/precinct-walls/. The wall may have been built in stages and has evidence of restorations and repairs of the Roman and Byzantine periods.
132 Amykles Research Project: https://amyklaion.gr/en/monuments/altar/
133 2017 report: https://amyklaion.gr/en/research/reports/51/; 2018 report: https://amyklaion.gr/en/research/reports/50/
134 *Ergon* (2019), 30–3.
135 See for example a fourth-century AD stele of Sextus Eudamon Onasikrates, who was a priest at the Hyakinthia; https://amyklaion.gr/en/sanctuary/buildings/.
136 https://amyklaion.gr/en/sanctuary/buildings/
137 Burkert (1975, 7–12) supports a 'Dorian' import of Apollo, which he finds derives from the Dorian word *apellon* – the Dorian institution of the assembly (1975, 16–20); *contra* Beeks (2003, 3–8), who supports a Near Eastern derivation (2003, 12–19), and Brown (2004, 245–9) who also argues for a Near Eastern origin, in particular from the Hittite *Apaliuna*. For further see Graf (2009, 134–6, 137–42).

138 The earliest epigraphic evidence for Apollo starts at c. 600 BC with an inscription on a bronze handle by someone called *Dorkonida* (Jeffery 1990, 198 no. 5; *SEG* XI.129.689).
139 Cartledge (1992, 49–55; 2002, 79–94). On the abandonment of many Laconian sites and the proof of 'Dorian' newcomers, see Demakopoulou (1982, 131) and Cartledge (2002, 75–100). The view of newcomers has been challenged and a more complex picture is drawn now, which sees various population movements, destruction and resettlement in the late Bronze Age. Demakopoulou (1982, 128–30; 2009b) gives a very good overview on the habitation and movement of population in Laconia during the LHIIIB–C periods.
140 Hatzisteliou-Price 1979, 226–7; Demakopoulou 1982, 94; 2009, 103; Vlizos 2009, 22.
141 Cartledge 2002, 80; Burkert 1985, 351 n.27 with references; Vlizos 2009, 22.
142 Eder 1998, 136–8.
143 Cartledge 2002, 70.
144 Tsountas 1892, 10; Calligas 1992, 34, fig. 13a–d; Demakopoulou 2009a, 103; 2015, 110.
145 Personal communication with Stavros Vlizos.
146 Cosmopoulos 2014.
147 Vlachou 2017b, 39. See eadem, 31–8 for dedications of spindle whorls and loom weights as indicatory of textile offerings and eadem 2018 for feasting at the Early Iron Age sanctuary.
148 Chapin and Hitchcock 2007, 255–62.
149 Cartledge 2002, 92–106.
150 While the ancient settlement of Amyklai has not been located, the discovery of twelve Proto-Geometric burials in the modern village of Amykles as well as Proto-Geometric and Geometric pottery suggests that it would have been situated somewhere between the hill of Agia Kyriaki (where the Amyklaion is situated) and the modern village of Amykles; *ArchDelt* (1996) vol. 51 (B1), 129–31; *ArchDelt* (1998) vol. 53 (B1), 172–3.
151 Vlachou 2017b, 41.
152 Pritchett 1985, 42.
153 Calame 1987, 184–5. On the topic see Nobili 2014, 138; Petropoulou 2011–12, 154.
154 On the foundation of Taras see Kõiv 2003, 108–18; Nafissi 1999, 254–8; Kennell 2010, 35–6.
155 Athens National Museum 8618; *SEG* XI.697; Lazzarini 1976, 296 no. 834.
156 Paris, Musée du Louvre B 118; Herfort-Kock 1986, K 122, pl. 16.7.
157 *SEG* XI. 696; Fiechter 1918, 220, 222, figs 74, 78; *LSAG*^{2}, 195 and 201 no. 51.
158 Massow 1926, 41ff. fig. 1.

159 There is no textual or other iconographic evidence of Hyakinthos in Sparta. Richer (2004, 86–7) suggests that the Taranto cup (Museo Nationale di Taranto 20909) shows Hyakinthos.
160 Hyakinthos is bearded (thus a mature man), which is in unlike his Attic iconographic tradition in which he is depicted as an un-bearded youth from 500 BC. Calame (2001, 180) regards it a reference to a 'first youthful beard'. Richer (2004, 78) takes it to symbolize the endangered adolescent who enters adulthood. Pettersson (1992, 38–41) sees this Hyakinthos as a mature man, while the young Hyakinthos was an Attic invention.
161 Nicias is dated to *c.* 332–29 BC since Pliny (35.133) informs that he collaborated on Praxiteles' statues; Corso 2007, 22.
162 See Pausanias (3.18.10–19.5) for the description of the entire iconographical programme and studies by Faustoferri (1993) and Nafissi (2020).
163 Sourvinou-Inwood (2005, 123–4) makes the same observation about the introduction of Herakles to Olympus. For Dionysus and Hermes on the throne at Amyklai, see Pipili (1991), who doubts that the scene is that of Dionysus being given to Zeus but argues that Hermes gives Dionysus to Ino and Athamas. Schefold (1992, 46) believes there was another scene of *apotheosis* (Paus. 3.19.3) where Dionysus leads Semele to Olympus. On the overall theme of mortality and apotheosis on the decorative programme of the Throne of Apollo, see Nafissi 2020.
164 This heritage follows the Thessalian tradition of Hyakinthos as attested in Hesiod *Eoiae* fr. 16 Evelyn-White (called Hymenaeus) and ps-Apollod. *Bibl.* 1.3.3.
165 cf. Nafissi 2020, 4.
166 Ino and Semele in some myths also join the gods at Olympus; see discussion and full references in Ehrenheim 2015, 356–7.
167 Pettersson 1992, 40.
168 cf. Ehrenheim 2015, 351; Nafissi 2020, 4. The length of the festival in the Classical period is debated but it may have lasted for three or nine days. See Richer (2004, 80) for a discussion of the evidence and the possibility that in the earlier days the festival may have lasted for ten days; *contra* Petropoulou (2015), who sees no change in the festival length and argues that it was a nine-day celebration.
169 Polykrates is quoted by Didymos the Grammarian (*c.* first century BC) and comes down to us from Athenaios (4. 139d–f.). He may have been a local historian of Laconian origin as Jacoby suggests in *FGrH* 588 F1. His date is essentially unknown (*BNJ* 588).
170 Hodkinson 1999, 5; see discussion and full references in Petropoulou 2015, 182–3.
171 Ehrenheim 2015, 353–7.
172 The myth of Apollo and Hyakinthos, together with the description of the Hyakinthia, has led some to interpret Hyakinthos as a dying vegetation god and his festival as an occasion concerned with renewal and initiation rituals. Jeanmaire

(1939, 526–31) interprets the Hyakinthia, together with the Karneia and the Gymnopaideia, as initiation rituals and Hyakinthos as a symbol of excellence for the adolescents. Brelich (1969, 141–8, 171–9) sees the festival as part of the Spartan *agoge* and initiation. Calame (2001, 317) also reads it as a tribal initiation festival. Sergent (1984, 107) views Hyakinthos as the *eromenos* of Apollo whose death expresses the death of adolescence and the step into adulthood. Pettersson (1992, 14–29) suggests that the Hyakinthia was a Mycenaean cult of the dead that continued in later times. Richer (2004, 84–9) views the Hyakinthia as a festival with Dionysiac elements together with the worship of Apollo and Hyakinthos.

173 See Chapter 1.
174 On this topic, see Knoepfler 2019.
175 Personal communication with Stavros Vlizos.
176 See for example Mercier and Sperber (2009) and Evans and Stanovich (2013).
177 Intuitive thought is characterized by automacity, speed and implicitness. 'It allows us to function in daily life without consciously calculating how to execute every movement and decision'; Larson 2016, 11–12, 375–6).
178 Reflective thought is characterized by 'slowness, effort, and explicitness. It involves, thinking, comparing and making decisions'; Larson 2016, 377.
179 Richert and Lesage 2019, 59.
180 The Apharidai were the sons of Aphareus, king of Messene.
181 A different version of the story has the incident happen, not during the stealing of the cattle of Idas and Lynkeus, but when they stole the Leukippidai (pseudo-Hyginus, *Fab.* 80).
182 Sanders 1992b, 206.
183 Most of the reliefs remain unpublished. See Sanders 1992 for the reliefs in the Sparta Museum. I provide a brief description here of the published Archaic and Classical reliefs. SM 5380: the Dioskouroi face each other and have long hair, and each holds a spear. The right Dioskouros has a small, pointed beard. The frame of the relief is decorated with snakes; SM 588: the dokana of the Dioskouroi, which are elaborate with several horizontal beams. The snakes are arranged in S-curves on the two main verticals. The serpents face toward the centre of the top beam, which is decorated with a lotus blossom. The rounded ends of the main horizontal beam are decorated with palmettes; SM 613: the relief shows two amphoras with peaked lids; SM 575: the Dioskouroi in profile face towards the centre. They have short, pointed beards and a *chlamys*. Between them are two amphorai. Over them are two snakes that face an egg in the centre; SM 477: the relief is broken at the top. The Dioskouroi face each other with a wreath in the middle. In between them there is an inscription: 'Pleistiades dedicated me to the Dioskouroi careful to avoid the wrath of the twin sons of Tyndareus' (*IG* V. 1.919).

184 The meaning of the amphorae in the cult of the Dioskouroi is unknown. Their peaked lids resemble panathenaic amphorae and may suggest an association of the Dioskouroi with athletics (Sanders 1992b, 206, n.7) as is attested in literary sources (*Il.* 3.238; *Od.* 11.278; *Catalogue of Women* 198–9 M/W; Pindar *N*.10.50; *O.* 3.36; *P.* 5.9; Paus. 3.14.7) or they may have funerary connotations (Gaifman 2012, 299).

185 Sanders 1992, 206; Gaifman 2012, 299–300. For the dokana as two wooden beams connected at the top and thus symbolizing the unity of the Dioskouroi, see Plut. *Mor.* 478B. Gaifman (2012, 303) highlights how in the early Dioskouroi reliefs, the iconography is not uniform and thus any symbolic meaning has to be 'locally construed'. There are many examples where the Dioskouroi are presented with the dokana: for example, the fourth-century 'Verona Relief' from Taras, which depicts the Dioskouroi and the two amphorae on an altar (Verona, Museo Maffeiano 555). A man with a boat and two dokana are also present in the imagery (*LIMC* III. I. 577, no. 122; Gaifman 2012, 297, fig. 7.9). A number of fourth- and third-century terracotta reliefs from Taras dedicated to the Dioskouroi also depict the dokana and amphorae (*LIMC* III. I. 574, nos 66–70). The dokana were also found on Hellenistic amphora stamps on Delos and in the Athenian agora (among Thasian objects); see references in Gaifman 2012, 296.

186 Lanéres 2008.

187 Walker 2015, 246–9.

188 Farnell 1921, 192; cf. Walker 2015, 252.

189 See Walker (2015, 2480) who suggests that these cults were important to the young people going through adolescence.

190 Enyalios is a deity connected with warfare, e.g. Athens (Arist. *Ath. Pol.* 58.1) and the fourth-century inscription of the ephebic oath from Acharnai; Kellogg (2013) with previous bibliography.

191 Kennell 1995, 138–42 for relationship between the Dioskouroi and the Spartan youths.

192 Flower 2018, 442.

193 Richer 2012, 318–19, 361.

194 Calame 2001, 185–91; Richer 2004, 79–82; 2012 343–82.

195 Burkert 1985, 212; Parker 1989, 147.

196 Diod. 8.32. The Locrians proceeded to accept the offer and prepared a *kline* on their ship for the Dioskouroi (Diod. 8.32); Platt 2018, 232.

197 Pritchett 1979, 206; Kennell 1995, 138.

198 The Dioskouroi had other roles, such as in relation to horsemanship (*Iliad* 3. 253–55; Alkman fr. 2 Page, *PMG*; Callimachus fr. 227), protectors of sailors (*Homeric Hymn* 27; Plato, *Euthydemus* 293a; Diod. 4.43.1). Complete references are not attempted here; for these, see Walker 2015, 43–71.

199 Nilsson 1967, 420.
200 The Dioskouroi were apparently hostile towards Messenia because two Messenian men, Panormus and Gonippus of Andania, disrespected a festival of the Dioskouroi that was held in Sparta (Paus. 4.27.1–3).
201 For the story relating to the instigation of hostilities between Sparta and Messenia at the sanctuary of Artemis Volimos in Messenia see Strabo 6.1.6; 6.3.3; Paus. 4.4.2–3 (Luraghi 2008, 80–3).
202 For *katabasis* and heroes: Georgiades 2017.

Chapter 5

1 Currie 2005, 100.
2 Fitzhardinge 1980, 30–1, 70, 80, 159; Hodkinson 1998; 2000, 271–2, 276; Förtsch 1998; 2001; Cartledge 2001, 173–8.
3 van Wees 2018a, 203, 226
4 On the topic see Davies 2018.
5 Hodkinson 2000, 216–56; 2018, 43; van Wees 2018a, 214–20.
6 Hodkinson 2018, 49.
7 Currie (2005, 172–8), who argues that the term implies religious honours. However, his examples all date to the fourth century and later.
8 cf. Hoffmann 2000.
9 Davies 2018, 487–9.
10 Hodkinson 1993, 157–9; Davies 2018, 493–6.
11 Cartledge 1987, 84.
12 Further discussion and references in Davies 2018, 491–2.
13 For full discussion of the powers of the ephors see Richer 1998, 453–523.
14 Hodkinson 2000, 307–28. For the victory monuments at Olympia see idem, 320, table 13; Palagia 2009; Nobili 2013, 65–6, esp. n.8.
15 For example, Olympic victors could fight before kings in battle (Plut. *Lyc.* 22.4) and could be colony founders; Hodkinson 1999, 167–9; 2000, 325–7. See also an example of an inscribed stele (*IG* V 1.708) for two men who died in war, one of whom was also an Olympic athlete as the inscription states. Still, he is commemorated not because he was an athlete but because he died at war; Hodkinson 1999, 170, n.50).
16 Hodkinson 2000, 303–7; Nafissi 2013; Christesen 2019.
17 Nobili 2013, 65.
18 Jeffery 1990, 201, no. 51
19 *LSAG*² 201, nos 41–2, 44–8, 50–2; Whitley 1997, 647; Hodkinson 1999, 152–3, 156–7.

20 Hodkinson 1999, 152–6; Kyle 2007, 188.
21 Nobili 2013.
22 Hodkinson 2018, 51. By the fourth century, this wealth inequality led to the decline of numbers of Spartans who could be *homoioi* since property concentrated into the hands of a few (Arist. *Pol.* 6.1307a34–6). The late fourth and early third centuries saw Sparta back into a plutocratic society that shed the masking of an equal society brought about by the state institutions (idem).
23 Hodkinson 2000, 432ff.
24 Agesilaos urged his sister Kyniska to compete in order to prove that winning in chariot competitions was a matter of wealth (Paus. 5.12.5; 6.1.6); Hodkinson 1999, 99; Pomeroy 2002, 21–4; Kyle 2007, 189–91; Millander 2009, 23–6.
25 Habicht 1970, 4; Cartledge 1987, 83–4; Flower 1988, 131–3. The Spartan acropolis also housed the statue of Euryleonis, a woman who also won an Olympic chariot race, and two statues of Pausanias – the latter were ordained by the Delphic oracle (Paus. 3.17.6–7).
26 See the recent collection of data in Christesen 2018.
27 Loraux (1986, 39), who argues for immortal glory rather than heroization for the Athenian war-dead (eadem, 39–42).
28 Bowra 1933, 277–8, 281; Boedeker 1998; 1998, 234, 242; Stehle 2001, 117–18.
29 Pritchett 1985, 246; Bremmer 2006, 21–2.
30 Fuqua 1981, 221, 221–4. Boedeker (1998, 232) Stehle (2001, 116) and Currie (2005, 98) do not argue for seventh-century heroization but perceive that the ideology was there since the seventh century and thus was expressed by Simonides as heroization for the Persian War dead.
31 Meier 1998, 285; Currie 2005, 98, with previous bibliography.
32 This view has been expressed by Faraone (2006, 43–4) but this opinion is older, see idem (43, n. 47) for bibliography. Faraone (2006, 40) explains that Tyrtaeus' 12 West is composed of two stanzas constructed of a *protasis* and an *apodosis* (lines 21–30: first stanza and lines 35–45: second stanza). The middle part (lines 31–4) does not fit the general composition, as it has high-flown rhetoric and may have been added later in a re-performance.
33 Tarkow 1983, 62.
34 See synthesis of evidence and discussion in Christesen 2018, 321–5. A group of four burials found south of Palaiokastro Hill was interpreted by the excavator Christou (*ArchDelt* [1964] 19 [A], 123–63, 283–5) as Archaic but the dating has found some doubts and a later date has been proposed; Steinhauer: *ArchDelt* 1972, vol. 27 (B1), 244 n.15; Hodkinson 2000, 239–40; Christesen 2018, Appendix 7. For the Archaic–Hellenistic Olive Oil cemetery see Tsouli 2013; 2016; Christesen 2018, 325–9.
35 Dawkins *Orthia*, 210, pl. cii 2–3; Fragkopoulou 2011.
36 Hodkinson 2000, 238.

37 *ArchDelt* [1964] 19 (A), 123–93; Fitzhardinge 1980, 52; Sourvinou-Inwood 1995, 210–1; 276–8; Kennell 2010, 98 consider these vessels as funerary. Hodkinson (2000, 242) has his reservations since none have been found by burials but only by cult sites and sanctuaries, as emphasized by Steinhauer: *ArchDelt* 1972 vol. 27 (B1), 244 n.15). They were probably mixing kraters.

38 Scholars warn that Sparta was not different to other Peloponnesian cities where burial markers and gifts are poor in comparison to Athens. Moreover, restrictions on funerary display are observed in other poleis (Morris 1992, 128–49; Hodkinson 2000, 248–9; Christesen 2018, 339–52; van Wees 2018a, 222).

39 The Parparonia festival is attested also in the Damonon stele (*c.* 400 BC, *IG* V 1.213 lines 44–9, 62–4). For a discussion of the Parparonia, see Robertson (1992, 179–203); Shaw (2003, 178–80); Pavlides 2018, 288–9. See also a dedication of a bronze bull with an inscription ΠΑΡΠΑΟ in Phaklaris (1990, 226–7) and Shipley (1996, 279, no. AA16).

40 Hesychios s.v. Παρπαρόνια; Plin. *nat.* 4.17.

41 For the festival, see also Xen. *Hell.* 6.4.16 and Plat. *nom.* 1.633. This battle may be that of Hysiae (669 BC, Paus. 2.24.7) or the battle of Thyrea (550 BC, Hdt. 1.82; Paus. 2.38.5), cf. Robertson 1992, 161. If Athenaios is correct that Thaletas and Alkman performed at the festivals, then the 669 BC date is more possible. Wade-Gery (1949, 79–80), Parker (1989, 167, n.39) and Shaw (2003, 176–7) speculate that this association arose after 370/69 with an amalgamation with the Parparonia. *Contra* Robertson (1992, 163).

42 The military character of Apollo in Laconia is attested by the celebration of the Karneia (Pettersson 1992, 57, 62–6). For the Gymnopaideia as a festival of Apollo in which young and adult men competed, see idem (74) and Robertson (1992, 147–9). See also the sanctuary of Apollo Maleatas in Laconia where hundreds of weapons were given as dedications to Apollo; Pavlides 2018.

43 *Etym Magn.* s.v. Gymnopaidia; Suda s.v. Gymnopaidia; Currie 2005, 99, n.56.

44 Fuqua 1981, 225, n.33. Currie (2005, 100) remains cautious.

45 Pritchett 1985, 243–6, Hodkinson 2000, 251; Low 2006, 85ff; cf Loraux (1986, esp. 15–56) on Athenian fifth-century public memorials.

46 Hodkinson 2000, 251; Low 2006: 88–9, map. 1; Pavlides 2020, 158.

47 Pritchett 1985, 243–6. On this topic, see Kucewicz (2021), who argues that in the Archaic period wealthy families in Sparta could have repatriated the remains of their family members, a practice that he suggests gradually changes in the late Archaic period.

48 Dillon 2007, 157.

49 Sparta was not the only place where restrictions on burial took place in the Archaic and Classical periods but was part of a wider Greek phenomenon: Solon's legislation in Athens (Demosth. 43.62; Cic. *leg.* 2.2.63; Plut. *Sol.* 21; 12.8) and three inscriptions

at Gortyn dating from Archaic period carry rules about burials (*LSAG*², 315, nos 2, 4, 8; *IG* IV 22, 46b, 76); Toher 1991, 169, n.40. Katane: Stob. *Flor.* 44.40; Alexiou 2002, 17. Syracuse: Diod. 11.38; Alexiou 2002, 17. Ioulis on Keos: *LGS* 93A, p. 261–2; Alexiou 2002, 15, n.76. Delphi: *LGS* C74; Alexiou 2002, 16. For funeral restrictions in general see Seaford (1994, 77), Alexiou (2002, 14–18) and Dillon (2007, 150, n.6).

50 Sourvinou-Inwood 1995, 140–7. Monumental tombs do not occur in Sparta until 200 BC; Cartledge and Spawforth 2002, 132–3.

51 The texts γυναικὸς τῶν ἱερῶς ἀποθανόντων (codex Laurentianus) or γυναικὸς τῶν ἱερῶν ἀποθανόντων (codex Seitenstettensis) were amended in 1926 by Latte to γυναικὸς [τῶν] λεχοῦς ἀποθανόντων (Brulé and Piolot 2004, 153–4). This changed the meaning from female priests to women who died in childbirth and became the dominant translation. The emendation of the text has been criticized by Richer (1994, 53–4), Brulé and Piolot (2004, 152–8) and Dillon (2007), who suggest a return to the original text to mean female priestesses. See below for the inscriptions of ἱεραί.

52 Pomeroy 2002, 57–8.

53 It is doubtful that Xenophon's work expresses real Spartan quotes, see Tigerstedt 1974, 23–30.

54 Dillon 2007, 154.

55 Guarducci 1974, 173; *LSAG*², 197. In fact, *IG* V 1.1128 is Roman and comes not from Sparta but Geronthrai. *IG* V 1.1277 is also not Spartan and comes from Tainaron. The latter is noteworthy because it gives a list of women's names. Of the women on the lists, only two have the λεχοῦς after their name. Hodkinson (2000, 261) suggest that, based on this stele, women who did not die in childbirth could also be commemorated.

56 These vary in date (including the imperial period) and some are undated (Richer 1994, 53–4; Brulé and Piolot 2004, 158–9, n.47–9). Evidence for priestesses also appears in Messenia although it is of later date (Brulé and Piolot 2004, 159–60). On this topic, see also more recently Christesen 2021, 45.

57 *IG* V 1.720–722 date from fifth century BC and are included in Pfohl and Wallace's studies on early Greek epitaphs (Pfohl 1961; Wallace 1970). *IG* V 1.721–22 are too fragmentary to be accepted as epigrams, Andronikos (1956, 276–9) accepts *IG* V 1.721 as funerary, but Wallace (1970, 100 n.13) rejects it. Wallace (idem) believes that *IG* V 1.722 could possibly be funerary but Andronikos (idem) does not. *IG* V 1.720 mentions a 'μνᾶμα Κάλας', which may indeed refer to a person's tomb. Both Andronikos (1956, 276–9) and Wallace (1970, 99–100 n.13) reject *IG* V 1.720 as funerary but neither of them discusses the term 'μνᾶμα Κάλας'.

58 Christesen 2021, 45 and n.136.

59 Valmin 1929, 147, no. 20. For [h]ιαροί, see Le Roy 1961, 228–34.

60 Wallace (1970 99, n.1) gives it a fifth-century date. Dillon (2007, 161) argues for an Archaic date due to the letter forms.
61 Brulé and Piolot 2004, 168, n.20.
62 See discussion and epigraphic evidence in Wallace 1970; Richer 1994, 53–4, 64–8; Hodkinson 2000, 260–2; Brulé and Piolot 2004: 153–4; Dillon 2007; van Wees 2018a, 220–2.
63 For the discussion of the translation priests versus *eirenes*, see Brulé and Piolot (2004, 156–7) with previous bibliography and Ducat (2006, 94–5).
64 Christesen 2021, 40–1,
65 Parker 1989, 143. Many inscriptions in the Roman period attest to priests; Cartledge and Spawforth 2002, 137, 164–5, 178–9.
66 Dillon (2007, 160, n.46) collects the evidence but all date to the Hellenistic and Roman periods.
67 Dillon 2007, 160.
68 See Parker (1989, 159–60), Richer (2007, 237–8), and Flower (2009, 198, 214–6; 2018, 447–8) on how Sparta's religiosity contributed to its internal stability.
69 See also Xenophon's account of the funeral of king Agis (*Hell.* 3.3.1).
70 Cartledge (1987, 339–41; 1988) bases his argument on the heroization of historical persons, such as Chilon, and the cult of mythical heroes, such as Orestes, whose bones were transferred to Sparta. Cartledge believes that because the bones of the kings who died abroad were brought to Sparta, this means that they were heroized; cf. Nafissi 1991, 290.
71 Parker 1988, 9–10; 1989, 169, n.51.
72 Lipka 2002, 248–51.
73 Kennell (2010, 95–9) points out that the kings were not considered *homoioi*. See also Carlier (1984, 249–72) on the position of the Spartan kings within the different institutions of Sparta and particularly on the vocabulary used by ancient authors in association with the kings.
74 Carlier 1984, 267–9; Powell (2009) argues that the need for the Spartan kings to control the oracles reflected the threat to their position.
75 Carlier 1984, 267; Parker 1989, 154–5.
76 Kennell 2010, 29.
77 West 1985, 74.
78 Parker 1989, 143.
79 The speech is set in the assembly where the Spartan allies led by Corinth met to discuss the demand by the Thebans to recognize the newly colonized city of Messene. In the discussion of whether to wage war with Thebes, Archidamos III makes this speech to urge the Spartans to fight and die for Messenia, which is their rightful possession.
80 Malkin 1994, 19. It is also worth mentioning the descent of King Demaratos from the hero Astrabacus; here, the hero had an offspring on the throne (Hdt. 6.64–9).

81 Christesen 2018, 333 notes a number of burials by the likely axis of the Aphetaid road and proposes that they could continue all the way to the burial grounds of the Eurypontid kings.
82 Flower (2009, 213) interprets the religious-political power of the Spartan kings as closer to that of Near-Eastern monarchs.
83 For a full discussion of the burial of Spartan kings, see Cartledge (1987, 331–43); Carlier (1984, 272–3).
84 For the text and previous bibliography on the topic see Cassio (2012).
85 Pritchett 1985, 241; Hodkinson 2000, 262–3; Scott 2005, 246–51. At Olympia Pausanias (6.4.9) saw the statue of King Archidamos. He goes on to explain that this is the only statue of a Spartan king and the reason for its existence and set up at Olympia is because he died abroad – the only king who missed burial.
86 Pritchett 1985, 243–6; Hodkinson 2000, 249–59.
87 Schaefer (1957, 228–9) argues that an effigy would be present only if the body of the king could not be recovered after dying in battle. *Contra* Toher (1999, 180) who claims that the effigy would always be present if the king died in battle because his body would probably be disfigured and not in position to be displayed for public view.
88 Cartledge (1987, 340) 'the funeral played the same sort of role as the preservation and presentation of king-lists'. Loraux (1986, 46–7) sees this as a community event that would unite the populace.
89 Schaefer 1957, 230.
90 Lipka 2002, 251, n.72.
91 Malkin 1987, 229. See also Rhodes (1998, 323). For the rituals connected with Brasidas and his heroization, see Ekroth (2002, 185–6).
92 Ekroth 2002, 206–12, esp. 208–9 with previous bibliography.
93 Ekroth 2002, 211.
94 ibid.
95 Parker 1988, 10.
96 Parke 1945.
97 Ekroth (2002, 330–1) notes the overlap of status between the dead and heroes expressed in sacrificial rituals.
98 For the Roman period Leonidea see Hupfloher 2000, 190–3; Cartledge and Spawforth 2002, 192–3.
99 Marincola 2016, 233.
100 Low 2011, 5–6; Marincola 2016.
101 The earliest evidence for the cult of the war-dead of Marathon is a second-century BC inscription (*IG* II² 1006.26–7) and Pausanias (1.32.4). Other evidence consists of three inscribed vases with similar dedications (one found in the Marathon plain: Ἀθεναῖοι ἆθλα ἐπὶ τοῖς ἐν τοι πολέμοι – *IG* II³ 523, 525; *SEG* XXVIII 26; all published by Vanderpool in *ArchDelt* (1969) vol. 24 (A), 1–5; Marchiandi 2010,

222–6. Amandry (1971, 612–26) interprets them as dedications from games in honour of the war-dead of either Plataia or Marathon. For an early cult, see Kearns (1989, 55) and Garland (1992, 95). Against this opinion, see Welwei (1991, 62), Parker (1996, 137 n.5) and Bremmer (2006, 21) who argues that Marathon acquired its pre-eminent position in Athenian cultural memory gradually in the course of the fifth century. For a recent discussion on the heroization of the war-dead, see Proietti (2014).

102 It is not until the third century BC that there is concrete evidence for a festival (the Eleutheria) for the Plataia war-dead with the Glaukon decree (*SEG* XXVII 65) and Heraclides Creticus (Austin 2006, 101). See also Strabo 9.2.31; Plut. *Arist.* 21.1–5; Paus. 9.2.5–6; Philostr. *Gymn.* 8 (Bremmer 2006, 22, n. 72). Evidence of honouring the Megarian dead at the battle of Plataia is also found in a fifth-century epigram attributed to Simonides, which was inscribed in the fourth century AD by the high-priest Helladios (*IG* VII 53; *SEG* XXXI 384). The text has an introduction by Helladios in which the war-dead are called heroes before then going into Simonides' text, which ends with the word *enagizein*. Ekroth (2002, 78) rejects the *enagizein* as a continuous tradition but may have been added later. As for the term 'heroes' at the start, the word is not part of Simonides' epigram but is the choice of Helladios. Wade-Grey (1933, 96) is sceptical about the attribution to Simonides, cf. Page 1981 213–5. Raaflaub (2004, 63–5) argues that the games were founded in the late fourth century BC in connection with the wars against the Persians pursued by Philip and Alexander; cf. Wallace 2011.

103 For Simonides as the writer of the epigram placed at the site of Thermopylai mentioned in Hdt. 7.228, see Lykourg. *Leocr.* 109; Cic. *Tusc.* 1.101; Kowerski 2005, 152, no. B.6. See also Molyneaux (1992, 6–7, n.6, 12–13, nos 38, 41, 43; 175ff.) and Petrovic (2007, 245–9) for a discussion of the epigram at the site of Thermopylai.

104 For example, the graves of the Spartans who died fighting in Athens in 403 BC were found in the Kerameikos in Athens; Pritchett 1985, 243–4; Kucewicz 2021, 83.

105 Boedeker 1998; 2001; Currie 2005, 92.

106 Ekroth 2002, 278. The offerings of the text resemble also those given for *theoxenia* (eadem, 179). Boedeker (1998, 240) also sees evidence of heroic cult for the Plataia war-dead in Isokrates' *Plataikos* (14.61). In this text, the Plataians attempt to gain Athens' support against the impending destruction of Plataia by Thebes, advising that if Plataia is destroyed, then the dead of the battle of Plataia will not receive the νομιζόμενα (customary funeral offerings), which Boedeker interprets as heroic cult. However, the νομιζόμενα, are usually connected with funeral offerings in general and not necessarily hero cult (Ekroth 2002, 87, 106).

107 Bowra 1933; 2001, 345. *Contra* Podlecki 1968, 258–62. Molyneaux (1992, 186–7) suggests that the poem may have been sung at Thermopylai and commemorated

all of the Thermopylai dead, not just the Spartans. For Simonides and the Persian Wars, see Bravi (2006, 42–7) with bibliography.
108 Goldhill 1991, 125. See also the fourth-century inscription from Thasos, which mentions the war-dead as ἀγαθοί (Pouillioux 1954, 271–2, no. 141, lines 3, 8, pl. 39.6).
109 Aischyl. *Choeph.* 106: Currie 2005, 13, n.15; Duris *FGrH* 76 F 34: Poltera 2008, 474, n.2.
110 Stehle 2001.
111 Young 1968, 62–3; Nagy 1979, 118–19. This is seen in much Archaic lyric poetry, such as the works of Sappho and Theognis, where immortality is metaphorical. Faraone (2002) analyses Pindar's use of *kleos* as a way to conquer death and see the discussion in Currie 2005, 71–4. Wiater (2005) argues for the metaphorical use of the word σηκός (precinct) in the Simonides 531 Page, *PMG* text above.
112 Kegel 1962, 28–37; *contra* Podlecki 1968, 261; Molyneaux 1992, 185.
113 Podlecki 1968, 258–62; *contra* Molyneaux 1992, 186. Pelliccia (2009, 245) looks at a variety of occasions for Simonides' work, both for festivals and private occasions.
114 Stehle 2001, 118; Molyneaux 1992, 186. For Simonides and Sparta, see Hutchinson 2001, 286.
115 Steiner 1999.
116 Currie 2005, 104–5. All the examples Currie cites to argue his point, except that of Brasidas, talk of honours or public burials not cult for the individual.
117 Parker 1996, 137.
118 Heroic epiphanies: Pritchett 1979, 11–46; Speyer 1980; Bravo 2004; Chaniotis 2005, 145–60; Platt 2011, 154–60; Petridou 2016, 107–70. Theseus and Echetlaios, a local Athenian hero, at Marathon: Plut. *Thes.* 35.5; the Dioskouroi at Aegospotamoi: Plut. *Lys.* 12.1; Phylakos and Autonoos protected Delphi during the Persian invasion: Hdt. 8.38–9; Mikalson 2003, 189; Ajax, Telamon, Aeakus, and Aeakidai at Salamis: Hdt. 8.64; cf. Plut. *Them.* 15.
119 It is impossible that Pausanias, the general of Plataia, transferred the bones of Leonidas forty years after the battled of Thermopylai because he would have been dead by then (Paus. 3.14.1). For alternative interpretations of the text, see Connor (1979) with bibliography and discussion; Low 2011, 8; Marincola (2016, 225 n.18) suggests amending the text to 'four years' rather than forty.
120 Chilon's time as ephor is dated *c.* 556/5 BC, during the fifty-fifth or fifty-sixth Olympiad (Diog. Laert. 1.68; Stibbe 1985, 7; Shaw 2003, 225; Christesen 2007, 105) but the precise dates are unknown: he is considered an old man by 570 BC (Diog. Laert. 1.72). Scholars estimate his death to the latter half of the sixth century (Shaw 2003, 225) or soon after his time as ephor (Stibbe 1985, 19).
121 Herodotus attributes the ephorship to Lykourgos (1.65.4).

122 Cartledge, 2001, 120. For Chilon and his involvement in Spartan military matters, see also Stibbe (1995; 1996, 20–1) and Welwei (2004, 127).
123 Wace 1937; Stibbe 1991, 12; Kourinou 2000, 148–9. Jeffery dates the [X]IΛON inscription to around 525 BC on the basis of the letter forms although she is uncertain (*LSAG2*, 200, n.26). Stibbe (1991, 9, fig. 7) pushes the date back to 550–530 BC based on style, while Salapata (2014, 347, no. R10) dates it to 510–500 BC, again, based on the style of the relief.
124 Wace 1937, 220; Salapata 1993, 190; Stibbe 1996, 224–5; Cartledge 2001a, 120.
125 Wace 1937; Stibbe 1991, 12; Kourinou 2000, 148–9.
126 See, for example, *IG* V 1.215; *SEG* II 64–80; *LSAG*^{2}, 198, no. 6, 199, n.7.
127 Lazzarini 1976, 58–9; Woodhead 1981, 43; Guarducci 2008, 305–6. For Archaic Spartan examples of votives inscriptions in the dative to Athena, Apollo or the Dioskouroi, see *LSAG*^{2} (199–200).
128 See *LSAG*^{2}, 199–200 for more examples.
129 Lazzarini 1976, 58–9.
130 Lykourgos is dated anytime between the twelfth and seventh centuries BC (Xen. *Lak. Pol.* 10.8; Aristot. fr.533 Rose; *Ath. pol.* 1313a 26f, Cartledge 2001a, 113–15.
131 *ThesCRA* 2, 163; For the Roman-period cult of Lykourgos, see Hupfloher 2000, 178–82.
132 Harrison 2000, 70, 125.
133 For Chilon as ephor and his involvement in Spartan military matters, see Stibbe (1995; 1996, 204–21) and Welwei (2004, 127).
134 Richer 1994, 63–70; Christesen *forthcoming*, 34–5. Richer (2007, 250) argues for a hierarchy of burial honours according to the bravery demonstrated in battle.
135 The Persian Stoa located in the agora was another such monument that commemorated and perpetuated the memory of the Spartan success over Persia (Paus. 3.13.3; Vitr. 1.1.6); Spawforth 2012, 118–19; Greco and Voza 2016.
136 Flower 2009, 212.
137 Thuc. 4.55; Xen. *Ages.* 9.6; Hodkinson 1999, 99. Agesilaos urged his sister Kyniska to compete in order to prove that winning in chariot competitions was a matter of wealth (Paus. 5.12.5; 6.1.6). She then had a bronze horse and statue group with an inscription declaring that she was the first female to win the wreath in the chariot events at the Olympic Games; Paus. 5.12; 6.1.6; *IG* V 1.1564a; Pomeroy 2002, 21–4; Kyle 2007, 189–91; Millander 2009, 23–6.
138 Hodkinson 1999, 165–6 suggests that the cult was instituted in accordance with a wider Greek phenomenon of heroization of athletes in the fifth century BC.
139 Boardman 1985, 80; Stewart (1990, 255–6). Myron is thought to have been active in the mid-fifth century and contemporary to Phidias and Polyclitus but a little older; Fullerton 2016, 163–4.

140 Christesen (2010) argues for fifth-century heroization due to the political motives of the Agiad kings with Cyrene, where Chionis was an oikistes. Hodkinson (1999, 165) views the setting up of the statue of Chionis at Delphi next to that of Astylos of Syracuse to be related to the dispute in 480 BC between Sparta and Syrace over the leadership against the Persians (Hdt. 7.157–9). Pausanias (6.15.8) also mentions a statue of a seventh-century youth, Eutelidas (Hodkinson 1999, 180, n.39 with bibliography). A statue, of course, does not indicate heroization, as Larson (2007–8, 202) notes.

Chapter 6

1 Boedeker 1993; McCauley 1999, 88–93; Nafissi 2016, 636, 639–40; Pavlides 2021, 29–39.
2 Wace 1905–6a, 293.
3 *ArchDelt* (1972) vol. 27 (B1), 242, 245–51.
4 *ArchDelt* (1996) vol. 51 (B1), 101–3; *ArchDelt* (1997) vol. 52 (B1), 160–2; *ArchDelt* (2001–4) vols 56–9 (B1), 272; cf. Flouris 2000, 4–5. The area also produced two later burials, one of which contained a marble urn; Poupaki 2009, 248.
5 Raftopoulou 1996–7, 276.
6 *ArchDelt* (1972) vol. 27 (B1), 247–8.
7 A similar story is attested by Polybios for the Spartan colony of Taras (8.30), where the dead are buried within the city.
8 *Contra* Kourinou (2000, 218) who argues that before the Hellenistic walls were built, Spartan burials were located at the boundaries of each *kome*, a custom that continued even after the walls were constructed, thus giving the impression that they were inside the inhabited area. See, however, Christesen 2018.
9 cf. Raftopoulou 1996, 273–6; Kourinou 2000, 216. For the geometric burials at Limnai also in the northern part see Kourinou 2000, 94; Zavvou and Themos 2009, 111; Tsouli 2016, 360, n.33; Christesen 2018, 318–21.
10 *ArchDelt* (1972) vol. 27 (B1), 244–5.
11 Flouris 2000, 4; *ArchDelt* (2001–4) vols 56–9 (B1), 179.
12 *ArchDelt* (2006) vol. 61, 275.
13 Zavvou and Themos 2009, 111–12, fig. 11. 10.
14 Tsouli 2016, 360, n.33.
15 Christesen 2018, 320–1, fig. 6.
16 *ArchDelt* (1972) vol. 27 (B1), 247–8.
17 *ArchDelt* (1972), vol. 27 (B1), 243, 244–5; Zavvou and Themos 2009, 119.
18 Tsouli 2016, 361, n.33. See further examples in Christesen 2018, 328–32, fig. 12.

19 Two further Geometric burials were discovered about 20 metres from the site (Raftopoulou 1996–7, 273). Other isolated examples of terracotta plaques have been found in the area; *ArchDelt* (2001–4) vols 56–9 (B1), 179; Salapata 2014, 332.
20 Cavanagh 2018, 68.
21 Tosti 2011, 103.
22 Pavlides 2011.
23 cf. Parker 2011, 289.
24 Parker (2011, 291) argues that evidence of ancestor cult as known from ethnographic descriptions is absent from the Greek world.
25 Boehringer 2001, 42–5. See idem (2001, 39ff) on the Anthesteria as a cult for the collective, anonymous dead and not the family dead as there was no visit to the grave. For a difference between hero cult and that to the ordinary dead see Ekroth 2002, 21.
26 See for example the seventh-century burials at Vari in Attica where the deceased were given burial gifts over a few decades; Alexandridou, 2012; 2017. There, burial rites address a family group that becomes the focus of veneration. There are earlier examples in the Greek world, at Vitsa in Epirus, Minoa on Amorgos and Eretria, for which see Alexandridou 2017, 289 with bibliography.
27 Kourou 2015, 93, 100–1.
28 Antonaccio 1995; 2003, 90; Bremmer 2006; Parker 2011, 291.
29 See Kourou (2015, 93–100) for discussion and further examples.
30 Alexandridou 2017. For other examples of family groups becoming the focus of veneration after death see eadem, 289.
31 See discussion of cult over Bronze Age tombs in Chapter 1.
32 Bravo; Kourou 2015.
33 The dates are based on Christesen 2018, 319.
34 Personal communication with the excavator Christos Flouris.
35 Raftopoulou 1998, 134–5, figs 12.18–19. Two-storey tombs in Sparta, which existed in the Archaic–Hellenistic periods, held in their lower part the primary burial and in their upper parts stored the bones of the earlier burials together with offerings (eadem, 134).
36 Tsouli 2013, 160–1; 2016, 369–71.
37 Earth with the remains of birds, sheep, and goats with traces of burning are suggestive of food preparation at the site. It is unclear whether this activity took place during the burial or at some later grave ritual (Tsouli 2016, 371–7; cf. Christesen 2018, 327).
38 Antonaccio 1995, 102–26.
39 Tsouli 2013, 159–60; 2016, 366–9.
40 Tsouli 2016, 370.
41 Van Wees 1999, 3–4; Hodkinson 2000, 2; 76.

42 Cavanagh 2018, 67; cf. Zavvou and Themos 2009, 112–13, fig. 11.10.
43 Halbwachs 1992, 200.
44 Assmann 2011, 18.
45 On the topic see Cartledge and Spawforth 2002, 176–95; Spawforth 2012, 117–30; Kennell 2018.
46 Cartledge and Spawforth 2002, 176–95.
47 On the topic see Schear 2003, 218–20.
48 Kennell 1995, 31–8; 2018.
49 Kennell 1995, 32.
50 Cartledge 2002, 86, 183.
51 Cartledge 2002, 186; Kennell 2018, 646–8.
52 Cartledge 2002, 94–5. Eurykles may have been responsible for the remodelling of the Persian Stoa and the Augustan theatre; Spawforth 2012, 218–20, 220–5.
53 Cartledge 2002, 90–1. There is little support of private patronage of civic buildings in Sparta in all periods apart from some limited evidence from Roman Sparta; Cartledge 2002, 124, App. I 25, 29. 41. See for example (*S.E.G.* xi.846) of an inscribed block belonging to the entablature of a building and dedicated by the priest Polydamas son of Phoebidas (first century BC?).
54 Alcock 1994, 230.
55 For a recent discussion of the topic of cultural memory in Roman Sparta, see Kennell 2018.
56 Kennell 2010, 189. On the topic see also Kennell 2018.
57 Kennell 2018.
58 Kennell 2018, 649–54.
59 Kennell 2018, 651–2. Other elements pertained to the cultural memory of Roman Sparta, such as the Messenian Wars, the festivals of the Hyakinthia and the Gymnopaidia, and individuals such as Chilon; idem for a full discussion.
60 Hupfloher 2000, 131; Lafond 2018, 411.
61 Hupfloher (2000, 117–18, 141). For other hereditary priesthoods see idem and Chrimes 1949, 471–4, Appendix V.
62 Spawforth, 1985, 196–7.
63 Some inscriptions indicate the generations of descent, e.g. in the forty-fourth generation of the Dioskouroi. See discussion and references in Lafond 2018, 411–12. For the inscription mentioning Lycurgus see Spawforth 1994, 437–8, no. 10.
64 Schachermeyr 1984.
65 *ArchDelt* (1972) vol. 27 (B1), 248.
66 *ArchDelt* (1972) vol. 27 (B1), 248; Stibbe 1989a, 92.
67 A number of scholars raise the possibility that a 'club-house', the *lesche*, in Sparta (and elsewhere) may be connected with hero cults; Nafissi 1991, 318–27; Burkert

2003, 140. Pausanias mentions the *lesche* of the Crotani, who are a group from the Pitanatans, near the tombs of the Agiad kings (3.14.2) and another called the painted *lesche* near the hero shrine of Cadmus, son of Agenor and his descendants Oeolycus and Aegeus (Paus. 3.15.8). Nafissi (1991, 318–27) notes the proximity of these hero shrines (and the graves of the Agiad kings) to the leschai. He suggests that both types of building would be related to the unity of a familial group and the memory of the ancestors; Nafissi 1991, 321–2. It is also suggested that the lesche would be built near the grave of one's ancestor and so a private part of religion would be celebrated associated with familial groups; Tosti 2011, 102. Thus, Nafissi (1991, 331–4) interprets a number of long buildings, such as Ergatikes katoikies (5), the Stavropoulos plot (6), and the one at the Laskari plot as examples of a *lesche* – a building where members would meet up, by the shrine of a hero. Tosti (2011) argues the same for the cult at Stauffert Street (8).

However, in general, *leschai* appear to serve as places for assembly of old men for conversation and dining (Hesychius s.v. λέσχη; λέσχαι; Etymologicum Magnum s.v. λέσχη; Bremmer 2008, 153–67, esp. 157–64). This is not unlike Plutarch's attestation (*Lyc.* 25.1) whereby old men spend their time at a *lesche* in Sparta or even Cratinus (fr.175=Athen.4.138e) where he mentions a *lesche* not in relation to a particular group or a hero but in connection with dining. In Plutarch (*Lyc.*16), a *lesche* in Sparta is a place where the tribal leaders (καθήμενοι τῶν φυλετῶν) examine the new-born infants. The connection between the *leschai* and hero shrines, as suggested by Nafissi, is possible and if so it would be a good example where kinship ties and religion merge in Sparta. However, their relationship is unclear to say the least; Pausanias could be describing what is near or around the hero shrines and does not make a clear link between the two. It is Pausanias' narrative style to often jump from monument to monument in the description of the topography. He is also selective and leaves behind buildings that do not interest him.

68 Laskaris: *ArchDelt* (1966) vol. 21 (B1), 154–5; *ArchDelt* (1967) vol. 22 (B1), 202–3; *ArchDelt* (1969) vol. 24 (B1), 137). 'Altar of Lykourgos': initially dated to the to the second century BC (Dickins 1905–6, 295–302), now it is dated to the fourth century BC: https://eurotas.wordpress.com/2015/09/29/1794/.
69 Stibbe 1989a, 84–93. Steinhauer 2009, 274–5; Doulfis 2019, 141. Nafissi (1991, 331-3) identifies them as *leschai*.
70 For Hellenistic burials in Sparta, see Raftopoulou 1998, 134–6; Schörner 2007, 66; Zavvou and Themos 2009, 119; see also at the Sourli plot *ArchDelt* (2013) vol. 68 (B1), 124–5; Tsouli 2016, 360–1 n.33.
71 *ArchDelt* (2001–4) vols 56–9 (B4), 226.
72 Cavanagh 2018, 83.
73 Raftopoulou 1998, 134; Cavanagh 2018, 83–4. On Hellenistic tombs in general, see Fedak 2006.

74 Spawforth 1978, 249–55; Flämig 2007, 213–14, no. I, 3; Fouquet 2017, 122. See further examples from Roman Sparta in Flämig 2007, 171–4, nos 69–73.
75 Cormack 2004, 45 on space and burial in the city; Flämig (2007, 130–8) on intra-mural burials in Roman Greece; Fouquet 2017 on intra-mural burials in Argos, Messene and Mantineia.

Bibliography

Abramson, H. 1978. *Greek Hero Shrines* (PhD Diss.). University of California, Berkeley, CA.

Abramson, H. 1979. A hero shrine for Phrontis at Sounion? *CSCA* 12: 1–19.

Adams, D. Q. 1987. Ἥρως and Ἥρα: of men and heroes in Greek and Indo-European. *Glotta* 65: 171–8.

Ahlberg-Cornell, G. 1992. *Myth and Epos in Early Greek Art: Representation and Interpretation* (Studies in Mediterranean Archaeology 100). Jonsered.

Albersmeier, S. (ed.). 2009. *Heroes: mortals and myths in ancient Greece*. Baltimore.

Alcock, S. E. 1991. Tomb cult and the post-Classical polis. *AJA* 95: 447–67.

Alcock, S. E. 1994. The heroic past in the Hellenistic present. *Échos du monde classique* 38: 221–34.

Alcock, S. E. 2002. *Archaeologies of the Greek Past: landscape, monuments and memory*. Cambridge.

Aleshire, S. B. 1989. *The Athenian Asklepeion: the people, their dedications, and the inventories*. Amsterdam.

Alexandridou, A. 2017. Special burial treatment for the 'heroized' dead in the Attic countryside: The case of the elite cemetery of Vari. In *Interpreting the Seventh Century BC: tradition and innovation*, edited by X. Charalambidou and C. Morgan: 281–91. Oxford.

Alexiou, M. 2002. *The Ritual Lament in Greek Tradition*, revised by D. Yatromanolakis and P. Roilos. Lanham, MD.

Allen, A. 1993. *The Fragments of Mimnermus: text and commentary*. Stuttgart.

Alroth, B. 1988. The positioning of Greek votive offerings. In *Early Greek Cult Practice: Proceedings of the Fifth International Symposium at the Swedish Institute at Athens, 26–29 June, 1986*, edited by R. Hägg, N. Marinatos and G. C. Nordquist: 195–203. Stockholm.

Amandry, P. 1971. Collection Paul Canellopoulos, I: armes et lébes de bronze. *BCH* 95: 585–626.

Ammerman, R. M. 2002. *The Sanctuary of Santa Venera at Paestum II: the votive terracottas*. Ann Arbour, MI.

Andersen, L. H. 1977. *Relief Pithoi from the Archaic Period of Greek Art* (PhD Diss.). The University of Michigan.

Andrews, A. 1956. *The Greek Tyrants*. London.

Andronikos, M. 1956. Λακωνικά Ανάγλυφα. *Peloponnesiaka* 1: 253–314.

Antonaccio, C. 1994. Contesting the past: hero cult, tomb cult, and epic in early Greece. *AJA* 98 (3): 389–410.

Antonaccio, C. 1995. *An Archaeology of Ancestors: tomb cult and hero cult in early Greece*. Lanham, MD.

Antonaccio, C. 1999. Colonization and the origins of hero cult. In Hägg 1999: 109–21.

Antonaccio, C. 2002. Warriors, traders, ancestors: the 'heroes' of Lefkandi. In *Images of Ancestors* (Århus Studies in Mediterranean Archaeology 5), edited by J. Munk Høtje: 13–42. Århus.

Antonaccio, C. 2005. Dedications and the character of cult. In Hägg and Alroth 2005: 99–112.

Antonaccio, C. 2006. Religion, *basileis* and heroes. In Deger-Jalkotzy and Lemos 2006: 381–95.

Arafat, K. W. 1996. *Pausanias' Greece: ancient artists and Roman rulers*. Cambridge.

Aravantinos, V. 2014a. The Sanctuaries of Herakles and Apollo Ismenios at Thebes: new evidence. In *Interpreting the Seventh Century* BC: *tradition and innovation*, edited by X. Charalambidou and C. Morgan: 221–230. Oxford.

Aravantinos, V. 2014b. The inscriptions from the sanctuary of Herakles at Thebes: an overview. In *The Epigraphy and History of Boeotia*, edited by N. Papazarkadas: 149–210. Leiden and Boston.

Arnaotouglou, I. 2015. Cult Associations and Politics: Worshipping Bendis in Classical and Hellenistic Athens. In *Private Associations and the Public Sphere: Proceedings of a Symposium held at the Royal Danish Academy of Sciences and Letters, 9–11 September 2010*, edited by V. Cabrielsen and C. A. Thomsen: 25–56. Copenhagen.

Asheri, D. 2007. 'Book I'. In *A Commentary on Herodotus Books I–IV*, edited by O. Murray and A. Moreno: 57–218. Oxford.

Assmann, J. 2011. *Cultural Memory and Early Civilization: writing, remembrance, and political imagination*. Cambridge.

Austin, M. M. 2006. *The Hellenistic World from Alexander to the Roman Conquest: a selection of ancient sources in translation* (2nd ed.). Cambridge.

Barfoed, S. 2015. The significant few: Miniature pottery from the Sanctuary of Zeus at Olympia. *World Archaeology* 47 (1): 170–88.

Barletta, B. 2001. *The Origins of the Greek Architectural Orders*. Cambridge.

Barletta, B. 2017. *The Sanctuary of Athena at Sounion*. Princeton, NJ.

Barr, J. P. 1996. Horse and rider plaques at Ilion: a preliminary study of Hellenistic hero-cult in Asia Minor. *Studia Troica* 6: 133–57.

Barrigón, C. 2000. La désignation des héros et héroïnes dans la poésie lyrique grecque. In Pirenne-Delforge and Suárez de la Torre 2000: 1–14.

Baudini, A. 2006. L'agorà di Sparta: dati, posizionamento e alcune considerazioni. In *Workshop di archeologia classica: paesaggi, costruzioni, reperti. 3.2006*, edited by F. Serra: 21–35. Pisa.

Beeks, R. S. 2003. The origin of Apollo. *Journal of Ancient Near Eastern Religions* 3: 1–21.

Bennett, E. L. Jr. and J-P. Olivier. 1973. *The Pylos Taplets Transcribed*. Rome.

Bennett, M. and A. J. Paul. 2002. *Magna Graecia: Greek art from south Italy and Sicily.* Cleveland.

Benton, S. 1938-9. Excavations in Ithaca, III; the cave at Polis, II. *ABSA* 39: 1-51.

Bentz, M. 1998. *Panathenäische Preisamphoren: eine athenische Vasengattung und ihre Funktion vom 6.-4. Jahrhundert v. Chr.* Basel.

Bérard, C. 1969. Note sur la fouille au sud de l'hérôon. *Antike Kunst* 12: 74-9.

Bérard, C. 1970. *L'Hérôon à la Porte de L'Ouest.* (Eretria. Fouilles et Recherches III). Berne.

Bérard, C. 1982. Récupérer la mort du prince: héroïsation et formation de la cité. In *La mort: les morts dans des sociétés anciennes,* edited by G. Gnoli and J. P. Vernant: 19-26. Cambridge.

Berger, E. 1970. *Das Basler Arztrelief.* Basel.

Berquist, B. 1990. Symbotic space: a functional aspect of Greek dining-rooms. In *Symbotica: the study of the symbosium,* edited by O. Murray: 38-65. Oxford.

Best, J. 2015. Roadside assistance: religious spaces and personal experience in Athens. In *Autopsy in Athens: recent archaeological research on Athens and Attica,* edited by M. M. Miles: 100-7. Oxford.

Bevan, E. 1986. *Representations of Animals in Sanctuaries of Artemis and Other Olympian Deities* (BAR international Series 315). Oxford.

Biers, W. R. 1971. Excavations at Phlius, 1924, the votive deposit. *Hesperia* 41 (4): 397-423.

Bilis, T. and M. Magnisali. 2011-12. Ζητήματα της αρχιτεκτονικής αναπαράστασης των μνημείων στο ιερό του Αμυκλαίου Απόλλωνα. *MusBenaki* 11-12: 125-36.

Blandin, B. 1998. Recherches sur les tombes à inhumation de l' Hérôon d' Erétrie. In *Euboica: L'Eubea e la presenza Euboica in Calcidica e in Occidente. Atti del convegno internazionale di Napoli, 13-16 Novembre 1996,* (AION suppl. 12), edited by M. Bats and B. d'Agostino: 135-46. Naples.

Blegen, C. W. 1937. *Prosymna: the Helladic settlement preceding the Argive Heraeum.* Cambridge.

Boardman, J. 1963. Artemis Orthia and chronology. *ABSA* 58: 1-7.

Boardman, J. 1966. Attic Geometric scenes, old and new. *JHS* 86: 1-5.

Boardman, J. 1978. *Greek Sculpture: the Archaic period.* London.

Boardman, J. 1985. *Greek Sculpture: the Classical period.* London.

Boardman, J. 1992. For you are the progeny of unconquered Herakles. In Sanders 1992a: 25-9.

Boardman, J. 2002, *The Archaeology of Nostalgia: how the Greeks re-created their mythical past.* London.

Boedeker, D. 1993. Hero cult and politics in Herodotus: the bones of Orestes. In *Cultural Poetics in Archaic Greece: cult, performance, politics,* edited by C. Dougherty and L. Kurke: 164-77. Oxford.

Boedeker, D. 1998. The new Simonides and heroization at Plataia. In *Archaic Greece: new approaches and new evidence,* edited by N. Fisher and H. van Wees: 231-49. Swansea.

Boedeker, D. 2001. Heroic historiography: Simonides and Herodotus on Plataea. In Boedeker and Sider 2001: 120–34.

Boedeker, D. 2008. Family matters: domestic religion in Classical Greece. In *Household and Family Religion in Antiquity*, edited by J. P. Bodel and S. M. Olyan: 229–47. Malden.

Boedeker, D. and D. Sider (eds). 2001. *The New Simonides: contexts of praise and desire.* Oxford.

Boehringer, C. 1980. Mégare: traditions mythique, espace sacré et naissance de la cite. *AC* 49: 5–22.

Boehringer, D. 2001. *Heroenkulte in Griechenland von der Geometrischen bis zur Klassischen Zeit: Attika, Argolis, Messenien.* Berlin.

Bol, P. C. 1989. *Argivische Schilde* (Olympische Forschunghen 17). Berlin.

Bonias, Z. 1988. *Ένα αγροτικό ιερό στις Αιγιές Λακωνίας.* Athens.

Bonfante, L. 1989. Nudity as a costume in Classical art. *AJA* 93 (4): 543–70.

Bookidis, N. 1993. Ritual dining at Corinth. In *Greek Sanctuaries: new approaches*, edited by N. Marinatos and R. Hägg: 34–50. London; New York.

Bookidis, N. 2003. The Sanctuaries of Corinth. In Williams and Bookidis 2003: 247–60.

Bookidis, N. and R. Stroud. 1997. *The Sanctuary of Demeter and Kore: topography and architecture* (Corinth vol. XVIII, part III). Princeton, NJ.

Bosanquet, R. C. 1905–6. Laconia: Excavations at Sparta, 1906. *ABSA* 12: 277–83.

Boss, M. 2000. *Lakonische Votivgaben aus Blei.* Würzburg.

Bowie, E. L. 1996. Past and present in Pausanias. In *Pausanias Historien* (Fondation Hardt, Entretiens sur l'antiquité classique 41) edited by J. Bingen: 207–39. Geneva.

Bowra, C. M. 1933. Simonides on the fallen of Thermopylae. *CPh* 28: 277–81.

Bowra, C. M. 2001. *Greek Lyric Poetry from Alcman to Simonides.* (2nd ed). Oxford.

Bradley, R. 1990. *The Passage of Arms: an archaeological analysis of prehistoric hoards and votive deposits.* Cambridge and New York.

Bravi, L. 2006. *Gli epigrammi di Simonide e le vie della tradizione.* Rome.

Bravo, J. J. III. 2004. Heroic Epiphanies: narrative, visual, and cultic contexts. In *Divine Epiphanies in the Ancient World*, edited by N. Marinatos: 63–84. Illinois.

Bravo, J. J. III. 2006. *The Hero Shrine of Opheltes/Archemoros at Nemea: a case study of ancient Greek hero cult* (PhD Diss.). The University of California, Berkeley, CA.

Bravo, J. J. III. 2009. Recovering the past: the origins of Greek heroes and hero cult. In Albersmeier 2009: 10–29.

Bravo, J. J. III. 2018. *Excavations at Nemea IV: The Shrine of Opheltes.* Oakland, CA.

Brelich, A. 1958. *Gli Eroi Greci: un problema storico-religioso.* Rome.

Brelich, A. 1969. *Paides e Parthenoi.* Rome.

Bremmer, J. N. 1983. *The Early Greek Concept of the Soul.* Princeton, NJ.

Bremmer, J. N. 1994. *Greek Religion.* Oxford.

Bremmer, J. N. 2006. The rise of the hero cult and the new Simonides. *ZPE* 158: 15–26.

Bremmer, J. N. 2008. *Greek Religion and Culture, the Bible and the Ancient Near East.* Leiden and Boston, MA.

Brisart, T. 2011. *Un art citoyen: Recherches sur l'orientalisation des artisanats en Grèce proto-archaïque.* Brussels.
Broneer, O. 1942. Hero shrines in the Corinthian agora. *Hesperia* 11 (2): 128–61.
Brown, E. L. 2004. In search of Anatolian Apollo. In ΧΑΡΙΣ: *Essays in Honor of Sara A. Immerwahr* (Hesperia suppl. 33), edited by A. P. Chapin: 243–57. Princeton, NJ.
Bruit, L. 1990. The meal at the Hyakinthia: Ritual consumption and offering. In *Sympotica: A symposium on the symposion*, edited by O. Murray: 162–74. Oxford.
Brulé, P. and L. Piolot. 2004. Women's way of death: fatal childbirth or *hierai*? Commemorative stones at Sparta and Plutarch, *Lycurgus*, 27. 3. In *Spartan Society*, edited by T. J. Figueira: 151–78. Swansea.
Bruneau, P. 1970. *Recherches sur les cultes de Délos a l'époque hellénistique et à l'époque impériale* (BEFAR 217). Paris.
Burgess, J. S. 1996. The Non-Homeric *Cypria*. *TAPA* 126: 77–99.
Burgess, J. S. 2001. *The Tradition of the Trojan War in Homer and the Epic Cycle*. Baltimore, MD.
Burgess, J. S. 2009. *The Death and Afterlife of Achilles*. Baltimore, MD.
Burkert, W. B. 1975. Apellai und Apollon. *RhM* 118: 1–21.
Burkert, W. B. 1985. *Greek Religion: Archaic and Classical*, translated by J. Raffan. Oxford.
Burkert, W. B. 1987. The Making of Homer in the Sixth Century BC: rhapsodes versus Stesichoros. In *Papers on the Amasis Painter and his World: colloquium sponsored by the Getty Center for the History of Art and the Humanities and symposium sponsored by the J. Paul Getty Museum*: 43–62. Malibu.
Burkert, W. B. 1992. *The Orientalizing Revolution: Near Eastern influence on Greek culture in the early Archaic Age.* Cambridge, MA; London.
Burkert, W. B. 1995. Greek *Poleis* and civic cults. In *Papers of the Copenhagen Polis Centre* 2 (Historia Einzelschriften 95), edited by M. S. Hansen and K. A. Raaflaub: 201–10. Stuttgart.
Burkert, W. B. 2003. *Kleine Schriften II: Orientalia*. Gottingen.
Burr, D. 1933. A Geometric house and a proto-Attic votive deposit. *Hesperia* 2: 542–640.
Busolt, G. and H. Swoboda. 1926. *Griechische Staatskunde* II. Munich.
Buschor, E. and W. von Massow. 1927. Von Amyklaion. *MDAI(A)* 52: 1–85.
Buxton, R. (ed.). 2000. *Oxford Readings in Greek Religion.* Oxford.
Calame, C. 1987. Spartan genealogies: the mythical representation of a spatial organization. In *Interpretations of Greek Mythology*, edited by J. Bremmer: 153–86. London.
Calame, C. 2001. *Choruses of Young Women in Ancient Greece: their morphology, religious role and social functions.* Lanham, MD.
Callaghan, P. J. 1978. KRS 1976: excavations at a shrine of Glaukos, Knossos. *ABSA* 73: 1–30.
Calligas, P. G. 1988. Hero cult in early Iron Age Greece. In Hägg, Marinatos and Nordquist 1988: 229–34.
Calligas, P. G. 1992. From the Amyklaion. In Sanders 1992a: 31–48.

Camp, J. M. II. 1986. *The Athenian Agora: excavations in the heart of Classical Athens.* London.

Campbell, D. A. 1982. *Greek Lyric Poetry: a selection of early Greek lyric, elegiac, and iambic poetry.* Bristol.

Campbell, D. A. 1991. *Greek Lyric III.* Cambridge, MA.

Carlier, P. 1984. *La Royauté en Grèce avant Alexandre.* Strasbourg.

Carpenter, T. H. 1986. *Dionysian Imagery in Archaic Greek Art: its development in black-figure vase painting.* Oxford.

Carter, J. B. 1985. *Greek Ivory-Carving in the Orientalizing and Archaic Periods.* New York.

Carter, J. B. 1987. The masks of Orthia. *AJA* 91: 355–81.

Cartledge, P. A. 1977. Hoplites and heroes: Sparta's contribution to the technique of ancient warfare. *JHS* 97: 11–27.

Cartledge, P. A. 1987. *Agesilaos and the Crisis of Sparta.* London.

Cartledge, P. A. 1988. Yes, Spartan kings were heroized. *LCM* 13 (3): 43–4.

Cartledge, P. A. 1992. Early Lacedaimon: The making of a conquest state. In Sanders 1992a: 49–55.

Cartledge, P. A. 2001a. *Spartan Reflections.* London.

Cartledge, P. A. 2001b. Sparta's Pausanias: another Laconian past. In *Pausanias: Travel and Memory in Roman Greece*, edited by S. E. Alcock, J. F. Cherry and J. Elsner: 167–74. Oxford.

Cartledge, P. A. 2002. *Sparta and Laconia: a regional history 1300–362 BC* (2nd ed.). London.

Cartledge, P. A. 2003. *The Spartans: the world of warrior-heroes of ancient Greece, from utopia to crisis and collapse.* New York.

Cartledge, P. A. 2007. Review of J. Ducat, *Spartan Education. New England Classical Journal* 34: 149–50.

Cartledge, P. and A. Spawforth. 2002. *Hellenistic and Roman Sparta: a tale of two cities.* London.

Cassio, A. C. 2012. L'eroe Lakedaimon e gli onori funebri per i re di Sparta (orac. ap. Herodot. 7, 220 = nr.100 Parke-Wormell). In *Venuste Noster: Scritti offerti a Leopoldo Gamberale*, edited by M. Passalacqua, M. De Nonno and A. M. Morelli: 37–42. Hildesheim.

Catling, H. W. 1976–7. Excavations at the Menelaion, Sparta, 1973–1976. *AR* 23: 24–42.

Catling, H. W. 1977. Excavations at the Menelaion, 1976–1977. *Lakonika Spoudai* 3: 406–16.

Catling, H. W. 1990. A Sanctuary of Zeus Messapeus: excavations at Aphyssou, Tsakona. *ABSA* 85: 15–35.

Catling, H. W. 1994. A fragment of an Archaic temple model from Artemis Orthia. *ABSA* 89: 269–75.

Catling, H. W. 2009. *Sparta. Menelaion I: the Bronze Age.* London.

Catling, H. W. and H. Cavanagh. 1976. Two inscribed bronzes from the Menelaion. *Kadmos* 15: 145–57.

Catling, R. 1986. Excavations at the Menelaion, 1985. *Lakonikai Spoudai* 8: 205–16.

Catling, R. 1992. A votive deposit of seventh-century pottery from the Menelaion. In Sanders 1992a: 57–75.

Catling, R. 1994. A fragment of an Archaic temple model from Artemis Orthia, *ABSA* 89: 269–75.

Catling, R. 1995. Archaic Laconian architecture: the evidence of a temple model, *ABSA* 90: 317–24.

Catling, R. 2002. The survey area from the early Iron Age to the Classical Period. In Cavanagh *et al.* 2002: 151–256.

Cavanagh, W. G. 2002. *Continuity and Change in a Greek Rural Landscape: The Laconia survey*, i: *methodology and interpretation* (ABSA suppl. 26). London.

Cavanagh, W. G. 2018. An Archaeology of ancient Sparta with reference to Laconia and Messenia. In Powell 2018: 61–92.

Cavanagh, W. G. *forthcoming*. The lead votives. *Menelaion II*.

Cavanagh, W. G. and R. R. Laxton. 1984. Lead figurines from the Menelaion and seriation. *ABSA* 79: 23–36.

Cavanagh, W. G. and S. E. C. Walker (eds). 1998. *Sparta in Laconia: proceedings of the 19th British Museum Classical colloquium*. London.

Cavanagh, W. G., C. Gallou and M. Georgiadis (eds). 2009. *Sparta and Laconia: from Prehistory to Premodern: proceedings of the conference held in Sparta, organized by the British School at Athens, the University of Nottingham, the 5th ephoreia of Prehistoric and Classical antiquities and the 5th ephoreia of Byzantine antiquities, 17–20 March 2005*. London.

Cavanagh, W. G., Crouwel, J., Catling, R. W. V., Shipley, G., Armstrong, P., Fiselier, J., Rackham, O., Van Berghem, J.-W. and M. Wagstaff. 1996. *Continuity and Change in a Greek Rural Landscape: the Laconia survey*, ii: *archaeological data* (ABSA suppl. 27). London.

Chaniotis, A. 2005. *War in the Hellenistic World: a social and cultural history*. Oxford.

Chapin, A. P and L. A. Hitchcock. 2007. Homer and Laconian topography: this is what the book says, and this is what the land tells us. In *EPOS: Reconsidering Greek Epic and Aegean Bronze Age Archaeology* (Aegaeum 28), edited by R. Laffineur and S. Morris: 255–62. Liège and Austin.

Chapouthier, F. 1935. *Les Dioscures au service d'une déese*. Rome.

Charalampidou, X. and C. Morgan (eds). 2017. *Interpreting the Seventh Century BC: tradition and innovation*. Oxford.

Chrimes, K. M. T. 1949. *Ancient Sparta: a re-examination of the evidence*. Manchester.

Christensen, L. B. 2009. "Cult" in the study of religion and archaeology. In *Aspects of Ancient Greek cult: context, ritual and iconography*, edited by J. T. Jensen *et al.*: 13–27. Århus.

Christesen, P. 2007. *Olympic Victor Lists and Ancient Greek History*. Cambridge.

Christesen, P. 2010. King playing politics: the heroization of Chionis of Sparta. *Historia* 59 (1): 26–73.

Christesen, P. 2018. The typology and topography of Spartan burials from the Protogeometric through Hellenistic periods: re-thinking Spartan exceptionalism and the ostensible cessation of adult intramural burials in the Greek World. *ABSA* 113: 307–63.

Christesen, P. 2019. *A New Reading of the Damonon Stele* (*Histos* Suppl. 10). Newcastle upon Tyne.

Christesen, P. 2021. Herodotus 9.85 and Spartiate Burial Customs. *Classica et Mediaevalia* 69, 1–72.

Clader, L. L. 1976. *Helen: the evolution from divine to heroic in Greek epic tradition.* Leiden.

Cleland, L. 2005. *The Brauron Clothing Catalogues: text, analysis, glossary and translation* (BAR International Series 1428). Oxford.

Cohen, A. P. 1985. *The Symbolic Construction of Community.* Chichester.

Comella, A. 2002. *I Rilievi Votivi Greci di Periodo Arcaico e Classico: diffusione, ideologia, committenza.* Bari.

Coldstream, J. N. 1968. *Greek Geometric Pottery: a survey of ten local styles and their chronology.* London.

Coldstream, J. N. 1976. Hero cults in the age of Homer. *JHS* 96: 8–17.

Coldstream, J. N. 2003. *Geometric Greece: 900–700 BC.* London.

Cole, S. G. 1988. The use of water in Greek sanctuaries. In Hägg, Marinatos and Nordquist 1988: 161–5.

Cole, S. G. 1994. Civic cult and civic identity. In *Sources for the Ancient Greek City State*, edited by M. H. Hansen: 292–325. Copenhagen.

Confino, A. 1997. Collective Memory and Cultural History: problems of method, *American Historical Review* 102: 1386–403.

Connor, W. R. 1979. Pausanias 3.14.1: a sideline of Spartan history, c. 440 BC? *TAPhA* 109: 21–7.

Constantinidou, S. 1998. Dionysiac elements in Spartan cult dances. *Phoenix* 52: 15–30.

Corso, A. 2007. *The Art of Praxiteles II: the mature years* (Studia Archaeologica 153). Rome.

Cosmopoulos, M. B. 2014. Cult, continuity, and social memory: Mycenaean Eleusis and the transition to the Early Iron Age, *AJA* 118 (3): 401–27.

Coudin, F. 2009a. *Les Laconiens et la Méditerranée à l'époque archaïque.* Naples.

Coudin, F. 2009b. Les vases laconiens entre Orient et Occident au vi^e sècle av. J-C: formes et iconographie. *RA* (2): 227–63.

Cook, J. M. 1950. Laconia. Kalývia Sokhás. *ABSA* 45: 261–81.

Cook, J. M. 1953. Mycenae, 1939–1952, part 3: the Agamemnoneion. *ABSA* 48: 30–68.

Cormack, S. 2004. *The Space of Death in Roman Asia Minor.* Wien.

Coulanges de, F. 1991. *Η Αρχαία Πόλη*, translated by L. Stamatiadi. Athens.

Costaki, L. 2008. Πάντα πλήρη θεῶν εἶναι: παρόδια ἱερὰ στήν ἀρχαία Ἀθήνα. In *Μικρός ἱερομνήμων μελέτες εἰς μνήμην Michael H. Jameson*, edited by A. P. Matthaiou and I. Polinskaya: 145–66. Athens.

Coulson, W. D. E. 1985. The Dark Age pottery of Sparta. *ABSA* 80: 29–84.

Crielaard, J. P. 1995. Homer, history and archaeology. In *Homeric Questions: essays in philology, ancient history and archaeology, including the papers of a conference organized by the Netherlands Institute at Athens (15 May 1993)*, edited by J. P. Crielaard: 201–88. Amsterdam.

Crielaard, J. P. 2002. Past or present? Epic poetry, aristocratic self-representation and the concept of time in the eighth and seventh centuries BC. In *Omero Tremila anni Dopo*, edited by F. Montanari: 239–65. Rome.

Crouwel, J. H. *et al.* 2001. Geraki: An akropolis site in Laconia. Preliminary report of the seventh season. *Pharos* 9: 1–32.

Currie, B. 2005. *Pindar and the Cult of Heroes*. Oxford.

Daux, G. 1983. Le calendrier de Thorikos au Musée J. Paul Getty, *AntCl* 52: 150–74.

Davies, G. 2005. On being seated: gender and body language in Hellenistic and Roman art. In *Body Language in the Greek and Roman Worlds,* edited by D. Cairns: 215–38. Swansea.

Davies, M. 1988a. Monody, choral lyric and the tyranny of the hand-book. *CQ* 38 (1): 52–64.

Davies, M. 1988b. Corinna's date revisited. *SIFC* 81: 186–94.

Davies, P. 2018. Equality and distinction within the Spartiate community. In Powell 2018: 480–99.

Dawkins, R. M. 1908-9. The seasons' work. *ABSA* 15: 1–4.

Delivorrias, A. 2009. The throne of Apollo at Amyklai: old proposals, new perspectives. In Cavanagh, Gallou, and Georgiadis 2009: 133–5.

de Elvira, A. 1992. Jacinto. *Myrtia* 7: 7–40.

Demakopoulou, K. 1982. *Το Μυκηναίκο Ιερό στο Αμυκλαίο και η ΥΕ ΙΙΙ Γ Περιόδος στη Λακωνία*. Athens.

Demakopoulou, K. 2009a. Το Μυκηναικό ιερό στο Αμυκλαίο: μια νέα προσέγγιση. In Cavanagh, Gallou and Georgiadis 2009: 95–104.

Demakopoulou, K. 2009b. Laconia LHIII C late and submycenaean: evidence from Epidauros Limera, Pellana, the Amyklaion and other sites. In *LH III C chronology and synchronisms III, LH III C Late and the transition to the Early Iron Age: proceedings of the international workshop held at the Austrian Academy of Sciences at Vienna, February 23rd and 24th, 2007*, edited by S. Deger-Jalkotzy and A. B. Bächle: 117–26. Vienna.

Demakopoulou, K. 2011–12. The early cult at the Amyklaion: the Mycenaean sanctuary. *MusBenaki* 11–12: 105–12.

Deoudi, M. 1999. *Heroenkulte in Homerischer Zeit* (BAR international series 806). Oxford.

Deoudi, M. 2008. *Ithake: Die Polis-Höhle, Odysseus und die Nymphen*. Thessaloniki.

Deger-Jalkotzy, S. 2006. Late Mycenaean warrior tombs. In Deger-Jalkotzy and Lemos 2006: 151–79.

Deger-Jalkotzy, S. 2009. From LHIII C Late to the Early Iron Age: the submycenaean period at Elateia. In *LH III C chronology and synchronisms III, LH III C Late and the transition to the Early Iron Age: proceedings of the international workshop held at the Austrian Academy of Sciences at Vienna, February 23rd and 24th, 2007*, edited by S. Deger-Jalkotzy and A. B. Bächle: 77–116. Vienna.

Deger-Jalkotzy, S. and I. Lemos (eds). 2006. *Ancient Greece: from the Mycenaean palaces to the Age of Homer* (Edinburgh Leventis Studies 3). Edinburgh.

Dentzer, J.-M. 1982. *Le Motif du Banquet couché dans le procheorient et le monde grec du VIIe ai IVe Siècle avant J.-C.* Rome.

Desborough, V. R. d' A. 1964. *The last Mycenaean and their Successors: an archaological survey c. 1200–1000 BC*. Oxford.

Devillers, M. 1988. *An Archaic and Classical Votive Deposit from a Mycenaean Tomb at Thorikos* (Miscellanea Graeca 8). Gent.

Dickins, G. 1905–6. Excavations at Sparta, 1906. The great altar near the Eurotas. *ABSA* 12: 295–302.

Dickins, G. 1906–7a. Laconia. Excavations at Sparta, 1907. The Hieron of Athena Chalkioikos. *ABSA* 13: 139–54.

Dickins, G. 1906–7b. Laconia. Excavations at Sparta, 1907. A sanctuary on the Megalopolis road. *ABSA* 13: 169–73.

Dickins, G. 1912. The growth of the Spartan policy. *JHS* 32: 1–42.

Dickins, G. 1929. Terracotta masks. In Dawkins, *Orthia*: 163–86.

Dietrich, B. C. 1975. The Dorian Hyacinthia: a survival from the Bronze Age. *Kadmos* 14: 133–42.

Dillon, M. A. 2007. Were Spartan women who died in childbirth honoured with grave inscriptions? *Hermes* 135: 147–65.

Dodds, E. R. 1973. The religion of the ordinary man in Classical Greece. In *The Ancient Concept of Progress and other Essays on Greek Literature and Belief*: 140–56. Oxford.

Donohue, A. A. 2005. *Greek Sculpture and the Problem of Description*. Cambridge.

Dougherty, C. 1993. Its murder to found a colony. In *Cultural Poetics in Archaic Greece: cult, performance, politics*, edited by C. Dougherty and L. Kurke: 178–98. Cambridge and New York.

Doulfis, G. 2019. Sacred Architecture in Roman Laconia. In *Listening to the Stones: Essays on Architecture and Function in Ancient Greek Sanctuaries in Honour of Richard Alan Tomlinson*, edited by E. C. Partida and B. Schmidt-Dounas: 139–52. Oxford.

Dreher, M. 2006. Die Primititivät der früen Spartanischen verfassung. In *Das Frühe Sparta*, edited by A. Luther, M. Meier and L. Thommen: 43–62. Stuttgart.

Dressel, H. and A. Milchhöfer. 1877. Die antiken Kunstwerke aus Sparta und Umgebung. *MDAI(A)* 2: 293–474.

Droop, J. P. 1908–9. Laconia: I excavations at Sparta, 1909. The Menelaion. The bronzes; the pottery. *ABSA* 15: 144–57.

D' Onofrio, A. M. 2001. Immagini di divinità nel materiale votivo dell' edificio ovale geometrico ateniese e indagine sull' area sacra alle pendici settentrionali dell' Areopago. *MEFRA* 113 (1): 257–320.

Ducat, J. 1990. *Les Hilotes* (BCH suppl. 20). Paris.

Ducat, J. 2006. *Spartan Education: youth and society in the Classical period*. Swansea.

Ducrey, P. (ed.). 2004. *Eretria: a guide to the ancient city*, translated by S. Rendall. Gollion.

Dunbabin, K. 1998. Ut Graeco More Biberetur: Greeks and Romans on the dining couch. In *Meals in a Social Context* (Aarhus Studies in Mediterranean Antiquity 1), edited by I. Nielsen and H. S. Nielsen: 81–101. Aarhus.

Dyggve, E., F. Poulsen and K. Romaios. 1934. *Das Heroon von Kalydon*. Copenhagen.

Eaverly, M. A. 1995. *Archaic Greek Equestrian Sculpture*. Ann Arbor, MI.

Edelmann, M. 1999. *Menschen auf griechischen Weihreliefs*. Munich.

Eder, B. 1998. *Argolis, Lakonien, Messenien: vom Ende der Mykenischen Palastzeit bis zur Einwanderung der Dorier*. Vienna.

Edmunds, L. 2007. Helen's divine origins. *Electronic Antiquity* 10 (2): 1–45.

Edmunds, L. 2016. *Stealing Helen: the myth of the abducted wife in comparative perspective*. Princeton, NJ and Oxford.

Effenberger, A. 1972. Das Symposion der Seligen. *FuB* 14: 128–63.

Ehrenheim von, H. 2015. Death and Ascent of Hyakinthos in Sparta: Ritual Mourning and Feasting. In *Actes du Colloque international Katábasis, la descente aux Enfers dans la tradition littéraire et religieuse de la Grèce ancienne, à Montréal et Québec 2–5 mai 2014. Les Études classiques*, 83: 351–64.

Eijnde, F. van den. 2010. *Cult and society in early Athens:. archaeological and anthropological approaches to state formation and group participation in Attica* (PhD diss.). University of Utrecht.

Ekroth, G. 1997–8. Review of C. Antonaccio, *An Archaeology of Ancestors: tomb cult and hero cult in early Greece. Opuscula Atheniensia* 22–3: 160–2.

Ekroth, G. 1998. Altars in Greek hero-cults: A review of the archaeological evidence. In Hägg 1998: 117–30.

Ekroth, G. 1999. Pausanias and the sacrificial rituals of Greek hero-cults. In Hägg 1999: 145–58.

Ekroth, G. 2000. Offerings of blood in Greek hero-cults. In Pirenne-Delforge and Suárez de la Torre 2000: 263–80.

Ekroth, G. 2002. *The Sacrificial Rituals of Greek Hero-cults in the Archaic to the Early Hellenistic Periods* (Kernos suppl. 12). Liège.

Ekroth, G. 2003. Small pots, poor people? In *Griechische Keramik im kulturellen Kontext. Akten des Internationalen Vasen-Symposium in Kiel vom 24.–28.9.2001 veranstaltet durch das Archäologische Institut der Christian-Albrechts-Universität zu Kiel*, edited by B. Schmaltz and M. Söldner: 35–7. Münster.

Ekroth, G. 2007. Heroes and hero-cults. In Ogden 2007: 100–14.

Ekroth, G. 2009. The cult of heroes. In Albersmeier 2009: 120–43.

Ekroth, G. 2012. Pelops joins the party: Transformations of a hero-cult within the festival at Olympia. In *What is a festival? A Conference held in Rosendal, Norway, May 19-May 22, 2006*, edited by R. Brandt and J. W. Iddeng, 95–138. Oxford.

Ekroth, G. 2015. Heroes – Living or dead? In *The Oxford Handbook of Ancient Greek Religion*, edited by E. Eidinow and J. Kindt: 383–96. Oxford.

Étienne, R. 2017. Introduction: can one speak of the seventh century BC? In Charalambidou and Morgan 2017: 9–14.

Erll, A. 2011. *Memory in Culture*, translated by S. B. Young. Hampshire and New York.

Evans, J. and K. E. Stanovich. 2013. Dual-process theories of higher cognition: advancing the debate. *Perspectives on Psychological Science* 8: 223–41.

Faraone, C. A. 2002. A drink from the daughters of Mnemosyne: poetry, eschatology and memory at the end of Pindar's Isthmian 6. In *Vertis in usum: studies in honor of Edward Courtney*, edited by J. F. Miller, C. Damon and K. S. Myers: 259–70. Munich.

Faraone, C. A. 2006. Stanzaic structure and responsion in the elegiac poetry of Tyrtaeus. *Mnemosyne* 59: 19–52.

Faraone, C. A. 2008. Household religion in ancient Greece. In *Household and Family Religion in Antiquity*, edited by J. P. Bodel and S. M. Olyan: 210–28. Malden.

Farnell, L. R. 1906–7. *The Cults of the Greek States*. IV. Oxford.

Farnell, L. R. 1921. *Greek Hero Cults and Ideas of Immortality*. Oxford.

Faustoferri, A. 1993. The throne of Apollo at Amyklai: its significance and chronology. In *Sculpture from Arcadia and Laconia* (Oxbow Monograph 30), edited by O. Palagia and W. Coulson: 159–66. Oxford.

Faustoferri, A. 1996. *Il Trono di Amyklai a Sparta: Bathykles al servizio del potere*. Naples.

Fedak, J. 2006. Tombs and commemorative monuments. In *Studies in Hellenistic Architecture* (Phoenix Suppl. 42; Toronto), edited by F. Winter: 71–95.

Ferguson, W. S. and A. D. Nock. 1944. The Attic Orgeones and the cult of heroes. *Harvard Theological Review* 37 (2): 61–174.

Ferrari, W. L. 1938. L' Orestea di Stesicoro. *Athenaeum* 16: 1–37.

Fiechter, E. 1918. Amyklae: Der Thron des Apollon. *JDAI* 33: 107–245.

Figueira, T. J. 1999. The evolution of the Messenian identity. In Hodkinson and Powell 1999: 211–44.

Figueira, T. J. 2003. The demography of Spartan helots. In *Helots and their Masters in Laconia and Messenia: histories, ideologies, structures*, edited by N. Luraghi and S. E. Alcock: 193–239. Cambridge, MA.

Figueira, T. J. 2018. Helotage and the Spartan economy. In Powell 2018: 565–94.

Finglass, P. J. 2007. *Pindar Pythian Eleven*. Cambridge.

Finglass, P. J. 2014. Introduction. In *Stesichorus: The Poems*, edited by M. Davies and P. J. Finglass: 1–91. Cambridge.

Finley, M. I. 1985. *The Ancient Economy*. London.

Fisher, N. 1994. Sparta re(de)valued: some Athenian public attitudes to Sparta between Leuctra and the Lamian War. In Powell and Hodkinson 1994: 347–400.

Fisher, N. and H. van Wees (eds). 1998. *Archaic Greece: new approaches and new evidence.* London.
Fitzhardinge, L. F. 1980. *The Spartans.* London.
Flämig, C. 2007. *Grabarchitektur der römischen Kaiserzeit in Griechenland.* Rahden and Westfalen.
Floren, J. 1987. *Die Griechische Plastik I: die Geometrische und Archaische Plastik.* Munich.
Flouris, C. 2000. *I Pinakes Fittili dell' area di Limnai a Spata: apsetti tecnici e iconografici. Il loro collegamento coi culti eroici* (PhD Diss.). Istituto Universitario Orientale di Napoli.
Flower, M. A. 1988. Agesilaus of Sparta and the origins of ruler cult. *CQ* 38 (1): 123–34.
Flower, M. A. 1991. Revolutionary agitation and social change in Classical Sparta. In *Georgica: studies in honour of George Cawkwell,* edited by M. A. Flower and M. Toher: 78–97. London.
Flower, M. A. 2002. The invention of tradition in Classical and Hellenistic Sparta. In Powell and Hodkinson 2002: 191–217.
Flower, M. A. 2009. Spartan 'religion' and Greek 'religion'. In *Sparta: comparative approaches,* edited by S. Hodkinson: 193–230. Swansea.
Flower, M. A. 2018. Spartan Religion. In Powell 2018: 425–51.
Fontenrose, J. 1960. *The Cult and Myth of Pyrros at Delphi* (University of California publications in Classical archaeology 4:3). Berkeley, CA; Los Angeles, CA.
Forrest, W. G. G. 1980. *A History of Sparta, 950–192.* London.
Förtsch, R. 1988. Spartan art: its many different deaths. In Cavanagh and Walker 1998: 48–54.
Förtsch, R. 2001. *Kunstverwendung und Kunstlegitimation im archaischen und frühklassischen Sparta.* Mainz am Rhein.
Fossey, J. M. 2014. A cult of the Horseman Hero in Boiotia, *Epigraphica Boeotica, 2. Further studies on Boiotian inscriptions,* 117–31. Leiden.
Foucart, P. 1918. *Le Culte des Héros chez les Grecs.* Paris.
Fouquet, J. 2017. Heroes of their times: Intra-mural burials in the urban memorial landscapes of the Roman Peloponnese. In *Strategies of remembering in Greece under Rome (100 BC–100 AD),* edited by T. M. Dijkstra, I. N. I. Kuin, M. Moser and D. Weidgenannt: 111–24. Leiden.
Fouquet, J. 2019. *Bauen zwischen Polis und Imperium: Stadtentwicklung und urbane Lebensformen auf der kaiserzeitlichen Peloponnes.* Urban Spaces 7. Berlin.
Fowler, R. L. 1987. *The Nature of Early Greek Lyric: three preliminary studies.* Toronto.
Fragkopoulou, F. 2011. Sanctuary dedications and the treatment of the dead in Laconia (800–600 BC): the case of Artemis Orthia. In *Honouring the Dead in the Peloponnese Proceedings of the conference held at Sparta 23–25 April 2009,* edited by H. Cavanagh, W. Cavanagh and J. Roy: 83–97. Nottingham.
Frölich, P. 2013. Funérailles publiques et tombeaux monumentaux intra-muros dans les cités grecques à l'époque hellénistique. In *Forgerons, élites et voyageurs d'Homère à*

nos jours: Hommages en mémoire d'Isabelle Ratinaud-Lachkar, edited by Ferries, M.-C., M. P. Castiglioni, and F. Létoublon: 227–309. Grenoble.

Fuchs, W. 1961. Attisches Weihrelief im Vatikan, *RM* 68: 167–81.

Fullerton, M. D. 2016. *Greek Sculpture*. Chichester.

Fuqua, C. 1981. Tyrtaios and the cult of heroes. *GRBS* 22: 215–26.

Furtwängler, A. 1882. Atlakonisches relief. *MDAI(A)* 7: 160–73.

Furtwängler, A 1883. Archaischen Sculpturen: aus Lakonien. *MDAI(A)* 8: 364–73.

Furtwängler, A 1883–87. *La collection Sabouroff I: monuments de l'art grec*. Berlin.

Gabrielsen, V. and C. A. Thomsen (eds). 2015. *Private Associations and the Public Sphere. Proceedings of a Symposium held at the Royal Danish Academy of Sciences and Letters, 9–11 September 2010*. Copenhagen

Gagarin, M. 2006. The unwritten monument speaking and writing Pericles' funeral oration. In *Γ΄ Διεθνές Συμπόσιο για τον Θουκυδίδη. Δημηγορίες*, edited by I. Theofanopoulou and A. Salimpa: 176–87. Athens.

Gaifman, M. 2012. *Aniconism in Greek Antiquity*. Oxford.

Gantz, T. 1993. *Early Greek Myth: a guide to literary and artistic sources*. Baltimore, MD.

Garland, R. 1992. *Introducing New Gods: the politics of Athenian religion*. Ithaka.

Gasparro, G. S. 2015. Daimonic Power. In *Oxford Handbook of Greek Religion*, edited by Eidinow E. and J. Kindt: 413–28. Oxford.

Gebhard, E. R. and M. W. Dickie. 1999. Melikertes-Palaimon, Hero of the Isthmian Games. In Hägg 1999: 159–65.

Gengler, O. 2005. Héraclès, Tyndare et Hippocoon dans la description de Sparte par Pausanias: mise en espace d'une tradition mythique. *Kernos* 18: 311–28.

Georgiades, R. 2017. To hell and back: the function of the ancient Greek hero's katabasis, *Classicum* 43 (2): 2–8.

Georgoudi, S. 1998a. Héraclès dans les pratiques sacrificielles des cités. In *Le Bestiaire d' Héraclès: IIIe Recontre héracléenne* (Kernos suppl. 7), edited by C. Bonnet, C. Jourdain-Annequin and V. Pirenne Delforge: 301–17. Liège.

Georgoudi, S. 1998b. Les douze dieux et les autres dans l'espace cultuel grec. *Kernos* 11: 73–83.

Gerber, D. E. 1999. *Greek Elegiac Poetry from the Seventh to the Fifth Centuries BC*. Cambridge, MA.

Giannakaki, Ch. 2008. *The River Eurotas Monuments*. Sparta.

Gill, D. and M. Vickers. 2001. Laconian Lead Figurines: Mineral Extraction and Exchange in the Archaic Mediterranean. *ABSA* 96: 229–36.

Gilula, D. 2003. Who was actually buried in the first of the three Spartan graves (Hdt. 9. 85. 1)? Textual and historical problems. In *Herodotus and his World: Essays from a conference in memory of George Forrest*, edited by P. Derow and R. Parker: 73–87. Oxford.

Goette, H. R. 2000. *Ὁ ἀξιόλογος δῆμος Σούνιον: Landeskundliche Studien in Sudost-Attika*. Rahden and Westfalen.

Goldhill, S. D. 1991. *The Poet's Voice: essays on poetics and Greek literature*. Cambridge.

Gomme, A. W. 1956. *A Historical Commentary on Thucydides*. Oxford.
Graf, F. 1985. *Nordionische Kulte: religionsgeschichtliche und epigraphische Untersuchungen zu den Kulten von Chios, Erythrai, Klazomenai und Phokaia* (Bibliotheca helvetica romana 21). Rome.
Graf, F. 2003. Initiation: a concept with a troubled history. In *Initiation in Ancient Greek Rituals and Narratives: new critical perspectives*, edited by D. B. Dodd and C. A. Faraone: 3–24. London.
Graf, F. 2009. *Apollo*. London; New York.
Graham, A. J. 2001. *Collected Papers on Greek Colonization* (Mnemosyne suppl. 214). Leiden.
Grandjean, Y. and F. Salviat. 2000. *Guide de Thasos*. Paris.
Greco, E. 2010. *Topografia di Atene: Sviluppo urbano e monumenti dale origini al III secolo d. C.* 1. Athens.
Greco, E. 2011. Alla ricerca dell'agora di Sparta. *ASAtene* 89 (3, 11.I): 53–77.
Greco, E. and O. Voza. 2016. For a reconstruction of the 'Round Building' at Sparta as the Skias. In *ΑΡΧΙΤΕΚΤΩΝ: Τιμητικός τόμος για τον καθηγητή Μανόλη Κορρέ*, edited by K. Zampas, V. Lambrinoudakis, E. Sirmantoni-Mournia and A. Ohnesorg: 343–50. Athens.
Green, P. 2006. *Diodorus Siculus Books 11–12.37.1. Greek History, 480–431. The alternative version*. Austin.
Grethlein, J. 2010. The *Iliad* and the Trojan War. In *Epic and History*, edited by D. Konstan and K. A. Raaflaub: 122–44. Chichester and Malden, MA.
Grethlein, J. 2012. Homer and heroic history. In *Greek Notions of the Past in the Archaic and Classical Eras*, edited by J. Marincola, L. Llewellyn-Jones and C. Maciver: 14–36. Edinburgh.
Grunaer-von Hoerschlmann, S. 1978. *Die Münzprägung der Lakedaimonier*. Berlin.
Guarducci, M. 1974. *Epigrafia Greca III*. Rome.
Guarducci, M. 2008. *Ελληνική Επιγραφική. Από τις απαρχές ως την ύστερη Ρωμαϊκή περίοδο*. Athens.
Guralnick. E. 1974. The Chrysapha relief and its connections with Egyptian art. *JEA* 60: 175–88.
Habicht, C. 1970. *Gottmenschentum und Griechische Städte*. Munich.
Hägg, R. 1983. Funerary meals in the Geometric necropolis at Asine? In *The Greek Renaissance of the Eighth Century B.C.: tradition and innovation. Proceedings of the second international symposium at the Swedish Institute in Athens, 1–5 June 1981*, edited by R. Hägg: 189–93. Stockholm.
Hägg, R. 1987. Gifts to the heroes in Geometric and Archaic Greece. In *Gifts to the Gods: proceedings of the Uppsala Symposium 1985* (Boreas 15), edited by T. Linders and G. Nordquist: 93–9. Uppsala.
Hägg, R. (ed.). 1998. *Ancient Greek Cult Practice from the Archaeological Evidence: proceedings of the 4th international seminar on ancient Greek cult, organized by the Swedish Institute at Athens, 22–24 October 1993*. Stockholm.

Hägg, R. (ed.). 1999. *Ancient Greek Hero Cult: proceedings of the 5th international seminar on ancient Greek cult, organized by the department of Classical archaeology and ancient history, Göteborg University, 21–23 April 1995.* Stockholm.

Hägg, R. (ed.). 2002. *Peloponnesian Sanctuaries and Cults. Proceedings of the ninth international symposium at the Swedish Institute at Athens, 11–13 June 1994.* Stockholm.

Hägg, R., N. Marinatos and G. C. Nordquist (eds). 1988. *Early Greek Cult practice: proceedings of the fifth international symposium at the Swedish Institute at Athens, 26–29, June, 1986.* Stockholm.

Hägg, R and B. Alroth (eds). 2005. *Greek Sacrificial Ritual, Olympian and Chthonian: proceedings of the sixth international seminar on ancient Greek cult, organized by the department of Classical archaeology and ancient history, Göteborg University, 25–27 April 1997.* Stockholm.

Halbwachs, M. 1992. *On Collective Memory.* Edited, translated and with an introduction by L. A. Coser. Chicago.

Hall, J. M. 1995. How Argive was the 'Argive' Heraion? The political and cultic geography of the Argive plain, 900–400. *AJA* 99 (4): 577–613.

Hall, J. M. 1997. *Ethnic Identity in Greek Antiquity.* Cambridge.

Hall, J. M. 1999. Beyond the polis: the multilocality of heroes. In Hägg 1999: 49–59.

Hall, J. M. 2000. Sparta, Lakedaimon, and the nature of the Perioikic dependency. In *Further Studies in the Ancient Greek Polis* (Papers from the Copenhagen Polis Centre 5), edited by P. Flensted-Jensen: 73–89. Stuttgart.

Hamilton, R. 2009. Basket case: altars, animals and baskets on Classical Attic votive reliefs. In *Aspects of Ancient Greek Cult: context, ritual and iconography,* edited by J. T. Jensen *et al.*: 29–53. Århus.

Hammond, N. G. L. 1998. *Miniature Votives from the Sanctuary of Athena Alea at Tegea.* Ann Arbor.

Hammond, N. G. L. 2009. Figurines, the miniature vase, and cultic space. In *Encounters with Mycenaean Figures and Figurines: Papers presented at a seminar at the Swedish Institute at Athens, 27–29 April 2001,* edited by A.-L. Schalin in collaboration with P. Pakkanen: 139–47. Stockholm.

Hansen, M. H. 2006. *Polis: an introduction to the ancient Greek city-state.* Oxford.

Harrison, E. 1912. *Themis: a study of the social origins of Greek religion.* Cambridge.

Harrison, E. 1977. Notes of Daedalic dress. *JWAG* 36: 37–48.

Harrison, T. 2000. *Divinity and History: the religion of Herodotus.* Oxford.

Haslam, M. 1978. The versification of the New Stesichorus (*P. Lille* 76abc). *GRBS* 19: 29–57.

Hatzisteliou-Price, T. 1973. Hero cult and Homer. *Historia* 22: 129–44.

Hatzisteliou-Price, T. 1979. Hero-cult in the 'Age of Homer' and earlier. In *Arktouros: Hellenic studies presented to Bernard M. W. Knox on the occasion of his 65th birthday,* edited by G. W. Bowersock, W. Burkert and M. C. J. Putnam: 219–28. Berlin.

Henrichs, A. 1983. The 'Sobriety' of Oedipus: Sophocles OC 100 Misunderstood. *HSCP* 87: 87–100.

Henrichs, A. 2010. What is a Greek god? In *The Gods of Ancient Greece: identities and transformations*, edited by J. Bremmer and A. Erskine: 19–41. Edinburgh.

Herfort-Koch, M. 1986. *Archaische Bronzeplastic Lakoniens* (Boreas 4). Münster.

Hermary, A. 1978. Images de l' apotheosis des Dioscures. *BCH* 102: 51–76.

Hibler, D. 1993. The hero-reliefs of Laconia: changes in form and function. In *Sculpture from Arcadia and Laconia: proceedings of an international conference held at the American School of Classical Studies at Athens, April 10–14, 1992* (Oxbow Monograph 30), edited by O. Palagia and W. Coulson: 199–204. Oxford.

Higbie, C. 2003. *The Lindian Chronicle and the Greek Creation of their Past*. Oxford.

Hinge, G. 2009. Cultic persona and the transmissions of the Partheneions. In *Aspects of Ancient Greek Cult: context, ritual and iconography*, edited by J. T. Jensen *et al*: 215–36. Århus.

Hodkinson, S. 1989. Inheritance, marriage and demography: perspectives upon the success and decline of Classical Sparta. In *Classical Sparta*, edited by A. Powell: 97–121. London.

Hodkinson, S. 1993. Warfare, wealth, and the crisis of Spartiate society. In *War and Society in the Greek World*, edited by J. Rich and G. Shipley: 146–77. London.

Hodkinson, S. 1994. 'Blind Ploutos'? Contemporary images of the role of wealth in Classical Sparta. In Powell and Hodkinson 1994: 183–222.

Hodkinson, S. 1997. The development of Spartan society and institutions in the archaic period. In *The Development of the Polis in Archaic Greece*, edited by L. G. Mitchell and P. J. Rhodes: 83–102. London.

Hodkinson, S. 1998a. Patterns of bronze dedications at Spartan sanctuaries, c. 650–350 BC: towards a quantified database of material and religious investment. In Cavanagh and Walker 1998: 55–63.

Hodkinson, S. 1998b. Laconian artistic production and the problem of Spartan austerity. In Fisher and van Wees 1998: 93–117.

Hodkinson, S. 1999. An agonistic culture? Athletic competition in Archaic and Classical Spartan society. In Hodkinson and Powell 1999: 147–88.

Hodkinson, S. 2000. *Property and Wealth in Classical Sparta*. London.

Hodkinson, S. 2002. Social order and the conflict of values in classical Sparta. In *Sparta*, edited by M. Whitby: 104–30. Edinburgh.

Hodkinson, S. 2003. Spartiates, Helots and the direction of the agrarian economy: towards an understanding of Helotage in comparative perspective. In *Helots and their Masters in Laconia and Messenia: histories, ideologies, structures*, edited by N. Luraghi and S. E. Alcock: 248–85. Cambridge, MA.

Hodkinson, S. 2005. The imaginary Spartan politeia. In *The Imaginary Polis* (Acts of the Copenhagen Polis Centre 7), edited by M. H. Hansen: 222–81. Copenhagen.

Hodkinson, S. 2006. Was classical Sparta a military society? In *Sparta and War*, edited by S. Hodkinson and A. Powell: 111–62. Swansea.

Hodkinson, S. 2009. Was Sparta an Exceptional Polis?' In *Sparta: comparative approaches*, edited by S. Hodkinson: 417–72. Swansea.

Hodkinson, S. 2009. Introduction. In *Sparta: comparative approaches*, edited by S. Hodkinson: ix–xxxiii. Swansea.

Hodkinson, S. 2018. An Exceptional Domination of State over Society? In Powell 2018: 29–57.

Hodkinson, S. and A. Powell (eds). 1999. *Sparta: new perspectives.* Swansea.

Hoffmann, G. 2000. Brasidas ou le fait d' armes comme source d' héroïsation. In Pirenne-Delforge and Suárez de la Torres 2000: 365–75.

Hoffmann, H. 1989. Rhyta and Kantharoi in Greek Ritual. *Greek Vases in the J. Paul Getty Museum*, 4: 131–66. Malibu.

Hölscher, T. 1999. Images and political identity: the case of Athens. In *Democracy, Empire and the Arts in Fifth century Athens*, edited by D. Boedeker and K. A. Raaflaub: 153–84. Cambridge, MA and London.

Hook, van. L. (ed.). 1944. *Isocrates III.* Cambridge MA.

Hooker, J. T. 1980. *The Ancient Spartans.* London.

Hughes, D. D. 1999. Hero cult, heroic honors, heroic dead: some developments in the Hellenistic and Roman periods. In Hägg 1999: 167–75.

Hupfloher, A. 2000. *Kulter im Kaiserzeitlichen Sparta: eine Reconstruktion anhand der Priesterämter.* Berlin.

Hornblower, S. 2015. *Lykophron: Alexandra. Greek text, translation, commentary, and introduction.* Oxford.

Hurwit, J. M. 2006. Lizards, lions and the uncanny. *Hesperia* 75: 120–6.

Hutchinson. G. O. 2001. *Greek Lyric Poetry: commentary on selected larger pieces.* Oxford.

Hutton, W. 2005. *Describing Greece: landscape and literature in the Periegesis of Pausanias.* Cambridge.

Huxley, G. L. 1962. *Early Sparta.* London.

Huxley, G. L. 1969. *Greek Epic Poetry: from Eumelos to Panyassis.* London.

Instone, S. 2009. *Greek Personal Religion: a reader.* Oxford.

Intzesiloglou, B. 2002. Aiatos et Polycléia. Du mythe à l'histoire. *Kernos* 15: 289–95.

Jackson, P. 2006. *The Transformations of Helen: Indo-European myth and the roots of the Trojan Cycle.* Dettelbach.

Jacob-Felsch, M. 1988. Compass-drawn concentric circles in vase painting: a problem of relative chronology at the end of the Bronze Age. In *Problems in Greek Prehistory: papers presented at the centenary conference of the British School of Archaeology at Athens, Manchester, April 1986*, edited by E. B. French and K. A. Wardle: 193–9. Bristol.

Jameson, M. H. 1990. Perseus, the Hero at Mykenai. In *Celebrations of Death and Divinity in the Bronze Age Argolid: Proceedings of the Sixth International Symposium at the Swedish Institute at Athens, 11–13 June 1988* (ActaAth, 40), edited by R. Hägg and G. Nordquist: 1990 (ActaAth, 40). Stockholm.

Jameson, M. H. 1994. Theoxenia. In *Ancient Greek cult practice from the epigraphical evidence: proceedings of the Second International Seminar on Ancient Greek Cult, organized by the Swedish Institute at Athens, 22–24 November 1991*, edited by R. Hägg: 35–57. Göteborg.

Jameson, M. H., D. R. Jordan and R. D. Kotansky. 1993. *A Lex Sacra from Selinous*. Durham, NC.

Jeanmaire, H. 1975. *Couroi et Courètes*. New York.

Jeffery, L. H. and P. Cartledge. 1982. Sparta and Samos: a special relationship? *CQ* 32: 243–65.

Jenkins, R. J. H. 1932–3. Laconian terracottas of the Daedalic style. *ABSA* 33: 66–79.

Jim, T. S. F. 2014. *Sharing with the Gods: Aparchai and Dekatai in Ancient Greece*. Oxford.

Johansen, F. 1951. *The Attic Grave-Reliefs of the Classical Period: an essay in interpretation*. Copenhagen.

Jones, C. P. 2010. *New Heroes in Antiquity: from Achilles to Antinoos*. Cambridge, MA.

Jones, N. F. 1999. *The Associations of Classical Athens: the response to democracy*. Oxford.

Jones, W. H. S. and H. A. Ormerod (trans.). 1926. *Pausanias' Description of Greece*. Cambridge MA.

Jost, M. 1985. *Sanctuaires et cultes d'Arcadie*. Paris.

Jung, H. 1982. *Thronende und sitzende Götter. Zum griechischen Menschenideal in geometrischer und früharchaischer Zeit* (Habelts Dissertationsdrucke. Reihe Klassische Archäologie 17). Bonn.

Junker, K. 1993. *Der ältere Tempel im Heraion am Sele. erzierte Metopen im architektonischen Kontext* (Arbeiten zur Archaologie). Koln.

Kahil, L. 1955. *Les enlèvements et le retour d'Hélène dans les textes et les documents figurés*. Paris.

Kahn, C. H. 1979. *The Art and Thought of Heraclitus: an edition of the fragments with translation and commentary*. Cambridge.

Kaltsas, N. 2002. *Sculpture in the National Archaeological Museum, Athens*, translated by D. Hardy. Malibu.

Kaltsas, N. (ed.). 2006. *Athens-Sparta*. New York.

Kardara, Ch. 1975. *Αχαϊκή Πολιτική της Σπάρτης: η υπό της Σπάρτης αναβίωσης της ηγεμονίας των Ατρείδων*. Athens.

Karouzou, S. 1985. Η Ελένη της Σπάρτης. Η μεγάλη πρόχους από την Ανάληψη της Κυνουρίας, *ArchEph* 124: 33–44.

Kästner, V. 1990. Scheibenförmige Akrotere in Griechenland und Italien, *Hesperia* 59 (1): 251–64

Kearns, E. 1989. *The Heroes of Attica* (BICS suppl. 57). London.

Kearns, E. 1992. Between god and man: Status and function of heroes and their sanctuaries. In *Le Sanctuaire Grec* (Entretiens sur l'Antiquité classique 37), edited by A. Schachter and J. Bingen: 65–99. Geneva.

Kearns, E. 2010. *Ancient Greek Religion: a sourcebook*. Chichester.

Kellogg, D. L. 2012. The place of publication of the Ephebic Oath and the 'Oath of Plataia', *Hesperia* 82 (2): 263-76.

Kennell, N. 1995. *The Gymnasium of Virtue: education and culture in ancient Sparta.* Chapel Hill.

Kennell, N. 2010. *Spartans: a new history.* Chichester.

Kennell, N. 2018. Spartan cultural memory in the Roman period. In Powell 2018: 643-62.

Kennell, N. and N. Luraghi. 2009. Laconia and Messenia. In *A Companion to Archaic Greece*, edited by K. A. Raaflaub and H. van Wees: 239-54. Chichester.

Kegel, W. J. H. F. 1962. *Simonides.* Groningen.

Kilian-Dirlmeier, I. 1979. *Anhänger in Griechenland von der Mykenischen bis zur Spätgeometrischen Zeit: griechisches Festland, Ionische Inseln, dazu Albanien und Jugoslawisch-Mazedonien.* Munich.

Kilian-Dirlmeier, I. 1984. *Nadeln der fruhhelladischen bis archaischen Zeit von der Peloponnes.* Munich.

Kilian-Dirlmeier, I. 1998. Elitäres Verhalten vom Ende der Bronzezeit bis zum Beginn der Eisenzeit. In *The History of the Hellenic Language and Writing from the Second to the First Millennium BC: Break or Continuity? Conference held at Ohlstadt/Oberbayern 3-6 October 1996*, edited by N. Dimoudis and A. Kyriatsoulis. Weilheim.

Kilmer, M. F. and R. Develin. 2001. Sophilos' vase inscriptions and cultural literacy in Archaic Athens. *Phoenix* 55 (1/2): 9-43.

King, H. 1983. Bound to Bleed. In *Images of Women in Antiquity*, edited by A. Cameron and A. Kuhrt: 109-27. London.

Kindt, J. 2009. Polis religion: A critical appreciation. *Kernos* 22: 9-34.

Kindt, J. 2012. *Rethinking Greek Religion.* Cambridge.

Kindt, J. 2015. Personal religion: a productive category for the study of ancient Greek religion? *JHS* 135: 35-50.

Knoepfler, D. 2019. Tombeaux de héros dans les sanctuaires des divinités olympiennes: De Hyakinthos le Laconien à l'Eubéen Narkittos. In *Des tombeaux et des dieux*, edited by J. Jouanna, A. Vauchez, J. Scheid and M. Zink: 31-74. Paris.

Kõiv, M. 2003. *Ancient Tradition and Early Greek History: the origins of states in Early-Archaic Sparta, Argos and Corinth.* Tallinn.

Kokkorou-Alevras, G. 2006. Laconian stone sculpture from the eighth century BC until the outbreak of the Peloponnesian War. In *Athens-Sparta: contributions to the research on the history and archaeology of the two city-states*, edited by N. Kaltsas: 89-103. New York.

Kopanias, K. 2009. Some ivories from the Geometric stratum of Artemis Orthia: interconnections between Sparta, Crete and the Orient in the late eighth century BC. In Cavanagh, Gallou and Georgiadis: 123-31.

Kopestonsky, T. 2018. Locating Lost Gifts: Terracotta Figurines as Evidence of Ephemeral Offerings. *Journal of Greek Archaeology* 3: 245-68.

Korres, G. S. 1981-2. Ἡ προβληματική δια τήν μεταγενεστέραν χρῆσιν τῶν Μυκηναϊκῶν τάφων Μεσσηνίας. *Peloponnesiana: Parartima* 2: 363-450.

Korres, G. S. 1988. Evidence for a Hellenistic chthonian cult in the prehistoric cemetery of Voïdokilia in Pylos (Messenia). *Klio* 70: 311-28.

Korres, M. 2011-12. Το βάθρο του αγάλματος, *MusBenaki* 11-12: 137-8.

Kourinou, E. 2000. Σπάρτη: συμβολή στη μνημειακή τοπογραφία της. Athens.

Kourinou-Pikoula, E. 1987-8. Ευρήματα μεγάλης πλαστικής σε πηλό από τη Σπάρτη. In *Peloponnesiaka: Parartima* 13 (2): 475-8.

Kourou, N. 2002. Tenos-Xobourgo. From a Refuge Place to an extensive fortified settlement. In *Excavating Classical Culture*, edited by M. Sematopoulou and M. Yerolanou: 258-62. Oxford.

Kourou, N. 2015. Early Iron Age mortuary contexts in the Cyclades: pots, function and symbolism. In *Pots, Workshops and Early Iron Age Society: function and role of ceramics in early Greece. Proceedings of the International Symposium held at the Université libre de Bruxelles, 14-16 November*, edited by V. Vlachou: 83-105. Brussels.

Kowerski, L. M. 2005. *Simonides on the Persian Wars: a study of the elegiac verses of the 'New Simonides'*. London.

Kranz, P. 1972. Frühe griechische Sitzfiguren. *MDAI(A)* 87: 1-55.

Kron, U. 1976. *Die Zehn Attischen Plylenheroen. Geschichte, mythos, kult und darstellungen* (MDAI(A)-Beiheft 5). Berlin.

Kron, U. 1999. Patriotic Heroes. In Hägg 1999: 61-83.

Kucewicz, C. 2021. The War-dead in Archaic Sparta. In *Brill's Companion to Greek Land Warfare Beyond the Phalanx*, edited by R. Konijnendijk, C. Kucewicz and M. Lloyd: 83-121. Leiden.

Kunze, E. 1950. *Archaische Schildbänder* (Olympische Forschungen 2). Berlin.

Kunze, E. 1956. *Bericht über die Augrabungen in Olympia V*. Berlin.

Kunst, K. 1924-5. *Die Schuld der Klytaimnestra*. WS 44: 18-32.

Kurtz, D. C. and J. Boardman. 1971. *Greek Burial Customs*. London.

Küster, E. 1913. *Die Schlange in der griechischer Kunst und Religion*. Giessen.

Kyle, D. G. 2007. *Sport and Spectacle in the Ancient World*. Malden.

Kyrieleis, H. 1969. *Thronen und Klinen: Studien zur Formgeschichte altorientalischer und griechischer Sitz- und Liegemöbel vorhellenistischer Zeit*. Berlin.

Kyrieleis, H. 2002. Zu den Anfängen des Heiligtums von Olympia. In *Olympia 1875-2000: 125 Jahre Deutsche Ausgrabungen; Internationales Symposion, Berlin 9-11 November 2000*, edited by H. Kyrieleis: 213-20. Mainz am Rhein.

Kyrieleis, H. 2006. *Anfänge und Frühzeit des Heiligtums von Olympia: Die Ausgrabungen am Pelopeion, 1987-1996* (Olympische Forschungen 31). Berlin.

Lafond, Y. 2018. Sparta in the Roman Period. In Powell 2018: 403-22.

Lalonde, G. V. 1980. A hero shrine in the Athenian Agora. *Hesperia* 49 (19): 97-105.

Lalonde, G. V. 2006. *Horos Dios (Ὅρος Διός): an Athenian shrine and cult of Zeus*. Leiden.

Lamb, W. 1926-7a. Excavations at Sparta, 1927: Bronzes from the Acropolis. *ABSA* 28: 82-95.

Lamb, W. 1926-7b. Excavations at Sparta, 1906-1910: Notes on some bronzes from the Orthia site. *ABSA* 28: 96-106.

Lambrinoudakis, V. 1988. Veneration of ancestors in Geometric Naxos. In Hägg, Marinatos and Nordquist 1988: 235-46.

Lane, E. 1933-4. Laconian vase-painting. *ABSA* 34: 99-189.

Lanéres, N. 2008. L'éphèbe au serpent de Magoula: propositions pour la relecture d'une inscription archaïque laconienne. *REG* 121 (1): 1-15.

Langefass-Vuduroglu. 1973. *Mensch und Pferd auf griechischen Grab und Votivesteinen*. Munich.

Larson, J. 1995. *Greek Heroine Cults*. Madison.

Larson, J. 2007-8. Review of B. Currie, *Pindar and the Cult of Heroes*. *CJ* 103.2: 201-4.

Larson, J. 2009. Arms and armour in the sanctuaries of goddesses: a quantitative approach. In *Le Donateur, l'Offrande et la Déesse: Systèmes votifs des sanctuaires de déesses dans le monde grec* (Kernos suppl. 23), edited by C. Prêtre: 123-33. Liège.

Larson, J. 2016. *Understanding Greek Religion: A cognitive approach*. London and New York.

Lauter-Bufé, H. 1974. Entstehung und Entwicklung des kombinierten lakonischen Akroters. *AM* 89: 205-30.

Lawall, M. L. 2003. In the sanctuary of the Samothracian gods: myth, politics, and mystery cult at Ilion. In *Greek Mysteries: the archaeology and ritual of Ancient Greek secret cults*, edited by M. B. Cosmopoulos: 79-111. London.

Lawton, C. 2016. The *Totenmahl* motif in votive reliefs of Classical Athens. In *Dining and Death: Interdisciplinary Perspectives on the 'Funerary Banquet' in Ancient Art, Burial and Belief*, edited by C. M. Draycott and M. Stamatopoulou: 385-404. Leuven, Paris, Bristol CT.

Lazzarini, M. L. 1976. Le formule dele dediche votive nella Grecia Arcaica. *MAL* 19: 45-354.

Leekley, D. and R. Noyes. 1976. *Archaeological Excavations in Southern Greece*. Park Ridge.

Léger, R. M. 2015. *Artemis and her Cult* (PhD Diss.). The University of Birmingham.

Lembessi, A. 1976. Οι στῆλες τοῦ Πρινιᾶ. Athens.

Le Roy, C. 1961. Λακωνικά. *BCH* 85: 206-35

Levaniouk, O. 2012. Οὐ χρώμεθα τοῖς ξενικοῖς ποιήμασιν: questions about evolution and fluidity of the Odyssey. In *Homeric Contexts: neoanalysis and the interpretation of oral poetry*, edited by in F. Montanari, A. Rengakos and C. Tsagalis: 369-409. Göttingen.

Lévêque, P. and A. Verbanck-Piérard. 1992. Héraclès, héros ou dieu? In *Héraclès: d'une rive à autre de la Mediterranée*, edited by C. Bonnet and C. Jourdain-Annequin: 43-65. Brussels.

Lindblom, M. and G. Ekroth. 2016. Heroes, ancestors or just and old bones? Contextualizing the consecration of human remains from the Mycenaean shaft graves at Lerna in the Argolid. In *Metaphysis Ritual, Myth and Symbolism in the Aegean Bronze Age (Aegaeum 39)*, edited by E. Alram-Stern, F. Blakolmer, S. Deger-Jalkotzy, R. Laffineur and J. Weilhartner: 235–43.

Link, S. 2000. *Das frühe Sparta: Untersuchungen zur spartanischen Staatsbildung im 7. und 6. Jahrhundert v. Chr.* St. Katharinen.

Lipka, M. 2002. *Xenophon's Spartan Constitutio: introduction, text, commentary.* Berlin; New York.

Loraux, N. 1977. La 'belle mort' spartiate. *Ktema* 2: 105–20.

Loraux, N. 1986. *The Invention of Athens: funeral oration in the Classical city*, translated by A. Sheridan. Cambridge MA.

Low, P. 2006. Commemorating the Spartan war-dead. In *Sparta and War*, edited by S. Hodkinson and A. Powell: 85–109. Swansea.

Low, P. 2011. The Power of the Dead in Classical Sparta: The Case of Thermopylae. In *Living Through the Dead: Burial and Commemoration in the Classical World*, edited by M. Carroll and J. Rempel: 1–20. Oxford.

Luginbill, R. D. 2002. Tyrtaeus 12 West: Come join the Spartan army. *CQ* 52: 405–14.

Luraghi, N. 2008. *The Ancient Messenians: constructions of ethnicity and memory.* Cambridge.

Luther, A. 2002. Chilon von Sparta. In *Gelehrte in der Antike: Alexander Demandt zum 65. Geburstag*, edited by A. Goltz, A. Luther and H. Schlange-Schöningen: 1–16. Köln.

Lyons, D. 1997. *Gender and Immortality: heroines in ancient Greek myth and cult.* Princeton.

Magnetto, A. 1997. *Gli Arbitrati Interstatali Greci, II: dal 337 al 196 a. C.* Pisa.

Mallwitz, A. 1972. *Olympia und seine Bauten.* Munich.

Malkin I. 1987. *Religion and Colonization in Ancient Greece.* Leiden.

Malkin I. 1994. *Myth and Territory in the Spartan Mediterranean.* Cambridge.

Malkin I. 1998. *The Returns of Odysseus: colonization and ethnicity.* Berkley, CA.

Marangou, E. L. 1969. *Lakonische Elfenbein und Beinschnitzereien.* Tübingen.

Marchiandi, D. 2010. Le consuetudini funerarie dell'élite ateniese: i lebeti bronzei di Myrina (Lemnos) *ASAA*, 88, 3.10, 221–36.

Margreiter, I. 1988. *Frühe Lakonische Keramik der Geometrischen bis Archaischen Zeit, 10. bis 6. Jahrhundert v. Chr.* Waldsassen-Bayern.

Marinatos, S. 1936. Le temple géométrique de Dréros. *BCH* 60: 214–85.

Marincola, J. 2016. The Historian as Hero: Herodotus and the 300 at Thermopylae. *TAPA* 146: 219–36.

Martin, R. 1978. Thasos: quelques problèmes de structure urbaine. *CRAI*: 182–201.

Martin, R. 1976. Bathyclès de Magnésie et le 'trône' d' Apollon a Amyklae. *RA* (2): 205–18.

Massow, von. W. 1926. Die Stele des Ainetos in Amyklai. *MDAI(A)* 51: 41–7.

Mattusch, C. 1988. *Greek Bronze Statuary: from the beginnings through the fifth century BC*. Ithaka.

Mays, L. W. 2010. A brief history of water technology during antiquity before the Romans. In *Ancient Water Technologies*, edited by L. W. Mays: 1–28. New York.

Mazarakis Ainian, A. 1999. Reflections on hero cults in early Iron Age Greece. In Hägg 1999: 9–36.

Mazarakis Ainian, A. 2007–8. Buried among the living in Early Iron Age Greece: some thoughts. In *Sepolti tra i vivi. Evidenza ed interpretazione di contesti funerari in abitato: Convegno Internazionale, Roma 26-29 aprile 2006* (Scienze dell' Antichità, 14), edited by G. Bartoloni and M. G. Benedettini: 365–98. Rome.

Mazarakis Ainian, A. 2017a. Heroes in early Iron Age Greece and the Homeric epics. In *Archaeology and Homeric Epic*, edited by S. Sherratt and J. Bennet: 101–15. Oxford.

Mazarakis Ainian, A. 2017b. Conservatism versus innovation: architectural forms in Early Archaic Greece. In *Interpreting the seventh century BC: Tradition and Innovation*, edited by X. Charalampidou and C. Morgan: 173–85. Oxford.

McPhee, I. 1986. Laconian Red-Figure from the British Excavations in Sparta. *ABSA* 81: 153–65.

McCauley, B. 1999. Heroes and power: the politics of bone transferal. In Hägg 1999: 85–98.

McNiven, T. J. 1982. *Gestures in Attic Vase Painting: use and meaning, 550-450 BC* (PhD Diss.). The University of Michigan.

Meiggs, R. and D. Lewis (eds). 1969. *A Selection of Greek Historical Inscriptions to the End of the Fifth Century BC*. Oxford.

Meier, M. 1998. *Aristokraten und Damoden: Untersuchungen zur inneren Entwicklung Spartas im 7. Janhundert v. Chr. und zur politischen Function der Dichtung des Tyrtaios*. Stuttgart.

Meier, M. 2006. Wann entstand das *homoios*-ideal in Sparta? In *Das Frühe Sparta*, edited by A. Luther, M. Meier and L. Thommen: 113–24. Stuttgart.

Mellink, M. J. 1943. *Hyakinthos*. Utrecht.

Mercier, H. and D. Sperber. 2009. Intuitive and reflective inferences. In *Two Minds: Dual Processes and Beyond*, edited by J. Evans and K. Frankish: 149–70. Oxford.

Meritt, B. D. 1936. Greek inscriptions. *Hesperia* 5: 355–441.

Merker, G. S. 2000. *The Sanctuary of Demeter and Kore: terracotta figurines of the Classical, Hellenistic, and Roman periods* (*Corinth* vol. 18.4). Princeton, NJ.

Merker, G. S. 2003. The terracotta figurines. In Williams and Bookidis 2003: 233–45.

Mertens, D. 2006. *Städte und Bauten der Westgriechen: Von der Kolonisation bis zur Krise am Ende des 5. Jh. v. Chr.* Munich.

Mikalson, J. D. 2003. *Herodotus and Religion in the Persian Wars*. Chapel Hill.

Mikkola, M. 2008. Heroa as described in the ancient written sources. In *Grapta Poikila II: saints and heroes* (Papers and Monographs of the Finnish Institute at Athens 14), edited by L. Pietilä and V. Vahtikari: 1–32. Helsinki.

Mili, M. 2015. *Religion and Society in Ancient Thessaly*. Oxford.
Millander, E. 2009. The Spartan dyarchy: a comparative perspective. In *Sparta: comparative approaches*, edited by S. Hodkinson: 1–67. Swansea.
Mitchell, L. 2007. *Panhellenism and the Barbarian in Archaic and Classical Greece*. Swansea.
Mitropoulou, E. 1975. *Libation Scenes with Oinochoe in Votive Reliefs*. Athens.
Mitropoulou, E. 1977. *Deities and Heroes in the Form of Snake*. Athens.
Mitsopoulos-Leon, V. 1984. Zur Verehrung des Dionysos in Elis: Nochmals Αξιε Ταυρε und die sechzehn heiligen Frauen. *MDAI(A)* 99: 275–90.
Molero, L. R. 1992. La serpiente guardiana en la antigua Grecia: Mito y realidad. In *Héroes, Semidioses y Daimones: Primer encuentro-coloquio de ARYS, Jarandilla de la Vera, diciembre de 1989*, edited by J. Alvar *et al*.: 11–31. Madrid.
Molyneaux, J. H. 1992. *Simonides: a historical study*. Wauconda.
Momigliano, A. 1945. The Locrian maidens and the date of Lycophron's *Alexandra*. *CQ* 39: 49–53.
Morgan, C. 1990. *Athletes and Oracles*. Oxford.
Morgan, C. 1993. The origins of pan-Hellenism. In *Greek Sanctuaries: New Approaches*, edited by N. Marinatos and R. Hägg: 18–44. London and New York.
Morgan, C. and T. Whitelaw. 1991. Pots and politics: ceramic evidence for the rise of the Argive state. *AJA* 95: 79–108.
Morris, I. 1987. *Burial and Ancient Society: the rise of the Greek city-state*. Cambridge.
Morris, I. 1988. Tomb cult and the 'Greek Renaissance': the past and the present in the eighth century BC. *Antiquity* 62: 750–61.
Morris, I. 1992. *Death Ritual and Social Structure in Classical Antiquity*. Cambridge.
Morris, I. 1996. The art of citizenship. In *New Light on a Dark Age: exploring the culture of Geometric Greece*, edited by S. Langdon: 9–43. Missouri, MO.
Morris, I. 2000. *Archaeology as Cultural History: words and things in Iron Age Greece*. Oxford.
Morris, I. 2001. The use and abuse of Homer. In *Oxford Readings in Homer's Iliad*, edited by D. Cairns: 57–91. Oxford.
Moustaka, A. 2005. Ο Ludwig Ross στην Πελοπόννησο. In *Ludwig Ross und Griechenland: Akten des Internationalen Kolloquiums, Athen, 2–3. Oktober 2002* (Internationale Archäologie. Studia honoraria 24), edited by H. R. Goette and O. Palagia: 251–61. Rahden/Westfalen.
Müller, V. K. 1915. *Der Polos, die griechische Götterkrone*. Berlin.
Mylonas, G. 1961. *Eleusis and the Eleusinian Mysteries*. Princeton.
Nafissi, M. 1991. *La Nascita del Kosmos: studi sulla storia e la società di Sparta*. Naples.
Nafissi, M. 1999. From Sparta to Taras: Nomima, ktiseis, and relationships between colony and mother city. In *Sparta: new perspectives*, edited by S. Hodkinson and A. Powell: 245–72. London/Swansea.
Nafissi, M. 2009. Sparta. In *A Companion to Archaic Greece*, edited by K. A. Raaflaub and H. van Wees: 117–37. Chichester and Malden.

Nafissi, M. 2013. La stele di Damonon (IG V 1, 213 = Moretti, IAG 16), gli Hekatombaia (Strabo 8,4,11) e il sistema festivo della Laconia d'epoca classica. In *La cultura a Sparta in età classica: atti del seminario di studi, Università statale di Milano, 5–6 maggio 2010. Aristonothos* 8: 105–74. Trento.

Nafissi, M. 2016. Oreste, Tisameno, gli Ephoreia e il santuario delle Moire a Sparta. In *Vestigia. Miscellanea di studi storico-religiosi in onore di Filippo Coarelli nel suo 80o anniversario*, edited by V. Gasparini: 633–44. Stuttgart.

Nafissi, M. 2018. Lykourgos the Spartan 'Lawgiver'. Ancient Beliefs and Modern Scholarship. In Powell 2018: 93–123.

Nafissi, M. 2020. Gli eroi del trono di Apollo ad Amicle tra apoteosi, immortalità elisia e destino di morte. *Mythos* 14: 1–24.

Nagy, G. 1979. *The Best of the Achaeans: concepts of the hero in Archaic Greek poetry*. Baltimore.

Nagy, G. 1990. *Pindar's Homer: The lyric possession of an epic past*. Baltimore.

Nagy, G. 1999. *The Best of the Achaeans: concepts of the hero in Archaic Greek poetry*. Baltimore.

Nagy, G. 2005. The Epic hero. In *A Companion to Ancient Epic*, edited by J. M. Foley: 71–89. Oxford.

Nagy, G. 2012. Signs of hero cult in Homeric poetry. In *Homeric Contexts. Neoanalysis and the Interpretation of Oral Poetry*, edited by F. Montanari, A. Rengakos, and C. C. Tsagalis: 27–71. Berlin.

Neumann, G. 1979. *Probleme des griechischen Weihreliefs*. Tübingen.

Nevett, L. C. 2012. *Domestic Space in Classical Antiquity*. Cambridge.

Nicholls, R. V. 1970. Greek votive statuettes and religious continuity, c. 1200–700 BC. In *Auckland Classical Essays presented to E. M. Blaiklock*, edited by B. F. Harris: 1–37. Auckland.

Nilsson, M. P. 1967. *Geschichte der Griechischen Religion*, 1. Munich.

Nilsson, M. P. 1972. *Cults, Myths, Oracles and Politics in Ancient Greece*. New York.

Nobili, C. 2013. Celebrating sporting victories in Classical Sparta: Epinician odes and epigrams. *Nikephoros* 26: 63–98.

Nobili, C. 2014. Performances of girls at the Spartan festival of the Hyakinthia. In *Mädchen im Altertum/ Girls in Antiquity*, edited by S. Moraw and A. Kieburg: 135–48. Münster.

Nock, A. D. 1944. The cult of heroes. *HThR* 37: 141–74.

Nora, P. 1984, 1986, 1992. *Les lieux de mémoire*, 3 vols. Paris.

Nora, P. 1989. Between memory and history: Les lieux de mémoire. *Representations* 26: 7–24.

O'Brien, V. J. 1993. *The Transformation of Hera: a study of ritual, hero and the goddess in the Iliad*. Lanham.

Ogden, D. 1994. Crooked Speech: the genesis of the Spartan Rhetra. *JHS* 114: 85–102.

Ogden, D. 1997. *The Crooked Kings of Ancient Greece*. London.

Ogden, D. (ed.). 2007. *A Companion to Greek Religion*. Oxford; Malden.

Ogden, D. 2013. *Drakon: dragon myth and serpent cult in the Greek and Roman worlds*. Oxford.

Ohnesorg, A. 2005. *Ionische Altäre: Formen und Varianten einer Architekturgattung aus Insel- und Ostionien* (Archäologische Forschungen 21). Berlin.

Orlandos, A. K. 1956. Μεθόρια Τεγεάτιδος καὶ Λακεδαίμονος. Βούρβουρα. Ἔργον: 83–5.

Osborne, R. 2004. Hoards, votives, offerings: the archaeology of the dedicated object. *World Archaeology* 36: 1–10.

Osborne, R. 2009. *Greece in the Making, 1200–479 BC*. 2nd ed. London.

Østby, E. 1995. I Templi di Pallantion. *Annuario della Scuola archaeological di Atene e delle Missioni italiane in Oriente* 68–9: 285–391.

Pache, C. O. 2004. *Baby and Child Heroes in Ancient Greece*. Urbana.

Page, D. L. 1981. *Further Greek Epigrams: Epigrams before A. D. 50 from the Greek Anthology and other sources, not included in 'Hellenistic Epigrams' or 'The Garland of Philip'*. Cambridge.

Palagia, O. 1993. Athena Promachos from the Acropolis of Sparta'. In *Sculpture from Arcadia and Laconia*, edited by O. Palagia and W. Coulson: 167–175. Princeton, NJ.

Palagia, O. 2003. The impact of *Ares Macedon* on Athenian Sculpture. In *The Macedonians in Athens, 322–229 BC*, edited by O. Palagia and S. Tracy: 140–51. Oxford.

Palagia, O. 2009. Spartan self-presentation in the panhellenic sanctuaries of Delphi and Olympia in the Classical period. In *Athens – Sparta*, edited by N. Kaltsas: 32–40. New York.

Palmisciano, R. 1996. Simonide 531 P. Testo, dedicatario e genere letterario. *QUCC* 54(3): 39–53.

Papadopoulos, J. K. 2003. *Ceramicus Redidivus: The Early Iron Age Potter's Field in the Area of the Classical Athenian Agora* (Hesperia suppl. 31). Princeton, NJ.

Papaefthimiou, V. 2001–2. Σύμπλεγμα τριῶν εἰδωλίων ἀπὸ τὸ ιερὸ της Δήμητρος κα τῶν Διοσκούρων της ἀρχαίας Μεσσήνης. *Peoponnesiaka. Parartima* 24(2): 129–46. Athens.

Papakonstantinou, Z. 2018. Athletics, memory and community in Hellenistic and Roman Messene. *BICS* 61 (1): 64–78.

Pariente, A. 1992. Le Monument Argient des 'Sept contre Thèbes'. In *Polydipsion Argos: Argos de la fin des palais mycéniens à la constitution de l État classique*, edited by M. Piérart (BCH suppl. 22): 195–225. Paris.

Parke, H. W. 1945. The Deposition of the Spartan Kings. *The Classical Quarterly* 39 (3/4): 106–12.

Parker, R. 1983. *Miasma: pollution and purification in early Greek religion*. Oxford.

Parker, R. 1986. Demeter, Dionysus and the Spartan pantheon. In Hägg, Marinatos and Nordquist 1986: 99–103.

Parker, R. 1987. Festivals of the Attic demes. In H. Hägg 1987: 137–47.

Parker, R. 1988. Were Spartan kings heroized? *LCM* 13 (1): 9–10.

Parker, R. 1989. Spartan religion. In *Classical Sparta: techniques behind her success*, edited by A. Powell: 142–72. London.

Parker, R. 1996. *Athenian Religion: a history*. Oxford.

Parker, R. 2003. The problem of the Greek cult epithet. *OAth* 28: 173–83.

Parker, R. 2005a. *Polytheism and Society at Athens*. Oxford.

Parker, R. 2005b. Ὡς ἥρωι ἐναγίζιν. In Hägg and Alroth 2005: 37–45.

Parker, R. 2011. *On Greek Religion*. Ithaca and London.

Parker, R. 2015. Public and Private. In *A Companion to the Archaeology of Religion in the Ancient World*, edited by R. Raja and J. Rüpke: 71–80. Chichester, Malden, MA, and Oxford.

Parker, R. *forthcoming*. The cult of Helen.

Parker, V. 1991. The dates of the Messenian Wars. *Chiron* 21: 25–43.

Parsons, P. 2001. These fragments we have shored against our ruin. In Boedeker and Sider 2001: 55–64.

Patera, I. 2012. *Offrir en Grèce: gestes et contexts*. Stuttgart.

Paton, J. M. 1904. Archaeological news. *AJA* 8 (3): 338–401.

Pavlides, N. 2011. Worshipping heroes: civic identity and the veneration of the communal dead in Archaic Sparta. In *Honouring the Dead in the Peloponnese. Proceedings of the Conference held in Sparta on the 23rd–25th of April 2009*, edited by H. Cavanagh, W. Cavanagh and J. Roy: 551–76. Nottingham.

Pavlides, N. 2018. The sanctuaries of Apollo Maleatas and Apollo Tyritas in Laconia: religion in Spartan-perioikic relations. *ABSA* 113: 279–305.

Pavlides, N. 2020. Non-Spartans in the Lakedaimonian army: the evidence from Laconia. *Historia* 69 (2): 154–84.

Pavlides, N. 2021. Heroes, politics, and the problem of ethnicity in Archaic Sparta. *Kernos* 34: 9–53.

Pedley, J. G. 2005. *Sanctuaries and the Sacred in the Ancient Greek World*. Cambridge.

Pelagatti, P. 1958. Kylix laconica con Herakle e le Amazoni. *BCH* 82: 482–94.

Patton, K. 2009. *Religion of the Gods: ritual, paradox, reflectivity*. Oxford.

Pelliccia, H. 2009. Simonides, Pindar and Bacchylides. In *The Cambridge Companion to Greek Lyric*, edited by F. Budelmann: 240–62. Cambridge.

Peppa-Papaioannou, I. 2012. *Πήλινα αναθήματα από την Πύλο: Ανασκαφή Βοϊδοκοιλιάς*. Athens.

Perdrizet, P. 1936. Hélène, soeur d'Aphrodite. *Annales du service des antiquités* 36: 5–10.

Petridou, G. 2016. *Divine Epiphany in Greek Literature and Culture*. Oxford.

Petropoulou, A. 2011–12. Hyakinthos and Apollo of Amyklai: identities and cults: A reconsideration of the written evidence. *MusBenaki* 11–12: 153–61.

Petropoulou, A. 2015. Hieromênia and sacrifice during the Hyakinthia. In *Dossier: Aitia: Causalité juridique, causalité philosophique* (Metis 38): 167–88. Paris and Athens.

Petrovic, A. 2007. *Kommentar zu den simonideischen Versinschriften* (Mnemosyne suppl. 282). Leiden.

Pettersson, M. 1992. *The Cults of Apollo at Sparta: the Hyakinthia, the Gymnopaidiai and the Karneia*. Stockholm.

Pfaff, C. 2003. Archaic Corinthian architecture, c. 600 to 480 BC. In Williams and Bookidis 2003: 95–140.

Pfaff, C. 2013. 'Artemis and a hero at the Argive Heraion', *Hesperia* 82: 277–99.

Pfister, F. 1909. *Die Reliquienkult im Altertum*. Giessen.

Pfohl, G. 1967. *Greek Poems on Stone, 1: epitaphs from the seventh to the fifth centuries BC* (Textus Minores 36). Leiden.

Phaklaris, P. 1990. Ἀρχαία Κυνουρία ἀνθρώπινη δρασηριότητα και περιβάλλον (Δημοσιεύματα του Αρχαιολογικού Δελτίου 43). Athens.

Phillips, D. D. 2003. The Bones of Orestes. In *Gestures: essays in ancient history, literature and philosophy presented to Alan L. Boegehold on the occasion of his retirement and his seventy-fifth birthday*, edited by G. W. Bakewell and J. Sickinger: 301–16. Oxford.

Picard, C. 1921. Fouilles de Thasos. *BCH* 45: 86–173.

Picard, C. 1940. L' Héroôn de Phrontis au Sounion. *RA* 16: 5–28.

Picirilli, L. 1967. Ricerche sul culto di Hyakinthos. *Studi Classici e Orientali* 16: 99–116.

Pikoulas, G. A. 1988. *Η νότια μεγαλοπολίτικη χώρα: ἀπὸ τὸν 8ο π.χ. αἰῶνα ὡς τόν 4ο μ.Χ. αῶνα. Συμβολή στὴν τοπογραφία της* (PhD Diss.). Athens.

Pilz, O. 2011. The uses of small things and the semiotics of Greek miniature objects. In *Gods of Small Things*, edited by A. C. Smith and M. E. Bergeon: 15–30. Toulouse.

Pipili, M. 1987. *Laconian Iconography of the Sixth Century BC* (Oxford Monographs 12). Oxford.

Pipili, M. 1991. Hermes and the child Dionysus: what did Pausanias see on the Amyklai Throne? In *Stips Votiva: Papers Presented to C. M. Stibbe*, edited by M. Gnade: 143–7. Amsterdam.

Pipili, M. 1998. Archaic Laconian vase-painting: some iconographical considerations. In Cavanagh and Walker 1998: 82–96.

Pipili, M. 2000. Vases from the Samian Heraion: shapes and iconography. In *Agathos Daimon, Mythes et cultes: Ètudes d' iconographie en l'honneur de Lilly Kahil* (BCH suppl. 38), edited by P. Lilant de Bellefonds: 409–21. Paris.

Pipili, M. 2001. Samos, the Artemis Sanctuary: The Laconian Pottery. *JDAI* 116: 12–102.

Pipili, M. 2018. Laconian Pottery. In *A Companion to Sparta, vol. 1*, edited by A. Powell: 124–53. Hoboken, NJ.

Pirenne-Delforge, V. 2004. La portée du témoignage de Pausanias sur les cultes locaux. In *Les cultes locaux dans les mondes grec et romain: actes du colloque de Lyon, 7–8 juin 2001*, edited by G. Labarre: 5–20. Lyon; Paris.

Pirenne-Delforge, V. 2006. Ritual Dynamics in Pausanias: the Laphria. In *Ritual and Communication in the Graeco-Roman World* (Kernos suppl. 16), edited by E. Stavrianopoulou: 111–29. Liège.

Pirenne-Delforge, V. 2008. *Retour à la source: Pausanias et la religion grecque* (Kernos Suppl. 20). Liège.

Pirenne-Delforge, V. and E. Suárez de la Torre (eds). 2000. *Héros et Héroïnes dans les Myths et les Cultes Grecs: Actes du colloque organisé à l' Universit de Valladolid du 26 au 29 Mai 1999* (Kernos suppl. 10). Liège.

Platt, V. J. 2011. *Facing the Gods: epiphany and representation in Graeco-Roman art, literature and religion.* Cambridge.

Platt, V. J. 2018. Double vision: epiphanies of the Dioscuri in Classical antiquity. *ARG* 20 (1): 229–56.

Podlecki, A. J. 1968. Simonides 480. *Historia* 17 (3): 257–75.

Podlecki, A. J. 1971. Stesichoreia. *Athenaeum* 49: 313–27.

Polignac, de. F. 1995. *Cults, Territory, and the Origins of the Greek City-State*, translated by J. Lloyd. Chicago.

Polignac, de. F. 2009. Sanctuaries and festivals. In *A Companion to Archaic Greece*, edited by K. A. Raaflaub and H. van Wees: 427–43. Oxford.

Poltera, O. 2008. *Simonides Lyricus: Testimonia und Fragmente. Einleitung, kritische, Ausgabe, Übersetzung und Kommentar.* Fribourg.

Pomeroy, S. B. 2002. *Spartan Women.* Oxford.

Popham, M. R., P. G. Calligas, and L. H. Sackett (eds). 1993. *Lefkandi II: The Protogeometric building at Toumba, part 2: the excavation, architecture and finds.* Athens.

Porter, J. I. 2001. Ideals and ruins: Pausanias, Longinus, and the Second Sophistic. In *Pausanias: Travel and Memory in Roman Greece*, edited by S. E. Alcock, J. F. Cherry and J. Elsner: 63–92. Oxford.

Pouilloux, J. 1954. *Recherches sur l'histoire et les cultes de Thasos. Vol. I. De la fondation de la cité à 196 avant J.-C* (Études Thasiennes 3). Paris.

Pouilloux, J. 1955. Glaukos, fils de Leptine, Parien. *BCH* 79: 75–86.

Poupaki, E. 2009. Marble urns in the Sparta museum. In Cavanagh, Gallou, and Georgiades 2009: 243–51.

Powell, A. 1998. Sixth-century Laconian vase-painting: continuities and discontinuities with the 'Lykourgan' ethos. In *Archaic Greece: new approaches and new evidence*, edited by N. Fisher and H. van Wees: 119–46. Swansea.

Powell, A. 2002. Dining groups, marriage, homosexuality. In *Sparta*, edited by M. Whitby: 90–103. Edinburgh.

Powell, A. 2009. Divination, royalty and insecurity in Classical Sparta. *Kernos* 22: 37–82.

Powell, A. and S. Hodinson (eds). 1994. In *The Shadow of Sparta*. London; New York.

Powell, A. (ed.). 2018. *A Companion to Sparta.* Hoboken, NJ and Chichester.

Powell, B. B. 1991. *Homer and the Origins of the Greek Alphabet.* Cambridge.

Prent, M. 2003. Glories of the past in the past: ritual activities in palatial ruins in early Iron Age Crete. In *Archaeologies of Memory*, edited by R. M. Van Dyke and S. E. Alcock: 81–103. Malden, MA

Pretzler, M. 2007. Making Peloponnesians: Sparta's allies and their regional identities. In *Being Peloponnesian: Proceedings of the conference held at the University of*

Nottingham 31st March–1st April 2007 (CSPS Online Publication, 1): 1–12. Nottingham.
Price, S. 1999. *Religions of the Ancient Greeks.* Cambridge.
Pritchett, W. K. 1953. The Attic Stelai. *Hesperia* 22: 225–99.
Pritchett, W. K. 1979. *The Greek State at War. Part III. Religion.* Berkeley, CA.
Pritchett, W. K. 1985. *The Greek State at War. Part IV.* Berkeley, CA.
Proietti, G. 2014. Annual games for war-dead and founders in classical times: between hero-cult and civic honors. *Nikephoros* 27: 199–213.
Prost, F. 2018. Laconian art. In *A Companion to Sparta*, edited by A. Powell: 154–76. Hoboken, NJ.
Prückner, H. 1968. *Die lokrischen Tonreliefs.* Mainz am Rhein.
Purvis, A. 2003. *Singular Dedications: founders and innovators of private cults in Classical Greece.* New York.
Raaflaub, K. A. 2004. *The Discovery of Freedom in Ancient Greece.* Chicago.
Rabinowitz, A. 2009. Drinking from the same cup: Sparta and late Archaic commensality. In *Sparta: comparative approaches*, edited by S. Hodkinson: 113–92. Swansea.
Raftopoulou, S. 1988. New finds from Sparta. In Cavanagh and Walker 1998: 125–40.
Raftopoulou, S. 1996–7. Ταφές της εποχής του Σιδήρου στη Σπάρτη. *Peloponnesiaka* (Parartima 22): 272–82.
Rask, K. A. 2016. Devotionalism, Material Culture, and the Personal in Greek Religion. *Kernos* 29: 9–40.
Ratinaud-Lachkar, I. 2000. Héros homériques et sanctuaires d'époque géométrique. In Pirennne-Delforge and Suáreze de la Torre 2000: 247–62.
Renfrew, C. 1985. *The Archaology of Cult: the sanctuary at Pylakopi* (ABSA suppl. 18). London.
Renfrew, C. 1994. The archaeology of religion. In *The Ancient Mind: elements of cognitive archaeology*, edited by C. Renfrew and E. B. W. Zubrow: 47–54. Cambridge.
Rhodes, P. J. 1998. *Thucydides. History IV. 1–V. 24.* Warminster.
Rhomaios, K. A. 1914. Tegeatische Reliefs. *MDAI(A)* 39: 189–235.
Richer, N. 1994. Aspects des funérailles à Sparte. *CCG* 5: 51–96.
Richer, N. 1998. *Les Éphores: Études sur l'histoire et sur l'image de Sparte (VIIIe–IIIe siècle avant Jésus-Christ).* Paris.
Richer, N. 2004. The Hyakinthia of Sparta. In *Spartan Society*, edited by T. J. Figueira: 71–102. Swansea.
Richer, N. 2007. The religious system at Sparta. In Ogden 2007: 236–52.
Richer, N. 2012. *La religion des Spartiates: croyances et cultes dans l'Antiquité.* Paris.
Richert, R. and K. Lesage. 2019. Do people think the soul is separate from the body and the mind? In *The Cognitive Science of Religion: a methodological introduction to key empirical studies*, edited by D. J. Slone and W. W. McCorkle: 55–62. London.
Ridgway, B. S. 1993. *The Archaic Style in Greek Sculpture.* Princeton, NJ.
Ridgway, B. S. 2004. *Second Chance: Greek sculptural studies revisited.* London.

Riethmüller, J. W. 1999. Bothros and Tetrastyle: The heroon of Asclepius in Athens. In Hägg 1999: 123–43.
Robertson, N. 1992. *Festivals and Legends: the formation of Greek cities in the light of public ritual.* Toronto.
Robertson, N. 1996. Athena and early Greek society: Palladium shrines and promontory shrines. In *Religion in the Ancient World: new themes and approaches*, edited by M. Dillon: 383–475. Amsterdam.
Robinson, D. M. 1906. Terracottas from Corinth. *AJA* 10: 159–73.
Rohde, E. 2000. *Psyche: the cult of souls and the belief in immortality among the Greeks*, translated by W. B. Hillis. London.
Roller, M. B. 2006. *Dining Posture in Ancient Rome: Bodies, Values, and Status.* Princeton, NJ and Oxford.
Rolley, C. 1976. Objets de metal. In *Médéon de Phocide V: tombes hellénistiques, objets de métal, monnaies*: 95–121. Paris.
Romano, I. B. 1980. *Early Greek Cult Images* (PhD Diss.). University of Pennsylvania.
Romano, I. B. 1995. *Gordion Special Studies, Volume II: The Terracotta Figurines and Related Vessels.* Philadelphia, PA.
Ross, L. 1855. Uebersicht. *Archäologische Aufsätze* I: 1–11.
Ross, L. 1861. Bleifigürchen vom Menelaion. *Archäologische Aufsätze* II: 341–4.
Rossi, D. 1982. Sei terrecotte tarantine e il culto di Hyakinthos. In *ΑΠΑΡΧΑΙ: nuove ricerche e studi sulla Magna Grecia e la Sicilia antica in onore di Paolo Enrico Arias*, edited by M. L. Gualandi, L. Massei, and S. Settis: 563–7. Pisa.
Rusch, S. M. 2011. *Sparta at War: Strategy, Tactics, and Campaigns (550–362).* London.
Rusten, J. S. 1983. Γείτων ἥρως. *HSPh* 87: 289–97
Rutherford, I. A. 1996. *Homer.* Oxford.
Rutherford, I. A. 2001. The New Simonides: towards a commentary. In Boedeker and Sider 2001: 33–54.
Salapata, G. 1993. The Laconian hero reliefs in the light of the terracotta plaques. In *Sculpture from Arcadia and Laconia: proceedings of an international conference held at the American School of Classical Studies at Athens, April 10–14, 1992*, edited by O. Palagia and W. Coulson: 189–97. Oxford.
Salapata, G. 1997. Hero warriors from Corinth and Laconia. *Hesperia* 66 (2): 245–60.
Salapata, G. 2001. Review of E. Kourinou-Pikoula, *Σπάρτη. Συμβολή στη μνημειακή τοπογραφία της* (Athens; 2000). *Bryn Mawr Classical Review.*
Salapata, G. 2002a. Myth into cult: Alexandra/Kassandra in Lakonia. In *Oikistes: studies in constitution, colonies and military power in the ancient world. Offered in honor of A. J. Graham*, edited by V. B. Gorman and E. Robinson: 131–59. Leiden.
Salapata, G. 2002b. Greek votive plaques: manufacture, display, disposal. *BaBesch* 77: 19–42.
Salapata, G. 2006. The tippling serpent in the art of Laconia and beyond. *Hesperia* 75 (4): 541–60.
Salapata, G. 2009. Female triads on Laconian terracotta plaques. *ABSA* 104: 325–340.

Salapata, G. 2011. The heroic cult of Agamemnon. *Electra* 1(1): 39–60.

Salapata, G. 2014. *Heroic Offerings: the terracotta plaques from the Spartan sanctuary of Agamemnon and Kassandra*. Ann Arbor, MI.

Salapata, G. 2018. Tokens of piety: inexpensive dedications as functional and symbolic objects. *Opuscula* 11: 97–109.

Sanders, J. M. (ed.). 1992a. Φιλολάκων: *Laconian studies in honour of Hector Catling*. London.

Sanders, J. M. 1992b. The early Laconian Dioskouroi reliefs. In Sanders 1992a: 205–10.

Santa, della M. 2014. Les conséquences de l'urbanisation hellénistique sur la description de Sparte par Pausanias le périégète. *Dialogues d'histoire ancienne* 11: 77–92.

Scanlon, T. F. 1988. Virgineum gymnasium: Spartan females and early Greek athletics. In *The Archaeology of the Olympics: the Olympics and other festivals in antiquity*, edited by W. J. Raschke: 185–216. Madison.

Schachermeyer, F. 1984. *Die griechische Rückerinnerung*. Vienna.

Schachter, A. 1981–94. *Cults of Boiotia* (BICS suppl. 38). Vol. I–IV. London.

Schaefer, H. 1957. Das Eidolon des Leonidas. In *Charites: Studien zur Altertumswissenschaft*, edited by K. Schauenburg: 223–33. Bonn.

Schattner, T. G. 1990. *Griechsche Housmodelle. Untersuchungen zur frühgriechischen Architektur* (Mitteilungen des Deutschen Archäologischen Instituts. Athenische Abteilungen. Beiheft 15). Berlin.

Scheer, T. S. 2003. The past in the Hellenistic present: myth and local tradition. In *A Companion to the Hellenistic World*, edited by A. Erskine: 216–31. Oxford.

Schefold, K. 1992. *Gods and Heroes in Late Archaic Greek Art*. Cambridge.

Schefton, B. B. 1954. Three Laconian vase-painters. *ABSA* 49: 299–310.

Schlesier, R. 1991–2. Olympian versus Chthonian religion. *Scripta Classica Israelica* 11: 38–51.

Schmitt Pantel, P. 2012. De l'espace privé à l'espace public dans le monde grec. *ThesCRA* 8: 1–7.

Schörner, H. 2007. *Sepulturae graecae intra urbem: untersuchungen zum Phänomen der intraurbanen Bestattungen bei den Griechen* (Boreas Beiheft 9). Möhnesee.

Schroder, B. 1904. Archaische Skulpturen aus Laconien 2: Inschriftstele aus Sparta. *AM* 29: 24–31.

Schwarzmaier, A. 1997. *Griechische Klappspiegel: Untersuchungen zu Typologie und Stil* (Mitteilungen des Deutchen Archäologischen Institutes, Beiheft 18). Berlin.

Scott, L. 2005. *Historical Commentary on Herodotus Book 6*. Leiden.

Scott, M. 2010. *Delphi and Olympia: the spatial politics of Panhellenism in the Archaic and Classical periods*. Cambridge.

Scullion, S. 1994. Olympian and Chthonian. *CA* 13: 75–119.

Scullion, S. 2000. Heroic and Chthonian sacrifice: new evidence from Selinous. *ZPE* 132: 163–71.

Seaford, R. 1994. *Reciprocity and Ritual: Homer and tragedy in the developing city-state*. Oxford.

Sergent, B. 1984. *L' Homosexualité dans la Mythologie Greque*. Paris.

Shapiro-Lapatin, K. D. 1992. A family gathering at Rhamnous? Who's who in the Nemesis base. *Hesperia* 61: 107–19.

Shapiro, H. A. 2012. Anonymous heroes: Reinterpreting a group of classical Attic votive reliefs. In *Kunst von unten? Stil und Gesellschaft in der antiken Welt -von der 'arte plebea' bis heute. Internationales Kolloquium anlässlich des 70. Geburtstages von Paul Zanker, Rom Villa Massimo, 8.–9. Juni 2007*. 111–20. Wiesbaden.

Shaw, P-J. 2003. *Discrepancies in Olympiad Dating and Chronological Problems of Archaic Peloponnesian History*. Wiesbaden and Stuttgart.

Shear, T. L. Jr. 1973. The Athenian Agora: excavations of 1972. *Hesperia* 42 (4): 359–407.

Shipley, G. 1992. *Perioikos:* the discovery of Classical Laconia. In Sanders 1992: 211–26.

Shipley, G. 1996. Survey site catalogue. In Cavanagh *et al.* 1996: 315–438.

Shipley, G. 2004. Messenia. In *An Inventory of Archaic and Classical Poleis*, edited by M. H. Hansen and T. H. Nielsen: 547–68. Oxford.

Shipley, G. 2006. Sparta and its Perioikic neighbours: a century of reassessment. *Hermathena* 181: 51–82.

Seiffert, O. 1911. Die Totenschlange auf lakonischen Reliefs. *Festschrift zur Jahrundertfeier der Universität Breslau*: 113–26. Breslau.

Sider, D. 2001. Fragments 1–22 W^2: text, apparatus criticus, and translation. In Boedeker and Sider 2001: 13–30.

Simantoni-Bournia, E. 2004. *La Céramique Grecque à Reliefs: ateliers insulaires du VIIIe au VIe siècle avant J.-C.* Geneva.

Simon, C. G. 1986. *The Archaic Votive Offerings and Cults of Ionia* (PhD Diss.). The University of California, Berkeley, CA.

Skutsch, O. 1987. Helen: her name and nature. *JHS* 102: 188–93.

Snodgrass, A. M. 1971. *The Dark Age of Greece: an archaeological survey from the eleventh to the eighth centuries BC*. Edinburgh.

Snodgrass, A. M. 1980. *Archaic Greece: the age of experiment*. London; Toronto.

Snodgrass, A. M. 1987. *An Archaeology of Greece: towards the history of a discipline*. Berkeley, CA.

Snodgrass, A. M. 1988. The archaeology of the hero. *AION* 10: 19–26.

Snodgrass, A. M. 1998. *Homer and the Artists*. Cambridge.

Snodgrass, A. M. 2006. *Archaeology and the Emergence of Greece: collected papers on early Greece and related topics (1965–2002)*. Edinburgh.

Smith, T. J. 1998. Dances, drinks and dedications: the Archaic komos in Laconia. In Cavanagh and Walker 1998: 75–81.

Smith, T. J. 2010. *Komast Dancers in Archaic Greek Art*. Oxford.

Sourvinou-Inwood, Ch. 1978. Persephone and Aphrodite at Locri: A model for personality definitions in Greek religion. *JHS* 98: 101–20.

Sourvinou-Inwood, Ch. 1983. A trauma in flux: death in the 8th century and after. In *The Greek Renaissance of the Eighth Century B.C.: tradition and innovation*.

Proceedings of the second international symposium at the Swedish Institute in Athens, 1–5 June 1981, edited by R. Hägg: 33–49. Stockholm.
Sourvinou-Inwood, Ch. 1995. *'Reading' Greek Death: to the end of the Classical period*. Oxford.
Sourvinou-Inwood, Ch. 2000. What is *Polis* religion? In Buxton 2000: 13–37.
Sourvinou-Inwood, Ch. 2005. *Hylas, the Nymphs, Dionysos and others: myth, ritual, ethnicity*. Stockholm.
Spallino, G. 2016. Athena Chalkioikos a Sparta: riesame dei dati archeologici e topografici del santuario. In *ΔPOMOI: Studi sul mondo antico offerti a Emanuele Greco dagli allievi della Scuola Archeologica Italiana di Atene*, edited by F. Longo, R. Di Cesare and S. Privitera: 695–710. Paestum.
Spawforth, A. J. S. 1978. Balbilla, the Euryclids and memorials for the Greek magnate. *ABSA* 73: 249–60.
Spawforth, A. J. S. 1985. Families at Roman Sparta and Epidaurus: Some prosopographical notes. *ABSA* 80: 191–258.
Spawforth, A. J. S. 1994. Sparta, the Roman Stoa, 1988-92: the inscriptions. *ABSA* 89: 433–41.
Spawforth, A. J. S. 2012. *Greece and the Augustan Revolution*. Cambridge.
Speyer, W. 1980. Die Hilfe und Epiphanie einer Gottheit, eines Heroen und eines Heiligen in der Schlacht. In *Pietas: Festschrift für Bernhard Köttin*, edited by E. Dassmann and K. S. Frank: 55–77. Münster.
Stafford, E. 2005. Héraklès: encore et toujours le problème du heros-theos. *Kernos* 18: 391–406.
Stavrianopoulou, E. 2006. Introduction. *Ritual and Communication in the Graeco-Roman World* (Kernos suppl. 16), edited by E Stavrianopoulou: 7–22. Liège.
Ste Croix de G. E. M. 2002. Sparta's foreign policy. In *Sparta*, edited by M. Whitby: 218–22. Edinburgh.
Stehle, E. 2001. A bard of the Iron Age and his auxiliary muse. In Boedeker and Sider 2001: 106–19.
Steiner, D. 1999. To praise, not to bury: Simonides fr. 531P. *CQ* 49 (2): 364–82.
Steinhauer, G. 1982. Πήλινες Αρχαϊκές μετόπες απο τη Σπάρτη. *ASAA* 60: 329–41.
Steinhauer, G. 2009. Παρατηρήσεις στην πολεοδομία της ρωμαϊκής Σπάρτης. In Cavanagh, Gallou and Georgiadis 2009: 271–8.
Steinhauer, G. 2020. Le téménos du Héros spartiate. In *ΚΥΔΑΛΙΜΟΣ. Τιμητικός Τόμος για τον Καθηγητή Γεώργιο Στυλ. Κορρέ* (Aura Supp. 4): 263–80. Athens.
Stelow, A. R. 2020. *Menelaus in the Archaic Period: not quite the best of the Achaeans*. Oxford.
Stewart, A. 1990. *Greek Sculpture: an exploration*. New Haven, CT.
Stibbe, C. M. 1972. *Lakonische Vasenmaler des sechsten Jahrunderts v. Chr, vols 1–2*. Amsterdam.
Stibbe, C. M. 1974. Il cavaliere Laconico. *MNIR* 36: 19–37.
Stibbe, C. M. 1976. 'Ein lakonischer Becher aus dem heraion von Samos'. *AM* 91: 63–74.

Stibbe, C. M. 1984. Lo Stamnos Laconico. *Bolletino d'Arte* 69: 1–12.
Stibbe, C. M. 1985. Chilon of Sparta. *MNIR* 46: 7–24.
Stibbe, C. M. 1989a. Beobachtungen zur Topographie des antiken Sparta. *BaBesch* 64: 61–99.
Stibbe, C. M. 1989b. *Laconian Mixing Bowls: a history of the krater Laconikos from the seventh to the fifth century B.C. Laconian black-glazed pottery, part 1.* Amsterdam.
Stibbe, C. M. 1991. Dionysos in Sparta. *BaBesch* 67: 1–62.
Stibbe, C. M. 1992. La lakaina. Un vaso laconico per pere. In *Lakonikà: ricerche e nuovi materiali di ceramica laconica*, edited by P. Pelagatti and C. Stibbe: 73–113. Rome.
Stibbe, C. M. 1993. Das Eleusinion am Fusse des Taygetos in Lakonien. *BaBesch* 68: 71–105.
Stibbe, C. M. 1994a. *Laconian Drinking Vessels and other Open Shapes: Laconian black-glazed pottery, part 2.* Amsterdam.
Stibbe, C. M. 1994b. Between Babyka and Knakion. *Babesch* 69: 63–102.
Stibbe, C. M. 1995. Lakonische bronzene Hopliten. Die erste Generation. *AK* 38: 68–80.
Stibbe, C. M. 1996. *Das andere Sparta.* Mainz am Rhein.
Stibbe, C. M. 2002. The 'Achilleion' near Sparta: some unknown finds. In Hägg 2002: 207–19.
Stibbe, C. M. 2004. *Lakonische Vasenmaler des sechsten Jahrhunderts v. Chr. Supplement.* Amsterdam.
Stibbe, C. M. 2006. *Agalmata: Studien zur griechisc-archaischen Bronzekunst* (BaBesch suppl. 11). Leuven; Paris; Dudley.
Stibbe, C. M. 2007. Mädchen, Frauen, Göttinnen. Lakonishe Weibliche Bronzestatuetten. *MDAI(A)* 122: 17–102.
Stibbe, C. M. 2008. Laconian bronzes from the sanctuary of Apollo Hyperteleatas near Phoiniki (Laconia) and from the Acropolis of Athens. *BaBesch* 83: 17–75.
Stillwell, A. N. 1952. *The Potter's Quarter* (Corinth XV 1). Princeton, NJ.
Straten van, F. T. 1981. Gifts for the gods. In *Faith, Hope and Worship: aspects of religious mentality in the ancient world*, edited by H. S. Versnel: 65–151. Leiden.
Straten van, F. T. 1995. *Iera Kala: Images of animal sacrifice in Archaic and Classical Greece.* Leiden.
Straten van, F. T. 2000. Votives and votaries in Greek sanctuaries. In Buxton 2000: 191–226.
Stratiki, K. 2004. The Greek heroes as 'Personifications'. In *Personification in the Greek World*, edited by E. Stafford and J. Herrin: 69–76. Aldershot and Burlington, VT.
Stroszeck, J. 2014. Laconian red-figure pottery: local production and use. In *The Regional Production of Red-figure Pottery: Greece, Magna Graecia and Etruria*, edited by S. Schierup and V. Sabetai: 138–58. Aarhus.
Svenson-Evers, H. 1996. *Die Griechischen Architekten Archaischer und Klassischer Zeit.* Berlin
Sweet, W. 1987. *Sport and Recreation in Ancient Greece: a sourcebook with translations.* Oxford.

Szeliga, G. 1981. *Dioskouroi on the Roof: Archaic and Classical equestrian acroteria in Sicily and South Italy* (PhD Diss.). Bryn Mawr College.

Taita, J. 2001. Indovini stanieri al servizio dello stato spartano. *Dike* 4: 39–85.

Taplin, O. 1992. *Homeric Soundings: the shaping of the Iliad.* Oxford.

Taplin, O. 2000. The spring of the Muses: Homer and related poetry. In *Literature in the Greek and Roman Worlds: a new perspective*, edited by O. Taplin: 22–57. Oxford.

Tarkow, T. A. 1983. Tyrtaeus, 9D: the role of poetry in the new Sparta. *AC* 52: 48–69.

Themelis, P. 1998. The sanctuary of Demeter and the Dioscouri at Messene. In Hägg 1998: 101–22. Jonsered.

Themelis, P. 2000. Ήρωες και ηρώα στη Μεσσήνη. Athens.

Theodoropoulou-Polychroniadis, Z. 2015. *Sounion Revisited: The sanctuaries of Poseidon and Athena at Sounion in Attica.* Oxford.

Thommen, L. 2000. Spartas Umgang mit der Vergangenheit. *Historia* 49: 40–53.

Thompson, H. A. 1958. Activities in the Athenian Agora: 1957. *Hesperia* 27 (2): 145–60.

Themelis, P. 1966. Activity in the Athenian Agora 1960–1965. *Hesperia* 35 (1): 37–54.

Thompson, H. A. and R. E. Wycherley. 1972. *The Athenian Agora XIV: The history, shape and uses of an ancient city center.* Princeton, NJ.

Thompson, M. S. 1908–9. Laconia: I excavations at Sparta, 1909. The Menelaion. The terracottas. Ivory and bone. *ABSA* 15: 116–44.

Thönges-Stringaris, R. N. 1965. Das griechische Totenmahl. *MDAI(A)* 80: 1–99.

Tigerstedt, E. N. 1974. *The Legend of Sparta in Classical Antiquity.* vol. 2. Stockholm.

Tillyard, H. J. W. 1906–7. Laconia: Excavations in Sparta. Inscriptions. *ABSA* 13: 174–94.

Tod, M. N. and A. J. B. Wace. 1906. *A Catalogue of the Sparta Museum.* Oxford.

Toher, M. 1990. Greek funerary legislation and the two Spartan funerals. In *Georgica: Greek studies in honour of George Cawkwell*, edited by M. A. Flower and M. Toher: 159–75. London.

Toher, M. 1999. On the *eidolon* of a Spartan king. *RhM* 142: 113–27.

Tomlinson, R. A. 1992. The Menelaion and Spartan architecture. In Sanders 1992a: 247–55.

Tomlinson, R. A. 2008. Ionian influence on Spartan architecture? In *Dioskouroi: studies presented to W. G. Cavanagh and C. B. Mee on the anniversary of their 30-year joint contribution to Aegean Archaeology* (BAR international series 1889), edited by C. Gallou, M. Georgiadis and G. M. Muskett. Oxford.

Tosti, V. 2011. Una riflessione sui culti eroici nella Sparta katà komas. L'edificio con banchina di odos Staufert. *ASAtene* 59, ser. III.11, vol. 1: 95–108.

Travlos, J. 1971. *Pictorial Dictionary of Ancient Athens.* London.

Tsagalis, C. 2017. *Early Greek Epic Fragments I: Antiquarian and Genealogical Epic.* Berlin and Boston, MA.

Tsountas, Ch. 1892. Εκ του Αμυκλαίου. *Archaiologiki Ephimeris*: 1–20.

Tsouli, M. 2013. Ανασκαφή κλασικού νεκροταφείου στην πόλη της Σπάρτη. In *Griechische Grabbezirke klassischer Zeit: Normen und Regionalismen: Akten des internationalen Kolloquiums Athen, 20–21 November 2009*, edited by K. Sporn: 151–66. Munich.

Tsouli, M. 2014. Μνημειώδη έργα κοροπλαστικής και πήλινα αναθήματα από ένα νέο ιερό της ρωμαϊκής Σπάρτης. In *Κοροπλαστική και Μικροτεχνία στον Αιγαιακό Χώρο από τους Γεωμετρικούς Χρόνους έως και τη Ρωμαϊκή Περίοδο*, edited by A. Giannikouri: 141–61. Athens.

Tsouli, M. 2016. Testimonia on funerary banquets in ancient Sparta. In *Dining and Death: interdisciplinary perspectives on the 'funerary banquet' in ancient art, burial and belief*, edited by C. Draycott and M. Stamatopoulou: 353–84. Leuven.

Ungern-Sternberg, J. von. 1985. Das grab des Theseus und andere Gräber. In *Antike in der Moderne, Xenia, Kostanzer Althistorische Vorträge und Forschungen* 15, edited by W. Schuller: 321–9. Konstanz.

Usener, H. 1896. *Gotternamen: Versuch einer Lehre von der Religiösen Begriffsbildung*. Bonn.

Usener, H. 1948. *Gotternamen: Versuch einer Lehre von der Religiösen Begriffsbildung*. Frankfurt.

Valmin, N. M. 1929. *Inscriptions de la Messénie*. Lund.

Vasilogamvrou, A., M. Tsouli and A. Maltezou. 2018. Η πόλη της Σπάρτης μέσα από τις πρόσφατες αρχαιολογικές ανασκαφές. In *Το Αρχαιολογικό Έργο στην Πελοπόννησο*, edited by E. Zymi, A.-V. Karapanagiotou and M. Xanthopoulou: 329–52. Kalamata.

Verbanck-Piérard, A. 1992. Herakles at feast in Attic art: a mythical or cultic iconography? In *The Iconography of Greek Cult in the Archaic and Classical Periods* (Kernos suppl. 1), edited by R. Hägg: 85–106. Athens and Liège.

Verbanck-Piérard, A. 2000. Les héros guérisseurs: des dieux comme les autres! In Pirenne-Delforge, and Suárez de la Torres 2000: 281–32.

Vikela, E. 2011. Τα μικρά ιερά της Αθήνας. *Archaiologiki Ephimeris* 150: 133–96.

Villing, A. 2002. For whom did the bell toll in Ancient Greece? Archaic and Classical Greek bells at Sparta and beyond. *ABSA* 97: 223–95.

Vlachou, V. 2011–12. The Spartan Amyklaion: the Early Iron Age pottery from the sanctuary. *MusBenaki* 11–12: 113–24. Athens.

Vlachou, V. 2017a. Ritual practices in early Iron Age and early Archaic Peloponnese. In *Regional Stories Towards a New Perception of the Early Greek World*, edited by A. Mazarakis Ainian, A. Alexandridou and X. Charalambidou: 249–78. Volos.

Vlachou, V. 2017b. From Mycenaean cult practice to the Hyakinthia festival of the Spartan polis: Cult images, textiles and ritual activity at Amykles: an archaeological perspective. In *Constructing Social Identities in Early Iron Age and Archaic Greece*, EA 12, edited by A. Tsingarida and I. S. Lemos: 11–42. Brussels.

Vlachou, V. 2018. Feasting at the sanctuary of Apollo Hyakinthos at Amykles: the evidence of the Early Iron Age. In *Feasting and Polis Institutions*, edited by F. van den Eijnde, J. Blok and R. Strootman: 93–124. Leiden and Boston.

Vlassopoulos, K. 2007. *Unthinking the Greek Polis: Ancient Greek history beyond Eurocentrism*. Cambridge.

Vlizos, S. 2009. The Amyklaion revisited: new observations on a Laconian Sanctuary of Apollo. In *Athens-Sparta: Contributions to the research on the history and archaeology of the two city-states*, edited by. N. Kaltsas: 11-23. New York.
Vlizos, S. 2017. Ο Θρόνος του Θεού. Ο Οικισμός και το ιερό των Αμυκλών, *Ανασκαφή* 124: 28-39.
Voyatzis, M. 1990. *The Early Sanctuary of Athena Alea at Tegea, and Other Archaic Sanctuaries in Arcadia*. Göteborg.
Voyatzis, M. 1992. Votive riders seated side-saddle at early Greek sanctuaries. *ABSA* 87: 259-79.
Wace, A. J. B. 1905-6a. Laconia II: excavations at Sparta, 1906. The Heroon. *ABSA* 12: 288-94.
Wace, A. J. B. 1905-6b. Laconia II: Excavations at Sparta, 1906. The Stamped Tiles. *ABSA* 12: 344-50.
Wace, A. J. B. 1906-7. Excavations at Sparta, 1907. The Stamped Tiles. *ABSA* 13: 17-43.
Wace, A. J. B. 1908-9. Laconia: I excavations at Sparta, 1909. The Menelaion. The lead figurines. *ABSA* 15: 129-41.
Wace, A. J. B. 1937. A Spartan Hero Relief. *Archaiologiki Ephimeris*: 217-20.
Wace, A. J. B. and F. W. Hasluck. 1904-5. Laconia. I. Excavations near Angelona. *ABSA* 11: 81-90.
Wace, A. J. B., M. S. Thompson and J. P Droop. 1908-9. Laconia: I excavations at Sparta, 1909. The Menelaion. *ABSA* 15: 108-57.
Wade-Gery, H. T. 1949. A note on the origin of the Spartan Gymnopaidai. *CQ* 43: 79-81.
Wallace, M. B. 1970. Notes of early Greek grave epigrams. *Phoenix* 24 (2): 93-105.
Wallace, S. 2011. The significance of Plataia for Greek Eleutheria in the early Hellenistic period. In *Creating a Hellenistic World*, edited by A. Erskine and L. Llewellyn-Jones: 147-76. Swansea.
Wallach, B. P. 1980. 'Epimone' and 'diatribe': dwelling on the point in ps.-Hermogenes. *Rheinisches Museum für Philologie* 123 (3/4): 272-322.
Wallensten, J. 2008. Personal protection and tailor-made deities: the use of individual epithets. *Kernos* 21: 81-95.
Walker, H. J. 2015. *The Twin Horse Gods: the Dioskouroi in mythologies of the ancient world*. London and New York, NJ.
Walter-Karydi, E. 2006. *How the Aiginetans Formed their Identity*, translated by J. Glough. Athens.
Warner, R. (trans.). 1972. *Thucydides: history of the Peloponnesian War*. London.
Waywell, G. 1999. Sparta and its topography. *BICS* 43: 1-26.
Wees, van H. 1992. *Status Warriors: war, violence and society in Homer and history*. Amsterdam.
Wees, van H. 1999. Tyrtaeus' *Eunomia*: nothing to do with the Great Rhetra. In Hodkinson and Powell 1999: 1-41.
Wees, van H. 2006. From kings to demigods: epic heroes and social change c. 750-600 BC. In Deger-Jalkotzy and Lemos: 363-79.

Wees, van H. 2018a. Luxury, austerity and equality in Sparta. In *A Companion to Sparta*, edited by A. Powell: 202–35. Hoboken, NJ.

Wees, van H. 2018b. The common messes. In Powell 2019: 236–68.

Welter, G. 1941. *Troizen und Kalaureia*. Berlin.

Welwei, K.-W. 1991. Heroenkult und Gefallenehrung im antiken Griechenland. In *Tod und Jenseits im Altertm* (Bochumer Altertumswissenschaftliches Colloquium), edited by G. Binder and B. Effe: 50–70. Trier.

Welwei, K.-W. 2004. *Sparta: Aufstieg und Niedergang einer antiken Großmacht*. Stuttgart.

West, M. L. 1970. Corinna. *CQ* 29: 277–87.

West, M. L. 1972. *Iambi et Elegi Graeci, II*. Oxford.

West, M. L. 1975. *Immortal Helen*. Castle Cary.

West, M. L. (ed.). 1978. *Hesiod, Works and Days*. Oxford.

West, M. L. 1985. *The Hesiod Catalogue of Women: its nature, structure and origins*. Oxford.

West, M. L. 1990. Dating Corinna. *CQ* 40: 553–7.

West, M. L. 1992. Alcman and the Spartan royalty. *ZPE* 91: 1–7.

West, M. L. 1999. The invention of Homer. *CQ* 49 (2): 364–82.

Whitby, M. 1994. Two Shadows: images of Spartans and helots. In Powell and Hodkinson 1994: 87–126.

Whitby, M. 2002. Introduction. In *Sparta*, edited by M. Whitby: 1–25. Edinburgh.

Whitley, J. 1988. Early states and hero cults: a reappraisal. *JHS* 108: 173–82.

Whitley, J. 1991. Social diversity in Dark Age Greece. *ABSA* 86: 341–65.

Whitley, J. 1995. Tomb cult and hero cult: the uses of the past in Archaic Greece. In *Time, Tradition and Society in Greek Archaeology: bridging the 'Great Divide'*, edited by N. Spencer: 43–63. London.

Whitley, J. 1997. Cretan laws and Cretan literacy. *AJA* 101 (4): 635–61.

Whitley, J. 2001. *The Archaeology of Ancient Greece*. Cambridge.

Whitley, J. 2002. Objects with attitude: biographical facts and fallacies in the study of Late bronze Age and early Iron Age warrior graves. *Cambridge Archaeological Journal* 12: 217–32.

Whittaker, H. 1997. *Mycenaean Cult Buildings: a study of their architecture and function in the context of the Aegean and the Eastern Mediterranean*. Bergen.

Wiater, N. 2005. Eine poetologische Deutung des σηκός in Simon. fr. 531 PMG. *Hermes* 133 (1): 44–55.

Wide, S. K. A. 1893. *Lakonische Kulte*. Leipzig.

Wide, S. K. A. 1909. Grabspende und Totenschlage. *Archiv für Religionswissenschaft* 12: 221–3.

Williams, C. K. II. 1978. Corinth, 1977: Forum Southwest. *Hesperia* 47 (1): 1–39.

Williams, C. K. II. 1981. The city of Corinth and its domestic religion. *Hesperia* 50 (4): 408–21.

Williams, C. K. II. 1989. *The Sanctuary of Demeter and Kore: The Greek Pottery* (Corinth 18. 1). Princeton, NJ.

Williams, C. K. II and N. Bookidis (eds). 2003. *Corinth: the centenary, 1896-1996* (Corinth 20). Princeton, NJ.
Williams, C. K. II and J. E. Fisher. 1972. Corinth, 1971: Forum Area. *Hesperia* 41 (2): 143-84.
Williams, C. K. II and J. E. Fisher. 1973. Corinth, 1972: The Forum Area. *Hesperia* 42 (1): 1-44.
Williams, C. K. II, J. MacIntosh and J. E. Fisher. 1974. Excavation at Corinth, 1973. *Hesperia* 43 (1): 1-76.
Winter, F. E. 2006. *Studies in Hellenistic Architecture*. Toronto.
Winter, N. A. 1993. *Greek Architectural Terracottas from the Prehistoric to the End of the Archaic Period*. Oxford.
Woodford, S. 2003. *Images of Myths in Classical Antiquity*. Cambridge.
Woodhead, A. G. 1981. *The Study of Greek Inscriptions*. Cambridge.
Woodward, A. M. 1908-9. Excavations at Sparta: Inscriptions. *ABSA* 15: 40-106.
Wycherley, R. E. 1957. *The Athenian Agora III: Literary and Epigraphical Testimonia*. Princeton, NJ.
Wycherley, R. E. 1959. Two Athenian shrines. *AJA* 63 (1): 67-72.
Wycherley, R. E. 1970. Minor shrines in ancient Athens. *Phoenix* 24: 283-95.
Wycherley, R. E. 1978. *The Stones of Athens*. Princeton, NJ.
Wypustek, A. 2013. *Images of Eternal Beauty in Funerary Verse Inscriptions of the Hellenistic and Greco-Roman Periods*. Leiden.
Wypustek, A. 2014. Beauty and heroization: the memory of the dead in the Greek funerary epigrams of the hellenistic and Roman ages. In *Attitudes Towards the Past in Antiquity Creating Identities: Proceedings of an International Conference held at Stockholm University, 15-17 May 2009*. Stockholm: 277-84.
Young, D. C. 1968. *Three Odes of Pindar: a literary study of Pythian 11, Pythian 3 and Olympian 7*. Leiden.
Zaitman, L. B. and P. S. Pantel. 1992. *Religion in the Ancient Greek City*, translated by P. Cartledge. Cambridge.
Zapheiropoulou, Ph. 1983. La necropoli geometrica di Tsikalario a Naxos. *Magna Grecia* 18 (5-6): 1-4.
Zapheiropoulou, Ph. 1999. I due polyandria dell' antica necropoli di Paros. *A.I.O.N.* 6: 13-24.
Zapheiropoulou, Ph. 2006. Geometric battle scenes on vases from Paros. In *Pictorial Pursuits*, edited by E. Rystedt and B. Wells: 271-7. Stockholm.
Zavvou, E. and A. Themos. 2009. Sparta from prehistoric to early Christian times: observations from the excavations of 1994-2005. In Cavanagh, Gallou and Georgiades 2009: 105-32.

Index

Page numbers in **bold** refer to figures.

Abramson, H., 23
Achaian heroes, appropriation of, 42
Achaian policy, 2, 42
Achilleion, the *see* Megalopolis road sanctuary
Achilles, 13, 59
Acropolis, the, 64, 81–2, 95, 96–8, 100, 101, 132, 169
Aelian, 155
affluence, display of, 68
Agamemnon, 13, 41–2
Agamemnon and Alexandra/Kassandra, cult of, 1, 22, 23, 24, 118, 163, 171
   architecture, 86, 89
   drinking groups, 66
   location, 39
   longevity, 90, 172
   reliefs, **36, 37, 38, 40**, 62
   sanctuary, 2
   site survey, 39–42
   votives, 3, 29, 35, 40–1, 62, 63–4, 64, 67, 69, 70, 71, 118
Agamemnoneion, Mycenae, 22–3
Agis, 165
agora, the, 98–9
Aiatos, 27
Aigeidai, the, 4
Aigidai clan, 94
Ainetos, 126
Ainian, M., 21
Aischylos, 16
Aithiopis, 15
Alexandra, 159
Alkman, 10, 44, 113, 126, 129, 133
Amyklai, 1, 4, 41, 125
Amyklaian deposit, 55
Amyklaion, the, 9, 109, 111, 120–4, 134, 163, 171
   architecture, 84, 84–5, 86
   chronology, 123–4

   monumentalization, 121, 126
   plan, **122**
   the sanctuary, 120–3
   throne of Apollo, 109, 115, 120, 121–2, 128
   votives, 35, 67, 120–1, 172
ancestor cults, 19, 21, 160–1
ancestor worship, 161
Andokides, 93
Andronikos, M., 32
animal bones, 50
antefixes, 86
Antiphanes, 26
Antiphon, 26
antiquarian tendencies, 165–6, 175
Antonaccio, C., 18–19
Apharidai, the, 131, 132
Aphetaid road, 96, 99
Apollo, 9, 120, 124, 126, 126–7, 128, 134
archaeological record, 173
   early, 17–20
   hero cults, 16–25
   mythical heroes, 22–3
   oikistai, 23–4
Archaic period, 1, 4–7
architecture, 84–91, 172
Arfani plot
   architecture, 89
   site survey, 55–6
   votives, 76
Argonauts, the, 129
Argos, 2, 24
Aristokles Relief, 34–5
Aristophanes, 93, 116, 117
Aristotle, 26, 141
Artemis Orthia, sanctuary of, 45, 58, 98, 100, 109, 141, 163, 165, 171
   architecture, 84, 86, 87
   disc acroteria, 86

votives, 35, 62, 64, 65, 67, 69, 79, 112, 172
Artemis Orthia, second temple of, 6
artistic production, 79–80, 136
Astrabacus, 1, 45, 89, 93, 95
Athena Poliachos (Chalkioikos), sanctuary of, 4, 64, 69, 84, 85, 87, 88, 97, 100, 109, 112
Athenaios, 128
Athens, 3, 8, 20, 21, 80–1, 81, 85, 87–8, 94, 97, 159
athletic commemorations, 98, 137–8

Bakchylides, 13
Barbios, 93
Battos, 24
Bilida plot
  site survey, 55
  votives, 76
Bion, 128
Boehringer, C., 12, 19
bone transfers, 157, 172
Bookidis, N., 81
Booneta, the, 99
Bouchalis plot, 159
Bougadis plot, Gitiada Street
  architecture, 87
  reliefs, 62
  site survey, 52–3
  votives, 62, 74
Bowra, C. M., 150–1
Brasidas, 12, 136, 147
Brelich, A., 12
Bremmer, J. N., 14
Bronze Age tombs, 106
bronze production, decline of, 79
building projects, 109
burial practices, 139–40, 141–2, 145–6, 148, 152, 156, 158, 161–2, 168–9
burials, 9–10, 17–18, 157–70
  catchment area, 161
  Ergatikes Katoikies, 165, 167–8, 170
  Hellenistic and Roman periods, 164–9, 170
  and hero cults, 159–60
  Homeric, 18
  monumental graves, 169
  proximity of hero shrines to, 158

Stauffert Street, 160–4, 169–70
Stavropoulos plot, 165, 168–9, 170
typology, 162–3
urban context, 159
Burkert, W. B., 12, 26

Cartledge, P. A., 4, 144
Catling, H. W., 104
Cavanagh, W. G., 69
Chatzis plot
  architecture, 89
  reliefs, 62
  site survey, 55–6
  votives, 62, 76
childbirth, death in, 142–3
Chilon, 1, 9, 32, 33, 83, 89, 97, 135, 153–4, 156, 168, 172, 174
Chionis, 138
Christesen, P., 96, 143, 159
Chrysapha, 30–2, **31**, **32**, 50
Chrysapha relief, 84
citizen militarization, 2
citizenship, 67, 136
civic ideology, 7
civic investment, 164
civic religion, 101
classes, 5
cognitive science, 128
Cohen, A. P., 6
collective memory, 154
colonization, 24
commensality, 65–6, 67, 68
communal investment, 7, 164
Corinna, 16
Corinth, 8, 20, 63, 80, 81, 89, 159
Cosmopoulos, M. B., 125
Coulanges de, F, 11
cremation, 17
cremation pyres, 18
cult, definition, 8
cult beings, categories of, 25–6
cult of the dead, 12
cult places, 8
cultic landscape, 156
cultic topography, 131–2
cultural memory, 6, 97, 98, 160, 164, 166, 174
Currie, B., 13, 151
Cypria, 15

daimones, 11
Damonon, 137–8
Damonon stele, 98, 152
dedications, 1, 8, 22–3, 35, 36–7, 61, 70, 71–8, 79–84, 98, 172
Delphic oracle, 152, 154
Demetrakopoulos plot, 159
Dimitrakopoulos, 159
Dionysus, 127
Dioskouroi, the 1, 9, 12, 27, 44, 79, 97, 109, 129–34, **130**, 134, 165, 172, 174
disc acroteria, 85–6
divinities, 11
Dorians, 97
double kingship, 132–3
Draco's law, 15–16
Dreros, 51
drinking, ritual, 64–8, 82, 112, 161–2
drinking groups, 66
drinking shapes, 64–5
Dromos, the, 131

earliest known, 1
Edmunds, L., 117, 118, 119
Eijnde, F. van den, 20
Eileithyia, sanctuary of, 48
Ekroth, G., 12, 19, 26, 147
Eleusinan Mysteries, 93
Eleusinion, the, 64
Eleusis, 21, 125
Ephorus, 154
Epic Cycle, 13, 15, 16
Eretria, 20–1, 66
Ergatikes Katoikies, 62, 98, 169
    architecture, 85
    burials, 158, 159, 165, 167–8, 170
    site survey, 46
    votives, 72
Eukosmos, 159–60
eunomia, 154
Euripides, 93, 114, 116, 117, 126, 127, 128, 132, 159
Eurotas Bridge drainage ditch, 96
    architecture, 86, 87
    Geometric *pithos* burial, 158
    site survey, 42–4, **43**
    votives, 64, 71
Eurotas River, 4
Eurotas River Heroon, 163, 171

architecture, 85, 86, 89
reliefs, 62
site survey, 44–5
votives, 62, 64, 68, 72
Eurybiades, 136, 155, 174

Farnell, L. R., 12
feasting, 66, 95, 161–2
Filippopoulou plot
    site survey, 54
    votives, 75, 83
Förtsch, R., 80
funerary connotations, 34
funerary stelai, 79
Fuqua, C., 139–40
Furtwängler, A, 31–2

Geometric graves, 7–8, 9–10, 20, 22, 27, 30, 83, 89–90, 135, 157–8, 158–9, 160–4, 171, 174–5
Georganta-Petrakou plot, 168
    site survey, 53–4
    votives, 74
Georgikon-Xinoneri, 19
Gerousia, the, 137
Gitiadas, 85
grave cults, 160–1
graves, location, 17
Great Rhetra, the, 5, 6
Grotta, 21
Gymnopaidia, the, 66, 95, 141

Hägg, R., 37
Halbwachs, M., 164
Harpy tomb, Xanthos, 31–2
Hatzisteliou-Price, T., 13
Helen, 111, 129, 132, 156
    divine status, 117–19
    literary evidence, 113–17
    status, 117, 147
Helen and Menelaus, cult of, 1, 3, 9, 103–4, **105**, 107, 165, 173–4. *see also* Menelaion, the literary evidence, 113–17
Hellenistic and Roman period burials, 164–9, 170
Herakleidai, the, 97, 145, 146
Herakleitos, 11, 14, 16
Herakles, 22, 23, 24, 27, 92, 127, 148, 166

hero cults, 7, 25–7
    absorption into the civic sphere, 163–4
    archaeological record, 16–25
    boom in, 24–5
    and burials, 159–60
    cult of the dead, 12
    duration, 18–19
    earliest instance, 15–16
    emergence of, 171
    growth, 172
    inconsistencies, 26–7
    in literary sources, 11–16, 14–16
    long tradition, 171
    longevity, 164, 172
    mythical heroes, 22–3
    for the recently deceased, 20–2
    terminology, 16–20
hero shrines, 1
    dedications, 35, 36–7
    funerary connotations, 34
    iconographical motifs, 32–3, 35–6, **36, 37, 38, 39, 40**
    identification, 30
    inscriptions, 30, 32, 34–5, **34**
    numbers, 3
    reliefs, 30–7, **31, 32, 33, 34, 36, 37, 38**
    size, 8
    votive deposits, 30, 35, 37
Herodotus, 10, 16–17, 66, 89, 93, 94, 95, 103, 113, 114, 117, 118, 132, 145–6, 146, 147, 149
heroes, 6–7
    anonymity, 83
    categories, 12, 26
    defining features, 27
    definition, 11, 11–14
    divine, 27
    divine descent and parentage, 14
    in Homer, 13–14
    immortality, 103
    lines of descent from, 166–7
    linguistic origin of word, 12–13
    in literary sources, 11–16
    mortality, 27
    popularity of, 1
    religious sense, 15–16, 27
    understanding, 7–8
heroic sacrifice, 12

heroic shrine topography, 90–101
    small shrines, 92–5
    Sparta, 95–101
heroic shrines, 2–3
    catchment area, 101
    civic importance, 88–9
    longevity, 88–90, 101
    typology, 88
heroine worship, 62–3
heroines, 16
heroization, 2, 9, 135, 138–9, 140, 144–56, 157, 172, 174
heroon, 16–17, 24–5
Heroon at Lefkandi, the, 17–18
Heroon at the Crossroads, 20, 22
Hesiod, 7, 13, 14, 15, 115
Hesychios, 112–13
Hipposthenes, 138
Hodkinson, S., 79, 94–5, 138
Homer, 7, 13–15, 18, 23, 42, 114, 125, 129
homoioi, 5
honours, 136
Hyakinthia festival, 120, 125, 126, 128, 132, 174
Hyakinthos, 120, 124, 134, 156, 174
    grave of, 121, 125, 126–7, 127–8, 134, 157
    immortality, 9
    literary sources, 126
    myth, 127–8
    status, 127–8

Ibykos, 13, 138
iconographical motifs, 1, 8, 32–3, 35, **36, 37, 38, 39, 40**, 68, 81, 82–3, 83–4
ideals of excellence, 136
Iliad (Homer), 13, 14, 42, 125, 129
immortality, 9, 15, 103, 114, 117–19, 129, 134, 139, 157, 173
influential dead, the, beliefs in, 19–20
inscriptions, 19, 24, 30, 31, 34–5, **34**, 142
internal crisis, 4–5
Isocrates, 117
Isokrates, 112, 113
Ithaka, 22, 22–3

Jeffery, L. H., 137
jewellery, 79

Kalatzis plot, 168
   architecture, 86, 88–9
   burials, 158
   site survey, 55
   votives, 76
Kalaureia, 66
Kalydon, 66
Kalydonian boar-hunt, 129
Kanellopoulos plot, 96
kantharoi, 34, 35, **36**
Karmoiris plot
   architecture, 86, 88
   site survey, 53
   votives, 74
Kastor, tomb of, 29, 131, 132, 157
Kinaithon, 115
kings, 94, 143, 152, 174
   heroization of, 2, 144–8, 156
Kladas, 63
Kladas-Voutianoi, 9
Kleomenes, 165
koinoniai, 94–5
Kokkynovrysi shrine, 81
Komast scenes, 65
Kyniska, 138
Kynosoura, 4
Kyrene, 24

Laconia, 8–9
Laconia Survey, 4–5, 8–9
Laconian Renascence, 4
Lakedaimon, 148, 152
Lanéres, N., 130–1
Larson, J., 117
Lathria, 159
lead figurines, 69, 71–8, 111, 112
Lefkandi, Toumba burial, 7, 17–18, 24
Lefkandi burial
Leonidas, King, 9, 97, 144, 146, 148–53, 174
Leukippidai, the, 132
Limnai, 4, 49, 81, 82, 95, 96, 98, 100–1, 101, 158–9, 163, 164, 174–5
Lipka, M., 146–7
literary sources, 10, 29
   Helen, 113–17
   heroes and hero cult in, 11–16
   Hyakinthos, 126

   small shrines, 93
   terminology, 16–20
local histories, lost, 159
local perspective, 173
Lokroi Epizephyrioi, 31
Loraux, N., 139
Lycurgus, 156, 174
Lycurgus, altar of, 44, 45
Lykourgian institutions, 154
Lykourgos, 5, 154, 156, 158
Lykourgos, sanctuary of, 98
Lykourgos and Karela plot, 96, 141, 163
   architecture, 86
   burials, 158
   site survey, 52
   votives, 73
Lysander, 138

Macedon, 165
Malkin I., 145
Marathon, Battle of, 149
Markou plot
   site survey, 55
   votives, 76
Massow, von. W., 126
material culture, 5–6
Megalopolis road sanctuary, votives, 63, 69, 78
Menelaion, the, 9, 22, 23, 24, 29, 103–20, **104**, 134, 163, 171
   architecture, 84, 85, 86, 87, 88
   artefacts, 104–5
   aryballos, **106**, 114
   chronology, 5, 6, 106–7, 109
   cistern, 112
   drinking groups, 66
   excavations, 2005, 109
   harpax, 104–5, **105**, 112
   inscriptions, 105
   Late Bronze Age remains, 105, 106–7, 119
   literary evidence, 113–17
   monumental terrace, 107
   ritual, 112–13, 119
   the sanctuary, 103–7, **108**, 109
   state importance, 90
   status, 109, 110
   stele, 114, **115**, **116**
   tile-stamps, 109

votive deposits, 35
votives, 63, 64, 65, 68, 69, 110–12, 112, 118–19, 172
Menelaus, 109, 110, 117–18, 133, 147, 156.
    see also Helen and Menelaus, cult of
Menidi tomb, 19, 83
mental representations, 128
Mesoa, 4
Messenia, 9, 11, 48, 133, 162, 171
Messenian Wars, 4–5, 139–40
messes, 67, 95
metal objects, 69–70, 71–8
metopes, 43, 44, 87
Metropolis, 27
military ethos, 133
Mimnermos, 15, 16
monumental graves, 169
monumentalization, 6
Morgan, C., 24
Morris, I., 18
mortality, 27, 173, 174
Mother of the Gods, sanctuary of the, 57
motivation, 2
Mycenae, 3, 18, 19, 22–3, 25, 63, 66
mythical heroes, 1, 22–3

Nafissi, M., 144
Nagy, G., 13, 14, 15
Naxos, 161, 162
Nemea, 24–5, 66, 81
New Simonides, 133
Niarchos plot, 163
    reliefs, 62
    site survey, 48
    votives, 62, 68, 73
Nikolarou plot
    site survey, 57
    votives, 77
Nilsson, M. P., 12
Nora, P., 6
nostalgia, 106
Nymphs, 23, 81, 92

O 13
    site survey, 45–6
    votives, 68, 72
Odysseus, 14–15, 22, 22–3
Odyssey (Homer), 13, 14–15, 23, 42, 114
offering tables, 51

oikistai, 3, 23–4, 135, 153
old market, 131
Olive Oil Cemetery, 33–4, 68, 140, 162, 162–3
Olympian gods, 25–6
Opheltes, cult of, 24–5
Orestes, 1, 2, 153, 157, 172
Orthia, sanctuary of, 4, 48, 111

Palaiokastro hill, 100
Panagopoulou plot
    site survey, 53
    votives, 74
panathenaic amphorae, 112
Pantel, P. S., 8
Parker, R., 116, 117–19, 144, 151
Paroikia, 21
Paros, 21
Parparonia, festival of the, 141
Partheniai, rebellion of the, 4–5
patronage, 165
Pausanias, 3, 10, 29, 39, 41, 42, 45, 48, 57, 84–5, 86, 89, 90, 93, 96–7, 98, 99, 109, 116, 119–20, 121, 126, 126–7, 128, 131, 132, 134, 137, 143–4, 145, 147, 148–9, 153, 154, 155–6, 159–60, 164–5, 172, 173
Peisistratus the Younger, 25–6
Peloponnese, the, hegemonic prospects, 2
Peloponnesian War, 145
Pelops, 17, 24
Persephone, 133
Perseus, 24–5
Persian Wars, 41–2, 99, 139, 150, 151, 152, 155, 174
personal prominence, 136–9
personal wealth, 138
Phoibaion, the, 131–2
Phrontis, cult of, 22, 23
Pindar, 16, 23, 26, 42, 92, 129, 131
Pitane, 4
pithos burials, 45
place, links to, 3
Plataia, Battle of, 109, 133, 149, 149–50
Plato, 26, 93
Pleistoanax, 145
Plutarch, 10, 66, 113, 133, 141, 142–3, 158
Podlecki, A. J., 151
political interpretation, 2

Polybius, 120
popularity, 1–2, 2–3
pottery and drinking shapes, 63–9, 71–8
priests and priestesses, 142–4
propaganda, 2
Proto-Geometric graves, 21, 27, 157–8, 159, 161, 175
Proto-Geometric period, 45
Psatha-Iliopoulou plot
  site survey, 56
  votives, 77
public buildings, 99

recently deceased, the, 135–56, 138–9, 157
  burial and commemoration, 139–44
  Chilon, 153–4, 156, 172, 174
  cults for, 20–2
  death in childbirth, 142–3
  heroization, 136–9, 140, 144–56, 157, 172, 174
  kings, 144–8, 156, 174
  Leonidas and the Thermopylai war dead, 9, 97, 148–53, 154–5, 174
  priests and priestesses, 142–4
  status, 136–9
  war-dead, 139–42, 156, 174
reliefs, 62, 71–8, 80, 98, 153
  Agamemnon and Alexandra/Kassandra, cult of, 62
  Bougadis plot, Gitiada Street, 52–3, 62
  Chatzis plot, 55–6, 62
  Chrysapha, 30–2, **32**, 50
  dedications, 36–7
  the Dioskouroi, 130–1, **130**
  Eurotas Bridge drainage ditch, 43, **43**
  Eurotas River Heroon, 62
  Filippopoulou plot, 54
  funerary connotations, 34
  heroes' shrines, 30–7, **31**, **32**, **33**, **34**, **36**, **37**, **38**
  iconographical motifs, 32–3, 35–6, **36**, **37**, **38**, **39**, **40**, 82–3, 83–4
  inscriptions, 31, 34–5, **34**
  Kalatzis plot, 55
  Niarchos plot, 62
  Sklavochori (Amyklai), Konidari plot, 59
  Stauffert Street cult site and burial, 50, 62

Stavropoulos plot, 47–8, 62
Tseliou plot, 54
Zaimis plot, 62
religious consolidation, 5
religious landscape, 3
religious significance, 2
religious topography, 7, 86, 101
religious tradition, 3, 9
remembering, 164
Renfrew, C., 8
Rhadamanthys, 166
Rhomaios, K. A., 32–3
Richer, N., 143
ritual boundaries, permeability of, 156
roads, 99
roadside shrines, 81, 96
Rohde, E., 11, 14
roof tiles, 54
Rusten, J. S., 92

sacrifice, 66, 95, 112, 114, 132
sacrificial pyres, 21
Salamis, battle of, 136, 155
Salapata, G., 8, 41, 48
sanctuaries, monumentalization, 6
shrines, 17
significance, 2
Simonides, 42, 109, 138, 139, 149
site survey, 38–59
  Agamemnon and Alexandra/Kassandra, cult of, 39–42
  Arfani plot, 55–6
  Bilida plot, 55
  Bougadis plot, Gitiada Street, 52–3
  Chatzis plot, 55–6
  Ergatikes Katoikies, 46
  Eurotas Bridge drainage ditch, 42–4, **43**
  Eurotas River Heroon, 44–5
  Filippopoulou plot, 54
  Georganta and Petrakou plot, 53–4
  Gitiada Street, 53
  Kalatzis plot, 55
  Karmoiris plot, 53
  Lykourgos and Karela plot, 52
  Markou plot, 55
  Megalopolis road sanctuary, 57–9
  Niarchos plot, 48
  Nikolarou plot, 57
  O 13, 45–6

Panagopoulou plot, 53
Psatha-Iliopoulou plot, 56
Sklavochori (Amyklai), Konidari plot, 59
Sourli plot, 56
Stathopoulos and Argeiti plot, 54
Stauffert street cult site and burial, 49–52, **49, 50**
Stavropoulos plot, 46–8, **47**
Stratakou plot, 57
Thermopylae Street, 56
Tseliou plot, 54
Valioti plot, 57
Zachariadi plot, 57
skeletal remains, 46
Skias, the, 99–100
Sklavochori (Amyklai), Konidari plot
    burials, 158
    votives, 78
small shrines, 92–5
Snodgrass, A.M., 18
social hierarchies, 137
social significance, 2
societal organization, 2, 5
socio-economic relations, 138
Sosibios, 141
Sotiriou, 159
Sounion, 22, 23
Sourli plot, 96, 159
    architecture, 87
    site survey, 56
    votives, 77
Sparta, **xiv(map)**
    peculiarities, 2
Sparta Museum Catalogue, 32
state formation, 4
Stathakos plot, 96
Stathopoulos and Argeiti plot
    site survey, 54
    votives, 69, 75
statues, 54
Stauffert street cult site and burial, 9–10, 30, 48, 95
    architecture, 86, 88, 89
    bench, 51
    burials, 158, 159, 160–4, 169–70
    burned area, 50
    disc acroteria, 86
    drinking groups, 66
    location, 163
    longevity, 163, 164
    monumentalization, 164
    reliefs, 50, 62, 84
    second phase, 52
    site survey, 49–52, **49, 50**
    votives, 49–50, 52, 62, 63, 64, 69, 73, 160
Stavropoulos plot, 96
    burials, 158, 165, 168–9, 170
    reliefs, 47–8, 62
    site survey, 46–8, **47**
    votives, 62, 73
Steinhauer, G., 43, 44, 54, 55, 168
stele, 114, **115, 116**, 126, 137–8, 142
Stesichoros, 10, 13, 42
Stibbe, C. M., 47–8, 168
Strabo, 126
Stratakou plot, votives, 77

Talthybiads, the, 94
Talthybios, 89, 94
Taras, 4
Tegea, 5
Tegea banquet reliefs, 32–3
Teisamenos, 2
Telegony, 15
Teleklos, King, 4
terracotta architectural models, 87
terracotta figurines, 62–3, 71–8, 110–11, 120
terracotta plaques, 39, 56, 57, 57–8
territorial consolidation, 4–5
Thasos, 24
Thebes, 22, 23, 24
Themistokles, 136
Theocritus, 116, 117
Theodoros of Samos, 99
Theognis, 13
Theogony (Hesiod), 15
Theomelida, 145
Theophrastus, 93
Therapne, 1, 113, 131, 132, 133–4, 134
Thermopylae Street
    site survey, 56
    votives, 76
Thermopylai, Battle of, 146
Thermopylai war-dead, 9, 97, 148–53, 154–5

Theseus, 12, 44, 129, 152
Thiokles relief, 130–1
Thorikos, 94
Thucydides, 4, 10, 86, 87, 146–7, 149–50
Timokles Relief, 34–5
Tod, M. N., 32
Toumba burial, Lefkandi, 17–18, 24
Trojan War, 14
Tseliou plot
  site survey, 54
  votives, 62, 64, 75
Tympanon Hill, 52
Tyndareus, 97, 166
Tyrtaeus, 4–5, 10, 139, 139–40, 141, 144, 155, 163

Underworld, the, 133

Valioti plot, site survey, 57
Vari, 81, 161
vase paintings, 65
Vathykles, 121, 127–8
Vathykles of Magnesia, 85
veneration, 25
visiting heroes, 39
Vlizos, Stavros, 120
votive wreaths, 54
votives, 2–3, 6, 8, 29, 30, 35, 37, 61–70, 90
  Agamemnon and Alexandra/Kassandra, 3, 29, 35, 40–1, 62, 63–4, 64, 67, 69, 70, 71, 118
  Amyklaion, 35, 67, 120–1, 172
  Archaic period, 80–3
  Arfani plot, 76
  Bilida plot, 76
  Bougadis plot, Gitiada Street, 62, 74
  Chatzis plot, 62, 76
  choice, 61
  dedications, 61, 70, 71–8, 79–84
  Ergatikes Katoikies, 72
  Eurotas Bridge drainage ditch, 64, 71
  Eurotas River Heroon, 62, 64, 68, 72
  Filippopoulou plot, 75, 83
  Georganta and Petrakou plot, 53–4, 74
  Kalatzis plot, 76
  Karmoiris plot, 53, 74
  lead figurines, 69, 71–8, 111, 112
  Lykourgos and Karela plot, 73
  Markou plot, 76
  Megalopolis road sanctuary, 63, 69, 78
  the Menelaion, 35, 63, 64, 65, 68, 69, 110–12, 112, 118–19, 172
  metal objects, 69–70, 71–8
  military character, 58
  Mycenaean tombs, 18
  Niarchos plot, 48, 62, 68, 73
  Nikolarou plot, 77
  O 13, 68, 72
  Panagopoulou plot, 74
  panathenaic amphorae, 112
  pottery and drinking shapes, 63–9, 71–8
  Psatha-Iliopoulou plot, 77
  reliefs, 62, 71–8, 80, 98
  sanctuary of Artemis Orthia, 62, 64, 65, 67, 69, 79, 112, 172
  sanctuary of Athena Chalkioikos, 112
  Sklavochori (Amyklai), Konidari plot, 78
  Sourli plot, 77
  Stathopoulos and Argeiti plot, 69, 75
  Stauffert street cult site and burial, 49–50, 52, 62, 63, 64, 69, 73, 160
  Stavropoulos plot, 62, 73
  Stratakou plot, 77
  terracotta figurines, 62–3, 71–8, 110–11, 120
  Thermopylae Street, 76
  Tseliou plot, 62, 64, 75
  typology, 172, 172–3
  Zachariadi plot, 77
  Zaimis plot, 62
Voyatzis, M., 111

Wace, A. J. B., 32
war-dead, 9, 97, 139–42, 148–53, 154–5, 156, 174
weapons, 58, 110
Wees, van H., 14
West, M. L., 15
Whitley, J., 18
Works and Days (Hesiod), 14, 15
worshippers, 83, 83–4, 93

Xenophon, 10, 66, 113, 144, 145, 146–7, 148, 156

Zachariadi plot
   site survey, 57
   votives, 77

Zaimis plot, 54, 62, 140, 161–2
   votives, 62
Zaitman, L. B., 8
Zeus, daughters of, 117–18
Zeus Messapeus, sanctuary of, 4, 64, 65

www.ingramcontent.com/pod-product-compliance
Lightning Source LLC
Chambersburg PA
CBHW071806300426
44116CB00009B/1216